T0207465

Communications
in Computer and Information Science 2097

Rationale

The CCIS series is devoted to the publication of proceedings of computer science conferences. Its aim is to efficiently disseminate original research results in informatics in printed and electronic form. While the focus is on publication of peer-reviewed full papers presenting mature work, inclusion of reviewed short papers reporting on work in progress is welcome, too. Besides globally relevant meetings with internationally representative program committees guaranteeing a strict peer-reviewing and paper selection process, conferences run by societies or of high regional or national relevance are also considered for publication.

Topics

The topical scope of CCIS spans the entire spectrum of informatics ranging from foundational topics in the theory of computing to information and communications science and technology and a broad variety of interdisciplinary application fields.

Information for Volume Editors and Authors

Publication in CCIS is free of charge. No royalties are paid, however, we offer registered conference participants temporary free access to the online version of the conference proceedings on SpringerLink (http://link.springer.com) by means of an http referrer from the conference website and/or a number of complimentary printed copies, as specified in the official acceptance email of the event.

CCIS proceedings can be published in time for distribution at conferences or as postproceedings, and delivered in the form of printed books and/or electronically as USBs and/or e-content licenses for accessing proceedings at SpringerLink. Furthermore, CCIS proceedings are included in the CCIS electronic book series hosted in the SpringerLink digital library at http://link.springer.com/bookseries/7899. Conferences publishing in CCIS are allowed to use Online Conference Service (OCS) for managing the whole proceedings lifecycle (from submission and reviewing to preparing for publication) free of charge.

Publication process

The language of publication is exclusively English. Authors publishing in CCIS have to sign the Springer CCIS copyright transfer form, however, they are free to use their material published in CCIS for substantially changed, more elaborate subsequent publications elsewhere. For the preparation of the camera-ready papers/files, authors have to strictly adhere to the Springer CCIS Authors' Instructions and are strongly encouraged to use the CCIS LaTeX style files or templates.

Abstracting/Indexing

CCIS is abstracted/indexed in DBLP, Google Scholar, EI-Compendex, Mathematical Reviews, SCImago, Scopus. CCIS volumes are also submitted for the inclusion in ISI Proceedings.

How to start

To start the evaluation of your proposal for inclusion in the CCIS series, please send an e-mail to ccis@springer.com.

Tammam A. T. Benmusa ·
Mohamed Samir Elbuni · Ibrahim M. Saleh ·
Ahmed S. Ashur · Nabil M. Drawil ·
Issmail M. Ellabib
Editors

Information and Communications Technologies

Second International Libyan Conference, ILCICT 2023
Tripoli, Libya, September 4–6, 2023
Proceedings

 Springer

Editors

Tammam A. T. Benmusa
University of Tripoli
Tripoli, Libya

Mohamed Samir Elbuni
University of Tripoli
Tripoli, Libya

Ibrahim M. Saleh
University of Tripoli
Tripoli, Libya

Ahmed S. Ashur
University of Tripoli
Tripoli, Libya

Nabil M. Drawil
University of Tripoli
Tripoli, Libya

Issmail M. Ellabib
University of Tripoli
Tripoli, Libya

ISSN 1865-0929   ISSN 1865-0937 (electronic)
Communications in Computer and Information Science
ISBN 978-3-031-62623-4   ISBN 978-3-031-62624-1 (eBook)
https://doi.org/10.1007/978-3-031-62624-1

This Springer imprint is published by the registered company Springer Nature Switzerland AG
The registered company address is: Gewerbestrasse 11, 6330 Cham, Switzerland

If disposing of this product, please recycle the paper.

Preface

The International Libyan Conference for Information and Communications Technologies (ILCICT 2023) was the second of a series of conferences to be held yearly. The conference's theme was "Accelerating the Digital Transformation through Smart Communications" and it was hosted in Tripoli, Libya, from September 4–6, 2023. It was supported by the General Authority for Communications and Informatics and supervised by the University of Tripoli's Faculty of Engineering. This was an extension of the first session (ILCICT 2022), which took place in the city of Tripoli from March 27 to March 30, 2022. Its activities included the presentation of a number of research papers, workshops, and keynote addresses from invited professors in the field of communications and informatics. It was estimated that there were more than 200 participants at that session.

The main objectives of the conference were to:

- Provide a forum for researchers, engineers, industry professionals, and economists interested in communication and information technology to exchange ideas and discuss new developments.
- Encourage research in communication and information technology that serves society and contributes to the development of the national economy.
- Disseminate the results of research in communication and information technology to a wider audience.

The conference program included five sessions of research papers, in addition to three specialized workshops related to the communications and informatics sector, and four keynote addresses from invited professors specializing in the conference field from Canada, the UK, and the UAE.

The publisher Springer was contacted by the scientific committee and agreed to publish the conference proceedings in the Communications in Computer and Information Science (CCIS) series.

Several conditions and requirements were established for submission of research papers according to the best international practices. Research papers have been solicited for acceptance in three main tracks, each covering several research points as follows:

Computers and Informatics Systems
Communication Systems
Image Processing, Computer Vision and Internet of Things

Professors, experts, and specialists from domestic and foreign universities, institutions, and research organizations submitted 57 papers. 55 papers were sent to the International Scientific Review Committee, and two papers were rejected due to non-compliance. The reviewing procedure was conducted using a double-blind method, with submissions receiving three reviews each on average. Only 26 papers were approved for the conference and included in the proceedings, as determined by the reviewers. This translates to a 46% acceptance rate of all articles submitted.

The research papers in the proceedings are arranged according to the conference tracks and the date of submission. They are published exactly as sent by the authors after the introduction of the auditors' observations, and the authors are therefore responsible for any typographical, spelling, linguistic, or organizational errors that may appear in their manuscript. The scientific committee is pleased to receive any suggestions or observations that could help to achieve the conference's objectives and to contribute to the success of future conferences.

We are grateful to the sponsors, the organizing committee, the reviewers, and the authors for their contributions to the success of the conference. We hope that the conference will be a valuable opportunity for all participants to share their knowledge and ideas, and to contribute to the development of communication and information technology in Libya and the world.

November 2023

Tammam A. T. Benmusa
Mohamed Samir Elbuni
Ibrahim M. Saleh
Ahmed S. Ashur
Nabil M. Drawil
Issmail M. Ellabib

Organization

General Chair

Tammam A. T. Benmusa   University of Tripoli, Libya

Program Committee Chairs

Tammam A. T. Benmusa   University of Tripoli, Libya
Mohamed Samir Elbuni   University of Tripoli, Libya
Ibrahim M. Saleh   University of Tripoli, Libya
Ahmed S. Ashur   University of Tripoli, Libya
Nabil M. Drawil   University of Tripoli, Libya
Issmail M. Ellabib   University of Tripoli, Libya

Steering Committee

Fouad Fadel (Chair)   Libyan Post, Telecommunication and IT Holding
                                     Company, Libya
Tammam A. T. Benmusa   University of Tripoli, Libya
Mohamed Samir Elbuni   University of Tripoli, Libya
Abdulkader J. Elzelitni   General Authority for Telecommunications &
                                     Informatics, Libya
Ali A. Albaroni   General Information Authority, Libya
Ahmed M. Elhmadi   National Information Security and Safety
                                     Authority, Libya

Program Committee

Shawki Areibi   University of Guelph, Canada
Mohamed Elmansouri   University of Colorado, USA
Ryan Riley   Carnegie Mellon University in Qatar, Qatar
Noureddin Sadawi   University of Oxford, UK
Khaled Rabie   Manchester Metropolitan University, UK
Crina Grosan   King's College London, UK
Khaled Shaban   Qatar University, Qatar

Ahmed Bouridane   University of Sharjah, UAE
Ahmad Kharaz   University of Derby, UK

Additional Reviewers

Abdoulmenim Bilh
Abdulatif Khrwat
Abdulbaset Ali
Abdulbaset Hamed
Abdulnaser Younes
Abdurhman Albasir
Abdurrahman Elbuni
Abubaker Abushofa
Abulgasim Shallof
Ahmad Kharaz
Ahmed Abougarair
Ahmed Alkilany
Ahmed Hussein
Ahmed Kagilik
Ali Elmelhi
Ali Elrowayati
Ali Ganoun
Alina Miron
Amna Elhawil
Ayad Ali
Benjamin Cross
Elbahlul Fgee
Elias Yaacoub
Gary Grewal
Hussein Magboub
Ibrahim Lahmer
Ismail Shrena
Jalal Miladi
Khaled Dadesh
Khaled Rabie
Khaled Shaban
Lutfi Arebi

Mahdi Hafi
Mahmoud Elfandi
Mohamed Buker
Mohamed Edardar
Mohamed Elalem
Mohamed Eljhani
Mohamed Elmansouri
Mohamed Ghretli
Mohamed Mussa
Mrwan Margem
Mustafa Alasswad
Mustafa Gabaj
Nabil Naas
Naser Telesi
Nizar Khemri
Nuredin Ahmed
Osama Abusaid
Osama Alkishriwo
Rudwan Husain
Salah Kanoun
Sarra Elrabiei
Seddeq Ghrare
Shawki Areibi
Suad El-Geder
Tarek Khalifa
Noureddin Sadawi
Nuri Benbarka
Haitham Amar
Wael Abughres
Yahya Ali
Yusra Maatug
Youssef Gdura

Contents

Communication Systems

A Hybrid Clipping and SLM Technique for PAPR Reduction in OFDM
Systems 3
  Omar Bouagila Algaderi and Abdulkhalek M. Zatout

AI-Driven Path Loss Optimization in 4G Networks Through PSO
Algorithm 20
  Hanane Djellab, Amel Bouchemha, Fouzia Maamri,
  Farouk Boumehrez, and Abdelhakim Sahour

Topology Discovery Tool for OpenFlow Controllers 27
  Mohamed Sati, Moad Emshiheet, Ahmed Majouk, and Salem Omar Sati

Performance Analysis of Classifying URL Phishing Using Recursive
Feature Elimination 42
  Marwa Albaser, Salwa Ali, and Hamouda Chantar

Performance Evaluation of Satellite Communication Link at Millimeter
Wave Based on Rain Fade Data Measured in Libya 55
  Asma Ali Budalal, Khaled Idris Sharif, Suleiman G H Hewadia,
  and Rogaya A H Budalal

BJT Based Voltage Reference Circuits Comparisons in 65 nm CMOS
Process 68
  Alharari Alsouri Alharari, Sami Saddek Bizzan, and Abdulmoied Omar

Computer and Information Systems

Solar Flare Classification via Modified Metaheuristic Optimized Extreme
Gradient Boosting 81
  Petar Bisevac, Ana Toskovic, Mohamed Salb, Luka Jovanovic,
  Aleksandar Petrovic, Miodrag Zivkovic, and Nebojsa Bacanin

Naïve Bayes Classifier with Genetic Algorithm for Phishing Website
Detection 96
  Hamouda Chantar, Salwa Ali, and Yousef Salem

Object-Relational Database Design Approaches: A Survey of Approaches
and Techniques 109
  Huda M. Bohalfaya, Abdelsalam M. Maatuk, and Esra A. Abdelnabi

Event Abstration in a Forensic Timeline 119
  Hudan Studiawan

Innovative SQL Query Generator Using an Arabic Language Description 130
  Salma Salah Ounifi, Mohamed Samir Elbuni, and Yousef Omran Gdura

Handling Imbalanced Datasets in Software Refactoring Prediction 145
  Ali Aburas

KnowAir: A Low-Cost PM2.5 Sensor Citizen-Based Air Pollution
Monitoring System for Real-Time 159
  Eiman M. Saleh, Sarah Al-Werfalli, Tariq Imbarak, Salwa Elakeili,
  and Howayda Elmajpri

Implementation of Qur'anic Question Answering System Based
on the BERT Model 173
  Ebtihal Alarabi and Issmail Ellabib

IT Security Office: The Way Forward for IT Governance for Libyan
Organizations 184
  Ibrahim E. Lahmer

Sentiment Analysis of Libyan Middle Region Using Machine Learning
with TF-IDF and N-grams 197
  Abdullah Habberrih and Mustafa Ali Abuzaraida

Data Quality Considerations for ERP Implementation: Techniques
for Effective Data Management 210
  Mohamed Elbadri, Ahmed Altaher, and Sharafedeen Alkawan

Fractional Calculus Application for PID Controller of a Nuclear Power Plant ... 221
  Hala Elhabrush, Mohamed Samir Elbuni, and Abdullah Ezzedin

Image Processing, Computer Vision and Internet of Things

Palm Print Recognition Based on a Fusion of Feature Selection Techniques 239
  Bothaina F. Gargoum, Ahmed Lawgali, Mohamed A. E. Abdalla,
  and Amina A. Abdo

Predictive Analytics Based on AutoML Email Spam Detection 248
 Tarek A. M. Nagem, Entesar H. Alfsai, Ebitisam K. Elberkawi,
 Fatma El-Deeb, and Salma Albar-Athe

Enhancing a System for Predicting Diabetes Utilizing Conventional
Machine Learning Approaches 257
 Qusay Karghli, Amina A. Abdo, Abdelhafid Ali Mohamed,
 and Fatma Banini

Enhanced Facial Expression Recognition Using Pre-trained Models
and Image Processing Techniques 269
 Rayhan S. Alshwihde and Wafa I. Eltarhouni

Identifying Bird Calls in Soundscapes Using Convolutional Neural
Networks 284
 Azer M. Eldukali and Amna Elhawil

Automated ECG Classification for Myocardial Infarction Diagnosis Using
CNN and Wavelet Transform 298
 Hajer Albraki and Issmail Ellabib

Detecting Chest Diseases with Chest X-Ray Using Convolutional Neural
Network 309
 Malik Miloud Alfilali, Yusra Maatug, and Ismail Ellabib

Real Time Arabic Sign Language Recognition Using Machine Learning:
A Vision - Based Approach 322
 Shahd Elgergeni and Nabil Drawil

Author Index 341

Communication Systems

A Hybrid Clipping and SLM Technique for PAPR Reduction in OFDM Systems

Omar Bouagila Algaderi[✉] and Abdulkhalek M. Zatout

Department of Communication Engineering, University of Derna, Derna, Libya
omar.algaderi@omu.edu.ly, abdulkhalek.m@uod.edu.ly

Abstract. The advantages of the orthogonal frequency division multiplexing system OFDM such as its efficient use of the spectrum and immunity against multipath fading make them the superior technology for the high data rate of wireline and wireless communication systems. However, the high peak-to-average power ratio PAPR of the OFDM signal is one of its main drawbacks. Consequently, many techniques, including selective mapping SLM and clipping-filtering CF, have been recommended to deal with the PAPR problem. The PAPR is decreased but the bit error rate is negatively impacted by the clipping approach. In contrast, the SLM technique decreases the PAPR of an OFDM signal without causing signal distortion, but it increases the complexity of the transmitter. In this paper, we provide a hybrid selective mapping-clipping scheme (HSLMC) for OFDM systems PAPR reduction. In order to decrease the computational complexity, the SLM is employed in iteration with a threshold of PAPR and four iterations; if the PAPR of the OFDM signal is still larger than the threshold after the fourth iteration, clipping is applied. The simulation results show that, in comparison to CF, the proposed method performs better in terms of bit error rate (BER). On the other hand, the computational complexity of the proposed technique is significantly lower than SLM with an equivalent PAPR decrease.

Keywords: OFDM · PAPR · SLM · Hybrid Technique · Computational complexity

1 Introduction

Orthogonal frequency division multiplexing OFDM is extensively employed in wired and wireless communication systems due to several notable advantages it offers in comparison to alternative techniques. These advantages include a high data transmission rate, immunity to frequency selective fading, and the ability to tolerate multipath delay spread. In addition, it should be noted that the OFDM system exhibits a reduced level of implementation complexity due to the use of the Fast Fourier Transform FFT technology for the execution of modulation and demodulation operations [1, 2].

Furthermore, the OFDM system exhibits superior performance compared to alternative multicarrier techniques. This can be attributed to its unique features, including the utilization of overlapping orthogonal subcarriers, which effectively optimize bandwidth

© The Author(s), under exclusive license to Springer Nature Switzerland AG 2024
T. A. T. Benmusa et al. (Eds.): ILCICT 2023, CCIS 2097, pp. 3–19, 2024.
https://doi.org/10.1007/978-3-031-62624-1_1

usage. Consequently, OFDM enables data transmission over low-bandwidth channels, thereby maximizing the efficiency of the available spectrum. In addition, OFDM mitigates the effects of multipath fading by partitioning the wide frequency selective fading channel into several narrowband channels with uniform fading characteristics. Flat fading enables the receiver to use straightforward equalization techniques in order to mitigate the effects of channel fading and Inter Symbol Interference ISI [3, 4].

OFDM has served as the foundation for a significant portion of commercial communication and broadcasting technologies. These include the wireless local area network (WLAN) IEEE.802.11a/b/g/n, worldwide interoperability for microwave access (WiMAX) IEEE.802.16, broadcast radio access network (BRAN), digital video broadcasting (DVB), digital audio broadcasting (DAB), digital television broadcasting (DTVB), Long Term Evaluation (LTE) standard for 4G mobile. Furthermore, it is now under consideration as the prevailing modulation technique for 5G networks and the Internet of Things (IoT) [5, 6].

Despite the many benefits offered by OFDM, its high PAPR is widely recognized as a significant negative that might potentially affect the performance of nonlinear elements within the system. This can result in in-band distortion IB and out-of-band radiation OOB in the OFDM system. The non-linear characteristics of the high power amplifier HPA in the transmitter may be identified as the cause of this phenomenon. Additionally, the elevated PAPR introduces intricacies in the utilization of some devices, such as analog-to-digital converters ADCs and digital-to-analog converters DACs. Consequently, the OFDM system necessitates a HPA that has a substantial dynamic range and a lengthy word length in order to accommodate the elevated PAPR value [7, 8].

Instead of using a pricey amplifier with a broad linear region, an alternate approach for the high PAPR issue in the OFDM system is to attempt to minimize the wide swings in the OFDM signal before attacking the nonlinear devices. Many strategies for reducing peaks in the OFDM signal have been developed, and they may be divided into three categories: signal distortion, multiple signaling and probabilistic techniques, and coding techniques [9]. The first group comprises clipping and filtering, peak windowing, active constellation extension ACE, and non-linear companding transforming, which minimizes high peaks in the OFDM signal by distorting the signal prior to amplification [9, 10]. The second category includes selective mapping SLM, partial transmit sequence PTS, tone reservation TR, and tone injection [11], while probabilistic strategies adjust various OFDM signal parameters in order to optimize them for least PAPR, multiple signaling techniques produce a variety of OFDM signals and choose the signal with the lowest PAPR for transmission. When it comes to coding categories, the idea for lowering PAPR mainly entailed picking code words with the lowest PAPR. This category includes block coding, interleaving technique, Golay codes, and Read-Muller codes [10, 12]. However, a fourth category, hybrid techniques, containing methods that combine two or more PAPR reduction techniques, will be introduced in this work.

Hybrid methods have acquired popularity in recent years as a result of their ability to combine characteristics of two or more techniques [13]. They can attain superior overall advantages, such as an enhanced PAPR reduction and improved system performance, with only a minor increase in system complexity.

The objective of this study is to provide a novel hybrid methodology that integrates a clipping-filtering technique with a selective mapping method in order to mitigate the PAPR in OFDM system. The clipping method, which is often used to mitigate the PAPR of OFDM signals, is known to experience a decline in performance. In this study, we aim to provide a hybrid model that effectively reduces the PAPR of OFDM signals to a predetermined threshold. Additionally, we ensure that the proposed system does not compromise the BER performance while simultaneously minimizing computational complexity.

The subsequent portions of this work are organized into four distinct parts. Section 2 of this paper offers the OFDM system model, accompanied by a comprehensive characterization of the PAPR. The strategies for reducing PAPR and the suggested solution are presented in Sect. 3. In Sect. 4, we provide the simulation results and conduct an analysis of the findings. In conclusion, Sect. 5 provides a comprehensive summary and finalizes the findings presented in this research.

2 OFDM System Model and PAPR Problem

2.1 OFDM System

The general OFDM transceiver model is shown in Fig. 1. The OFDM signal is generated by combining all N modulated subcarriers by the IFFT operation, while ensuring that the subcarriers maintain orthogonality with each other. In order to comprehend the concept of OFDM, it is necessary to regard X(k) as the complex representation of input data block symbols subsequent to the constellation mapping operation. Specifically, X(k) denotes the k_{th} transmit symbol at the kth subcarrier. k = 0, 1, 2,....N−1. The expression for the baseband OFDM signals in the continuous-time domain, consisting of N subchannels (also known as subcarriers), is as follows: [14]

$$x(t) = \frac{1}{\sqrt{N}} \sum_{k=0}^{N-1} X(k)e^{j2\pi f_k t} \quad 0 < t < T_{sym} \tag{1}$$

where T_{sym} represents the total time of symbol, and $f_k = k/T_{sym}$ represent the different subcarriers and N is the number of subcarriers, and $j = \sqrt{-1}$. The bandwidth of the symbol is $B = N. \Delta f$, and Δf is set as $1/T_{sym}$ in order to guarantee the orthogonality among the subcarriers inside the symbol.

Therefore, the baseband OFDM signal can be represented as follows:

$$x(t) = \frac{1}{\sqrt{N}} \sum_{k=0}^{N-1} X(k)e^{j2\pi kt/T_{sym}} \quad 0 < t < T_{sym} \tag{2}$$

The sampled form of the OFDM signal x(t) in Eq. (2), designated as x(n), can also be expressed as x(n) = x(nT_s), where T_s represents the sampling interval and is equal to T_{sym}/N, conforming to the Nyquist rate.

$$x(n) = \frac{1}{\sqrt{N}} \sum_{k=0}^{N-1} X(k)e^{j2\pi \frac{k}{T_{sym}} \frac{nT_{sym}}{N}} \quad n = 0, 1, \cdots, N-1 \tag{3}$$

$$x(n) = \frac{1}{\sqrt{N}} \sum_{k=0}^{N-1} X(k)e^{j2\pi \frac{k}{N}n} \quad n = 0, 1, \cdots, N-1 \tag{4}$$

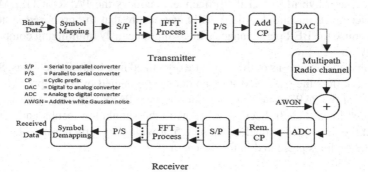

Fig. 1. Block diagram of transceiver in an OFDM system.

where n represents the discrete time index, therefore the discrete OFDM vector can be expressed as

$$x(n) = [x_0, x_1 \ldots x_{N-1}]^T \tag{5}$$

2.2 PAPR

The PAPR of OFDM signal is mathematically expressed as the division of the highest instantaneous power by the average power of the signal. Which can be written as [15]

$$PAPR(x(n)) = \frac{\max\limits_{0 \le n \le N-1} |x(n)|^2}{\frac{1}{N} \sum_0^{N-1} |x(n)|^2} \tag{6}$$

The discretization of the OFDM signal can be achieved by the use of the over-sampling technique. As a result, this approach ensures that certain signal peaks, which may not be captured in the PAPR calculation, are recorded by this procedure. In order to enhance the precision of the PAPR calculations, it is enough to sample the discrete baseband signal with a value of L that is greater than or equal to 4 [16], and this is accomplished by inserting (L-1)N zero-padding between the samples, where L is the oversampling factor. Accordingly, the oversampled OFDM signal is expressed as

$$x(n) = \frac{1}{\sqrt{NL}} \sum_{k=0}^{NL-1} X(k)e^{j2\pi \frac{k}{NL}n} \quad n = 0, 1, \cdots, NL-1 \tag{7}$$

And the PAPR will be represented by,

$$PAPR(x(n)) = \frac{\max\limits_{0 \le n \le NL-1} |x(n)|^2}{\frac{1}{NL} \sum_0^{NL-1} |x(n)|^2} \tag{8}$$

2.3 PAPR Distribution

The complementary cumulative distribution function (CCDF) is a commonly used approach for evaluating the performance PAPR. The CCDF offers a better understanding by monitoring the probability of the PAPR surpassing a certain level. Based on central limit theorem [9, 17], for a large number of subcarriers N, Complex OFDM symbols are composed of real parts and imaginary parts. The real and imaginary components of this variable are distributed according to a Gaussian distribution with a mean of zero and a variance of 0.5. Hence, the magnitude of the signal |x(n)| conforms to a Rayleigh distribution, whereas the power distribution of the signals assumes a central chi-square distribution with two degrees of freedom.

The evaluation of most PAPR reduction approaches is often conducted using the CCDF measure, which is represented as CCDFPAPR (γ) and computed as follows:

$$CCDF_{PAPR}(\gamma) = P_r(PAPR \geq \gamma) = 1 - P_r(PAPR \leq \gamma) \tag{9}$$

$$CCDF_{PAPR}(\gamma) = 1 - \left(1 - e^{-\gamma}\right)^N \tag{10}$$

where γ is the given threshold (also represented by PAPR0 in this paper). Furthermore, when the process of oversampling L is executed, the CCDF of OFDM signal can be formulated as

$$CCDF_{PAPR}(\gamma) = 1 - \left(1 - e^{-\gamma}\right)^{NL} \tag{11}$$

Hence, the CCDF of the OFDM signal exhibits a high level of accuracy when the number of subcarriers N is sufficiently big, specifically when N is more than or equal to 128 [18].

3 PAPR Reduction Techniques

In order to mitigate the issue of a PAPR, a number of solutions have been proposed, which may be classified into four distinct groups. Signal distortion (SD), multiple signaling and probabilistic (MSP), coding, and hybrid techniques [10]. In the context of signal distortion methods, the reduction of a PAPR is achieved by eliminating the high peak of the OFDM signal in the time-domain before passing the signal to the HPA. This process significantly decreases the PAPR value but at the expense of introducing in-band distortion and out-of-band radiation [19]. Consequently, the OFDM system will suffer a decline in BER performance and an increase in frequency spectrum spreading. Multiple signaling approaches use probabilistic methods and rely on generating various representations of the OFDM sequence. The selection of the signal with the lowest PAPR plays an important role in transmission [20]. These approaches provide the benefits of preserving the quality of the transmitted signal and achieving a significant reduction in PAPR. Nevertheless, these systems exhibit significant limitations, including a reduction in data speed caused by the transmission of many side information bits and a rise in complexity.

The coding category is determined by the process of encoding the data block bits in the transmitter and selecting code-words that effectively minimize the PAPR [21], the process does not induce any kind of distortion and does not generate any radiation beyond the designated frequency range. However, a drawback of this approach is its limited bandwidth efficiency due to the reduction in coding rate. Furthermore, the system encounters challenges in terms of the complexity involved in identifying optimal codes and managing extensive lookup tables for encoding and decoding, particularly when dealing with a substantial number of subcarriers. Furthermore, methods which integrate more than one approach to reduce PAPR can be referred to as hybrid techniques [22]. Hybrid methods are frequently accepted as a viable solution for reducing PAPR due to their ability to integrate the advantages of many techniques. Slight increases in complexity may lead to better overall results, including a greater decrease in peak-to-average power ratio (PAPR) and improved system performance. Figure 2 provides a summary of examples for each category.

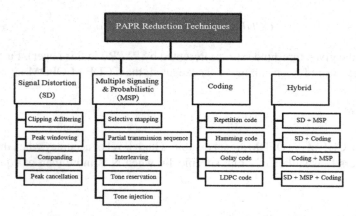

Fig. 2. Classifications of PAPR reduction techniques.

This work presents a novel hybrid approach for mitigating PAPR by integrating the techniques of clipping-filtering and SLM. The objective of this approach is to enhance the system by achieving a substantial decrease in PAPR, improving BER performance compared to the clipping technique, and minimizing complexity in comparison to the traditional SLM technique. The following sections will provide a description of the clipping-filtering and SLM approaches, followed by an outline of the model for the proposed methodology.

3.1 Clipping and Filtering Technique

This method is often regarded as the most straightforward approach to reducing PAPR. It involves a simple procedure of clipping the transmitted signal by limiting the peak amplitude to a predetermined threshold [23]. The resulting signal from the clipping process can be expressed as

$$\hat{x}(n) = \begin{cases} x(n) & |x(n)| < A \\ Ae^{j\angle[x(n)]} & |x(n)| > A \end{cases} \tag{12}$$

where $\angle[x(n)]$ represents the phase of $x(n)$, A is the maximum permissible amplitude over which the signal is clipped. The clipping ratio (CR) is defined as,

$$CR = \frac{A}{\sqrt{P_{in}}} \tag{13}$$

where P_{in} is the average input power of the OFDM signal before clipping.

However, the act of clipping produces non-linear distortion in the OFDM outcome. The introduction of nonlinear distortion results in an increase in both the radiation inside and beyond the desired frequency range. Figure 3 displays the power spectral density PSD of both the clipped signal and the unclipped signal. Both the distortion of the in-band signal and the out-of-band signal induced by clipping are perceptible. To mitigate the occurrence of out-of-band radiation, it is suggested to include a filtering mechanism subsequent to the process of clipping. Nevertheless, it is incapable of reducing in-band distortion, hence affecting the overall performance of the system..

Figure 4 shows the transmitter block diagram of an N sub-carrier OFDM system using the method of clipping and filtering.

It should be noticed that when the OFDM signals get direct clipping, the resultant noise from clipping will be entirely located within the frequency band of interest (referred to as in-band noise). Consequently, this in-band noise cannot be mitigated or decreased by the use of filters [24]. To overcome this aliasing problem, padding the original input data symbols X with zeros and applying these data with zero padding as the input to IFFT and the output from IFFT is called oversampling OFDM signal.

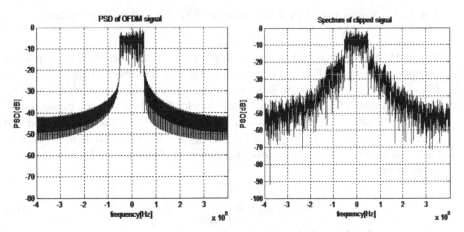

Fig. 3. PSD performance of un-clipped and clipped signal.

Fig. 4. Transmitter side of an OFDM system with envelope limiter.

3.2 Selective Mapping Technique SLM

SLM has been widely recognized as one of the most effective approaches for reducing PAPR [25]. Since the SLM is a multiple signaling technique, the concept of SLM differs from clipping technique. The concept here is any one single data vector of the transmitter signal can have multiple representations. The time domain vector with the lowest PAPR is chosen for transmission from the available options. The use of this approach yields the lowest PAPR, nevertheless, the complexity of the system increases due to the need of several IFFT operations [26]. The effect of SLM on the PAPR reduction and BER performance of the OFDM system will be evaluated in the sections that follow. The Fig. 5 illustrates the block diagram of N sub-carrier OFDM system using SLM technique.

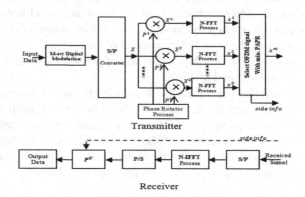

Fig. 5. Block diagram of the selective mapping SLM technique for PAPR reduction.

The SLM approach requires the multiplication of a data vector consisting of N symbols $X = [X(0), X(1), \ldots X(N-1)]^T$ by U phase sequences $P^u = [P_0^u, P_1^u, \cdots, P_{N-1}^u]$, $1 \leq u \leq U$ to generate U alternative symbol sequences that represents the same information as the original data block. P^u is the U_{th} block phase vector, where $P_v^u = e^{j\varphi_v^u}$ and $\varphi_v^u \in [0, 2\pi)$ for and $u = 1, 2, \cdots, U$. As a result, the modified data is then represented by $X^u = [X_1^u, X_2^u, \cdots, X_{N-1}^u]^T$. IFFT is performed for each of the U alternative symbol sequences, and then the one with the lowest PAPR is selected for transmission.

$$x^m(n) = \underset{1 < u \leq U}{\operatorname{argmin}} \left\{ \frac{max |x^u(n)|^2}{E|x^u(n)|^2} \right\} \tag{14}$$

To get back the original input data vector, it is necessary to transmit information about the chosen phase sequence to the receiver as supplemental information [27].

3.3 The Proposed Hybrid Technique

As previously stated, the conventional SLM method involves the following process: the generation of a set of phase-rotated data blocks by multiplying the original OFDM data block (using array multiplication) with U-independent phase sequences. All data blocks are representative of identical information, and the data block exhibiting the lowest PAPR will be selected for transmission. In other words, for each OFDM data block, the conventional SLM scheme will need to do U mappings and U IFFT computations. The problem is whether all U phase mappings for each OFDM data block are necessary. We should be able get lower computational complexity if we can find a way to reduce the number of phase mappings. In any practical system, the peak power of transmission power amplifier is limited, which translates to fixed a clipping level. So it is not necessary to further reduce the PAPR if the PAPR of the candidate OFDM data block is low enough to avoid clipping. According to this reasoning, we should set a PAPR threshold based on the peak power of the power amplifier to avoid the unnecessary mappings. Once the PAPR of the candidate signal is below the threshold, the phase mapping procedure will stop immediately and the current candidate signal will be transmitted.

Consequently, it is important to take into account the PAPR threshold γ_{th}, which is determined by the power amplifier limit. In this study, an amplifier with an 8-dB power back-off was used [28]. Therefore, based on the SLM approach, how many phase rotations do we need to make sure the PAPR of the OFDM signal is below a particular threshold level of 8 dB? Keep in mind that reducing the number of IFFT processes (phase mappings) will minimize the complexity of the SLM approach and therefore the need for additional computational effort.

To answer this question we simulate a large number of OFDM symbols modulated using the QPSK modulation. We next examine how using various numbers of phase rotations affects the PAPR. According to Fig. 6, the probability of using one phase rotation is approximately 0.79, meaning that 79% of all OFDM symbols will have PAPR values below the threshold level after using just one phase rotation. Additionally, the probability of using more than four phase rotations is only 2% meaning that 2% of all OFDM symbols need to more than 4 phase rotation to reach the threshold level.

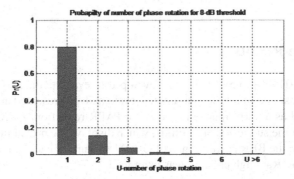

Fig. 6. Probability mass function of using different number of phase rotation to reach 8 dB threshold level.

We propose the hybrid SLM-clipping procedure showed in Fig. 7 depending on these results. Where γ_{th} is the PAPR threshold, which is defined according to the fixed clipping level of the power amplifier. There are two decision blocks in the system. While one is used to compare the PAPR value of phased rotated signal after mapping with the threshold γ_{th}, another is used to determine whether the current phase sequence is the last one. Compared to conventional SLM, the new scheme performs the next mapping only if the PAPR value of current phase rotated signal is bigger than the threshold. For example, when an OFDM data block enters the proposed system. It will be scrambled with the first phase sequence P^1. If the PAPR value of the first phase rotated signal is below or equal to the threshold γ_{th}, the candidate signal will be sent out directly without trying more phase sequences. Otherwise, if the current phase sequence is not the last one, the original data block will be scrambled with the next phase sequence P^2 to get a new candidate signal. The new generated signal's PAPR will be compared with γ_{th} again to determine whether to transmit it or start the next mapping.

The same procedure will be repeated until a PAPR value below the threshold is achieved or the system reaches the last phase sequence U $= 4$ (4th iteration) (since the PAPR of 98% of OFDM symbols will be under threshold ($\gamma_{th} = 8$ dB). If the procedure stops at the last phase sequence with a PAPR larger than the threshold, the OFDM data block will pass through clipping and filtering process.

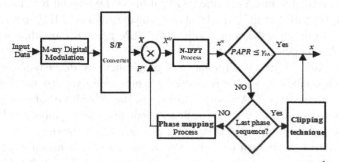

Fig. 7. Block diagram of the proposed hybrid SLM-Clipping technique.

4   Simulation Results

A MATLAB (R2019b) programmer was developed to evaluate the performance of the suggested methods. The simulation parameters evaluated are presented in Table 1. CCDF curve was picked as a performance measure for PAPR reduction. A CCDF curve was drawn for each of the suggested algorithms, which displays the probability vs the PAPR in dB furthermore the BER performance of OFDM system for each reduction technique across AWGN and Rayleigh channel was examined.

Table 1. Simulation Parameters

Simulation Parameter	Value
Number of subcarriers (N)	256
Modulation scheme	QPSK
Number of Symbols	10^5
over sampling factor L	4
guard interval type	cyclic extension
cyclic prefix length	0.25 * size of OFDM symbol
channel models	AWGN & Rayleigh fading

4.1 Simulation Results of Clipping and Filtering Technique for Different Values of CR

To evaluate the PAPR reduction capability of clipping technique the CCDF of the PAPR is recorded during the simulation. Figure 8 shows the PAPR performance of the clipped signal, and for sake of comparison, the PAPR of the un-clipped signal is also shown. Different clipping ratios are considered. Clearly, clipping largely compresses the dynamic range of the signal amplitudes. With CR = 0.6 reducing the PAPR 5.8 dB at CCDF of 10^{-3} is achievable. And with CR = 1.2 the PAPR can be reduced 5 dB at CCDF of 10^{-3}.

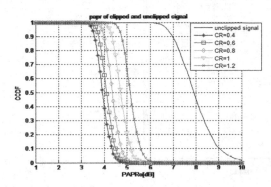

Fig. 8. PAPR performance of un-clipped and clipped signals

Effect of Clipping on BER performance of OFDM system is also studied through simulation analysis. Different clipping ration values (0.6, 0.8, 1, and 1.2) are chosen. Figure 9 (a, b) shows that the BER performance as a function of the received signal-to-noise ratio (SNR) with AWGN and Rayleigh channel respectively.

Although the filtering reduce out of band radiation, the in-band noise still exists, which causes a degradation in the bit error rate performance (BER). in additive white Gaussian noise (AWGN) channel Fig. 9-a. For CR = 0.8 the performance degradation is more than 4 dB at 10^{-3} BER level. However, when CR = 1 the degradation is about

2 dB at 10^{-3} BER level. Also in Rayleigh channel the BER degrades noticeably with the increase of clipping level as shown in Fig. 9-b.

4.2　Simulation Results of Selective Mapping Technique for Different Values of U

Figure 10 shows the performance of SLM scheme for PAPR reduction in a 2, 4, 8 and 16 phase mapping scenarios respectively. The measured PAPR at a given CCDF of 10^{-3} is presented in Table 2.

Table 2. SLM at CCDF $= 10^{-3}$, measured PAPR in dB

No. of U	2	4	8	16	Without SLM
PAPR(dB)	10.4	9.2	8.65	8.15	11.2

From Table 2 it can be seen that SLM technique achieves a PAPR gain of 0.8, 2, 2.5 and 3.1 dB from the original OFDM signal for 2, 4, 8 and 16 number of phase vectors respectively. From the Fig. 10, it is evident that the performance of SLM algorithm improves as we go on increasing the number of phase vectors U.

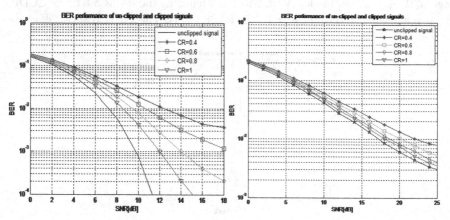

Fig. 9. BER performance for the Clipping technique and conventional OFDM signal over (a) AWGN channel (b) Rayleigh channel

Simulation results of BER vs. SNR using SLM techniques through AWGN channel and Rayleigh fading channel are given below (Fig. 11 a, b). It can be seen that in spite of the difference in number of phase rotation process in the SLM scheme, the bit error rates simulated are nearly identical with the original OFDM signal(without SLM). Which indicates that the OFDM signal is not damaged by SLM technique. Although Selective Mapping (SLM) is a distortion less technique that can reduce PAPR efficiently without increase in power requirement and decrease BER, the computational complexity of SLM increases with U, which is a major drawback of SLM technique.

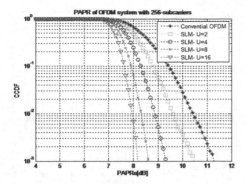

Fig. 10. PAPR performance of SLM technique for different number of phase mapping-U

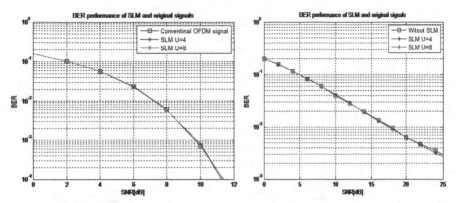

Fig. 11. BER performance for the SLM technique and conventional OFDM signal over (a) AWGN channel (b) Rayleigh channel

4.3 Simulation Results of the Proposed Hybrid Technique

Figure 12 shows the CCDFs of the PAPR of the unmodified OFDM data block and the reduced PAPR after proposed technique is used. It is shown that for 4 phase sequences (U = 4), the probability that the PAPR of the modified data block exceeds the threshold will drop to 10^{-6}, which is a very good PAPR reduction performance.

In addition The Fig. 13 presents the simulation results of BER vs SNR obtained by employing the proposed technique over an AWGN channel and a Rayleigh fading channel (Fig. 13). It is observed that as the signal to noise ratio (SNR) increases, the proposed scheme achieves better performance. Moreover, the performance of the proposed hybrid technique is better than that of the clipping scheme. For example, at a BER level of 10^{-3} for QPSK and AWGN channel the minimum required SNR of hybrid scheme with U = 4, CR = 0.8 is around 9.8 dB, which surpasses clipping scheme (CR = 0.8) 4 dB It is also found that the minimum required SNR for the proposed scheme with U = 4, CR = 0.8 over Rayleigh channel is around 17 dB when BER = 10^{-2}. Therefore, we can see the effectiveness of the proposed hybrid technique compared to the clipping technique.

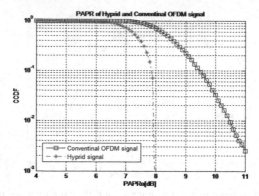

Fig. 12. PAPR performance of hybrid technique and conventional OFDM signals

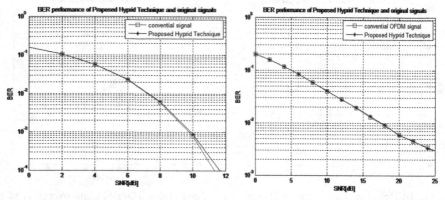

Fig. 13. BER performance for proposed technique and conventional OFDM signal over (a) AWGN channel (b) Rayleigh channel

As stated earlier the Conventional OFDM system is computationally efficient since it only uses IFFT and FFT at the transmitter and receiver sides. However the computational complexity of SLM–OFDM system increases with the rise of the number of phase mapping U. Therefore the computational complexity of SLM can be determined as,

$$C_{SLM} = U\left(\frac{N}{2}log_2N\right) \tag{15}$$

where N -point IFFT requires $(N/2)log_2N$ complex multiplications [3]. On the other hand, in the proposed scheme, for each OFDM data block, the next mapping will happen only if the PAPR of the current phase rotated signal exceeds γ_{th}. In other words, there will be no more mapping if the PAPR of the current phase rotated signal is below γ_{th} and this mean there will be on average U possible mappings for each ODFM data block. Therefore the computational complexity can be determined as,

$$C_{hyp} = E[U]\left(\frac{N}{2}log_2N\right) \tag{16}$$

we can derive the expected number of phase mappings for each OFDM block, E[U], by calculating the sum of the product of each possible number of mappings and the probability of the mapping will stop at that specific phase sequence, i.e.,

$$E[U] = \sum_{u=1}^{U} u\Pr(u) \tag{17}$$

To measure the reduction ratio of the our proposed hybrid technique compared to conventional SLM method, The computational complexity reduction ratio CCRR is adopted [27]. Therefore, the CCRR can be defined as:

$$CCRR = 1 - \left(\frac{\text{complexity of } hybrid \text{ } technique}{\text{complexity of conventional SLM method}} \right) \times 100\% \tag{18}$$

According to the Fig. 6, in our proposed technique, the average number of phase mappings is about 1.32 for one data block. Comparing with the conventional SLM scheme for the same PAPR performance, there is 92% savings on IFFT computations, on average. This clearly shows that the proposed technique provides much lower computational complexity than conventional SLM scheme while keeping an acceptable PAPR reduction performance.

5 Conclusion

OFDM systems have several advantages over traditional single-carrier systems such as FDM (Frequency Division Multiplexing). These include better spectral efficiency, improved robustness against multipath propagation, and support for high data rates. However, one of the main challenges with OFDM systems is the high PAPR which can lead to distortion in the transmitted signal. Several PAPR reduction techniques have been proposed in order to overcome the OFDM peak power problem. Among those techniques, Clipping is a simple and computationally efficient PAPR reduction scheme but it introduce more distortion in the signal. SLM, on the other hand, is a powerful and efficient PAPR reduction scheme without nonlinear distortion. However, the computational complexity of the SLM process is relatively high due to U − 1 additional IFFTs.

In this research work, a hybrid scheme that combines clipping and SLM is proposed to reduce the PAPR of OFDM systems. It works by repeatedly modifying the phase of each subcarrier in the OFDM signal and measuring the PAPR in each iteration, with the goal of reducing the peak power of the signal to the PAPR threshold, which is specified by the fixed clipping level of the power amplifier. The clipping and filtering process will be applied to the OFDM signal if the process is terminated at the last iteration with a PAPR that is greater than the threshold.

Simulation results show the effectiveness of the proposed technique in decreasing the PAPR by 4.1 dB relative to the original OFDM signal at a CCDF of 10^{-3}. Moreover, the BER performance of the hybrid technique is superior to that of the clipping technique for the same clipping level, as the minimum required SNR of the hybrid scheme is approximately 4 and 2 dB lower than that of the clipping technique for AWGN and Rayleigh fading channels, respectively, at BER = 10^{-3} and 10^{-2} for both channels.

Furthermore comparing the proposed technique to the conventional SLM scheme for the same PAPR reduction performance, IFFT computations are reduced by 92% on average, indicating that the proposed technique has a significantly lower computational complexity while achieving an acceptable PAPR reduction performance.

References

1. Barneto, C.B., et al.: Full-duplex OFDM radar with LTE and 5G NR waveforms: challenges, solutions, and measurements. IEEE Trans. Microw. Theor. Tech. **67**(10), 4042–4054 (2019)
2. Mishra, H., Rai, D.K.: Review paper on orthogonal frequency division multiplexing (OFDM). Int. Res. J. Modernization Eng. Technol. Sci. **3**, 1295–1301 (2021)
3. Jawhar, Y.A., et al.: A review of partial transmit sequence for PAPR reduction in the OFDM systems. IEEE Access **7**, 18021–18041 (2019)
4. Sundararajan, M., Govindaswamy, U.: Multicarrier spread spectrum modulation schemes and efficient FFT algorithms for cognitive radio systems. Electronics **3**(3), 419–443 (2014)
5. Dixit, S., Katiyar, H.: Performance of OFDM in time selective multipath fading channel in 4G systems. In: 2015 Fifth International Conference on Communication Systems and Network Technologies, pp. 421–424. IEEE (2015)
6. Nagul, S.: A review on 5G modulation schemes and their comparisons for future wireless communications. In: 2018 Conference on Signal Processing and Communication Engineering Systems (SPACES), pp. 72–76. IEEE (2018)
7. Mounir, M., El_Mashade, M.B., Berra, S., Gaba, G.S., Masud, M.: A novel hybrid precoding-companding technique for peak-to-average power ratio reduction in 5G and beyond. Sensors **21**(4), 1410 (2021)
8. Xing, Z., Liu, K., Rajasekaran, A.S., Yanikomeroglu, H., Liu, Y.: A hybrid companding and clipping scheme for PAPR reduction in OFDM systems. IEEE Access **9**, 61565–61576 (2021)
9. Rahmatallah, Y., Mohan, S.: Peak-to-average power ratio reduction in OFDM systems: a survey and taxonomy. IEEE Commun. Surv. Tutor. **15**(4), 1567–1592 (2013)
10. Sandoval, F., Poitau, G., Gagnon, F.: Hybrid peak-to-average power ratio reduction techniques: review and performance comparison. IEEE Access **5**, 27145–27161 (2017)
11. Mahajan, K.A., Mukhare, S.V.:Comparison of signal scrambling PAPR reduction techniques with signal distortion techniques in OFDM signal. In: International Conference on Recent Trends in Information Technology and Computer Science (ICRTITCS), pp. 18–22 (2012)
12. Hori, Y., Ochiai, H.: A new uplink multiple access based on OFDM with low PAPR, low latency, and high reliability. IEEE Trans. Commun. **66**(5), 1996–2008 (2018)
13. Akurati, M., Pentamsetty, S.K., Kodati, S.P.: Optimizing the reduction of PAPR of OFDM system using hybrid methods. Wirel. Pers. Commun. **125**(3), 2685–2703 (2022)
14. Thota, S., Kamatham, Y., Paidimarry, C.S.: Analysis of hybrid PAPR reduction methods of OFDM signal for HPA models in wireless communications. IEEE Access **8**, 22780–22791 (2020)
15. Nguyen, Q., Nguyen, T.K., Nguyen, H.H., Berscheid, B.: Novel PAPR reduction algorithms for OFDM signals. IEEE Access **10**, 77452–77461 (2022)
16. Tang, B., Qin, K., Mei, H.: A hybrid approach to reduce the PAPR of OFDM signals using clipping and companding. IEEE Access **8**, 18984–18994 (2020)
17. Kanti, R.D., Rao, R.C.S.: Systematic comparison of different PAPR reduction methods in OFDM systems. Int. J. Electron. Commun. Eng. **7**(1), 21–30 (2017)
18. Jiang, T., Wu, Y.: An overview: peak-to-average power ratio reduction techniques for OFDM signals. IEEE Trans. Broadcast. **54**(2), 257–268 (2008)

19. Kakkar, A., Garsha, S.N., Jain, O.: Improvisation in BER and PAPR by using hybrid reduction techniques in MIMO-OFDM employing channel estimation techniques. In: 2017 IEEE 7th International Advance Computing Conference (IACC), pp. 170–173. IEEE (2017)
20. Gangwar, A.K.S., Bhardwaj, M.: An overview: peak to average power ratio in OFDM system & its Effect (2012)
21. Falconer, D.D.: Linear precoding of OFDMA signals to minimize their instantaneous power variance. IEEE Trans. Commun. **59**(4), 1154–1162 (2011)
22. Haque, M.D., Rana, M.M., Tithy, T.A.: PAPR reduction and bit error rate evaluation in OFDM system using hybrid techniques. Int. J. AdHoc Netw. Syst. (IJANS) **12** (2022)
23. Beena, A., Pillai, S.S., Vijayakumar, N.: Hybrid PTS-clipping scheme for PAPR reduction in MIMO-OFDM systems. Int. J. Appl. Eng. Res. **13**(11), 9924–9928 (2018)
24. Rajkumarsingh, B., Rajarai, R.R., Hosany, M.: Performance analysis of hybrid filtering technique for reduction of Papr in alamouti coded mimo-ofdm systems (2022)
25. Mhatre, K., Khot, U.P.: Efficient selective mapping PAPR reduction technique. Procedia comput. Sci. **45**, 620–627 (2015)
26. Mahadevaswamy, U.B., Geetha, M.N.: A comparative survey on PAPR reduction in OFDM signal. In: 2016 International Conference on Electrical, Electronics, Communication, Computer and Optimization Techniques (ICEECCOT), pp. 123–126 (2016)
27. Hu, C., Wang, L., Zhou, Z.: "A modified SLM scheme for PAPR reduction in OFDM systems. In: 2020 IEEE 10th International Conference on Electronics Information and Emergency Communication (ICEIEC), pp. 61–64. IEEE (2020)
28. Saad, P., Hou, R., Hellberg, R., Berglund, B.: A 1.8–3.8-GHz power amplifier with 40% efficiency at 8-dB power back-off. IEEE Trans. Microw. Theor. Tech. **66**(11), 4870–4882 (2018)

AI-Driven Path Loss Optimization in 4G Networks Through PSO Algorithm

Hanane Djellab[1]([⊠]), Amel Bouchemha[2], Fouzia Maamri[3], Farouk Boumehrez[4], and Abdelhakim Sahour[3]

[1] Laboratory of LTI, Department of Electrical Engineering,
Echahid Cheikh Larbi Tebessi University, Tebessa, Algeria
djellab@univ-tebessa.dz

[2] Laboratory of LAVIA, Department of Electrical Engineering,
Echahid Cheikh Larbi Tebessi University, Tebessa, Algeria

[3] Laboratory of SATIT, Department of Industrial Engineering, Khenchela, Algeria

[4] Laboratory of LTI, Department of Industrial Engineering,
Khenchela University, Khenchela, Algeria

Abstract. This paper investigates signal attenuation in the mobile user interface of a 4G cellular network and proposes an AI-driven strategy to enhance path loss prediction. Employing the Particle Swarm Optimization (PSO) algorithm coupled with AI techniques, it analyzes and forecasts path losses. Measurements were conducted at 1800 MHz and 2100 MHz frequencies in a suburban area of Tebessa. The objective was to minimize the Root Mean Square Error (RMSE) between theoretical and observed path losses by optimizing parameters for the COST231 and Ericsson models using AI-supported PSO. The optimized models, benefiting from the synergy between AI and PSO, exhibited superior performance compared to unoptimized empirical models.

Keywords: mobile network · propagation model · 4G LTE network · Path loss models · metaheuristic · PSO · RMSE

1 Introduction

In recent times, significant strides have been made in advancing mobile network development, a domain increasingly pivotal in modern society. With a growing demand for connectivity everywhere and burgeoning user populations, the deployment and evolution of multiple mobile technology networks have become imperative. Mobile operators are thus tasked with meticulous network coverage planning, integrating radio wave propagation models and optimization algorithms. Long Term Evolution (LTE) and LTE Advanced (LTE-A) are the latest breakthroughs in mobile network technology representing a substantial leap from earlier 3G networks to more sophisticated 4G networks. These technologies operate using a shared frequency spectrum [1, 2], Path loss models play a crucial role in predicting coverage areas, conducting interference analysis, assigning frequencies, and determining cell parameters, making them indispensable components of

T. A. T. Benmusa et al. (Eds.): ILCICT 2023, CCIS 2097, pp. 20–26, 2024.
https://doi.org/10.1007/978-3-031-62624-1_2

mobile communication system projects [3], The transition to 4G networks, specifically utilizing the LTE Advanced standard, significantly boosts user bandwidth and enhances various quality of service parameters. The work of scientist Okumura in Tokyo, Japan, forms a cornerstone in this field. Okumura conducted experiments measuring signal loss at different frequencies and distances, culminating in the development of the Hata-Okumura planning model. This model, accompanied by graphical curves tailored to different environments, such as urban, suburban, and quasi-open areas, has served as a foundation for various derived models, including the well-known Cost-Hata model. Empirical propagation models [4], designed for specific propagation environments, have been developed based on distinct propagation characteristics. While several attempts have been made to design propagation models for different regions, this study primarily focuses on optimizing the path loss of different LTE radio models [5, 6], The Particle Swarm Optimization (PSO) algorithm [7], inspired by collective behavior observed in social organisms, is employed to refine existing models and adapt them to the specific conditions in the Tebessa (eNodB 12668) milieu. The objective is to identify and refine the most precise model through the utilization of the PSO algorithm, ultimately enhancing performance within the examined setting. The precision of the optimized model will be verified using the root mean square error (RMSE) to improve path loss prediction in tested environments. We detail the experimental setup in Sect. 4. Section 5 illustrates the optimization results obtained through the application of PSO. Lastly, in Sect. 6, we encapsulate the essence of the paper by summarizing the findings and delving into the implications of the proposed work.

2 Particle Swarm Optimization PSO

E Particle Swarm Optimization (PSO) algorithm, first introduced by Kennedy and Eberhart [10], is a metaheuristic approach [9] inspired by the collective behavior of birds navigating through a multidimensional space to find an optimal position. Through the adaptation of their movements and distances, a swarm of particles aims to enhance their search capabilities. PSO shares similarities with the genetic algorithm (GA) and operates as a dynamic computational method. Within the proposed PSO framework, every particle in the initial random population possesses its unique fitness value, which is determined by the objective function's output. These particles subsequently navigate the search space by aligning their movements with the current optimal value among the particles [11–13]. Following each iteration, the particle's movement is calculated employing the formula:

$$V\_i(t + 1) = V\_i(t) + C\_1 * r\_1(P\_best - X\_i(t)) + r\_2(G\_best \ X\_i(t)) \quad (1)$$

$$X_i(t + 1) = X_i(t) + V_i(t + 1) \quad (2)$$

Vi is the velocity, Xi is the position. The particle's Pbest represents its own currently optimal position, while the Gbest represents the best position achieved by the entire swarm up to the present moment. The variables r1 and r2 are random variables with values ranging from 0 to 1, and C1 and C2 denote the acceleration coefficients.

The following diagram illustrates the sequential steps of the PSO algorithm (Fig. 1).

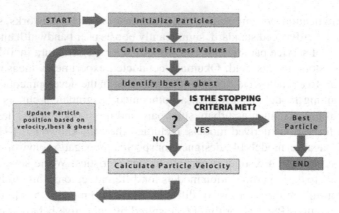

Fig. 1. Flowchart of the proposed PSO Algorithm [14]

3 Empirical Models

This study incorporates the following propagation models: the Okumura Hata Model.

3.1 Okumura Hata Model

The Okumura-Hata model is an empirical formulation of data graphical path loss for the 150–1500 MHz band [14, 15]. The study considers a distance range of 1 to 20 km between the transmitter and the receiver. The Path loss for the model as given in Eq. (5):

$$PL_{urbain} = 69 \cdot 55 + 26 \cdot 16 \log(f) - 13 \cdot 82 \, \log(h_b)$$
$$+ (44 \cdot 9 - 6 \cdot 55 \log(h_b)) \log(d) - a(h_m) \tag{3}$$

Within the study, the following variables are employed: f denotes the frequency in MHz, d represents the distance in kilometers, h_b signifies the height of the mobile antenna in meters, and h_m corresponds to the height of the base station antenna in meters. The expression of path loss for a suburban environment is shown below

$$PL_{suburban} = PL_{urban}(dB) - 2[\log(f/28)]^2 - 5 \cdot 4 \tag{4}$$

4 Experimental Setup

4.1 Measurements Procedure

Path loss calculations are performed using the previously discussed path loss equations for RF propagation models. The resulting data is then visualized by generating graphs using MATLAB. Various parameters are taken into account in our calculations, including carrier frequencies, distances between the transmitter and receiver, receiver height, and base station height. Table 2 provides the simulation parameters for the propagation models. Our study focused on analyzing the coverage area of eNodeB 12668, specifically investigating its performance within a distance of 1 km while continuously recording the received signal strengths (RSRP). To evaluate the outdoor coverage of eNodeB 12668 in the suburban area of Tebessa City, we conducted a comparative analysis on path loss using different radio propagation models, including Ericsson, Okumura Hata, Cost 231, and Egli models. The accuracy of these models was assessed using Root Mean Squared Error (RMSE) as a metric to evaluate their performance. Simulation parameters for the propagation models include the suburban area designation, a transmitter antenna height of 24 m, a mobile station antenna height of 2 m, and operating frequencies of 1800 MHz and 2100 MHz.

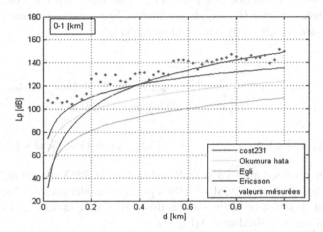

Fig. 2. Path loss of measurements data and empirical models

Lower RMSE values signify superior model accuracy. In our study, empirical Cost 231 and Ericsson models exhibited the lowest RMSE values compared to others, indicating their effectiveness. RMSE [18] was calculated by comparing measured data with predictions from empirical models, and signal strength measurements were then converted to path loss (PL_m) as illustrated in Fig. 2. Notably, the path loss values corresponding to the received power and empirical models are detailed in Table 1.

Table 1. RMSE between measured data and empirical model

Model	Cost231	Okumura Hata	Ericsson	Egli
RMSE	13.40	24.3612	18.7283	40

5 Optimization Results by PSO

To determine the best path loss prediction model, we used Root Mean Squared Error (RMSE). The models with the lowest RMSE, COST-231 and Ericsson, were deemed most accurate for Tebessa's conditions. Thus, we selected them as the optimal options for path loss prediction in the Tebessa region.

5.1 Optimization Strategy

We optimize Cost 231 and Ericsson models based on the study. For Cost231, a single equation with five variables (K_1–K_5) is formulated. Ericsson model uses four variables (A_0–A_3) to ensure compatibility with field measurements.

- *Cost231*

$$PL_{\cos t231} = 46.3 + 33.9\log(f) - 13.82\log(h_b) - a(h_m)$$
$$+ \left[44.9 - 6.55\log(h_b)\right]log(d) + C \tag{5}$$

$$K_1 = 46.3, K_2 = 33.9, \ K3 = 13.82, K_4 = 44.9, K_5 = -6.55.$$

The simulation results, based on default parameters of PSO algorithm, show lower Root Mean Squared Errors (RMSEs) in the optimized model compared to the original Cost 231 model. Test number 2 emphasizes this observation, indicating the validity and effectiveness of the optimized model (Fig. 3).

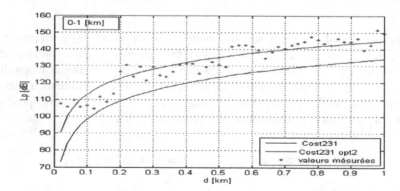

Fig. 3. Comparison between COST231 and COST231-Opt 2.

Figure 4 presents a comparison of measured and predicted path loss for selected models. The figure illustrates the performance of PSO with the optimum solution. Results show the COST 231 model at 1800 MHz offers the most accurate prediction, while the Ericsson model improves at 2100 MHz. Table 5 compares optimized Cost 231 and Ericsson models.

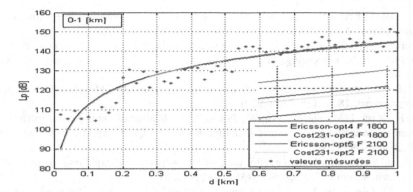

Fig. 4. Comparison between Cost231-opt and Ericsson-opt

6   Conclusion

This study aimed to optimize a propagation model for accurately predicting path loss in a 4G LTE network in Tebessa. Various models were analyzed, and comparison with measured path loss at 1800 MHz and 2100 MHz was conducted. The Particle Swarm Optimization (PSO) algorithm optimized path loss, and link margin was evaluated using RMSE. Results showed precise predictions by the COST 231 model at 1800 MHz and exceptional suitability of the Ericsson model at 2100 MHz.

References

1. Shabbir, N., Sadiq, M.T., Kashif, H., Ullah, R.: Comparison of radio propagation models for long term evolution (LTE) network. Int. J. Next-Gener. Netw. **3**(3), 27–41 (2011)
2. Cavalcanti, B.J., Cavalcante, G.A.: A hybrid path loss prediction model based on artificial neural networks using empirical models for LTE and LTE-A at 800 MHz and 2600 MHz. J. Microwaves Optoelectron. Electromagnet. Appl. **16**(3), 708–722 (2017)
3. Nkordeh, N.S., et al.: LTE network planning using the hata-okumura and the COST-231 Hata Pathloss models. In: Proceedings of the World Congress on Engineering, London, UK (2014)
4. Mollel, M.S., Kisangiri, M.: "Comparison of empirical propagation path loss models for mobile", communication. Comput. Eng. Intell. Syst. **5**(9), 1–10 (2014)
5. Ibhaze, A.E., Imoize, A.L., Ajose, S.O., John, S.N., Ndujiuba, C.U., Idachaba, F.E.: An empirical propagation model for path loss prediction at 2100 MHz in a dense urban environment. Indian J. Sci. Technol. **10**(5), 1–9 (2017)
6. Ajose, S.O., Imoize, A.L.: Propagation measurements and modeling at 1800 MHz in Lagos Nigeria. Int. J. Wirel. Mob. Comput. **6**(2), 165–174 (2013)
7. Misra, D.D., et al.: Optimal routing in the 5G ultra dense small cell network using GA, PSO and hybrid PSO-GA evolutionary algorithms. In: 24th International Conference on Circuits, Systems, Communications and Computers (CSCC), pp. 39–44 (2020)
8. Imoize, A.L., et al.: Analysis of key performance indicators of a 4G LTE network based on experimental data obtained from a densely populated smart city, Data Brief (2020)
9. Maamri, F., et al.: The Pachcondela Apicalis metaheuristic algorithm for parameters identification of chaotic electrical system. Int. J. Parallel Emerg. Distrub. Syst. **33**(1), 1–13 (2018)

10. Kennedy, J., Eberhart, R.: Particle swarm optimization. In: Proceedings IEEE International Conference on Neural Networks, Perth, Australia (1995)
11. Eberhart, R.C., Shi, R.: Comparing inertia weights and constriction factors in particle swarm optimization. In: Proceedings of the 2000 Congress on Evolutionary Computing, pp. 84–89 (2000)
12. Sylia, Z., et al.: New strategy for resource allocation using PSO-PFS hybrid. Int. J. Wirel. Mob. Comput. 18(2), 175–182 (2020)
13. Qi, H., Ruan, L.M., Shi, M., An, W., Tan, H.P.: Application of multi-phase particle swarm optimization technique to inverse radiation problem. J. Quant. Spectrosc. Radiat. Transf. 109(3), 476–493 (2008)
14. Waleed, S., et al.: Resource allocation of 5G network by exploiting particle swarm optimization. Iran J. Comput. Sci. 4(3), 211–219 (2021)
15. Erceg, V., Greenstein, L.J., et al.: An empirically based path loss model for wireless channels in suburban environments. IEEE J. Sel. Areas Commun. 17, 1205–1211 (1999)
16. Gadze, J.D., et al.: Improved propagation models for LTE pathloss prediction in urban & suburban Ghana. Int. J. Wirel. Mob. Networks (IJWMN). 11(6) (2019)
17. Michael, S., et al.: An overview of various propagation model for mobile communication. In: Proceedings of the 2nd Pan African International Conference on Science, Computing and Telecommunications, pp. 148–153 (2014)
18. Zielinski, K., Laur, R.: Stopping criteria for differential evolution in constrained single-objective optimization. In: Chakraborty, U.K. (ed.) Advances in Differential Evolution, pp. 111–138. Springer, Heidelberg (2008). https://doi.org/10.1007/978-3-540-68830-3_4

Topology Discovery Tool for OpenFlow Controllers

Mohamed Sati, Moad Emshiheet, Ahmed Majouk,
and Salem Omar Sati(✉)

IT Faculty, Misurata University, Misurata, Libya
{m09191148,m09191167,a.almagouk,salem.sati}@it.misuratau.edu.ly

Abstract. Decoupling the control plane from the forwarding plane is suggested by Software Defined Networks (SDNs). The OpenFlow SDN control protocol can be used to deploy SDN for virtual switches communications in this new architecture, which provides centralized management and monitoring. The creation of SDN technology based on software programming necessitates tests and measuring equipment that can assess performance. However, the open-source performance tools for SDN architecture that are currently available only test the fundamental attributes, despite the fact that there are numerous SDN controllers that require evaluation with relation to topology discovery time. As a performance monitoring tool for SDN controllers, this study suggests the Topology Discovery Tool (TDT). This tool can measure how quickly various topology sizes converge. The northbound interface of Python programming was used to create this utility. The tool is used in the research to evaluate the performance of well-known SDN controllers in systems with various topology sizes and out-of-band control strategies, including an Open Network Operating System, OpenDaylight, and Floodlight.

Keywords: Controller Performance · ODL Controller · ONOS Controller · Floodlight Controller · SDN Tool

1 Introduction

SDN (Software Defined Networking) [19] is a novel technology with new network requirements. Control in SDN networks is logically concentrated in the central component known as the controller. The OpenFlow protocol [15] appears to be the most often used protocol for SDN networks. The SDN controller offers a variety of signaling protocols and standards for virtual switches' connection with this SDN controller. The controller may connect with virtual switches using the OpenFlow protocol, which is regarded as an open protocol. Many SDN controllers have been proposed with different vendors and programming language and characteristics. These controllers such as, NOX [20] open-source controller which implemented by Nicira. This controller is programmed using C++. where

Supported by Misurata University.

POX [11] also an open-source SDN controller. This controller is inspired from the NOX controller, however, the POX controller is implemented using Python. The other Python controller is RYU [5] controller. On the other side, there are three SDN controllers implemented using Java which are Open Network Operating System (ONOS) [4], OpenDayLight (ODL) [14] and Floodlight [8] controllers. Hence, it may be difficult for a administrator to choose the best controller. Furthermore, the administrator will face the question *how he decides which controller is fast and suitable for large-scale SDN network ?*. An objective and programmable evaluation tool will be very helpful for administrators, that SDN tool should measure the SDN performance metrics. The tool which will evaluate the performance of SDN controllers can help administrators and designers to take the right decision. In this research, a Python performance monitoring tool for SDN controllers is proposed and implemented. OpenFlow is used as the tool's communication and control protocol. Regardless of the size of the network, managers can use this tool to measure the SDN controllers' topology discovery time. This paper employed a benchmarking tool to contrast the three well-known SDN controllers, ODL, Floodlight, and ONOS. The results of the studies demonstrate that ONOS and ODL outperform Floodlight in terms of performance. The paper is structured as follows. Section 2 shows the related topics and researches. In Sect. 3, the paper introduces the concepts of SDN. Section 4 demonstrates the features of the OpenFlow protocol. The Sect. 5 shows the popular controllers and it deploys them to validate the implemented tool. Section 6 shows the architecture and functionalities of the SDN tool proposed by the paper. The paper discuss the numerical results collected by the test scenario in Sect. 7. Finally, Sect. 8 introduces the paper directions for future work.

2   Related Works

Many papers compare SDN controllers concerning SDN architecture and efficiency. For example, The OFCBenchmark tool was suggested by the paper's authors [10]. This program is a benchmarking tool for OpenFlow. It builds a topology of virtual switches, and this tool may save switch statistics. The switches can be adjusted to simulate a particular scenario. The topology switches' reaction time, rate, and number of dropped packets are all provided by the OFCBenchmark tool. Numerous statistics are provided for certain virtual switches by the OFCBenchmark utility. In the paper [9], two distributed Open-Flow controllers—ONOS and OpenDaylight—are evaluated. In this paper, the Cbench tool is used. The article provided measures for two java-based controllers' throughput, latency, and software scalability in both real-world and virtualized environments. The study's findings show that when compared to the Open-Daylight controller, the ONOS controller offers higher throughput and reduced latency. The study [18] offers a queueing theory-based analytical performance model for OpenFlow. They suggested a packet forwarding approach that made use of OpenFlow switches and the Packet-In control message. The queueing systems that are being modeled are MX/M/1 and M/G/1, respectively. While the

study [6] offers an analysis of the performance of POX and Floodlight. Throughput and latency were examined throughout this evaluation using the Mininet
emulator. The study employs four topologies for the controller-to-controller evaluation. The paper's findings show that, in terms of latency and throughput, the
Floodlight controller superior to the POX controller. In this work [12], Open-
Daylight and Floodlight, two SDN controllers, are evaluated. This comparison
is made in terms of packet loss and latency. The Mininet is used in the study
with various topologies and traffic levels. According to the paper's findings, the
OpenDaylight controller works better than the Floodlight in terms of latency.
Additionally, under heavy traffic loads, the Floodlight controller works better
than the OpenDaylight controller. In the study [13], an OpenFlow network emulator called EstiNet is proposed. The controllers RYU and NOX are compared
in the paper. The study examined how SDN controllers act when they identify network loops. The outcomes of the simulation demonstrate that the RYU
and NOX controllers behave differently when identifying link failure. This study
[17] suggests a method for monitoring software-defined data planes in massively
distributed SDN networks. The procedure collects other specific monitor data
as well as forwarding path monitoring data. The designs shown in the paper
are compatible with many OpenFlow switches. Mininet simulation is used to
assess performance. It demonstrates the improved performance of the suggested
strategy. The study [16] makes use of the RYU SDN, Floodlight, and ONOS controllers. The results of the paper gave unique performance and scalability views
when the throughput and topology discovery time were measured. By sorting
the nodes into various topology forms, such as a tree, linear, ring, grid, and
random, this research [1] analyzes the assessment of both RPL metric functions.
The research also evaluates the RPL performance in terms of overhead, delay,
convergence time, and packet delivery ratio. The Cooja simulator is used to conduct the evaluation. The findings indicate a connection between topology and
RPL performance, particularly in terms of delay and overhead. This study [3]
contrasts the POX and RYU controllers, two open-source SDN controllers. This
comparison's focus was on controller effectiveness. The Mininet emulator is used
in the paper to simulate experiments based on various network topologies. The
results demonstrate that in terms of throughput, delay, and overhead, the RYU
controller superior to the POX controller. This study [2] examines how SDN
controllers perform in data center networks. The Mininet emulator is used in
the paper to account for the topology of various host counts. Based on POX and
RYU controllers with various server densities, the paper evaluates the performance of data centers. Throughput, overhead, delay, and convergence time are
compared between POX and RYU in this evaluation. According to the findings,
the POX controller performs better for data centers than the RYU.

3   Software Defined Networking (SDN)

Data communications networks require management and maintenance because
it provides critical services. Initially, the traditional networks were difficult to

manage, but as the internet grows the number of different intermediate devices increases. These devices come in a variety of configuration and from various manufacturers. Network administration methods were needed to make administrative tasks easier. These protocols included simple network management protocols that worked with many different manufacturers, but they had relatively few provisions for managing devices that used proprietary protocols. In order to enhance the management and servicing of networks, Software Defined Networks (SDNs) [19] were implemented. The SDN concept is founded based on a set of techniques that make network management and control programmable. The traditional network devices are modified and now include separated two planes which are data and control plans. SDN is a new technology that decouples the control plane from the data plane. The data plane as a forwarding plan is responsible for the data storage, and reception of data. The control plane of SDN switches is physically separated from their data plane, therefore, the routing protocol decisions are taken outside the switches and routers, and the SDN decision is made in a centralized component called the SDN controller. This controller function is dedicated to responding to requests from connected SDN switches. These controllers are configured through API programming. Generally, the structure of a software-defined network consists of an overlay, a control layer, and underlay. All control plane operations, such as routing and security, are carried out by the central controller, as was already mentioned. These activities have to do with the SDN control plane. When a packet reaches the SDN switch, it checks its flow table for a corresponding entry. If the current flow is listed in the flow table, the switch will transmit the packet via that particular output port. The processed packet is encapsulated by the virtual switch if there isn't a matching entry in the switch flow table. As a Packet-In OpenFlow control message, it then transmits a request to the particular or related SDN controller. The SDN controller uses this information to decide if the packet flow is accessible in the network. If so, the SDN controller locates a network flow path for this flow packet. Additionally, it inserts the necessary entries to each switch along the packet path's flow table. The virtual switches then forward the flow's packet using the entry that the SDN controller has defined. Through the southbound API interface, the SDN controller and topology switches communicate using established protocols. The OpenFlow protocol [15] is one of the most widely used SDN control protocols. The controller's primary job is to manage the network topology's flow tables. A northbound API is used for the SDN controller's management. This programmable interface makes network communication more user-friendly. This API access can be completed without having to deal with the network's basic functionality. Developers of SDN networks can construct applications that carry out certain functions without having to understand how SDN devices work under the SDN application layer of the overlay, allowing designers to abstract these notions from their applications. This feature allows easy development and deployment of new SDN applications. Where these SDN applications configure OpenFlow protocol for specific needs in terms of SDN performance.

4   Open Flow Control Plane Protocol

OpenFlow protocol is an open standard signaling protocol designed as a communication rule between SDN devices. OpenFlow was developed by Stanford University in the year 2008 [7]. SDN constructed as a centralized form of the control plane and it generates multiple packet flows using programmable properties specified by a high abstraction. In order to test the present designs that define and build new technology networks, users and designers can experiment with the new control protocols utilizing the OpenFlow protocol. The control plane should be separated from the data and forwarding plane, according to the OpenFlow protocol's design principles. The control plane is taken into account by the SDN controller in this design. It also takes into account that the data plane is created by the network SDN switches. There are two types of OpenFlow switches and control schemes. The out-of-band control plane is the first, or "dedicated" plane. A "hybrid" plan is the second kind, also known as the in-band control plane. The first type of switches are unable to process at the layer 2 and 3 levels. While the second type of switches are regarded as both switches and routers. The OpenFlow SDN control protocol is supported by these switches and routers. Similar to data plan interfaces for packet transmission and receiving are these OpenFlow control ports. There are three types of switch ports: physical, logical, and reserved. Logical and reserved ports are virtual ports. The number of switch ports available for processing is thus specified by the OpenFlow protocol. A minimum of one flow table must be defined by an OpenFlow virtual switch. Where each flow table entry in the switch is connected to a flow action. In addition to a private channel in the control plane that handles communications with the controller. The OpenFlow flows that control the data plane are determined by these flow tables. The table entries are filled based on packet flows for a virtual switch to be high-performance at minimal cost. The flow table's flow entries each include instructions that go along with them. A list of actions or a modification to these instructions may be present. Some of these directives have the ability to route the packet to a different flow table. The operations of the virtual switch are used if the flow searching procedure through the flow table is inconclusive. A series of operations control packets. These actions are originally pointless. With particular instructions, the flow entries change these actions. This series of operations follows the packet through the switches along the path's flow tables. Until the end of the OpenFlow navigation, they can also be changed in each flow table. All of the actions specified on the path will be carried out after this navigation is finished. A control plan channel is used to exchange the OpenFlow control messages between the SDN controller and the virtual switches. The OpenFlow header is the first part of the OpenFlow communication. The version of the OpenFlow control protocol is identified by this message header. Three different message kinds can be used to categorize OpenFlow protocol communications. The first kind is controller-to-switch communication: These messages may or may not have a switch control message response and are issued by the controller to switches to handle or inspect the state of the connected switch. Symmetric messages are the second type. Without previous authorization, these messages are delivered in both directions between the controller and switches. Hello, one of these messages. When OpenFlow establishes the connection, it is typically sent and received between the controller and linked switches. Asynchronous messages are the final type and are control messages that the switch sends to the controller without first requesting them. The Packet-in control messages, which the switch may generate to transfer a packet to the SDN controller, are a typical example of these messages. When there is no flow table entry matching the flow of the received packet, the switch generates this message.

5   SDN Controllers Tested Using the Tool

The controller in SDN architecture is the main component. It is also considered an SDN control plane core. The communication that travels through the switches is centralized by the controller's location and purpose. The SDN network architecture is controlled and monitored by the controller. An SDN controller is defined as a software system that works together to handle things like network topology and the SDN architecture. It also captures the relationship between managed network resources. The application programming interface API which responsible of expose the different services offered by the controller. Designers and developers of SDN applications need to validate the performance measurement of their implemented tool, they use several different SDN controllers to evaluate their implemented SDN tool. Therefore this paper implemented a new performance tool for SDN controllers. It uses OpenDaylight, Floodlight, and ONOS controllers to test the new SDN tool. The choice of selected controllers was based on the industry use and supported features. Furthermore, the commercial competitiveness of large-scale and enterprise solutions and designers, where the use of the SDN controller in different projects and solutions is commonly applied by different vendors and companies.

5.1   OpenDaylight (ODL)

OpenDaylight is an open-source SDN controller. This controller is implemented based on the Linux Foundation in collaboration with famous and commercial companies. Such businesses like Cisco Systems, Dell, HP, and others have a lengthy history in the networking industry. This behavior enables users and designers to reduce operational complexity and increase the lifespan of their networks. ODL controller functions as the core element of its SDN topology. Users are now able to develop new services and capabilities that are exclusive to SDN. One of the major SDN projects is the ODL project, which aims to create an open-source and commercial SDN controller. Java programming is used in the creation of ODL controller. There are numerous updated distributions. ODL features a number of software elements that enable greater application-controller interaction. For instance, ODL is able to interact with Karaf, a platform that offers all of the features and services necessary to build servers based on the Open Service Gateway Initiative (OSGi). ODL controller does not need any specific functionalities. When the ODL controller is installed, Using Karaf, users, and designers can choose the preferred functionalities from a list. ODL controller has the southbound API interface. This interface connects the controller with underlay virtual switches in network topology. ODL can run multiple control protocols such as OpenFlow version 1.0 and 1.3, in addition, to BGP as a signaling protocol. Service Abstraction Layer (SAL), another component of the controller's software, is used. The ODL controller's advanced modules software can access services thanks to this functionality. Additionally, it complies with the various services that are asked for, regardless of the underlying protocol that the controller uses to connect with the virtual switches. This behavior protects protocol or version changes of the protocol itself over the time.

5.2   Open Network Operating System (ONOS)

ONOS controller is programmed in Java and it provides a multi-domain SDN applications platform. The ONOS controller system offers a REST API interface, it also has CLI and an extensible and user-friendly web-based GUI. ONOS applications can be run and stopped dynamically through a REST API or GUI interface, these features can be run without restarting the cluster or its switches. The ONOS controller architecture has much functionality. The ONOS architecture's top layer consists of business applications. The middle layer in the ONOS controller architecture is the distributed software core. This layer allows the physical decoupling of data and control planes. This core or middle layer is the logically centralized view of the access to the SDN control plan. The core is separated from the overlay and underlay boundaries using namely Southbound and Northbound API interfaces. The Southbound API interface is the south-facing API interface that makes the controller interacts with the virtual switches environment. ONOS controller as a core works based on control plane protocols such as OpenFlow, NETCONF, and OVSDB. The ONOS controller has CLIs and a Northbound API interface which help to collect information about the underlay virtual switches of the topology, The controller software provides a network management interface for controlling and monitoring underlay virtual switches. ONOS controller interacts with the underlying virtual switches through its Providers' ONOS applications which are based on OSGi components. These ONOS applications can be enabled or disabled at the ONOS controller run time. The primary purpose of provider applications is to make the management, control, and configuration functions of specific OpenFlow or NETCONF-compatible devices. Further, the ONOS controller has communicate with underlay devices using different control and management plane protocols such as OpenFlow, and NETCONF in addition to SNMP protocol.

5.3   Floodlight

Floodlight controller is another java based OpenFlow controller. There is a Big Switch Networks community that supports this controller. The SDN topology is monitored or controlled by a group of apps on the overlay of the floodlight controller. The controller is capable of controlling and monitoring the SDN network topology, among other things. In order to address user application requirements via the network, the controller applications are targeted at various network activities. A Java modular platform is thought of as having the Floodlight controller architecture. Underlay and overlay are connected to the floodlight controller via the southbound and northbound lanes, respectively. The controller modules are given through APIs in the northbound API interface utilizing REST port programming. By sending HTTP-REST queries, any controller program can communicate with the Floodlight controller. These requests or orders enable the controller to provide the necessary response or answer. The Device Manager, Link Discovery, Topology Manager, and Performance Monitor, among other network operations, are just a few of the numerous specialized modules that make up this controller. Applications must be able to recognize these various network operations in order to respond on the opposite side of the underlying network. On the other hand, the Southbound Floodlight Controller API interface makes use of a specific TCP port for the OpenFlow control protocol. With SDN switches, this port was once used to start an OpenFlow control channel. The interface for the westbound API enables the creation of Java programming modules and controls how they communicate with the floodlight controller. When the controller starts up, the Floodlight Controller modules are run, which enables the controller to communicate with the network. Additionally, it offers a quick response to network topology events such switch communication and detection.

6   Proposed Topology Discovery Tool

This paper proposes a software tool as a performance evaluation tool for Open-Flow SDN controllers. In the SDN test tools, there is an open-source test tool called the "Cbench.". This tool is commonly used for testing OpenFlow controllers. It provides test results for measuring throughput and latency tests of OpenFlow controllers. Recently, the Cbench tool does not update last year, where it deals with OpenFlow version 1.0 only. It also does not measure the discovery time consumed by the controller to detect the topology. Therefore, this paper proposes a software tool that collects the topology information from the northbound SDN controller. TDT Tool targets for OpenFlow controller benchmark is his tool. TDT tool is compatible with OpenFlow 1.3. It also has an architecture based on a standalone centralized controller model. The proposed tool is programmed based on Python programming language due to its flexibility, and extensive and available documentation. Figure 1 shows the Python code of the TDT tool.

The TDT proposed tool communicates with the specified and connected SDN controller to get the current number of virtual switches, these virtual switches are connected with the OpenFlow controller via an out-of-band control plane channel. if the current number detected by the TDT tool is zero, this means the Mininet emulator and its topology are not connected with the virtual machine of

```
if(nodes == 0):
    self.start_time = int(time.time() * 1000)
    self.start_flag = True
if(nodes >= max_nodes):
    if(self.start_flag) :
        self.end_time = int(time.time() * 1000)
        QMessageBox.about(MainWindow, "Done", "The test finished !!!!"+ "\n
Discovery Time = " +  str(self.end_time - self.start_time) + "ms")
        self.timer.stop()
        self.stop_countdown()
        self.start_flag = False
    else :
        self.stop_countdown()
        QMessageBox.about(MainWindow, "Error" , "Please Disconnect the
mininet topology before starting the test !!!")
```

Fig. 1. TDT Calculation Code.

the SDN controller, where there is no detection for the controller by the Mininet emulator. At this time the SDN controller is not connected yet with the Mininet emulator. The user starts the topology discovery tool and it stores the current time of this response in the format of milliseconds. Then the TDT tool waits until the user enters the maximum switches number and connects the topology with the Mininet emulator which is already connected to the controller. The tool monitors the virtual switches detected by the controller via the northbound API interface. Then TDT tool waits until the current number of detected switches reaches the total number of switches that have been specified by the user at the beginning, At this moment the TDT tool stores the last response time which at detecting the last switch in the topology in milliseconds format. Finally, the TDT tool calculates the exact topology discovery time of the tested topology. Where discovery time is equal to the last switch detection time subtraction the first switch detection time in milliseconds. Then the time will be shown as an output window to the user. Figure 2 demonstrates the Python code of ODL API code. This ODL controller provides a large number of API endpoints. These endpoints provide flexibility to the controller application programmer. The proposed tool uses the topology inventory endpoint. This endpoint gives the tool brief information about the currently connected switches of the topology with the ODL controller. Also, the ODL controller has the default login credentials which are admin for the username and admin for the password. Therefore, These access username and password are included in the API request header. This can be observed from the fifth line of Fig. 2. The response of the TDT tool is in JSON format. Therefore, the tool counts the number of nodes as detected switches of tested topology in the response of the JSON format. Then the TDT tool displays the computed result of the discovery time to the user with a GUI output window.

Figure 3 shows the Python code of the ONOS controller northbound API. ONOS Controller API is much Simpler than ODL controller API. The user credentials of the ONOS controller have the following login credentials which are onos for the username and rocks for the password. Therefore, These access username and password are included in the ONOS controller API request header. This can be observed from the fifth line of Fig. 3. The response of the TDT tool is in JSON format, TDT tool with ONOS controller uses an endpoint that

```
class odl:
    def __init__(self, socket):
        self.baseUrl = ('http://' + socket +'/restconf')
        self.h = httplib2.Http(".cache")
        self.h.add_credentials('admin', 'admin')

    def get_all_wrapper(self,typestring):
     try:
      url = self.baseUrl + typestring
      logging.debug('url %s', url)
      _,content = self.h.request(url, "GET")
      allContent = json.loads(content)
      allrows=allContent['nodes']
      if allrows == {}:
        return "error"
     except:
       return "error"
     return allrows

    def get_all_nodes(self):
        node_list = self.get_all_wrapper('/operational/opendaylight-
inventory:nodes')
        return node_list

    def get_nodes(self):
      node_list = self.get_all_nodes()
      if(node_list=='error'):
         return 0
      return (len(node_list['node']))
```

Fig. 2. TDT Code For ODL Controller.

```
class onos:
    def __init__(self, socket):
        self.baseUrl = ('http://' + socket +'/onos/v1')
        self.h = httplib2.Http(".cache")
        self.h.add_credentials('onos', 'rocks')

    def get_all_wrapper(self,typestring):
     url = self.baseUrl + typestring
     logging.debug('url %s', url)
     _,content = self.h.request(url, "GET")
     allContent = json.loads(content)
     allrows=allContent['devices']
     return allrows

    def get_all_nodes(self):
     node_list = self.get_all_wrapper('/devices')
     return node_list

    def get_nodes(self):
     node_list = self.get_all_nodes()
     counter = 0
     for switch in node_list:
       if(switch['available'] == True):
         counter = counter+1
     return (counter)
```

Fig. 3. TDT Code For ONOS Controller.

gives the response of connected switches states, The response provides a count or list of all switches that are currently or have been connected with ONOS controller at any time, so For counting the topology detected switches, TDT tool uses the available attribute as observed from the Fig. 3. This attribute indicates whether the ONOS controller is currently connected (true) or not (false). The last part of the code in Fig. 3 shows the counter which counts the total detected switches of the topology. These switches are connected with the ONOS controller via an out-of-band control plane as an OpenFlow version 1.3 control channel. Figure 4 shows the Python code of the Floodlight API interface. The API Of the FloodLight controller is also a simple API interface. The response of the floodlight controller will be in JSON format as the other controllers. The tool uses the switches endpoint to give the current connected and detected switches by the floodlight controller. The Floodlight API interface has no authentication for accessing the northbound API. After getting the response from the API interface of the floodlight controller, the code of Fig. 4 just counts how many detected switches in the connected topology using the JSON response. Finally, the TDT tool shows the number of current connected switches as a GUI output window.

```
class floodlight:

    def __init__(self, socket):
        self.baseUrl = ('http://' + socket +'/wm')
        self.h = httplib2.Http(".cache")

    def get_all_wrapper(self,typestring):
        url = self.baseUrl + typestring
        logging.debug('url %s', url)
        _,content = self.h.request(url, "GET")
        allContent = json.loads(content)
        allrows=allContent
        return allrows


    def get_all_nodes(self):
        node_list = self.get_all_wrapper('/core/controller/switches/json')
        return node_list

    def get_nodes(self):
        node_list = self.get_all_nodes()
        return (len(node_list))
```

Fig. 4. TDT Code For Floodlight Controller.

7   Tool Test Results

This section describes the tool test performed with the TDT tool of SDN Open-Flow controllers, to evaluate the fulfillment of the proposed TDT tool. All the topology discovery tests were done in this paper using three java based SDN controllers. The simulated topology has a standalone controller which connected with kernel space virtual switches. The control plane of the topology was an out-of-band control plane. Furthermore, the OpenFlow version selected is 1.3. Figure 5 shows the user interface of the TDT tool which has the field of the controller IP and port number. This IP and port number are the socket parameters of the specific northbound API interface of the controller. The second field is used by the user to choose the controller type and version. The last input field used by the user is the total number of switches in the tested topology. The following step describes how to use the TDT tool to calculate the topology discovery time:-

1. Run the SDN controller to be ready for testing by the TDT tool.
2. Run the TDT tool and enter the socket information of the northbound interface which are IP and port number.
3. Choose the desired controller and version from the pop-down menu of the controller version TDT tool.
4. Enter the maximum number of the switches in the tested topology at the number of switches field of the TDT tool.
5. Finally press the start test button to execute the tool and get the output as Fig. 6 shows.

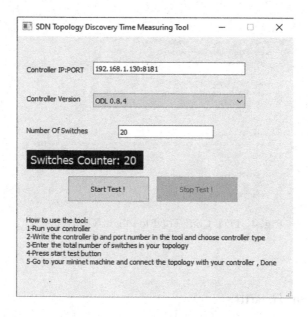

Fig. 5. TDT Tool User Interface.

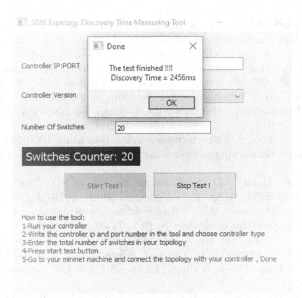

Fig. 6. TDT Tool Output.

8   Conclusion and Future Work

This paper proposes a topology discovery time evaluation tool for SDN controllers. This tool was developed using the Python programming language. This TDT tool evaluates SDN controllers in standalone mode, The tested topology is emulated using Mininet and it has virtual OpenFlow switches. The research performed topology testing using a number of well-known Java SDN controllers, including ODL, ONOS, and floodlight, to validate the TDT tool. Users can measure the out-of-band SDN controllers' discovery or convergence times using the TDT tool. The device is regarded as a tool for northbound SDN controllers. The tool is simple to use and gives the discovery time based on the northbound API controller responses. The authors want to create new functionalities and modules as future works in order to measure the out-of-band control plane's capacity. They also will consider SDN data plane scalability based on the maximum number of switches that may be attached to the controller.

References

1. Alatersh, F.M., Sati, S., Sullabi, M.: Impact of network topologies on RPL performance. In: 22nd International Arab Conference on Information Technology, ACIT 2021, Muscat, Oman, 21–23 December 2021, pp. 1–7. IEEE (2021)
2. Alzarog, J., Almhishi, A., Alsunousi, A., Abulifa, T.A., Eltarjaman, W., Sati, S.O.: Pox controller evaluation based on tree topology for data centers. In: 2022 International Conference on Data Analytics for Business and Industry (ICDABI), pp. 67–71 (2022). https://doi.org/10.1109/ICDABI56818.2022.10041622

3. Alzarog, J., Almhishi, A., Alsunousi, A., Elasaifer, A., Eltarjaman, W., Sati, S.O.: SDN controllers comparison based on network topology. In: 2022 Workshop on Microwave Theory and Techniques in Wireless Communications (MTTW), pp. 204–209 (2022). https://doi.org/10.1109/MTTW56973.2022.9942565

4. Berde, P., et al.: ONOS: towards an open, distributed SDN OS. In: Akella, A., Greenberg, A.G. (eds.) Proceedings of the Third Workshop on Hot Topics in Software Defined Networking, HotSDN 2014, Chicago, Illinois, USA, 22 August 2014, pp. 1–6. ACM (2014)

5. Bhardwaj, S., Panda, S.N.: Performance evaluation using RYU SDN controller in software-defined networking environment. Wirel. Pers. Commun. **122**(1), 701–723 (2022)

6. Bholebawa, I.Z., Dalal, U.D.: Performance analysis of SDN/openflow controllers: POX versus floodlight. Wirel. Pers. Commun. **98**(2), 1679–1699 (2018)

7. Boucadair, M., Jacquenet, C.: Software-defined networking: a perspective from within a service provider environment. RFC **7149**, 1–20 (2014)

8. Chen, X., Guo, D., Ma, W., He, L.: FloodSight: a visual-aided floodlight controller extension for SDN networks. In: Chen, Y., Christie, M., Tan, W. (eds.) SG 2015. LNCS, vol. 9317, pp. 75–86. Springer, Cham (2017). https://doi.org/10.1007/978-3-319-53838-9_6

9. Darianian, M., Williamson, C., Haque, I.: Experimental evaluation of two openflow controllers. In: 25th IEEE International Conference on Network Protocols, ICNP 2017, Toronto, ON, Canada, 10–13 October 2017, pp. 1–6. IEEE Computer Society (2017)

10. Jarschel, M., Lehrieder, F., Magyari, Z., Pries, R.: A flexible openflow-controller benchmark. In: European Workshop on Software Defined Networking, EWSDN 2012, Darmstadt, Germany, 25–26 October 2012, pp. 48–53. IEEE Computer Society (2012)

11. Jmal, R., Fourati, L.C.: Implementing shortest path routing mechanism using openflow POX controller. In: The International Symposium on Networks, Computers and Communications, ISNCC 2014, Hammamet, Tunisia, 17–19 June 2014, pp. 1–6. IEEE (2014)

12. Lantz, B., Heller, B., McKeown, N.: A network in a laptop: rapid prototyping for software-defined networks. In: Xie, G.G., Beverly, R., Morris, R.T., Davie, B. (eds.) Proceedings of the 9th ACM Workshop on Hot Topics in Networks. HotNets 2010, Monterey, CA, USA, 20–21 October 2010, p. 199. ACM (2010)

13. Lantz, B., O'Connor, B.: A mininet-based virtual testbed for distributed SDN development. In: Uhlig, S., Maennel, O., Karp, B., Padhye, J. (eds.) Proceedings of the 2015 ACM Conference on Special Interest Group on Data Communication, SIGCOMM 2015, London, United Kingdom, 17–21 August 2015, pp. 365–366. ACM (2015)

14. Medved, J., Varga, R., Tkacik, A., Gray, K.: Opendaylight: towards a model-driven SDN controller architecture. In: Proceeding of IEEE International Symposium on a World of Wireless, Mobile and Multimedia Networks, WoWMoM 2014, Sydney, Australia, 19 June 2014, pp. 1–6. IEEE Computer Society (2014)

15. Narisetty, R., et al.: Openflow configuration protocol: Implementation for the of management plane. In: 2013 Second GENI Research and Educational Experiment Workshop, Salt Lake City, UT, USA, 20–22 March 2013, pp. 66–67. IEEE Computer Society (2013)

16. da Silva, J.B., da Silva, F.S.D., Neto, E.P., Lemos, M.O.O., Neto, A.: Benchmarking of mainstream SDN controllers over open off-the-shelf software-switches. Internet Technol. Lett. **3**(3), e152 (2020)

17. Wang, Y., Bi, J., Zhang, K.: A tool for tracing network data plane via sdn/openflow. Sci. China Inf. Sci. **60**(2), 22304 (2017)
18. Xiong, B., Yang, K., Zhao, J., Li, W., Li, K.: Performance evaluation of openflow-based software-defined networks based on queueing model. Comput. Netw. **102**, 172–185 (2016)
19. Xu, F., He, J., Wu, X.: First study on supply and demand network with multi-functional and opening characteristics for enterprise (SDN). In: Proceedings of the IEEE International Conference on Systems, Man & Cybernetics: The Hague, Netherlands, 10–13 October 2004, pp. 2108–2113. IEEE (2004)
20. Yao, G., Bi, J., Xiao, P.: Source address validation solution with openflow/nox architecture. In: Proceedings of the 19th annual IEEE International Conference on Network Protocols, ICNP 2011, Vancouver, BC, Canada, 17–20 October 2011, pp. 7–12. IEEE Computer Society (2011)

Performance Analysis of Classifying URL Phishing Using Recursive Feature Elimination

Marwa Albaser, Salwa Ali, and Hamouda Chantar$^{(\boxtimes)}$ (iD)

Faculty of Information Technology, Sebha University, Sebha 18758, Libya
{marw.albaser,sal.ali1,ham.chantar}@sebhau.edu.ly

Abstract. Phishing is a popular cyber-attack that tricks users into revealing confidential data such as login passwords or account details, on a website that appears official. Many methods for identifying phishing attacks, particularly the use of machine learning, have been presented in recent years. This study examines the impact of using the Recursive Feature Elimination technique on the classification accuracy of phishing websites by analyzing several Machine Learning algorithms for identifying phishing websites based on URL attributes. According to the experimental findings, RFE (Recursive Feature Elimination) was essential in reducing the effect of irrelevant features on the accuracy of various classifiers. We also assessed the key features included in both datasets, which are crucial for classifying URL-based phishing websites. Our research uncovered four essential features: Page Rank, Links in Tags, Statical_Report and Having_Sub_Domain.

Keywords: Phishing website · Machine learning · URL · Classification models · Recursive Feature elimination

1 Introduction

With the web's quick development, the risk of keeping attackers like criminals, or non-malicious individuals away from confidential information such as passwords, loggings, and personal credit card data has increased; typically as a result of the massive volume of transactions conducted online every day. In general, phishing is a form of fraudulent activity in which a fraudster or online criminals contact one or more targets (such as individuals) via email, phone, or text message [1]. These scammers attempt to trap individuals into uncovering sensitive data such as passwords, character subtle elements, bank or credit card points of interest by imagining to be a solid and legitimate company or person. The data is then used to gain access to fundamental accounts or administrations, which can lead to identity theft and financial distress. Clients drop casualty to these sorts of assaults for different reasons. One of the reasons is the need of understanding of fake URLs. Another reason is that muddled URLs anticipate clients from perusing full site addresses; Subsequently, successful reaction strategies ought to be utilized to diminish the affect of phishing attacks [2].

Machine learning, heuristic-based techniques, blacklists, and white lists are only a few of the ways to prevent phishing URL websites. According to one study, it only takes

T. A. T. Benmusa et al. (Eds.): ILCICT 2023, CCIS 2097, pp. 42–54, 2024.
https://doi.org/10.1007/978-3-031-62624-1_4

a few hours for phishing URLs to be identified as hazardous; 63% are blacklisted within two hours, whereas 47% to 83% are white listed after 12 h [13]. This is due to the fact that a user clicks on a link to a phishing site and acquires a notification authorizing them to quit the site instantly, this demonstrates that the URL has been restricted or classified as vulnerable in the form of blacklists and white lists techniques. It is clear from the design of these blacklists why they cannot distinguish 0-day phishing attacks. Despite the fact that they may not be as exact and adaptable as other techniques such as similarity and heuristic-based models, which may be capable of distinguishing 0-day phishing attempts, [4].

Only frameworks based on machine learning have the flexibility and accuracy to identify new phishing attempts. These frameworks have been thoroughly investigated and added to well-known browsers like Chrome and Edge. They function by spotting distinctive patterns in the URLs, HTML, and visual presentation of authentic and phishing websites. Machine learning algorithms can forecast similar patterns and distinguish between secure and phishing websites by studying these patterns. The features employed and these models' resistance to repeated phishing attacks determine how effective they are. This study uses a variety of machine learning techniques to categorize phishing websites using feature selection. The effectiveness of algorithms like Gradient, Support Vector Machine, Random Forest, K Nearest Neighbors, Decision Trees, and K Nearest Neighbors.

The following sections describe the background of the study, suggested method and experimental results.

2 Background and Related Work

2.1 Machine Learning Classifiers

In this work, six machine learning classifiers including Decision Trees classifier (DT), K Nearest Neighbors (KNN), Support Vector Machine (SVM), Random Forest (RF), Logistic Regression (LR) and Gradient Boosting are employed for phishing website detection.

The decision tree machine learning method differs from others in that it can be used for classification and regression without extensive data pre-processing. It can be used in conjunction with supervised learning methods to estimate values based on decision criteria derived from data properties. Decision trees, unlike other models, can split attributes into nodes a decision is taken and prunes out unimportant features. This leads to a model with fewer features that can enhance its predictions.

Support vector machines are supervised learning algorithms used to solve problems such as classification, regression, and outlier detection. The purpose of this ma-chine learning algorithm is to define a hyper plane that classifies data points into N dimensions (number of attributes). Hyper planes can have variable diameters depending on the number of layers required for classification [16–18].

When the target variable is in conflict, a classification technique known as logistic regression is utilized to forecast its probability. It is a binary logistic regression with only two possible categorical probability values. A polynomial logistic regression model categorizes the variable of interest. The third type of logistic regression is ordinal regression, which categorizes the target variable [16–19].

A Random Forest classifier is an aggregation technique that can be used to address regression or classification issues. It is generated by building many decision trees; the more trees there are, the better the accuracy. The output of a classification problem is the class selected by the majority of the trees. The output of a regression problem is the average of the different trees [16–18].

KNN (or k-NN) is a technique for supervised learning. It is also known as k-NEAR neighbor. KNN organizes data in space based on predefined features. To make a classification decision, the algorithm compares a new data class to the k nearest data. It chooses the most common class for classification problems. It computes the average label for regression problems.

Gradient boosting is a class of machine learning techniques that employs weak learners to build strong models. The loss function, weak learner, and additive model are its three main components. The loss function assesses the model's ability to predict a set of data. A weak learner model, for example, is one that has a high error rate and incorrectly classifies a target variable. In additive models, weak learners are gradually added until the final model accurately predicts the class value [16–19].

2.2 Feature Selection

Feature selection (FS) process has a significant impact on the performance of ML classifiers. In data classification, FS is mainly applied to detect and remove noisy and uninformative features that affect the performance of machine learning classifiers. In general, FS technique can be either filter or wrapper. In wrapper FS, a search algorithm in conjunction with a machine learning classifier are used for feature selection. On the other side, filter FS approaches rely on statistical methods such as chi-square and mutual information in determining the best subset of features [15, 22]. In this work, we applied the wrapper FS approach, Recursive Feature Elimination (RFE) method to select the most informative features for classifying URLs into phishing or legitimate. Recursive Feature Elimination (RFE) is a wrapper feature selection approach that fits a classification model and eliminates the most weak feature from the feature space until the desired number of features is met. It employs a machine learning classifier to assess the importance of features [23]. In this work, Logistic regression classifier is used with RFE to remove irrelevant features. The basic methodology in this study is based on a logistic regression classifier since it allows to discover the best characteristics and reject those that are detrimental to algorithm performance.

2.3 Performance Metrics

In data classification, evaluating the performance of machine learning classifiers is an important step. Usually, a part of data named training is preserved to build the classifier. The other part of the data is used to examine the classification performance of the obtained classifier. Two popular methods comprise accuracy and F1-score are used to assess the ability of ML classifiers in predicating the right class of the instances in test set. The classification accuracy of a ML classifier is determined as follows:

$$Acc = \frac{TP + TN}{TP + FP + TN + FN}$$

Assume the URLs in the test portion of the dataset that is class R. The classifier assigns a class label for each URL, and that predictions will be one of four classes with regard to category R [10].

- TP (true positive): the set of URLs that are in class R, and were correctly assigned to R.
- TN (negative): the set of URLs that do not belong to R, and were labeled to be in another class than R.
- FP (false positive): the set of URLs that were assigned to be related to class R, but in fact they belong to another class.
- FN (false negative): the set of URLs that were assigned to be in another class than R, but they actually belong to class R.

F1-Score is obtained based on precision and recall measures using the following formulas [10, 20]:

$$F1 - Score = 2\frac{recall * precision}{recall + precision}$$

Precision and Recall can be calculated as follows:

$$Precisin = \frac{TP}{TP + FP}$$

$$Recall = \frac{TP}{TP + FN}$$

2.4 Related Work

Identifying fraudulent websites is the first step in preventing online fraud. Recent technological advances have been made in a variety of application areas such as aerospace, voice processing, healthcare technology, border security, object recognition, crime detection, cybercrime, smart cities, and so on [7]. Similarly, many technological advancements have been made in the field of cyber security, particularly in the automatic detection of phishing attacks. However, as the frequency of phishing incidents rises and malicious attackers develop new techniques, there is still room for improvement [12]. Importantly, many recent studies on the topic of phishing URL detection have been published, each with a different approach (phishing or legitimate). Several research have focused on rule-based approaches, machine learning, and natural language processing (NLP).

Several surveys have shown that Unified Source Locator URL detection (phishing) is highly accurate, but less effective on mobile phones and other devices. Some image similarity-based methods use image processing to determine a web page's URL. Systems may request access to a variety of parts, including HTML [11] (Hypertext Markup Language), JavaScript elements, HTML tags, and HTML links, depending on the level. complexity of the scam scheme. This consumes more battery power and makes the calculation of the method more difficult [10–13]. In a 2017 study, Zouina and Outtaj in [8] created an AI-based solution that efficiently identifies URL phishing attempts while consuming less memory and can be used with low power. smart phone. This method takes advantage of six characteristics of URLs, including the presence of an IP, number of dots, number of numeric characters, and number of hyphens. The authors' use of the Hamming distance increased and improved accuracy, yielding a hit rate of 95.80%. SVM, logistic regression, Naive Bayes and random forest are just some of the machine learning techniques used in a study of [6]. They trained these algorithms using the page attribute, the lexical-based attribute, and the server-based attribute, which are the three features of the URL. Its page-level attributes such as Page Rank and Traffic Rating, reveal a page's popularity based on how often users visit it. Server-based ownership shows who is responsible for the page and the location of the server, along with details like WHOIS, domain age, blacklisting, and geographic features. The lexical characteristics are determined by the characteristics of the URL string, not by the content of the web page. This includes a number of features, including domain name registration deadlines, IP addresses, suspicious characters, and dot numbers. Random Forest outperformed all other algorithms, reaching 96.1% when the training data was split at 60% and 94.4% when at 90%.

Another study, on the other hand, created an adaptive machine learning (AML) system [4]. A phishing adaptive classifier and an attribute extractor were used to build this adaptive ML system. A feature extractor is essential for detecting phishing attacks. From the site's content and URLs, the feature model extracted 38 distinct attributes. Based on the feature type, these attributes were divided into four groups. The groups were as follows: Features associated with length Features associated with numbers Information about hyperlinks features URLs that are suspicious.

In one study, eight features were used to create a pattern by combining a binary and non-binary number. The non-binary characteristics include: URL Length Domain Length Frequency of the domain The link rate The researchers devised two new features: Domain frequency and domain length The following non-binary characteristics were present: Persistence over HTTP domain-matching-page-title Domain names with non-alphabetical letters Copyright symbols on domain names There were five machine learning algorithms employed. For method evaluation, two ensemble methods were employed. There were two experiments: In the initial test, the average classifier accuracy was 97.74%. The average classifier accuracy increased to 98 when all criteria were applied.

The new features were extracted using Natural Language Processing (NLP), and word vectors were then used to create a real-time phishing detection program [6]. K-nearest neighbor, naive bayes, k-star, ran-dom forest, adaboost, decision tree, and sequential minimal optimization classification methods are all trained using these features. They used NLP features from earlier studies in addition to the new ones from this one. Since there are only 40 NLP features in total, feature reduction is not used. The vector generator is used to convert each URL into a vector, and the CfsSub setEval algorithm is used to reduce the features from 1701 to 102. The results of combining NLP and word vectors show that certain features are more suitable for each algorithm. The random forest method performs best, with a 97.98% accuracy rate. In a previous study, the researchers used different feature selection strategies to improve accuracy, including filtering and packing methods. Four filtering methods and three envelope-based filtering methods were used in this study. Three separate datasets were used to evaluate the performance of machine learning algorithms and the significance of the dataset characteristics. Boruta, Classification Subset Evaluation, and Wrapper Subset Evaluation are three more wrapper-based filtering methods. In this study, ML algorithms have been investigated using three distinct datasets to determine their performance and the significance of data features in all three datasets. The research was created using a variety of machine learning and data analysis tools, including Pandas, KERAS, Numpy, and Scikit Learn. Along with PCA-based and dimensionality reduction feature importance measurement, five machine learning (ML) techniques were used, including decision trees, SVM, random forest, Naive Bayes NB, K near neighbors (KNN), and artificial neural network (ANN). Some of the gold standards used to evaluate the effectiveness of ML models are accuracy, specificity, precision, recall, and F1 scores. The statistical findings demonstrated PCA's significant contribution to weight loss.

According to the research results mentioned above, a lot of effort has been made into categorizing phishing websites using different ML-based algorithms. The effectiveness of the ML algorithms across various datasets as well as across reduced features from all datasets, however, would be useful to explore the effect of dimensionality reduction on classification performance. As a result, recursive feature deletions are done in two datasets for feature analysis and dimensionality reduction, using classifier performance against outcomes obtained from an uncompressed set of attributes. The aim of this study is to improve the accuracy and resistance of machine learning-based phishing detection models through the application of feature selection methods.

3 Proposed Method

Figure 1 shows the proposed URL phishing detection model in this work. The process consists of the following steps:

1. Loading URLs phishing dataset. It contains both phishing and legitimate URLs.
2. Apply feature selection using RFE method.
3. Divide reduced dataset into training and test.
4. Construct a machine learning model that is able to detect phishing URLs.

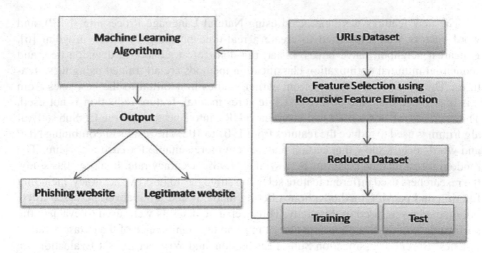

Fig. 1. Proposed URL phishing Detection Model

3.1 Model Description

The proposed model starts with crawling relevant URLs. Since the data is clean, it does not require any normalization. The only important features, in addition to the weak predictive characteristics for the classification problem, are chosen during the feature selection phase to limit the number of dimensions. We used the recursive feature removal (RFE) method, a wrapper-like method. RFE begins with all features (variables) in the dataset and then iteratively eliminates the least significant ones until the desired (optimal) number of features is obtained. RFE is included in the machine learning algorithm. In the study, we employed a classifier for logistic regression, which serves as the foundation for this method. Logistic regression assists in selecting the best characteristics and removing less helpful features that degrade algorithm performance. If the amount of features cannot be given, the RFE approach decreases the features by 50% automatically.

Once the data is prepared, the RFE-selected features are utilized to train the machine learning classifiers on both datasets. These are the most popular machine learning algorithms that were used: Decision Tree, Support Vector Machine (RBF & Poly), Logistic Regression, Random Forest, KNN, and Gradient Boosting. On the two datasets, we will run five experiments. The first experiment is to identify the most effective classifier for phishing websites. The three further experiments look at how Recursive Feature Elimination affects classifier prediction when ML algorithms are trained using RFE. The final experiment will pinpoint the key traits that emerge in both datasets following the use of RFE.

3.2 Data Sets

Two phishing URL datasets from various sources were used in this study to evaluate the efficiency of ML classifiers using the RFE technique. The description of each dataset is presented in Table 1. Data1 has a total of 30 features that can identify phishing URLs and are collected from [2]. The binary classifier was used as the target variable, with 1 indicating legit and -1 indicating scam. The information is pulled from a number of resources including MillerSmiles, PhisTank, and Google. Data 2 was collected from [21]. The dataset has 88 features, most of which are similar to the first dataset with some minor differences. With "Scam" replaced by 1 and "legitimate" by 0, the target class is also binary. Domain-based features, address bar features, anomalous features, and Javascript and HTML features are the four groups that Dataset 1 is divided into. In contrast, the categories in the two datasets are distinct; They are classified according to the following aspects: URL-based features, content-based features, and external-based features. A practice game is 80% of each dataset and a test game is 20%.

Table.1. Phishing website datasets

Dataset	Data1	Data2
Total number of URLs	11055	11430
Number of phishing URLs	4898	5715
Number of Legitimate URLs	6157	5715
Number of features	30	88

4 Result and Discussion

4.1 Pre-recursive Feature Elimination Classification Performance

This section discusses the results using the Precision, Recall, and F1-score measures. Table 2 shows the classification results for Data1 before applying the Recursive Feature Elimination (RFE) approach. Support Vector Machine (RBF and Poly) classifiers performed the worst, with an accuracy of 0.548, while Random Forest classifiers performed the best, with an accuracy of 0.96.6. Table 2 shows the results of the experiment on the second dataset. Random Forest was the most accurate model, with the highest accuracy (0.967), followed by Gradient Boosting (0.947). The support vector machine algorithm is the least accurate, with a poly accuracy of 50.2. While the first dataset's accuracy was higher than LR's, it fell to 78.3 percent when compared to LR's accuracy.

Despite the fact that the first dataset is more accurate than the LR, the accuracy drops to 78.3%. As a result, the classifier's performance is determined by the characteristics of both datasets. Tables 2 and 3 show that all of the ML classifiers performed well. With the exception of SVM (poly & RBF), which performed poorly on the first dataset but significantly better on the second. Tables 2 and 3 show that RF and XGBOOST learners produce higher percentage F1 scores on both datasets than other techniques. It's worth noting that these algorithms use multiple learning algorithms to improve prediction performance. KNN also performs poorly on dataset 1 but is more accurate on dataset 2. His could imply that KNN performs better with more features, given dataset one contained just 30 features whereas dataset two contained 88.

Table 2. Detailed accuracy evaluation for eight classifiers on Dataset1 before feature selection

Classifier	Accuracy	Precision	Recall	F1-score
RF	**0.966**	**0.960**	**0.978**	**0.969**
DT	0.924	0.903	0.965	0.933
XGBOOST	0.930	0.927	0.948	0.937
KNN	0.615	0.748	0.450	0.562
SVM	0.834	0.833	0.872	0.852
SVM (rbf)	0.548	0.548	1.000	0.708
SVM (poly)	0.548	0.548	1.000	0.708
LR	0.921	0.916	0.942	0.929

Table 3. Detailed accuracy evaluation for eight classifiers on Dataset2 before feature selection

Classifier	Accuracy	Precision	Recall	F1-score
RF	**0.967**	**0.965**	**0.968**	**0.966**
DT	0.927	0.919	0.934	0.926
XGBOOST	0.947	0.942	0.951	0.947
KNN	0.822	0.905	0.714	0.798
SVM	0.884	0.868	0.903	0.885
SVM (rbf)	0.548	0.522	1.000	0.686
SVM (poly)	0.502	0.497	0.970	0.657
LR	0.783	0.780	0.779	0.779

4.2 The Effectiveness of Classification Following Recursive Feature Elimination

Tables 4 and 5 show the results of machine learning classifiers after feature selection. When the recursive feature elimination strategy was used, The first dataset's total number of features, as shown in Table 4, decreased from 30 to 15 by 50%, suggesting a reduction in the number of features. Following the removal of recursive features, SVM (poly) and SVM (rbf) performed 0.94 and 0.913 better, respectively.

Table 5 shows the performance of the classifiers over Dataset2 after feature selection. Random Forest outperformed other classifiers when only RFE-selected features were

Table 4. Detailed accuracy evaluation for eight classifiers on Dataset1 after feature selection

Classifier	Accuracy	Precision	Recall	F1-score
RF	0.956	0.950	0.972	0.961
DT	0.951	0.952	0.959	0.956
XGBOOST	0.932	0.928	0.949	0.938
KNN	0.929	0.933	0.938	0.935
SVM	0.920	0.913	0.943	0.928
SVM (rbf)	0.913	0.901	0.944	0.922
SVM (poly)	0.940	0.925	0.970	0.947
LR	0.921	0.933	0.938	0.935

used to train and test them, followed by LR and SVM linear. Finally, as shown in Figs. 2 and 3, feature selection influenced the majority of the classifiers used. As a result, we could conclude that the RFE technique had a positive effect on all classifiers on both datasets.

Table 5. Detailed accuracy evaluation for eight classifiers on Dataset2 after feature selection

Classifier	Accuracy	Precision	Recall	F1-score
RF	**0.959**	**0.957**	**0.960**	**0.959**
DT	0.929	0.926	0.931	0.929
XGBOOST	0.932	0.928	0.949	0.938
KNN	0.918	0.902	0.935	0.918
SVM	0.938	0.941	0.933	0.937
SVM (rbf)	0.914	0.914	0.911	0.913
SVM (poly)	0.825	0.757	0.950	0.842
LR	0.939	0.926	0.952	0.939

The findings of the experiments demonstrate that the elements in Table 6 appeared in both datasets, showing that they are the primary features in identifying phishing websites based on URL.

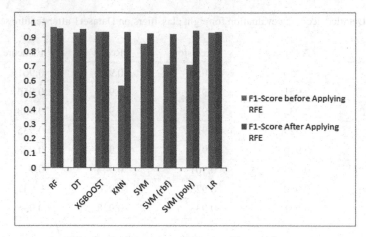

Fig. 2. Performance of ML classifiers on Data1

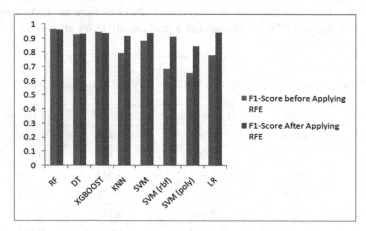

Fig. 3. Performance of ML classifiers on Data2

Table 6. Same features selected by RFE form the two applied datasets

Feature
Links_in_tag
Page_Rank
Statical_Report
Having_Sub_Domain

5 Conclusion

In conclusion, this paper explored a number of machine learning techniques for categorizing phishing websites based on URL attributes. It additionally examined at how feature selection using the Recursive Feature Elimination (RFE) method affected the results. As a consequence of the experimental findings, it was clear that applying RFE was essential for identifying and removing the irrelevant characteristics that had a negative impact on the effectiveness of various classifiers. The study also identified the most significant elements, or "core features," that are present in both datasets and are essential for classifying phishing websites according to their URLs. It is suggested that in subsequent research, features be divided into groups and then merged into two groups at a time to identify which elements are most beneficial in classifying phishing websites based on URLs. As Machine learning proves its effectiveness in detecting phishing URLs, It is recommended to apply machine learning approach using RFE to classify other types of attacks malwares and intrusions.

References

1. Tang, L., Mahmoud, Q.H.: A Survey of machine learning-based solutions for phishing website detection. Mach. Learn. Knowl. Extr. **3**(3), 672–694 (2021). https://doi.org/10.3390/make30 30034
2. Khan, S.A., Khan, W., Hussain, A.: Phishing attacks and websites classification using machine learning and multiple datasets (a comparative analysis). In: Huang, D.S., Premaratne, P. (eds.) Intelligent Computing Methodologies: 16th International Conference, ICIC 2020, Bari, Italy, October 2–5, 2020, Proceedings, Part III, pp. 301–313. Springer, Cham (2020). https://doi.org/10.1007/978-3-030-60796-8_26
3. Basit, A., Zafar, M., Liu, X., Javed, A.R., Jalil, Z., Kifayat, K.: A comprehensive survey of AI-enabled phishing attacks detection techniques. Telecommun. Syst. **76**(1), 139–154 (2020). https://doi.org/10.1007/s11235-020-00733-2
4. Yadollahi, M.M., Shoeleh, F., Serkani, E., Madani, A., Gharaee, H.: An adaptive machine learning based approach for phishing detection using hybrid features, In: 2019 5th International Conference on Web Research (ICWR), pp. 281–286. IEEE (2019)
5. Sundararajan, A., Gressel, G., Achuthan, K.: Feature selection for phishing detection with machine learning. Int. J. Eng. Adv. Technol. **8**(6s3), 1039–1045 (2019). https://doi.org/10.35940/ijeat.F1331.0986S319
6. Sahingoz, O.K., Buber, E., Demir, O., Diri, B.: Machine learning based phishing detection from URLs. Exp. Syst. with Appl. **117**, 345–357 (2019). https://doi.org/10.1016/j.eswa.2018.09.029
7. Pang, S., Li, Y.: Artificial intelligence techniques for cyber security applications. Int. J. Adv. Inf. Commun. Technol., 89–94 (2020)
8. Zouina, M., Outtaj, B.: A novel lightweight URL phishing detection system using SVM and similarity index. HCIS **7**(1), 1–13 (2017). https://doi.org/10.1186/s13673-017-0098-1
9. Shirazi, H.: Unbiased phishing detection using domain name based features. Ph.D. dissertation, Colorado State University (2018)
10. Hannousse, A., Yahiouche, S.: Towards benchmark datasets for machine learning based website phishing detection: an experimental study. Eng. Appl. Artif. Intell. **104**, 104347 (2021)

11. Jain, K., Gupta, B.B.: A machine learning based approach for phishing detection using hyperlinks information. J. Ambient. Intell. Humaniz. Comput. **10**(5), 2015–2028 (2019)
12. James, J., Sandhya L., Thomas, C.: Detection of phishing URLs using machine learning techniques. In: 2013 International Conference on Control Communication, pp. 304–309. IEEE (2013)
13. Chen, J.L., Ma, Y.W., Huang, K.L.: Intelligent visual similarity-based phishing websites detection. Symmetry **12**(10), 1681 (2020). https://doi.org/10.3390/sym12101681
14. Tupsamudre, H., Singh, A.K., Lodha, S.: Everything is in the name – a URL based approach for phishing detection. In: Dolev, S., Hendler, D., Lodha, S., Yung, M. (eds.) Cyber Security Cryptography and Machine Learning: Third International Symposium, CSCML 2019, Beer-Sheva, Israel, June 27–28, 2019, Proceedings, pp. 231–248. Springer, Cham (2019). https://doi.org/10.1007/978-3-030-20951-3_21
15. Chandrashekar, G., Sahin, F.: A survey on feature selection methods. Comput. Electr. Eng. **40**(1), 16–28 (2014)
16. Korkmaz, M., Sahingoz, O.K., Diri, B.: Detection of phishing websites by using machine learning-based URL analysis. In: 2020 11th International Conference on Computing, Communication and Networking Technologies (ICCCNT), Kharagpur, India, pp. 1–7 (2020)
17. Alam, M.N., Sarma, D., Lima, F.F., Saha, I., Ulfath, R.E., Hossain, S.: Phishing attacks detection using machine learning approach. In: 2020 Third International Conference on Smart Systems and Inventive Technology (ICSSIT), Tirunelveli, India, pp. 1173–1179 (2020)
18. Awad, M., Khanna, R.: Support vector machines for classification. In: Awad, M., Khanna, R. (eds.) Efficient Learning Machines: Theories, Concepts, and Applications for Engineers and System Designers, pp. 39–66. Apress, Berkeley, CA (2015). https://doi.org/10.1007/978-1-4302-5990-9_3
19. Sahoo, D., Liu, C., Hoi, S.C.H.: Malicious URL detection using machine learning: a survey. arXiv arXiv:1701.07179 [cs], August 2019
20. Singh, G.A.P., Gupta, P.K.: Performance analysis of various machine learning-based approaches for detection and classification of lung cancer in humans. Neural Comput. Appl. **31**(10), 6863–6877 (2018). https://doi.org/10.1007/s00521-018-3518-x
21. Hannouss, A., Yahiouche, S.: Web page phishing detection. Mendeley Data. V2. https://doi.org/10.17632/c2gw7fy2j4.2
22. Chantar, H.K., Corne, D.W.: Feature subset selection for Arabic document categorization using BPSO-KNN. In: 2011 Third World Congress on Nature and Biologically Inspired Computing, Salamanca, Spain, pp. 546–551 (2011)
23. Chen, X.W., Jeong, J.C.: Enhanced recursive feature elimination. In: Sixth International Conference on Machine Learning and Applications, ICMLA 2007, Cincinnati, OH, USA, pp. 429–435 (2007)

Performance Evaluation of Satellite Communication Link at Millimeter Wave Based on Rain Fade Data Measured in Libya

Asma Ali Budalal[1]([⊠]), Khaled Idris Sharif[1], Suleiman G H Hewadia[1], and Rogaya A H Budalal[2]

[1] College of Electrical and Electronic Technology, Benghazi, Libya
{asma.budalal,Khaled.Sharif,suleiman.hewadia}@ceet.edu.ly
[2] College of Computer Technology, Benghazi, Libya

Abstract. Many outage probability events have recently been recorded in Libya because of rain attenuation impact, especially at millimetre wave (mmWave) spectrum in terrestrial and satellite links. Therefore, accurate prediction of rain attenuation phenomena is highly recommended to mitigate outages due to rain fade. Rainfall statistical data measured for long-term data of 30 years were collected from five locations in Libya. Collected data were analysed and processed to convert into one–minute rain rate cumulative distribution. The model proposed by ITU-R has been utilised to predict and investigate rain fade based on converted 1-min rain rate data for sites in various climate regions in Libya in the zenith paths of the Hylas 2 satellite. The impact of different parameters such as frequency (GHz), satellite elevation (degrees), polarisation, and percentage of the year on rain fade prediction has been tested. Additionally, the essential properties of link performance have been investigated in determining dependable fade margin. The impact of rain attenuation at 28 GHz was considered for performance analysis at Benina ($R_{0.01\%}$ 21.7 mm / h) and Tripoli airport $R_{0.01\%}$ 35.8 mm / regarding link efficiency in bps/Hz and throughput in Mbps utilising Matlab. At V-band, rain fade is more challenging than at Ka in northern and most coastline zones but negligible in southern zones. V-band downlink shows that 99.99% availability is possible in all the Sothern part stations in Libya. This paper provides valuable insights into designing reliable earth-to-satellite communication links over mmwave frequencies in Libya. This data can be used to design and optimize the link budget and to select appropriate modulation and coding schemes to mitigate the effects of rain fade.

Keywords: Rain fade · millimetre wave links performance · satellite to Earth · performance · link efficiency · throughput

K. I. Sharif—IEEE, Member

T. A. T. Benmusa et al. (Eds.): ILCICT 2023, CCIS 2097, pp. 55–67, 2024.
https://doi.org/10.1007/978-3-031-62624-1_5

1   Introduction

Recently, (mm-Wave) operating at 30 to 300 GHz has been used to develop fifth-generation (5G) and sixth-generation (6G) cellular technologies, radio access, and back-haul systems. (Mm-Wave) links provide wide bandwidths, high directivity, and spatial resolution to meet quality and ultra-reliable communication criteria [1–3]. The large bandwidth available in (mmWave) bands has recently been considered as a means to maximize communication data rates through satellite links.

Satellite communication utilising (mm-Wave) is considered a Key Enabler of the 6G Era [1–3] to provide ubiquitous broadband access cost-efficiently, especially in some remote areas where terrestrial links architectures and network infrastructure are infeasible to be deployed. Additionally, 6G research is focused on developing non-terrestrial communication for third-dimensional (3D) coverage by combining on-the-ground infrastructures with aerial platforms, including satellites. [4, 5]. Weather factors affecting the signal propagation path of mm waves and beyond, such as rain, dust, and sand storms, have been highlighted. Consequently, these factors should be extensively considered in evaluating wireless link performance and channel modeling. Besides rain fades, there are several factors that can affect the performance of satellite communication links at millimeter waves in Libya. Some of these factors include atmospheric attenuation, antenna misalignment, multipath interference, and equipment failure [2]. However, few studies have been implemented in the Libyan climate considering long-term measured data.

2   Rain Fade Effect on Satellite Spectrum

Various links within the satellite system in outdoor millimeter wave wireless communication have been utelized such as Uplink, Downlink, Forward link, and Reverse link. The research community stated that rain attenuation is the most significant impairment in (mmWave) frequencies for various path losses [6]. Rainfall on propagation paths becomes even more critical for frequencies above 7 GHz, particularly in the rainy season. Raindrops absorb and scatter radio waves leading to rain attenuation, reducing the performance of (mmWave) band links, and increasing the possibility of outages, reducing the system's reliability. Thus, the move toward (mmWave) radio communications operating at 30 to 300 GHz requires improvement in the prediction of propagation impairments [6]. The new applications of indoor and outdoor communication systems need a high level of reliability, so we have to investigate the actual value of SNR that allows the link at higher frequencies to work accurately. Therefore, rain-induced attenuation on propagation paths must be considered when planning and designing satellite systems. The existing production models of rain attenuation can be classified into two types: a satellite communication model and a ground mobile communication model, such as on terrestrial links. One of the most commonly used models proposed by the International Telecommunication Union-Radio Wave Propagation ITU-R P.618 [3] defined the rain attenuation model.

Attenuation models can be divided into two categories. The first is a statistical model that uses long-term observations of rainfall intensities in the time domain to generate a probability distribution of $R_{0.01}$ mm/h. This prediction model analysed and calculated rain attenuations ($A_{0.01}$) dB. [7–9]. Based on a large amount of empirical data, these models are performing satisfactorily on a global scale. The other type is real-time rain attenuation models, e.g. Synthetic storm models [10], which incorporate rainfall intensity time series into their observation time to calculate rain attenuation. In [11–13], this model was used to analyse rain attenuation over time. Therefore, the empirical method is the most used methodology to predict rain fade.

Libya is a country located in North Africa, home to a population of over 6 million people. The increasing use of technology has led to the emergence of satellite links as a viable option in recent years. In many parts of Libya, the current telecommunications infrastructure still cannot provide reliable and consistent high-speed internet, which is crucial in some sectors. The country has been in political and economic turmoil since 2011, significantly impacting Internet services' availability and quality. Lack of infrastructure is the main challenge facing satellite links in Libya. Investments in the infrastructure necessary to support a reliable connection have not been made by the country.

Besides that, some technical reports presented by Almadar Aljadid company in 2023 highlighted that last winter in Libya, some communication links at different sites faced many performance degradations because of rain at Ka and E bands. Technical reports provide detailed information about the technical aspects of the company's operations, projects, and products. Additionally, the technical reports documented that attenuation due to rainfall is the most important factor to consider for various path losses. Hence, satellite link designers must accurately predict rain fade before system implementation based on climate conditions in Libya.

Predicting rain attenuation is primarily based on rainfall rate. One minute of integration time is also required for rain fade prediction methods proposed in the literature. However, rainfall statistical data measured and recorded in Libya are collected at a 3-h integration time for 30 years. The Libyan National Meteorological Center (LNMC) collected a long-term cumulative rainfall dataset. A reference period for this study is the climatic period (1981–2010). This makes the value of rain fade in dB inaccurate in the link budget. Also, a lack of satellite propagation studies in Libya based on long-term accurate rain measurements and monitoring its impact on the received signal strength., especially for higher frequency bands. This kind of analysis has a critical role in enhancing the link budget accuracy and avoiding outages for optimum link utilisation. The most significant additional losses on the free space that the link experiences in the given reliability threshold are to be kept at 0.01% (99.99% reliability) and have to be investigated for the provision of satellite backup services. Thus, this paper contributes effectively to providing earth-to-space link designers with a handy tool for designing reliable fixed satellite communication service terminals in Libya's coastal, mountainous, and arid areas by investigating the effect of rain on (mmWave) radio systems operating at 20,28,38, 40,50 GHz.

Ka-band satellites solve the rising need for internet-based and data-driven applications thanks to their increased capacity and throughput advantages. Wafa's Ka-band satellite internet services provider is amongst the most affordable solutions—Ka-band satellite internet services for all of Libya. Depending on the coverage areas and satellite footprint, satellite internet over Libya is offered on the Hughes, iDirect, and TooWay platforms using both Ka and Ku bands. It is operational on the Hylas-2 satellite, offering speeds of up to 6 Mbps to its users spread across the entire coverage beam. The satellite has a bandwidth of 72 MHz. In every major city in Libya, including Benghazi, Tripoli, Misratah, Zuwarah, Tobruk, Ghadamis, Sabha, Al Burayqah, etc., they are the only satellite ISP offering Ka-band-based high-speed satellite broadband internet. With only a dish size range of 72 to 98 cm, coverage of the Libya Ka-band is provided, as seen in Fig. 1. The most commonly used millimeter wave antennas for satellite communication are parabolic reflector antennas and horn antennas.

The Hylas 2 beams are located in Jordan, Afghanistan, Armenia, Georgia, Azerbaijan, Syria, Turkey, and Iraq. Hylas 2, the intended satellite, was launched into Long's geostationary orbit. 1 Position: 31° E (31° E), with six gateway beams and 24 active Ka-band user beams to transport high-speed data to Eastern Europe, the Middle East, and Northern and Southern Africa. Figure [1] shows a Satellite dish pinpointing Hylas 2Ka-band: Libya & Tunisia. Additionally, they have a steerable spot beam that can offer coverage anyplace on Earth that a satellite can see. In the uplink, the operational frequency is 28 GHz; in the downlink, it is 17.7 GHz. Hylas 2Ka-band in Libya can also be used as a primary or a backup path transmission. Hylas 2 Ka-band is known for its high reliability and availability, making it a suitable option for backup path transmission. However, the reliability of the transmission may depend on several factors, such as weather conditions, equipment maintenance, and network congestion. It is always recommended to have a backup plan in case of any unexpected disruptions.

3   Motivation and Contributions

This paper is a prototype to explain how to design a broadband satellite link in Libya that works in the Ka- V- and W-band frequency. This further provides an important ground for the link budget of the broadband satellite at mm-wave frequency. By determining the value of link efficiency in bps/Hz and throughput in Mbps we can get an insight into factors to consider while selecting a modulation scheme. Furthermore, the outcomes of this paper can support a technology that automatically adjusts the working mode based on channel quality, such as Adaptive modulation and adaptive channel. Further studies can be conducted using the measured data's proposed dependable rain fade margin (FM) value. This analysis will also be oriented to find the outage probability due to rain when the radio-link fade margin is smaller than A dB.

4   Simulation and Analysis

The critical performance indicators assessment is still needed to establish Libya's high-speed satellite broadband internet. Therefore, in this work, the link key performance indicators such as throughput and spectral efficiency have been predicted. Additionally, the broadband satellite links' link availability and link margin have been investigated by considering the impact of rain during the worst months in Libya. Libyan National Centre of Meteorology reports that the maximum period of rainfall occurs in December, particularly during the winter season.

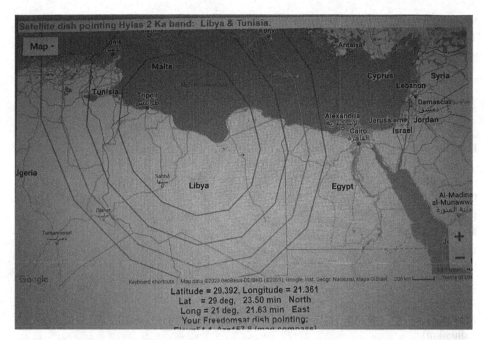

Fig. 1. The Beams are in Nothern and Southern Africa, Eastern Europe,e and the Middle East

Furthermore, in this simulation, we have determined the fade margin at different reliability levels. As we know, the new indoor and outdoor communication system applications need a high level of reliability, so we have to investigate the actual value of SNR that allows the link at a higher frequency to work accurately in the Libyan climate while considering rain fade. Thus, in the simulation, it's assumed that fade margins have reduced SNR at clear sky conditions at a reliability level of 99.99%.

4.1 Simulation Parameters

Simulation results have been provided in this section to confirm the validity of the theoretical analysis. Extensive simulations were conducted to validate the feasibility of using mm-wave communication systems to provide access connectivity to on-the-ground users through satellite communication in Libya. The most significant parameters used to perform the simulation have been presented in Table 1. Rain attenuation is expected in the Hylas 2 radio links at different polarisation. Additionally, the power margin to compensate for rain attenuation A, then P(A) is also the outage probability of the radio link can be determined by considering rain fade in five stations in Libya, namely, Shahat, Tripoli, Airport of Tripoli, Benina, and Sebha. We thought of these specific sites because of the % of availability of the collected data sheet rain-rate time series R(t) (mm/h) for 30 years [13]. Based on converted 1-min rain rate data, the ITU-R model predicts and examines rain fade. In performance analysis (Beninna and Tripoli airports) have been considered. Because we wish to show system-oriented results, we limited the power margin/attenuation in the range of 30.04 and 33.43 dBs, and the frequency is 28 GHz.

Also, the average signal-to-noise ratio was limited to the range of 10 to 40 dBs of the Hylas 2 radio links. Therefore, the rain attenuation expected in the Hylas 2 radio links at vertical polarisation has been predicted.

Table 1 Illustration of some Inputs Parameter at five different locations in Libya

Inputs Parameter	Tripoli	Shahat	Tripoli airport	Benina	Sebha
Frequency (GHz)	Ku, Ka, V, and W-band downlink	12–20-28, 38,40,50			
rainfall rate for 0.01% (mm\h)	45	51.74	35.8	21.7	4.18
Height of ES above MSL (km)	0.025	0.621	0.081	0.129	0.432
Latitude of ES (degrees)	32.54	32.49	32.40	32.05	27.01
Satellite elevation (degrees)	47.60	51.15	48.02	51.23	53.82
Effective Earth radius(km)	8500				
Polarisations	LP-H, LP- V, CP				
Percentage of the year	0.001% 0.0876 h/y	0.01% 0.876 hours/y	0.1% 8.76 hours/y	1% 87.6 hours/y	

Table 2. 0.01% Rain Fade (dB) was calculated for Benina and Tripoli airport stations at different polarisations for the C, Ku, and Ka bands.

Downlink Frequency band	Rain Attenuation $A_{0.01}$ (dB) at at Benina $R_{0.01\%}$ 21.7 mm / h			Rain Attenuation $A_{0.01}$ (dB) at Tripoli airport $R_{0.01\%}$ 35.8 mm / h		
	LP-H	LP-V	CP	LP-H	LP-V	CP
4 GHz	0.07	0.06	0.06	0.14	0.10	0.11
12 GHz	4.65	4.13	4.40	6.95	6.21	6.56
20 GHz	13.54	12.04	12.75	19.64	17.20	18.36
28 GHz	28.22	24.36	24.8	37.67	33.43	34.09
30 GHz	29.97	26.94	27.01	41.7	37.28	38
40 GHz	41.02	37.83	39.42	56.63	51.99	54.31
50 GHz	58.39	56.45	57.03	77.14	72.35	73.01

Table 3. Rain fades $A_{0.01}\%$ (B) for Uplink and Downlink frequency in Tripoli

Frequency band	$A_{0.01}\%$ (dB) at horizontal polarisation	$A_{0.01}\%$ (dB) at vertical polarisation	$A_{0.01}$ (dB) at Circular polarisation
4 GHz	0.18	0.13	0.13
6 GHz	1.09	0.8	0.95
12 GHz	8.19	7.29	7.72
14 GHz	11.46	10.28	10.82
20 GHz	25.22	22.03	21.40
28 GHz	44.45	39.25	49.02
30 GHz	44.59	39.65	42.12
40 GHz	65.13	59.69	62.40
50 GHz	77.7	72.93	79.49

4.2 Rain Attenuation Analysis

According to the data collected, it's noted that rainfall statistical data was recorded in Libya with a 3-hor integration time. Until now, the research center at the College of CEET in Benghazi couldn't collect rainfall data at a short integration time. This is considered a significant factor in designing the reliability of terrestrial networks and satellite links operating in the themmWave spectrum. It's worth mentioning that applying the empirical model presented in the recommendations ITUR P.837 and ITU-R P.838 to predict rainfall losses. Still, because of the sizeable Libyan area, it can underestimate or overestimate rain fade at the study area of interest. The country is the fourth-largest in Africa, the Arab world, and the world, with an area of almost 1.8 million km^2. Thus, one-minute rain rate cumulative distributions were generated from collected data. Several prediction models have been developed for converting one-minute rain rates by considering different climatic conditions worldwide. Budalal et al. recommended a suitable prediction model to predict one-minute rain rate distribution for millimeter wave link design in the Libyan environment. Chieko and Yoshio were recommended to calculate the cumulative distribution of the one-minute rain rate under Libyan climatic conditions [14].

Additionally, the model proposed by (ITU-R) is used to predict and investigate rain fade based on converted 1-min rain rate data under various parameters that significantly impact the expected rain fade. A comparison of rain attenuation for horizontal polarisation in Shahat city in the Est of Libya at v band downlink frequencies has been presented in Fig. 2.

It is found that rain attenuation can be neglected at C, Ku band downlink working at 4–12 GHz in Libya. Tables 2 and 3 compare the rain fade effects on Tripoli airport and Benina airport to the Ka- V and W bands with those of the Ku-band. Even though Ka-band (20 - 30 GHz) antenna gains are 4 to 6 dB higher than Ku-band(11 – 14 GHz)antennas of similar size, Ku-band rain effects are more minor at Ku-band [15]. Consequently, this increased gain in Ka-band may provide a degree of rain fade mitigation if Ka-band has

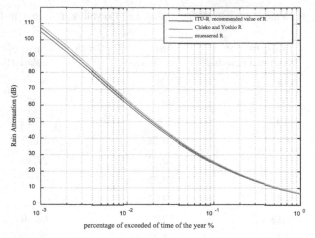

Fig. 2. Comparison of Rain Attenuation prediction in Shahat City at V downlink frequencies band (elevation angle = 51°, horizontal Polarisation)

been used. The current results will be a good tool for satellite system designers to shift to a frequency band higher than the Ku band. However, in some areas in Libya, rain effects present a larger challenge to overcome at V- band. The site diversity or power adaption techniques can be utilised to overcome the link outage probability because of rain fade. Figure 3 shows a comparison of horizontal polarisation rain attenuation at 5 different locations for the V-downlink frequency band [16]

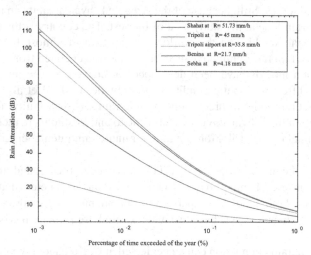

Fig. 3. shows a comparison of horizontal polarisation rain attenuation at five different locations for the V-downlink frequency band.

The other result shows a fade marginal difference of about 15 dB between Ku- and Ka-band frequencies for 99.99%-time availability in coastal regions. As well as the results obtained at V-band downlink shows that 99.99% availability is possible in all the southern part stations in Libya. However, Libya is exposed to dust and sand storms frequently. Thus, a real downlink improvement for satellite communication at mm-wave frequency has to be re-designed by considering the rain and dust attenuation parameters. Moreover, the simulation results showed that the ITU-R model underestimates the rain attenuation in the northeast and northwest of the Libyan coastal line. Rain attenuation is predicted for five selected locations based on a 1-min rainfall rate from ITU-R P. 837–6, 2017[18] model recommendation. Also, one-minute $R_{0.01\%}$ distributions were predicted using Chieko and Yoshio model, which is considered the best model for a one-minute rain rate according to Libyan climatic condition parameters.

Chieko and Yoshio are recommended in [17] for the calculation of one-minute rain rate cumulative distribution under Libyan climatic conditions. Comparative simulation results are shown in Fig. 2.

Using long-term data on rainfall intensity, Fig. 2 shows the attenuation due to rain in different zones of Libya when the signal is horizontally [19] polarised at 40 GHz for different percentages of time and various frequency bands. It's clear that the rain effect increases with an increase in frequency, a one-minute rain rate in mm/h, and a decrease in elevation angle [20].

4.3 Performance Analysis

It is possible to provide mobile broadband (MBB) connectivity using the mm-wave bands at (V/Q), which offer a lot more bandwidth(hundreds of MHz to a few GHz), even similar to fiber to the home (100 MB/s), especially at high antenna gain. They are, however, more susceptible to absorption and scattering by raindrops which may reduce the availability of the links below 99%[21]. The following section assesses the performance of two Libyan airports based on their link spectral efficiency in bps/Hz and throughput in Mbps (Tripoli Airport and Biennia Airport) [4].

The spectral efficiency and throughput of downlink satellite-to-earth microwave links were changed with transponder bandwidth. The rain fade margin (FM) value obtained from measured data on system average SNR dB at the receiver and neglecting interference at clear air conditions at particular reliability has been utilised. During rain events, this value of SNR would be decreased by FM. This value and the bandwidth used for the transmission provide an upper bound of the maximum achievable bit rate R_{max}. The formula (2&3)has been utilised to estimate link efficiency in bps/Hz and throughput in Mbps at vertical polarisation at 28 GHz. When the power margin in the Hylas 2 radio links provides Ka-band satellite internet services for all of Libya is equal to A (dB), and P(A) represents the outage probability.

The proposed fade margin (FM) is defined as:

$$MF = \frac{Gt\,Gr\,Pt}{kT_sRLoL_{sm}\left(\frac{E_b}{N_o}\right)} \tag{1}$$

where Gr is the receive antenna gain, Gt is transmit antenna gain, Pt is the transmitted power(dBm), R is the data rate in bps, L0 represents circuit losses, k is Boltzmann's constant $1.38 \times 10 - 23$ J/K, Ts is the effective system noise temperature, $\frac{E_b}{N_o}$ is the required energy per bit to noise spectral density ratio, L_{sm} L_{sm} is the modified free space path loss with consideration of rain fade.

$$Pr = EIRP + Gr - (l_{ta} + l_{ra} + l_{atm} + l_{rain} + l_{pol} + l_{pt}) \qquad (2)$$

where
l_{ta} –Attenuation due to transmit antenna, l_{ra} –Attenuation due to.

receive antenna, l_{atm} –Atmospheric attenuation, l_{rain} – Attenuation due to precipitation, l_{pol} –Attenuation due to polarisation, l_{pt} –Antenna pointing misalignment related attenuation. To determine the throughput, we must initially ascertain the value of the spectral efficiency as a function depending on SNR and FM, as shown in the formula below:

$$\text{Spectral efficiency} = \log(1 + \frac{SNR}{FM})/\log 2 \qquad (3)$$

The spectral efficiency value obtained during rainy events is considered the essential factor to determine of link throughout, as presented in Eq. (4).

$$\text{Throughput} = \text{Spectral efficiency} \times \text{Transponder Bandwidth} \qquad (4)$$

As shown in Figs. 4 and 5 over the whole SNR range, analytical results show an increase in 28 GHz Hylas 2 -sat link spectral efficiency and throughput with the increase of system SNR considering 30.4 dB as the fade margin in at Benina ($R_{0.01\%}$ 21.7 mm / h).Tripoli airport $R_{0.01\%}$ 35.8 mm / h at high SNR shows that the asymptotic SE curves closely

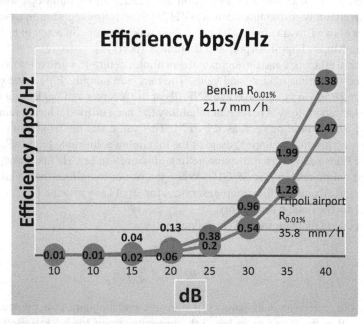

Fig. 4. The link efficiency in bps/Hz versus transmit SNR in dB varying the Parameter of satellite links with FM = 30.25 dB, F = 28 GHz, Hylas 2 -sat transponder BW = 72 MHz

reflect the actual findings. The throughput of the link in this scenario refers to the average rate of successful delivery of symbols over a communication channel considering rain fade.

Thus, it's important to identify the guaranteed capacity modulation scheme. Shifting of the modulation scheme and channel bandwidth on the mm-wave link caused by weather changes and the impact of the shifting on service throughput and reliability it's our future work.

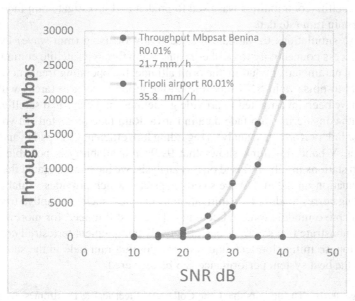

Fig. 5. The link throughput in Mbps versus transmit SNR in dB varies in the Parameter of satellite links with FM = 30.25 dB, F = 28 GHz, Hylas 2 -sat transponder BW = 72 MHz

5   Conclusion

Rain fade data is significant in evaluating the performance of satellite communication links at millimeter waves in Libya because it provides information on the attenuation caused by rainfall which can affect the signal quality and reliability. This data can be used to design and optimize the link budget and to select appropriate modulation and coding schemes to mitigate the effects of rain fade.

Many outage probability events in terrestrial and satellite links have recently been recorded in Libya because of rain attenuation impact, especially at higher frequencies. Therefore, in this paper, rain attenuation phenomena have been accurately predicted to mitigate outages due to rain fade. An analytical prediction was derived from rainfall statistics collected from five locations in Libya over the past 30 years. One of the limation of our data was metrological weather stations recorded rain rate data every three hours. However, a rain attenuation prediction method requires a minute of integration time.

Thus, collected data were analysed and processed to convert into one–a minute rain rate cumulative distribution in Libya. Several prediction models for converting one–minute rain rates have been utilised by considering different climatic conditions. From the comparison, Chieko and Yoshio's models proved by Japanese researchers are most suitable and recommended for use in the Libyan climate.

Based on the zenith paths of the Hylas 2 satellite, a relationship has been estimated between the annual average probability distribution of rain attenuation and the carrier wave (mm-Wave) in various climate regions in Libya. The model recommended by ITU-R for satellite communities was used to predict and investigate rain fade based on converted 1-min rain rate data

Extensive simulations to validate the feasibility of using (mm-wave) frequencies to provide access connectivity to on-the-ground users through satellite communication. Thus, several parameters, including the orbit altitude, the operating frequency, the value of the signal-to-noise ratio SNR, and the on-the-ground scenario (areas with distinct climates), have been investigated to provide guidelines on the optimal satellite configuration(s) with considering rain fade data in Libya. Rain fade predicted at two locations was used for link performance analysis regarding link efficiency in bps/Hz and throughput in Mbps. V-band downlink shows that 99.99% availability is possible in all the Sothern part stations in Libya. Based on this analysis, we have investigated the influence of rain attenuation on the mm-Wave satellite system, which provides valuable insights into designing corresponding fade mitigation techniques, such as adaptive transmission schemes, adaptive modulation, and coding. There is still a need for more research in Libya to demonstrate that satellites can effectively complement terrestrial communications and propose mitigation techniques in overcoming rain fade in the satellite-Earth link so that the best system performance can be delivered.

Acknowledgements. The authors thank the College of Electrical & Electronics Technology of Benghazi, Libya. They also thank the Libyan National Meteorological Center (LNMC) for their assistance and technical support during data collection.

References

1. Budalal, A.A., Islam, M.R.: Path loss models for outdoor environment—with a focus on rain attenuation impact on short-range millimeter-wave links. e-Prime – Adv. Electr. Eng., Electron. Energy **3**, 100106 (2023). https://doi.org/10.1016/j.prime.2023.100106
2. Zhao, X., Wang, Qi., Suiyan Geng, Yu., Zhang, J.Z., Li, J.: Path loss modification and multi-user capacity analysis by dynamic rain models for 5G radio communications in millimetre waves. IET Commun. **13**(10), 1488–1496 (2019)
3. Guo, Y., Kong, H., Huang, Q., Lin, M., Zhu, W.-P., Amindavar, H.: Performance analysis for the forward link of multiuser satellite communication systems. Int. J. Satell. Commun. Network. **39**(5), 560–569 (2021)
4. He, Y., Jiao, J., Liang, X., Wu, S., Wang, Y., Zhang, Q.: Outage performance of millimeter-wave band NOMA downlink system in satellite-based IoT. In: 2019 IEEE/CIC International Conference on Communications in China (ICCC), pp. 356–361. IEEE (2019)
5. Jia, M., Gu, X., Guo, Q., Xiang, W., Zhang, N.: Broadband hybrid satellite-terrestrial communication systems based on cognitive radio toward 5G. IEEE Wirel. Commun. **23**(6), 96–106 (2016)

6. Fukuchi, H., Chodkaveekityada, P.: Propagation impairments along satellite-to-earth path and their mitigation technologies. In: IEEE Wireless Communications, vol. 23, no. 6, pp. 96–106 (2019)

7. EMEA Satellite Operators Association, "Satellite Communication Services: An integral part of the 5G Ecosystem," White Paper (2017)

8. Sweeting, M.N.: Modern small satellites-changing the economics of space. Proc. IEEE **106**(3), 343–361 (2018)

9. Budalal, A.A., Islam, M.R., Habaebi, M.H., Rahman. T.: Millimeter wave channel modeling–present development and challenges in tropical areas. In: 2018 7th International Conference on Computer and Communication Engineering (ICCCE), pp. 23–28. IEEE (2018)

10. Giordani, M., Zorzi. M.: Satellite communication at millimeter waves: a key enabler of the 6G era. In: 2020 International Conference on Computing, Networking and Communications (ICNC), pp. 383–388. IEEE (2020)

11. Islam, M.R., Budalal, A.A.H., Habaebi, M.H., Badron, K., Ismail.,A.F.: Performance analysis of rain attenuation on earth-to-satellite microwave links design in Libya. In: IOP Conference Series: Materials Science and Engineering, vol. 260, no. 1, pp. 012041. IOP Publishing (2017)

12. Recommendation ITU-R P.618: propagation data and prediction methods required for the design of earth-space telecommunication systems. In: International Telecommunication Union, Geneva, Switzerland, Rec. ITU-R, P. 618-13 (2017)https://www.itu.int/rec/R-REC-P.618/

13. Budalal, A.A.H.: Rain attenuation prediction on earth-to-satellite microwave link in Libya as a case study. Master's Thesis, Kuala Lumpur: International Islamic University Malaysia, 2017 (2017)

14. Budalal, A.A.H., Islam, M.R., Habaebi, M.H., Ahmed, M.M.: Rain rate distribution for satellite to earth microwave links design in Libya. In: 2016 International Conference on Computer and Communication Engineering (ICCCE), pp. 443–448. IEEE (2016)

15. Kodheli, O., Guidotti, A., Vanelli-Coralli, A.: Integration of Satellites in 5G through LEO Constellations. CoRR abs/1706.06013, 1–6 (2017)

16. Ali Ahmad, R., Lacan, J., Arnal, F., Gineste, M., Clarac, L.: Enhancing satellite system throughput using adaptive HARQ for delay tolerant services in mobile communications. In: 2015 Wireless Telecommunications Symposium (WTS), New York, NY, pp. 1–7 (2015)

17. Guidotti, A., et. al.: Satellite-enabled LTE systems in LEO Constellations. In: 2017 IEEE International Conference on Communications (ICC), Paris, pp. 876–881 (2017). https://doi.org/10.1109/ICCW.2017.7962769

18. Recommendation ITU-R P. 837-6 Characteristics of precipitation for propagation modelling (2017)

19. Ito, C., Hosoya, Y.: The Thunterstorm Ratio as a Regional Climate Parameter: Its Effects on Different-Integration-Time Rain Rate Conversion, Rain Attenuation, Site-Diversity and Rain Depolarization, vol. 1, pp. 10–13

20. ITU-R P. 816–10 Propagation data and prediction methods required for the design of Earth-space (2017)

21. Matricciani, E., Riva, C.: Outage probability versus carrier frequency in geosurf satellite constellations with radio-links faded by rain. Telecom **3**(3), 504–513 (2022). https://doi.org/10.3390/telecom3030027

BJT Based Voltage Reference Circuits Comparisons in 65 nm CMOS Process

Alharari Alsouri Alharari, Sami Saddek Bizzan$^{(\boxtimes)}$, and Abdulmoied Omar

EEE Department, University of Tripoli, Tripoli, Libya
{al.alharari,s.bizzan,aa.omar}@uot.edu.ly, sbizzan@gmail.com

Abstract. Selected bandgap voltage reference circuits based on bipolar transistors from the literature are implemented and simulated using the same process node. This allowed us to compare their performance parameters. The process node used for the simulation is 65 nm PTM which is publicly available. Out of the four designs selected, design II shows the best overall results with temperature coefficient of 17.3 ppm/ °c, supply voltage ranges from 0.7 to 1.21 V, PSRR of -120 @ 10 Hz, and reasonable gate area.

Keywords: Bandgap Voltage Reference · Subthreshold Voltage Reference · Temperature Compensated Reference

1 Introduction

Bandgap voltage reference (BVR) is a circuit that provides a voltage reference independent of supply voltage variation and temperature variation. Voltage references are one of among the most important building blocks in analog and digital circuits. It is used in analog to digital converters or in digital to analog converters for setting up the full-scale level. The reference voltage is also used to generate bias currents for various analog blocks such as analog amplifiers, voltage-controlled oscillators, sense amplifiers, and charge pump phase locked loops.

With the tremendous efforts made in integrated circuit design and manufacturing where billions of transistors are constructed in a single die, certainly, voltage reference circuits must be incorporated in such circuits. These circuits range from data processors and memory chips to power electronics, which means that voltage reference circuits appear in almost all electronic integrated circuits.

One of the first classical bandgap voltage reference circuit is introduced by David Hilbiber in 1964 [1]. He used the Avalanche diodes to generate a reference voltage source. The output voltage is 1.25 V with temperature coefficient of 10 ppm/ °c.

In 1971, Robert Widlar introduced a reference circuit which later became known as the Widlar bandgap voltage reference circuit [2]. The circuit uses bipolar transistors to generate stable low temperature coefficient voltage reference over temperature range from -55 °c to 125 °c. Shortly after in 1973, Kuijk presented a voltage reference circuit which generates a low temperature coefficient voltage over temperature range from 0 °c to 60 °c. He used the conventional bipolar technology process [3].

© The Author(s), under exclusive license to Springer Nature Switzerland AG 2024
T. A. T. Benmusa et al. (Eds.): ILCICT 2023, CCIS 2097, pp. 68–78, 2024.
https://doi.org/10.1007/978-3-031-62624-1_6

CMOS process dominates the integrated circuit fabrication industry for its well-known benefits such as low power consumption and high transistor density. As Moore's law predicts, transistor feature size has shrunk tremendously in recent years which led to the need to reduce power supply voltage accordingly. This reduction in power supply voltage has increased IC manufacturing yield by reducing the stress exerted on the silicon oxide di-electric underneath the gate of MOS transistors and hence reducing di-electric failure. Power supply voltage reduction added the benefit of reducing power consumption since node toggling throughout the chip switches to reduced voltage level.

Supply voltage less than 1.2 V imposes yet another stringent condition on designing bandgap voltage reference circuits. The reference voltage must be less than 1 V and hence, the traditional circuit design techniques must be modified to obtain portion of the bandgap voltage which inherits the characteristics of the full bandgap voltage. This type of circuits which operate with supply voltage less than 1 V is known as sub-1 V voltage reference circuits [4].

One of among the first sub-1 V bandgap voltage reference is proposed by Neuteboom et al., which is based on resistive division technique and provides an output voltage less than 1.23 V and the supply voltage can be as low as 0.9 V in 1997 [5]. Another technique to lower the supply voltage is given by Banba [6]. It uses resistive sub-division to further decrease the minimum required supply voltage and it implemented in CMOS process.

2 Operating Principle of Bandgap Circuit

In the circuit shown in Fig. 1, the first and the second transistors, Q1 & Q2, are operating at different current densities, J1 & J2, to produce Proportional-To-absolute Temperature voltage (PTAT) across R3.

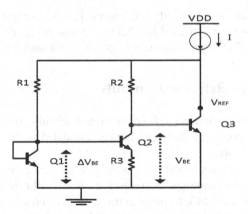

Fig. 1. Widlar Voltage Reference Circuit.

A third transistor Q3 is added to generate V_{BE} voltage at the collector of Q2. Q3 sets the output voltage such that $V_{REF} = V_{BE3} + \left(\frac{R_2}{R_3}\right)\Delta V_{BE}$. When the output voltage is set to approximate the bandgap voltage of silicon, the voltage across R2 will have a temperature variation that negates the voltage variation of V_{BE} of transistor Q3 [2].

In other words, the thermal voltage V_T extracted from ΔV_{BE} of two BJTs with different emitter areas and, hence, different current densities will generate the PTAT voltage, while the base-emitter voltage V_{BE} of the BJT will generate Complementary-To-Absolute Temperature voltage CTAT voltage.

In this circuit, Q1 is operating at a relatively high current density. The current density of Q2 is usually about 10 times lower than that of Q1 and the emitter-base voltage differrence ΔV_{BE} between the two devices appears across R3.

A simplified analysis is given as follows. The collector current I_C of a BJT transistor is shown by Eq. (1),

$$I_C = I_0 \left[\exp\left(\frac{V_{BE}}{\eta V_T} - 1 \right) \right] \tag{1}$$

where I_0 is a process-dependent constant, V_{BE} is the base-emitter voltage, η is the emission coefficient, and V_T is the thermal voltage.

If two transistors are operated at different current densities J_i, then the distinction of their base-producer voltages is given by Eq. (2),

$$\Delta V_{BE} = V_T \ln\left(\frac{J_1}{J_2} \right) \tag{2}$$

In Fig. 1, one can see that the output voltage of the bandgap voltage reference (BGR) is given by the sum of the base-emitter voltage of Q3 and the PTAT voltage across R3, as shown by Eq. (3)

$$V_{REF} = V_{BE} + \frac{R_2}{R_3} \Delta V_{BE} \tag{3}$$

The circuit is simple and can be easily implemented in BJT integrated circuit process. The circuit also can be implemented in CMOS process; however, the performance is degraded since the BJT characteristics is not optimized for such process

3   Various Voltage Reference Circuits

In this section, selected bandgap voltage reference circuits from the literature are explained and discussed. Then these circuits are simulated in the same process node to generate fair comparisons.

Design I [7] is a low power resistor-less voltage reference circuit implemented in $0.18\mu m$ CMOS process technology. The reference circuit is illustrated in Fig. 2. The circuit contains PMOS M2 and M3, forming a current mirror and giving bias current to the diode connected PMOS M5, working as a resistor whose resistance changes with temperature. The reference voltage V_{REF} is obtained by combining the junction voltage V_E (V_E equal to emitter to base voltage of bipolar transistor) which generate Complementary-To-Absolute Temperature voltage (CTAT) and the voltage obtained across the PMOS M5 which generate Proportional-To-absolute Temperature voltage (PTAT).

Design II [8] is a low power voltage reference with resistors shown in Fig. 3. It is implemented in a standard 180 nm CMOS process technology. This voltage reference

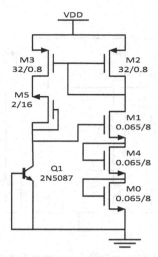

Fig. 2. Schematic of the Low Power Resistor-less Voltage Reference

circuit employ subthreshold current. The circuit provides a stable reference voltage at the output independent of variations in power supply and temperature. The reference voltage V_{REF} is obtained by combining the junction voltage V_E (V_E is complementary to absolute temperature) and the voltage across the transistor PMOS M5.

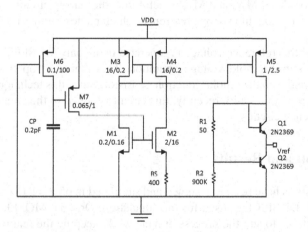

Fig. 3. Schematic of the Low Power with Resistors Voltage Reference

Design III [10] is a bandgap reference circuit with an inherent curvature-compensation property. It is implemented in TSMC 90 nm process technology. The reference circuit is illustrated in Fig. 4. The circuit is self-biasing to keep the currents flowing through the BJTs equal. One effective technique is the use of β-multiplier circuit.

Design IV [9] is a temperature and supply compensated subthreshold voltage reference circuit. It is shown in Fig. 5. The circuit is implemented in 45 nm CMOS technology

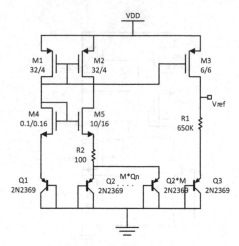

Fig. 4. Schematic of Bandgap Reference with an Inherent Curvature-Compensation Property

and can be divided into five parts. The first part includes transistors M_4, M_5, M_{10}, M_{11} and resistor R_2, , which generate current source Proportional-To-absolute Temperature (PTAT). The second part includes transistors M_{15}, M_{16}, M_{17}, and resistor R_3, , which generate current source Complementary-To-Absolute Temperature (CTAT). The third part is an operation amplifier made of transistors M_6, M_7, M_8, and M_9. The fourth part made of transistors M_{12}, M_{13}, and M_{14} which forms the startup circuit. The last part is responsible for generating the voltage reference, which made of transistors M_1, M_2, M_3, and resistor R_1.

It is clear that this reference voltage is generated using only MOSFETs and employs the principle of sub-threshold voltage operation. This region of operation possesses similar characteristics to the bipolar junction transistor. Since this technique is common among the research community recently, this circuit is added to the comparison of the BJT based reference circuits.

4   Simulation and Results

The selected designs have been redesigned and simulated in 65 nm PTM publicly available process [1]. LT SPICE is used for the simulation. Original MOSFET dimensions are sized up or down to suit the process at hand while keeping the relative dimensions intact. Supply voltage is set to 1.1 V as required by the process. Since the process has no models for bipolar transistors (it is a CMOS process), we have added external bipolar transistor models to facilitate the simulation. These models are available in LT SPICE.

Figure 6 Through Fig. 17. Shows the simulation results for the selected circuits under investigation.

Table 1: shows the performance parameters and comparison for the existing circuits.

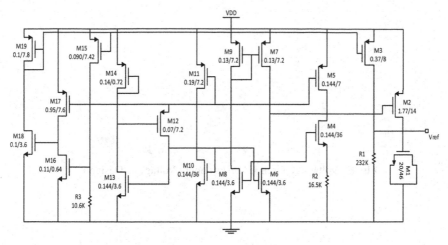

Fig. 5. Schematic of Temperature and Supply Compensated Voltage Reference

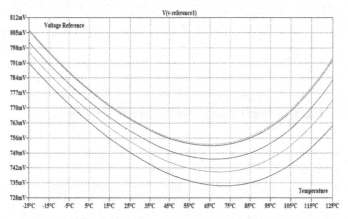

Fig. 6. Voltage Reference Versus Temperature of Design I

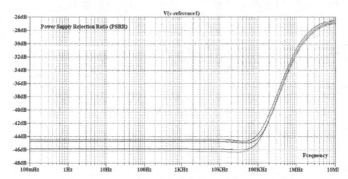

Fig. 7. Power Supply Rejection Ratio (PSRR) of Design I

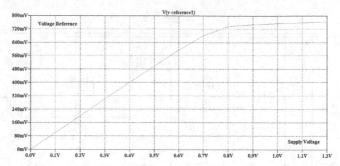

Fig. 8. Voltage Reference Versus Supply Voltage of Design I

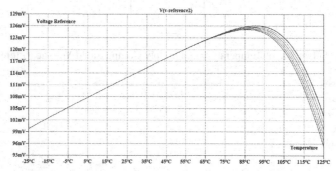

Fig. 9. Voltage Reference Versus Temperature of Design II

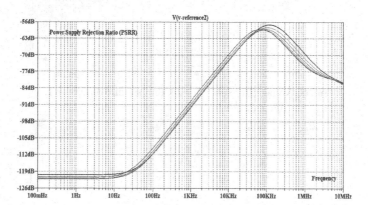

Fig. 10. Power Supply Rejection Ratio (PSRR) of Design II

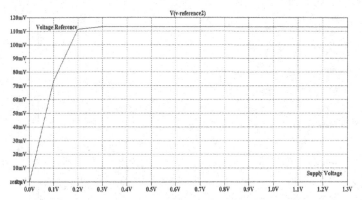

Fig. 11. Voltage Reference Versus Supply Voltage of Design II

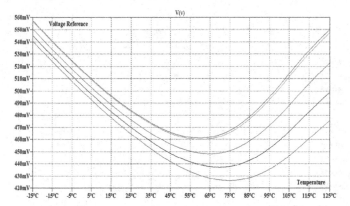

Fig. 12. Voltage Reference Versus Temperature of Design III

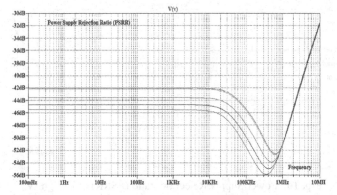

Fig. 13. Power Supply Rejection Ratio (PSRR) of Design III

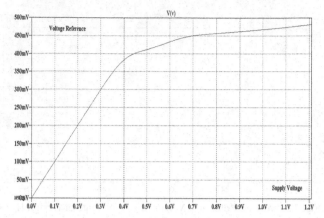

Fig. 14. Voltage Reference Versus Supply Voltage of Design III

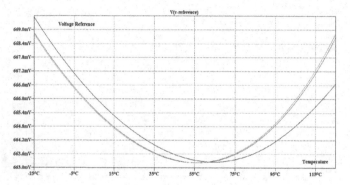

Fig. 15. Voltage Reference Versus Temperature of Design IV

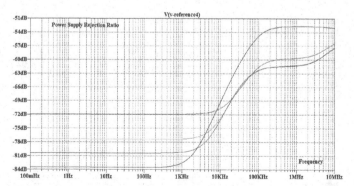

Fig. 16. Power Supply Rejection Ratio (PSRR) of Design IV

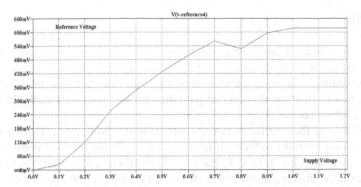

Fig. 17. Voltage Reference Versus Supply Voltage of Design IV

Table 1. Performance Comparisons of Voltage Reference Circuits

IV [9]	III [10]	II [8]	I [7]	Design
45nm	90nm	180nm	180nm	CMOS Technology
0.6	1.15	0.95	1.2	Minimum Supply Voltage [V]
0.6 to 1	NA	095 to 2.5	1.2 to 1.8	Supply Voltage Range [V]
-25 to 85	-0 to 100	-20 to 100	-45 to 125	Temperature Range [°c]
19	43.5	NA	11	Temperature Coefficient [ppm/°c]
193.2	720	169.4	1150	Voltage Reference [mV]
Results for 65nm PTM Process Listed Below				
-25 to 125	-25 to 125	-25 to 125	-25 to 125	Temperature Range [°c]
5.68	74	17.3	49	Temperature Coefficient [ppm/ °c]
1	0.9	0.7	0.9	Minimum Supply Voltage [V]
1 to 1.21	0.9 to 1.21	0.7 to 1.21	0.9 to 1.21	Supply Voltage Range [V]
669.5	550	126	798	Voltage Reference @ Minimum Supply Voltage [mV]
673	560	126	805	Voltage Reference @ Minimum Supply Voltage + 10% [mV]
-72	-46	-120.9	-45	10Hz	Power Supply Rejection Ratio [dB]
-71	-48	-112	-45	100kHz	
-62	-51	-59	-32	1MHz	
-56	-32	-80	-27	10MHz	
19	15	9	7	Transistor Count	
50.96	308.016	93.762	54.76	Gate Area [μm^2] (excluding Bipolar)	

5 Conclusion

This work allowed us to compare different bandgap voltage reference circuits implemented in the same process, namely, 65 nm PTM. Design II shows the best overall results. Even though these selected circuits originally implemented in different process nodes, this work allowed us to compare their performance parameters in the same publicly available process node.

Design IV gave the best temperature coefficient of 5.68 ppm/ °c. However, design II shows the best overall results with temperature coefficient of 17.3 ppm/ °c, supply voltage ranges from 0.7 to 1.21 V, PSRR of -120 @ 10 Hz, and reasonable gate area.

Unfortunately, silicon area for bipolar transistors is not given for the selected circuits in their original process. Furthermore, since the PTM process, we have used, has no models for BJTs, hence, silicon area size comparison is not accurate and further work needs to be carried out.

References

1. Hilbiber, D.F.: A new semiconductor voltage standard In: International Solid-State Circuits Conference ISSCC (1964)
2. Widlar, R.J.: New developments in IC voltage regulators. IEEE J. Solid-State Circuits 1, 2 (1971)
3. Kuijk, K.E.: A precision reference voltage source. IEEE J. Solid-State Circuits 3, 6 (1973)
4. Hande, V., Baghini, M.S.: Survey of bandgap and non-bandgap based voltage reference techniques. Sci Iranica 23(6), 2845–2861 (2016). https://doi.org/10.24200/sci.2016.3994
5. Neuteboom, B.M.J.K.A.M.J.H.: A DSP-based hearing instrument IC. IEEE J. Solid-State Circuits. 32(11), 1790–1806 (1997)
6. Banba, H.S.A.U.T.M.H.: A CMOS bandgap reference circuit with sub-1V operation, IEEE J. Solid-State Circuits. 34(5), 670–674 (1999)
7. Gupta, R.S.M.: Design of Ultra low power, Temperature Independent Resistorless Bandgap Reference Circuit in 180 nm CMOS. In: International Conference on Signal Processing and Integrated Networks (SPIN), IEEE, pp. 868–871 (2018)
8. Lin, C.J.L.H.: A sub-1v bandgap reference circuit using subthreshold current, IEEE, pp. 4253–4256 (2005)
9. Singh, S.S.K.S.R.: Design and optimization of a low power voltage reference generator circuit in 45 nm CMOS technology. In: International Journal of Innovative Research & Development, pp. 298–303 (2014)
10. Lee, T.S.L.P.D.H.K.K.: A sub-micro w bandgap reference circuit with an inherent curvature-compensation property. IEEE J. Solid-State Circuits 28, 1–9 (2015) (2014)

Computer and Information Systems

Solar Flare Classification via Modified Metaheuristic Optimized Extreme Gradient Boosting

Petar Bisevac[1] , Ana Toskovic[2] , Mohamed Salb[1] , Luka Jovanovic[1] ,
Aleksandar Petrovic[1] , Miodrag Zivkovic[1] , and Nebojsa Bacanin[1(✉)]

[1] Singidunum University, Danijelova 32, 11000 Belgrade, Serbia
{pbisevac,aleksandar.petrovic,nbacanin}@singidunum.ac.rs,
{mohamed.salb.16,luka.jovanovic.191,mzivkovic}@singimail.rs
[2] Teacher Education Faculty, University of Pristina in Kosovska Mitrovica,
Pristina, Serbia
ana.toskovic@pr.ac.rs

Abstract. Intense electromagnetic phenomena occurring on the Sun's surface give rise to solar flares. Energetic solar flares have the potential to reach Earth, causing significant interference with telecommunication systems. Particularly powerful solar events can even disrupt satellite and ground communication infrastructure, posing a substantial risk of extensive damage. To mitigate these risks, comprehensive monitoring systems and robust forecasting techniques are essential for early detection and warning. This research proposes an approach utilizing the extreme gradient boosting (XGBoost) algorithm for solar flare classification. Recognizing that the performance of XGBoost is heavily influenced by appropriate hyperparameter selection, a modified metaheuristic algorithm is introduced to optimize the network's hyperparameters. To evaluate the efficacy of the proposed methodology, a real-world dataset is utilized, and a thorough comparative analysis is conducted, encompassing several contemporary algorithms that address the same solar flare classification task under identical conditions. The objective is to identify the advantages and strengths of the proposed modified metaheuristic approach in comparison to existing methods.

Keywords: Solar flare · Metaheuristic Optimization · Classification · Swarm Intelligence · Extreme Gradient Boosting

1 Introduction

A solar flare is a sudden and intense release of energy from the Sun's surface. It is characterized by a rapid increase in brightness and the emission of a vast amount of electromagnetic radiation across the entire spectrum, from radio waves to X-rays and gamma rays [1]. Solar energetic particles or solar cosmic rays, can be hazardous to astronauts and can also disrupt satellite operations and communication systems on Earth. Solar flares are classified based on their brightness

T. A. T. Benmusa et al. (Eds.): ILCICT 2023, CCIS 2097, pp. 81–95, 2024.
https://doi.org/10.1007/978-3-031-62624-1_7

in X-rays, with the most powerful ones belonging to the X-class category [2]. A robust system for solar flare classification is needed to take timely preemptive measures to protect communication networks on Earth as well as in space.

One potential approach to address this challenge is the utilization of artificial intelligence (AI) techniques. By framing the problem of solar flare prediction as a classification task, advanced AI algorithms can be employed to assess the severity of forthcoming solar events. Among the effective methods for both regression and classification, Extreme Gradient Boosting (XGBoost) [3] has been recognized. XGBoost exhibits efficient capabilities in dealing with complex problems owing to its scalable implementation. Nevertheless, despite its overall strong performance, hyperparameter tuning is necessary to optimize its effectiveness in addressing the specific task at hand.

The use of metaheuristic algorithms has gained significant popularity among researchers as an effective approach for tackling hyperparameter optimization. This is particularly relevant because hyperparameter optimization [4] can be categorized as an NP-hard problem, necessitating the utilization of algorithms capable of handling such complex tasks. In this context, swarm intelligence algorithms have demonstrated their suitability and effectiveness. However, as no one approach works best, as stated by the no free lunch (NFL) theorem [5], experimentation is needed to determine the most suitable algorithm for the task at hand.

In this study, we introduce an adapted variant of a widely recognized metaheuristic algorithm that is employed to optimize the hyperparameters of XGBoost in the context of solar flare classification. Furthermore, a range of contemporary algorithms has been applied to the same real-world dataset to investigate their efficacy in this task. A comprehensive comparative analysis has been conducted to discern the benefits and strengths of the proposed modified metaheuristic approach.

The primary contributions of this work can be summarized as the following:

- A proposal for a robust methodology for determining the class of solar flares based on the XGBoost technique
- The introduction of a modified metaheuristic algorithm specifically for tuning hyperparameters for solar flare classification
- The application of the introduced approach to a real-world dataset consisting of relevant solar flare data

The remainder of this work is structured as per to following: Sect. 2 presents works relating to the topic addressed in this study. In Sect. 3 the introduced methods are described in detail. Section 4 and Sect. 5 present details about the experimental setup, utilized dataset, and evaluation metrics followed by the experimental outcomes and their discussion. Finally, Sect. 6 gives a conclusion to the work and presents proposals for future research.

2   Related Works

Solar flares represent a prominent celestial phenomenon within our solar system, extensively documented by the scientific community. The observation and recording of solar flares have been ongoing since the 1800s, generating a substantial volume of data. Various sources have contributed to this extensive dataset, including space-based observatories like NASA's Solar Dynamics Observatory (SDO) [6] and the Solar and Heliospheric Observatory (SOHO) [7], as well as ground-based observatories worldwide.

The abundance of available data pertaining to solar flares has motivated numerous researchers to employ diverse prediction methodologies for analyzing these solar events. Initially, conventional statistical techniques showed promise in this domain [8]. However, in recent years, deep learning methods have emerged as a novel approach for this purpose [9]. The accurate classification of solar flares has stimulated the development of a range of techniques [10].

One prominent deep learning technique that has shown promising results in the classification of solar flares is Convolutional Neural Networks (CNNs) [11]. CNNs are a type of neural network particularly well-suited for image recognition tasks, making them applicable to the analysis of solar flare data [12]. In addition to solar flare classification, deep learning techniques have also been employed for the prediction of flare occurrence. Recurrent Neural Networks (RNNs) [13] have shown promise in this regard, as they can effectively model the temporal dependencies within the solar flare data. By analyzing the sequential nature of solar flare events, RNNs can capture the underlying patterns and dynamics that precede flare eruptions. This temporal modeling enables the prediction of future flare activity based on historical data. Several studies have demonstrated the effectiveness of RNNs in solar flare prediction, showcasing their ability to provide early warnings for potentially hazardous solar events [14].

Overall, the utilization of deep learning methodologies, such as CNNs for classification and RNNs for prediction, represents a significant advancement in solar flare research. These techniques offer new avenues for understanding the complex dynamics of solar flares and provide valuable insights into their behavior. By harnessing the power of deep learning, researchers can unlock further knowledge about these captivating celestial events and contribute to our ability to forecast and mitigate their potential impact on Earth and space-based systems.

2.1   XGboost

Employing objective function optimization as its guiding principle, the XGBoost method [3] adopts an additive training strategy. At each stage of the optimization process, the outcomes from previous iterations are taken into account, influencing subsequent results. The Eq. (1) is employed to articulate the objective function for the t-th instance in XGBoost.

$$F_o{}^i = \sum_{k=1}^{n} l\left(y_k, \hat{y}_k^{i-1} + f_i\left(x_k\right)\right) + R(f_i) + C, \tag{1}$$

In this context, the loss component of the $t-th$ iteration is denoted as l, the constant term is represented by C, and the regularization parameter of the model is denoted as R. The specific definition of the regularization parameter can be found in Eq. (2).

$$R(f_i) = \gamma T_i + \frac{\lambda}{2} \sum_{j=1}^{T} w_j^2 \qquad (2)$$

Typically, opting for higher values of the γ and λ parameters leads to the creation of simpler tree structures. The mathematical expressions for the first derivative (g) and the second derivative (h) of the model are provided by the following:

$$g_j = \partial_{\hat{y}_k^{i-1}} l \left(y_j, \hat{y}_k^{i-1}\right) \qquad (3)$$

$$h_j = \partial_{\hat{y}_k^{i-1}}^2 l \left(y_j, \hat{y}_k^{i-1}\right) \qquad (4)$$

The solution can be derived using the following formulas:

$$w_j^* = -\frac{\sum g_t}{\sum h_t + \lambda} \qquad (5)$$

$$F_o^* = -\frac{1}{2} \sum_{j=1}^{T} \frac{(\sum g)^2}{\sum h + \lambda} + \gamma T, \qquad (6)$$

In this context, F_o^* refers to the score of the loss function, while w_j^* represents the solution for the weights.

2.2 Metaheuristic Optimization

The increasing complexity of emerging AI algorithms has created a need for advanced techniques for optimization. As the number of control parameters increased, the challenge of locating optimal values becomes more difficult and can be considered an NP-hard problem. Metaheuristic algorithms have emerged as the preferred approach for tackling NP-hard problems in various domains. Among these algorithms, swarm intelligence has demonstrated exceptional effectiveness.

Many of these algorithms draw inspiration from diverse animal and insect species, seeking to replicate nature's behavioral patterns, including foraging, hunting, and mating processes. To achieve this, mathematical models are formulated to encapsulate the essence of these natural behaviors. Some notably efficient optimization algorithms include the Firefly algorithm (FA) [15], Particle swarm optimizer (PSO) [16] as well as the Bat algorithm (BA) [17]. Evolution has severed as a of source inspiration for the notably efficient genetic algorithm (GA) [18]. However, more abstract sources of inspiration have given rise to powerful methods such as the COLSHADE [19] optimization algorithm.

Due to the excellent performance demonstrated when tackling general opti-
mizations, metaheuristic algorithms have found many applications across several fields. Some interesting examples include computer system security [20–23],
fraud detection [24,25], tackling complex challenges in emerging industries [26–
28], as well as healthcare [29–31] applications. Furthermore, metaheuristics have
demonstrated admirable performance when tackling optimization related to time
series forecasting [32–34] making them an ideal candidate for tackling solar flair
classification. Other examples of metaheuristics and hybrid techniques exist in
literature [35–38].

3   Methods

The following section describes the original FA algorithm in detail. This is
then followed by an in-depth discussion of the observed shortcomings. Finally,
the introduced modified version is introduced and the internal mechanisms are
explained in depth.

3.1   Original FA

The behavior of fireflies is modeled by the FA [15]. In this algorithm, the
brighter fireflies are more attractive to those with less illumination. Each firefly
is attracted to any other firefly that is brighter than itself. In cases where no
brighter firefly is available, the firefly's movements are determined randomly.
The brightness of each firefly is determined based on the evaluation function's
results for a specific location in the search space.

For maximization problems, the light intensity I of a firefly at location x can
be represented as $I(x) \propto f(x)$, where $f(x)$ denotes the objective function. However, the attractiveness β is relative and depends on the observations of fireflies,
considering the distance r_{ij} between fireflies i and j. Additionally, the propagation of light is influenced by the medium through which it travels, resulting in
the absorption of a certain amount of radiated light. This absorption coefficient
of the medium affects the attractiveness between fireflies. The simplest form of
attraction follows the inverse square law, as shown in Eq. (7).

$$I(r) = \frac{I_s}{r^2} \tag{7}$$

the variable I_s symbolizes the light intensity at the source location. The distance
between the source and a specific point is denoted as r, while $I(r)$ represents
the light intensity at that distance. Additionally, by considering the media's
light absorption coefficient, the determination of light intensity can be achieved
through the utilization of Eq. (8).

$$I(r) = I_0 e^{-\gamma r}, \tag{8}$$

where the light absorption coefficient specific to the medium is denoted as γ,
I_0 represents the initial brightness and r, signifies the distance. It is crucial to

prevent division by zero when r equals zero. This equation combines the inverse square law and approximates the absorption effect using a Gaussian form, as shown in Eq. (9).

$$I(r) = I_0 e^{-\gamma r^2} \tag{9}$$

If a slower and more gradual convergence is desired, Eq. (10) can be utilized as a substitute for this approximation.

$$I(r) = \frac{I_0}{1 + \gamma r^2} \tag{10}$$

When dealing with smaller search spaces and shorter distances, both Eq. (8) and Eq. (10) yield highly similar outcomes. This similarity arises from the series expansion conducted around $r = 0$.

$$e^{-\gamma r} \approx 1 - \gamma r^2 + \frac{1}{2}\gamma^2 r^2 + ..., \qquad \frac{1}{1 + \gamma r^2} \approx 1 - \gamma r^2 + \gamma^2 r^4 + ... \tag{11}$$

which are equivalent up to the order of $O(r^3)$.

The level of attraction among fireflies is influenced by the brightness they perceive in others. This attractiveness is further influenced by various factors, including the intensity at the source, properties of the medium, and the positions of individual fireflies. Taking all these aspects into consideration, the attractiveness of a specific firefly can now be precisely defined using Eq. (12).

$$\beta(r) = \beta_0 e^{-\gamma^2} \tag{12}$$

with β_0 representing attractiveness at $r = 0$.

In cases where computation speed may play an important factor, computing $1/(1 + r^2)$ is faster than working with an exponential equation. As such when necessary, the equation may be replaced with Eq. (13)

$$\beta(r) = \frac{\beta_0}{1 + \gamma r^2} \tag{13}$$

Additionally, Eq. (12) can be used to define characteristic distance Γ given in Eq. (14)

$$\Gamma = 1/\sqrt{\gamma} \tag{14}$$

With a fixed value for γ, characteristic length becomes $\Gamma = \gamma^{-1/m} \to 1$ as $m \to \infty$. Suitably, with a given scale size Γ for a certain optimization, parameter γ can be utilized as a usual initial value according to Eq. (15). It is worth noting that when scaling across different dimensions, it is advised to replace α with αS_k, where $S_k(k = 1, 2, ..., d)$ are scaling parameters in d dimensions defined by actual dimensional scales for the problem in question.

$$\gamma = \frac{1}{\Gamma^m} \tag{15}$$

Distance between any two fireflies can be determined using Cartesian distance according to Eq. (16)

$$\gamma = \frac{1}{\Gamma^m} \tag{16}$$

for fireflies i and j at location x_i and $x + j$, $x_{i,k}$ defines the $k - th$ special component for special coordinate x_i.

When working in two-dimensional space Eq. (17) can be used.

$$r_{ij} = \sqrt{(x_i - x_j)^2 + (y_i - y_j)^2} \tag{17}$$

Fireflies are attracted to their brighter counterparts. For firefly i attracted to firefly j due to higher light intensity, the movement can be computed using Eq. (18)

$$x_i = x_i + \beta_0 e^{-\gamma r_{ij}^2}(x_j - x_i) + \alpha(rand - \frac{1}{2}) \tag{18}$$

The second term in the equation relies on attraction mechanisms, while the third term introduces an element of randomness. The randomization parameter, denoted as α, determines the degree of randomization. The variable $rand$ represents a random number selected from a uniform distribution between 0 and 1. Typically, it is assumed that α lies within the range of $[0, 1]$, and B_0 is set to 1. However, it is also possible to adjust the random distribution to other types of distributions if needed.

The parameter γ now governs the variations in attraction, playing a crucial role in determining convergence rates and shaping the behavior of the Firefly Algorithm (FA). While theoretically, γ can range from 0 to infinity, it is usually constrained to be around the order of 1, as defined by the specific optimization problem's characteristics denoted by Γ. In most cases, the value of γ falls between 0.01 and 100.

3.2   Genetically Inspired FA

While the original FA demonstrated admirable performance, extensive testing with standard CEC functions [39] suggested that certain executions can result in sub-optimal outcomes, due to the algorithm focusing on less promising areas of the search space. Accordingly, this work incorporates a mechanism in the hope of improving exploration power and the effect of this shortcoming.

Following each iteration, a new solution is generated, that combines the current best agent with a randomly selected individual from the population. This generated solution combines the characteristics of each solution in accordance with an introduced uniform crossover control parameter pc, which has been empirically determined as $pc = 0.1$. Each parameter in the generated solution is also subject to mutation. Accordingly, the mutation is governed by a mutation parameter mp with an empirically determined value $mp = 0.1$.

When a mutation occurs, a pseudo-random value from a range $[\frac{lb}{2}, \frac{ub}{2}]$, where ub represents the upper bound and lb the lower bound for a given parameter, is added or subtracted from said solution parameter. Whether the value is added or subtracted is again decided by an additional control parameter that dictates mutation direction md. A pseudo-random value ψ is generated from a uniform distribution in range $[0, 1]$. Should $\psi < md$ subtraction is used, otherwise addition is utilized. For this research, the md parameter has been set to $mt = 0.5$.

Once a new solution has been generated, it is used to replace the worst-performing solution is replaced by the newly generated solution. Following generation and replacement the performance of the new solution is not evaluated until the next iteration. By doing so, the computational complexity of the modified algorithm remains the same as the original. The resulting algorithm is dubbed the Genetically Inspired FA (GIFA) due to the fact that it draws some inspiration from the GA. The pseudocode for the said algorithm is shown in Algorithm 1.

Algorithm 1. Pseudocode for the introduced GIFA

Set initial algorithm parameters
Create population P
Evaluate P using objective function
for i = 1 to iteration limit **do**
  for each solution **do**
    for each better soltuin **do**
      if soltuin is beter **then**
        Determine attraction with respect to distance
        Adjust location towards the better solution
      end if
    end for
    Evaluate and update solutions in population P
    Generated new solution using genetic crossover mechanism
    Subject new solution to mutation
    Replace the worst-performing agent with a newly generated solution
  end for
  Return best-performing solution
end for

---

4   Experimental Setup

In this study, an evaluation of performance was conducted by employing a reduced version of compounded recorded magnetic attributes and solar flare data [40]. Due to the significant computational requirements involved, a limited set of features was utilized for the research. It is worth noting that the dataset employed in this study is publicly available[1].

---

[1] https://zenodo.org/record/4603412.

Several key parameters were selected for predicting the incidence of an M- or X-class solar flare (referred to as "FLARE NUMBER"). These parameters include the total magnitude of the Lorentz force (TOTBSQ), the total photospheric magnetic free energy density (TOTPOT), the average gradient of the total magnetic field (MEANGBT), the average vertical current density (MEANJZD), a quality flag derived from SHARP indicating the data's noise level (QUALITY). To train the predictive model, 70% of the dataset was allocated, while the remaining 30% was reserved for testing and evaluating the model's performance.

In order to make predictions, each XGBoost model was assigned the responsibility of classifying solar events. To enhance the classification performance of the model, metaheuristics were employed to optimize the selection of hyperparameter values. The process involved identifying the optimal parameter values from their respective ranges from the following: Learning Rate $[0.1, 0.9]$, Minimum Child Weight $[1, 10]$, Subsample $[0.01, 1]$, Colsample by Tree $[0.01, 1]$, Maximum Depth $[3, 10]$, and Gamma $[0, 0.8]$.

The compared metaheuristics include the introduced modified algorithm, as well as the original versions of the algorithms that formed the hybrid FA [15] and GA [18]. Alongside these, the well-known PSO [16] and BA [17] have also been evaluated and compared as well as the COLSHADE [19] algorithm. Each algorithm was allocated 20 agents for their respective populations and allowed 15 iterations to improve outcomes. Additionally, to account for the randomness inherent in metaheuristic algorithms the experiments have been carried out over 30 independent runs to ensure a fair comparison.

In order to assess the effectiveness of the proposed approach, a set of commonly used metrics has been employed. Given that the objective was to classify the solar events into two classes (M or X), performance evaluation was conducted using the classification metrics of Accuracy, Recall, and F1 score. Additionally, due to the inherent class imbalance in the dataset, Cohen's kappa metric was utilized as the objective function, as indicated by Eq. (19).

$$\kappa = \frac{P_o - P_e}{1 - P_e} \tag{19}$$

where P_e and P_o denote the expected and observed values respectfully. Metaheuristics where tasked with maximizing the value of the objective function though proper parameter selection. The optimization process can therefore be considered a maximization problem.

5 Experimental Outcomes

The objective function outcomes tracked over independent executions for the best, worst, mean, and median runs as well as the standers deviation and variance for negative classification are shown in Table 1. These are followed by Table 2 which shows positive classification outcomes for class X flares.

The outcomes demonstrated by the introduced metaheuristics suggest that it attained the best results compared to all other evaluated algorithms applied

Table 1. Overall objective function outcomes for non-X class flare classification

Method	Best	Worst	Mean	Median	Std	Var
XG-GIFA	**0.753128**	**0.732782**	**0.742876**	**0.741121**	**0.006301**	**3.97E-05**
XG-FA	0.735049	0.708212	0.721260	0.720949	0.008507	7.24E-05
XG-GA	0.745955	0.719348	0.728346	0.726774	0.007208	5.20E-05
XG-PSO	0.739400	0.707490	0.721174	0.721468	0.009731	9.47E-05
XG-BA	0.736105	0.711404	0.720468	0.718451	0.006306	3.98E-05
XG-COLSHADE	0.739400	0.716549	0.727113	0.726774	0.006954	4.84E-05

Table 2. Overall objective function outcomes for X class flare classification

Method	Best	Worst	Mean	Median	Std	Var
XG-GIFA	0.018059	0.018811	0.018548	0.018623	**0.000414**	**1.71E-07**
XG-FA	0.019564	**0.021445**	0.020128	0.020316	0.000635	4.03E-07
XG-GA	0.018059	0.019564	0.019074	0.019187	0.000447	2.00E-07
XG-PSO	0.018435	0.020692	0.019676	0.019752	0.000734	5.39E-07
XG-BA	**0.019940**	0.020316	**0.020278**	0.020316	0.000489	2.39E-07
XG-COLSHADE	0.018435	0.019564	0.019488	0.019564	0.000439	1.92E-07

to negative classifications shown in Table 1. While positive classifications remain a difficult challenge for all methods, the introduced algorithm demonstrated admirable stability across all intended runs as shown in Table 2.

Compression of the accuracy outcomes obtained by each metaheuristic optimized model in their respective best execution are shown in Fig. 3.

Table 3. Accuracy comparison between the best performing models optimized by each metaheuristic

	XG-GIFA	XG-FA	XG-GA	XG-PSO	XG-BA	XG-COLSHADE
Accuracy	0.981941	0.980436	0.981941	0.981565087	0.980060196	0.981565087

As suggested by Table 3 the best accuracy outcome in the respective best run has been attained by the originally introduced metaheuristic. The performance has been matched by the original GA. To visually demonstrate the stability of each metaheuristic distribution plots are presented for both the objecting as well as the error functions in Fig. 1

As demonstrated in Fig. 2, the modifications made to the introduced metaheuristic made a clear improvement to convergence rates over the original version. Furthermore, the introduced improvement helped the metaheuristic avoid local minimum, and converge towards a more promising solution.

Figure 3 demonstrates the KDE plots of the objective and error functions.

As it can be observed in Fig. 3 the introduced modification consistently demonstrated an improvement over the tested metaheuristic, including the original version of the algorithm. The improvements are evident in both the objective and error functions.

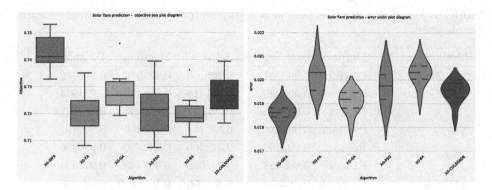

Fig. 1. Objective and error function distribution plots

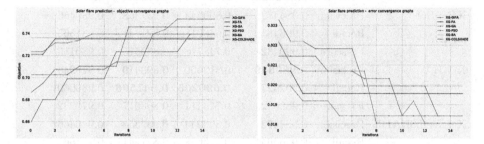

Fig. 2. Objective and error function convergence plots

Further detailed metrics for the best-performing models optimized by each evaluated metaheuristic are shown in Table 4.

The parameter selections made by each metaheuristic for models that demonstrated the best outcomes are shown in Table 5.

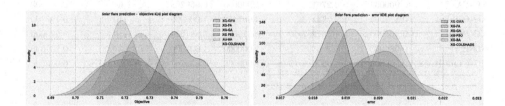

Fig. 3. Objective and error KDE plots

Table 4. Detailed metric comparison of best-performing models optimized by each metaheuristic

Method	Metric	Non X-Class	X-Class	Macro avg	Weighted avg
XG-GIFA	Precision	0.985987	0.865169	0.925578	0.980850
	Recall	0.995285	0.681416	0.838350	0.981941
	F1-score	0.990614	**0.762376**	0.876495	**0.980911**
XG-FA	Precision	0.985586	0.835165	0.910376	0.979191
	Recall	0.994106	0.672566	0.833336	0.980436
	F1-score	0.989828	0.745098	0.867463	0.979424
XG-GA	Precision	0.984854	**0.891566**	**0.938210**	**0.980888**
	Recall	0.996464	0.654867	0.825665	0.981941
	F1-score	**0.990625**	0.755102	0.872864	0.980612
XG-PSO	Precision	0.984472	0.890244	0.937358	0.980466
	Recall	0.996464	0.646018	0.821241	0.981565
	F1-score	0.990432	0.748718	0.869575	0.980156
XG-BA	Precision	**0.986339**	0.812500	0.899419	0.978948
	Recall	0.992927	**0.690265**	**0.841596**	0.980060
	F1-score	0.989622	0.746411	0.868017	0.979282
XG-COLSHADE	Precision	0.984472	0.890244	0.937358	0.980466
	Recall	0.996464	0.646018	0.821241	0.981565
	F1-score	0.990432	0.748718	0.869575	0.980156
	Support	2545	113	2658	2658

Table 5. Parameter selections made by each metaheuristic for the respective best-performing models

Method	Learning Rate	Min child weight	Subsample	Colsample by tree	Max Depth	Gamma
XG-GIFA	0.850526	3.178469	0.778974	0.854656	9	0.076786
XG-FA	0.900000	2.276111	1.000000	0.960290	6	0.800000
XG-GA	0.867565	2.274113	0.985452	1.000000	10	0.198300
XG-PSO	0.900000	1.501287	0.812608	0.881294	10	0.000000
XG-BA	0.900000	7.389393	1.000000	1.000000	5	0.800000
XG-COLSHADE	0.900000	1.020902	1.000000	0.933967	10	0.000000

6   Conclusion

Monitoring solar flares plays a vital role in various aspects, including predicting space weather, safeguarding satellites and spacecraft, ensuring the well-being of astronauts, sustaining the functionality of aviation and GPS systems, and propelling scientific research focused on understanding the Sun's influence on Earth and the cosmos. However, to take preemptive measures and protect infrastructure a robust system for timely identification is required. This work explores the potential of optimization metaheuristics applied to optimizing XGBoost hyper-parameters for solar flare classification. A modified version of a metaheuristic is introduced specifically for this research. Alongside it, several well-established metaheuristics are subjected to a comparative analysis when optimizing the hyperparameter selection of XGBoost applied to a real-world publicly available solar flare dataset. The modified metaheuristics demonstrated admirable performance when optimizing parameters, with the optimized models attaining the best outcomes.

Future works will focus on further improving the solar flare classification methodology and further improving classification outcomes. Furthermore, additional implementations for the introduced metaheuristic will be explored for tackling pressing real-world challenges.

References

1. Korchak, A.: On the origin of solar flare x-rays. Sol. Phys. **18**, 284–304 (1971)
2. Gao, P.-X., Xu, J.-C.: Solar flare count periodicities in different x-ray flare classes. Mon. Not. R. Astron. Soc. **457**(3), 2839–2844 (2016)
3. Chen, T., Guestrin, C.: Xgboost: a scalable tree boosting system. In Proceedings of the 22nd ACM Sigkdd International Conference on Knowledge Discovery and Data Mining, pp. 785–794 (2016)
4. Feurer, M., Hutter, F.: Hyperparameter optimization. In: Automated Machine Learning: Methods, Systems, Challenges, pp. 3–33, 2019
5. Wolpert, D.H., Macready, W.G.: No free lunch theorems for optimization. IEEE Trans. Evol. Comput. **1**(1), 67–82 (1997)
6. Woods, T.N., et al.: Extreme ultraviolet variability experiment (eve) on the solar dynamics observatory (SDO): overview of science objectives, instrument design, data products, and model developments. Sol. Phys. **275**, 115–143 (2012)
7. Domingo, V., Fleck, B., Poland, A.: Soho: the solar and heliospheric observatory. Space Sci. Rev. **72**, 81–84 (1995)
8. Wheatland, M.: A statistical solar flare forecast method. Space Weather **3**(7) (2005)
9. Huang, X., Wang, H., Xu, L., Liu, J., Li, R., Dai, X.: Deep learning based solar flare forecasting model. I. Results for line-of-sight magnetograms. Astrophys. J. **856**(1), 7 (2018)
10. Leka, K., et al.: A comparison of flare forecasting methods. II. benchmarks, metrics, and performance results for operational solar flare forecasting systems. Astrophys. J. Suppl. Ser. **243**(2), 36 (2019)
11. Gu, J.: Recent advances in convolutional neural networks. Pattern Recogn. **77**, 354–377 (2018)
12. Zheng, Y., Li, X., Wang, X.: Solar flare prediction with the hybrid deep convolutional neural network. Astrophys. J. **885**(1), 73 (2019)
13. Salehinejad, H., Sankar, S.,, Barfett, J., Colak, E., Valaee, S.: Recent advances in recurrent neural networks. arXiv preprint arXiv:1801.01078 (2017)
14. Muzaheed, A.A.M., Hamdi, S.M., Boubrahimi, S.F.: Sequence model-based end-to-end solar flare classification from multivariate time series data. In: 2021 20th IEEE International Conference on Machine Learning and Applications (ICMLA), pp. 435–440. IEEE (2021)

15. Yang, X.-S., Slowik, A.: Firefly algorithm. In: Swarm Intelligence Algorithms, pp. 163–174. CRC Press (2020)
16. Eberhart, R., Kennedy, J.: Particle swarm optimization. In: Proceedings of the IEEE International Conference on Neural Networks, vol. 4, pp. 1942–1948. Citeseer (1995)
17. Fister, I., Yang, X.-S., Fong, S., Zhuang, Y.: Bat algorithm: recent advances. In: 2014 IEEE 15th International Symposium on Computational Intelligence and Informatics (CINTI), pp. 163–167. IEEE (2014)
18. Mirjalili, S., Mirjalili, S.: Genetic algorithm. In: Evolutionary Algorithms and Neural Networks: Theory and Applications, pp. 43–55 (2019)
19. Gurrola-Ramos, J., Hernàndez-Aguirre, A., Dalmau-Cedeño, O.: Colshade for real-world single-objective constrained optimization problems. In: 2020 IEEE Congress on Evolutionary Computation (CEC), pp. 1–8. IEEE (2020)
20. Zivkovic, M., Jovanovic, L., Ivanovic, M., Bacanin, N., Strumberger, I., Joseph, P.M.: XGBoost hyperparameters tuning by fitness-dependent optimizer for network intrusion detection. In: Sharma, H., Shrivastava, V., Kumari Bharti, K., Wang, L. (eds.) Communication and Intelligent Systems. LNNS, vol. 461, pp. 947–962. Springer, Singapore (2022). https://doi.org/10.1007/978-981-19-2130-8_74
21. AlHosni, N., et al.: The xgboost model for network intrusion detection boosted by enhanced sine cosine algorithm. In: Chen, J.I.Z., Tavares, J.M.R.S., Shi, F. (eds.) ICIPCN 2022. LNCS, pp. 213–228. Springer, Heidelberg (2022). https://doi.org/10.1007/978-3-031-12413-6_17
22. Salb, M., Jovanovic, L., Zivkovic, M., Tuba, E., Elsadai, A., Bacanin, N.: Training logistic regression model by enhanced moth flame optimizer for spam email classification. In: Smys, S., Lafata, P., Palanisamy, R., Kamel, K.A. (eds.) Computer Networks and Inventive Communication Technologies: Proceedings of Fifth ICCNCT 2022, pp. 753–768. Springer, Heidelberg (2022). https://doi.org/10.1007/978-981-19-3035-5_56
23. Bačanin Džakula, N., et al.: Arithmetic optimization algorithm for spam detection. In: Sinteza 2022-International Scientific Conference on Information Technology and Data Related Research, pp. 406–413. Singidunum University (2022)
24. Djuric, M., Jovanovic, L., Zivkovic, M., Bacanin, N., Antonijevic, M., Sarac, M.: The adaboost approach tuned by SNS metaheuristics for fraud detection. In: Proceedings of the International Conference on Paradigms of Computing, Communication and Data Sciences: PCCDS 2022, pp. 115–128. Springer, Heidelberg (2023). https://doi.org/10.1007/978-981-19-8742-7_10
25. Petrovic, A., Antonijevic, M., Strumberger, I., Jovanovic, L., Savanovic, N., Janicijevic, S.: The xgboost approach tuned by TLB metaheuristics for fraud detection. In: Proceedings of the 1st International Conference on Innovation in Information Technology and Business (ICIITB 2022), vol. 104, p. 219. Springer, Heidelberg (2023)
26. Gajevic, M., Milutinovic, N., Krstovic, J., Jovanovic, L., Marjanovic, M., Stoean, C.: Artificial neural network tuning by improved sine cosine algorithm for healthcare 4.0. In: Proceedings of the 1st International Conference on Innovation in Information Technology and Business (ICIITB 2022), vol. 104, p. 289. Springer, Heidelberg (2023)
27. Jovanovic, L., Bacanin, N., Zivkovic, M., Antonijevic, M., Jovanovic, B., Sretenovic, M.B., Strumberger, I.: Machine learning tuning by diversity oriented firefly metaheuristics for industry 4.0. Expert Syst. **41**(2), e13293 (2024)

28. Strumberger, I., Bezdan, T., Ivanovic, M., Jovanovic, L.: Improving energy usage in wireless sensor networks by whale optimization algorithm. In: 2021 29th Telecommunications Forum (TELFOR), pp. 1–4. IEEE (2021)
29. Zivkovic, M., Jovanovic, L., Ivanovic, M., Krdzic, A., Bacanin, N., Strumberger, I.: Feature selection using modified sine cosine algorithm with COVID-19 dataset. In: Suma, V., Fernando, X., Du, K.-L., Wang, H. (eds.) Evolutionary Computing and Mobile Sustainable Networks. LNDECT, vol. 116, pp. 15–31. Springer, Singapore (2022). https://doi.org/10.1007/978-981-16-9605-3_2
30. Jovanovic, L., et al.: Tuning xgboost by planet optimization algorithm: an application for diabetes classification. In: Proceedings of Fourth International Conference on Communication, Computing and Electronics Systems: ICCCES 2022, pp. 787–803. Springer, Heidelberg (2023). https://doi.org/10.1007/978-981-19-7753-4_60
31. Jovanovic, L., Zivkovic, M., Antonijevic, M., Jovanovic, D., Ivanovic, M., Jassim, H.S.: An emperor penguin optimizer application for medical diagnostics. In: 2022 IEEE Zooming Innovation in Consumer Technologies Conference (ZINC), pp. 191–196. IEEE (2022)
32. Jovanovic, L., et al.: Multi-step crude oil price prediction based on LSTM approach tuned by SALP swarm algorithm with disputation operator. Sustainability 14(21), 14616 (2022)
33. Bacanin, N., Zivkovic, M., Jovanovic, L., Ivanovic, M., Rashid, T.A.: Training a multilayer perception for modeling stock price index predictions using modified whale optimization algorithm. In: Smys, S., Tavares, J.M.R.S., Balas, V.E. (eds.) Computational Vision and Bio-Inspired Computing. AISC, vol. 1420, pp. 415–430. Springer, Singapore (2022). https://doi.org/10.1007/978-981-16-9573-5_31
34. Jovanovic, L., Milutinovic, N., Gajevic, M., Krstovic, J., Rashid, T.A., Petrovic, A.: Sine cosine algorithm for simple recurrent neural network tuning for stock market prediction. In: 2022 30th Telecommunications Forum (TELFOR), pp. 1–4. IEEE (2022)
35. Jovanovic, L., et al.: The explainable potential of coupling metaheuristics-optimized-xgboost and shap in revealing vocs' environmental fate. Atmosphere 14(1), 109 (2023)
36. Petrovic, A., Jovanovic, L., Zivkovic, M., Bacanin, N., Budimirovic, N., Marjanovic, M.: Forecasting bitcoin price by tuned long short term memory model. In: 1st International Conference on Innovation in Information Technology and Business (ICIITB 2022), pp. 187–202. Atlantis Press (2023)
37. Zivkovic, M., et al.: An improved animal migration optimization approach for extreme learning machine tuning. In Intelligent and Fuzzy Systems: Digital Acceleration and The New Normal-Proceedings of the INFUS 2022 Conference, vol. 2, pp. 3–13. Springer, Heidelberg (2022)
38. Jovanovic, L., Bacanin, N., Antonijevic, M., Tuba, E., Ivanovic, M., Venkatachalam, K.: Plant classification using firefly algorithm and support vector machine. In: 2022 IEEE Zooming Innovation in Consumer Technologies Conference (ZINC), pp. 255–260. IEEE (2022)
39. Luo, W., Lin, X., Li, C., Yang, S., Shi, Y.: Benchmark functions for cec 2022 competition on seeking multiple optima in dynamic environments. arXiv preprint arXiv:2201.00523 (2022)
40. Larsen, E.E.: Predicting solar flares with machine learning (2021)

Naïve Bayes Classifier with Genetic Algorithm for Phishing Website Detection

Hamouda Chantar[(✉)] [iD], Salwa Ali, and Yousef Salem

Faculty of Information Technology, Sebha University, Sebha 18758, Libya
{ham.chantar,sal.ali1,you.salem}@sebhau.edu.ly

Abstract. Online phishing is one of the most serious cyber-attacks, with the goal of fraudulently obtaining sensitive information from internet users. Site and Common Resource Locator (URL) phishing occurs when attackers use phishing websites that appear identical to legitimate websites to trick end users into disclosing personal information. Passwords and credit card numbers are examples of sensitive factors. Several techniques have been proposed to address this issue. Machine learning algorithms have proven to be extremely effective in this field. This paper describes a method for detecting phishing websites that is based on the Naive Bayes classifier (GA) and the genetic algorithm (GA). These algorithms are combined to form a wrapped feature selection algorithm, which searches the feature space for a useful and relevant feature. This will then aid in determining whether the sites are genuine or fraudulent. To discover the optimal subset, GA was used to generate feature subsets and the NB classifier was used to evaluate the classification accuracy of feature subsets generated with GA. The proposed method has been tested on three phishing site datasets. On all data sets, experimental results show that NB combined with GA can achieve accuracy of up to 91%. Furthermore, less than 40% of the features in all datasets considered were identified as informative and important, while other features were excluded from the feature space.

Keywords: Feature selection · Genetic Algorithm · Machine learning · Naïve Bayes classifier · Phishing website

1 Introduction

Phishing is the most common sort of cybercrimes. It is a deception technique that uses the web to steal electronic identification and financial information from internet users (customers) [1]. In general, phishing attempts that target end-users in order to steal their sensitive information take numerous forms, including email phishing, voice phishing (Vishing), SMS phishing (Smishing), search engine phishing, URL (Uniform Resource Locators) or website phishing, and others [2, 3, 32].

Nowadays, information about anything is easily accessible via websites, where companies, banks, universities, organizations, and others provide end-users with information about their services and products via their official websites. Websites also offer services such as chatbots and instant messages to assist clients who are having troubles. Furthermore, websites save the information of their visitors. Because a website assists its visitors in collecting information, cybercriminals might exploit it as a trap to acquire personal information such as end-user usernames and passwords [2, 4]. Cybercriminals do not need to execute sophisticated procedures to crack cypher codes or breach robust firewalls when using URL or website-based phishing. Alternatively, they send sensible, critical, or emotive e-mails to end-users, requesting that they introduce their personal information by clicking on a link associated with received emails [4]. This redirects targeted viewers to counterfeit web pages that appear identical to authentic web pages [4]. As a result, recipients become like fish, being caught in fraudulent websites [2, 4].

Because of the harm and danger that phishing websites pose, many researchers have concentrated their efforts on developing effective methods for detecting phishing websites. There are a variety of phishing website detection strategies available, including list-based, heuristic-based, visual similarity-based, and machine learning-based [2]. Machine learning algorithms have been shown to be the most accurate and trustworthy for website phishing detection [5, 6]. Typically, the data needed to train machine learning models is supplied as vectors of features collected from real legitimate and fraudulent URLs. These aspects include information such as IP address, HTTP tokens, port numbers, Google index, page rank, and so on [4].

In general, machine learning (ML) approaches have been widely employed for data classification in a variety of sectors. Data preparation is a crucial step in classifying information before using a machine learning classifier. It has a significant impact on machine learning classifier performance [7]. One of these steps is feature selection (FS). It is recognized as a critical phase that aims to locate and remove noisy and uninformative features in the data under categorization. FS techniques are broadly classified into two types: filter and wrapper. The filter paradigm assigns a score to each feature in the feature space based on the classes of data using a statistical method such as information gain or gain ratio. Then, features with ratings lower than a predefined threshold are deemed useless and removed from the feature space. The wrapper model selects features using the search method and the machine learning classifier. The search mechanism's goal is to generate a large number of feature subsets, while the ML classifier is used to assess the quality of the generated feature subsets. This method is typically repeated until the best feature selection with the highest possible classification accuracy is found [7, 8]. Meta-heuristic algorithms like Genetic Algorithm (GA) and Particle Swarm Optimization (PSO) have shown to be extremely effective as search engines in FS methods. [9] Wrapper-based.

This paper explores the performance of the Naive Bayes classifier (NB) and the Genetic algorithm (GA) in the subject of phishing website identification. The two algorithms comprise a wrapper FS technique in which GA is used to generate subsets of features and NB is used to evaluate the generated subsets of features by GA.

2 Background and Related Works

2.1 Related Works

Previous research has revealed that several machine learning-based approaches for detecting online phishing have been developed. Shirazi et al. [10], for example, investigated the performance of various classifiers in detecting phishing websites. Only seven attributes were used, including URLs and web page content. Among the classifiers used, the gradient boosting classifier had the highest classification accuracy (97%). Similarly, Zaini et al. [11] used five machine learning models to detect website phishing. Furthermore, 15 characteristics from various classes were used. The results of the experiments revealed that the random forest classifier had the greatest detection rate of 94.79%. Researchers in [12] built a random forest classifier (RF) on a dataset of 35 variables taken from web page content to detect website phishing. The random forest-based phishing detection model achieved 98.25% accuracy. Furthermore, Jain et al. [13] investigated several machine learning methods for online phishing detection, using twelve features collected from hyperlinks in web pages. The results of the experiments indicated that logistic regression had the highest detection accuracy. Another work was conducted by Jain et al. in [14] for phishing website detection using machine learning, where an SVM classifier was applied over phishing data from a website. SVM classifier obtained 90% detection accuracy, according to the results.

Furthermore, several feature selection strategies were used in some research to improve the performance of machine learning-based phishing website detection models. For example, Rajab et al. [15] suggested a feature ranking methodology for online phishing detection that incorporates chi-square and information gain feature scores. Experiment results using a website phishing dataset from the UCI repository and two machine learning classifiers, JRIP and C4.5, indicated that the selected features by the suggested FS technique boosted the accuracy of the C4.5 classifier by up to 95.5%. Moreover, Hannousse and Yahiouche [4] studied the effect of several feature selection approaches on the performance of a machine learning classifier in a phishing detection problem. The researchers concluded that combining filter-based and incremental removal of low important features approaches increased the accuracy of machine learning classifiers by up to 96.83% when compared to wrapper FS approaches. In general, prior study shows that FS has a considerable favorable effect on the accuracy of machine learning classifiers in detecting phishing websites. In addition, previous studies reveal that the use of wrapper mode of feature selection for phishing website detection is limited [31].The objective of this work is to demonstrate the efficiency of wrapper feature selection in phishing website detection domain through integrating Genetic Algorithm with Naïve Bayes machine learning classifier and apply the proposed approach to categorize websites into either phishing or legitimate.

2.2 Naïve Bayes Classifier

The Naive Bayes (NB) classifier is a classifier for probabilistic machine learning that is based on the Bayes theorem. It is regarded as an effective and simple classifier [16, 17]. It is assumed in the NB classifier that feature values are conditionally self-contained in relation to target categories [16]. Assume there are a series of training examples, with each case E represented by a target category and a set of attribute values $< A1, A2, An >$. Let C represent a set of groups that define the goal function. Based on the attribute values, NB assigns the label of the category with the highest probability to the unlabeled test case (d)

[16]. The likelihood that a particular instance E belongs to a category G_j can be calculated as follows [30]:

$$P(G_j|E) = \frac{P(E|G_j)P(G_j)}{P(E)}$$

$P(G_j|E)$ denotes the probability of the class G_j given an instance E. $P(E)$ is equal for all given categories hence, it can be omitted

$$P(G_j|E) = P(E|G_j)P(G_j)$$

Considering the assumption in Bayes theorem that states features are conditionally separated. Therefore, the probability of category G_j can be transformed as given below [30]

$$P(G_j|E) = P(G_j) \prod_{i=1}^{m} P(A_i|G_j)$$

m denotes the number of attributes A_i that shape the set of training instances. The predicted category of the test instance E is set by NB classifier as follows:

$$V_{NB} = \underset{g \in G}{\operatorname{argmax}} P(G_j) \prod_{i=1}^{m} P(A_i|G_j)$$

V_{NB} denotes the output of Naïve Bayes classifier which determines the category of the test instance E

2.3 Genetic Algorithm

The Genetic Algorithm (GA) is an evolutionary optimization approach first proposed by J. Holland in the 1970s. GA simulates the concept of biological evaluation. The GA algorithm was primarily designed to exploit the adaptive nature of natural systems to solve inflexible and non-linear problems (30). The GA algorithm starts from a population of random chromosomes. Each chromosome represents a potential solution to the optimization problem under discussion, and each element in the chromosome represents a gene. Using a fitness (assessment) function, each chromosome is assigned a fitness score that is used to determine whether it will be selected for the future generation or destroyed. Each parent (chromosome) undergoes a crossover operation based on a pre-specified crossover probability in order to produce new offspring. The new individuals are then subjected to mutation operations based on a predetermined mutation probability. At the conclusion of the crossover operation, new chromosomes are introduced into the population. This process is repeated until a predetermined stopping point is reached [18]. Several GA-based feature selection techniques for FS problems have been developed [19–22]. Individuals are represented as binary strings in the GA algorithm. The most prevalent operators in GA algorithms are mutation and crossover. The most common operators in GA algorithms are mutation and crossover. On a randomly chosen chromosome, the mutation operator is used to flip a selected bit from 1 to 0 or vice versa. The crossover operator, on the other hand, is used to produce offspring from a pair of chromosomes [19, 20].

3 Proposed Method

The performance of a machine learning classifier is highly dependent on the quality of the features that represent the data, with relevant and informative features greatly improving classification accuracy and noisy and irrelevant features having a direct negative impact. It is critical to identify high informative features before applying a machine learning classifier to data. The selection of feature subsets is treated as a hard binary optimization problem, with alternative solutions represented as binary vectors. Each cell in the vector corresponds to a dataset feature. When the value of a cell is one, the related feature is chosen. Otherwise, it is deemed irrelevant and is thus excluded from the chosen subset of traits. The vector's length is equal to the number of features in the dataset. The proposed GA and NB phishing site detection method is depicted in Fig. 1. The method starts with an n-chromosome population, each of which represents a subset of features. The population's chromosomes are then evaluated using the fitness function. The chromosome with the lowest fitness function (highest classification accuracy) contains the best subgroup of features and is thus retained as the best solution for the population. Following that, the processes of selection, mutation, and crossover are carried out in turn. The steps are repeated until a stopping condition (i.e., a set number of generations) is reached.

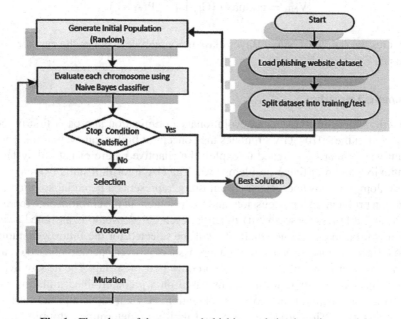

Fig. 1. Flowchart of the proposed phishing website detection model

The method begins with a population of N chromosomes, with each chromosome representing a subset of traits. Following that, each chromosome in the population is evaluated using a fitness function. The chromosome with the lowest fitness function (highest classification accuracy) has the best subset of features, so it is retained as the best solution in the population. Then, in that order, selection, mutation, and cross-over operations are carried out. The stages are repeated until the stopping condition (e.g., a predetermined number of generations) is met. The pseudo code of the GA algorithm is presented in Algorithm 1.

Algorithm 1. Pseudo Code of the Genetic Algorithm.

Initialize the parameters of GA
Generate random population of N chromosomes
Estimate the fitness value of each chromosome using NB classifier
While (Stopping condition is not satisfied)
Randomly select two parents P1 and P2 (chromosomes)
Perform crossover between P1 and P2 to form offspring (child)
Mutate the child
Estimate the fitness value of the child using NB classifier
Add child to population
Remove the worst solution (lowest fitness) from the population
Return best solution (most fit chromosome in the population)

The fitness of each chromosome in the population is calculated to measure the quality of potential solutions. It is a minimization fitness function that is used to decrease the rate of the classification error over the test set. It is widely employed in feature selection to estimate the quality of selected subset of features [7, 8].

$$\text{Fitness} = (\alpha * \text{ER}) + \text{\ss} * \left(\frac{S}{N}\right)$$

where ER is the NB classifier's error rate over a subset of features chosen by a specific chromosome, which is equal to (1-accuracy). α and $\text{\ss}$ are two parameters for achieving the required balance between the size of the selected subset of features and classification accuracy. $\text{\ss}$ is obtained by (1-α) and is a number in the range [0, 1]. S and N represent the number of preserved subsets of features and the overall number of features. Figure 2 shows that each gene in the chromosome represents a feature, and the length of the chromosome corresponds to the number of features in the dataset. If the value of the gene is one, the matching feature is chosen. Otherwise, it is deemed uninformative and is removed from the list of selected features.

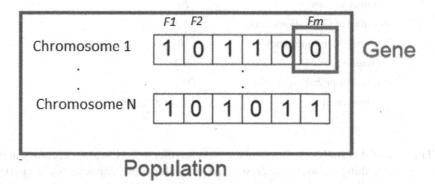

Fig. 2. Population of N chromosomes (search agents) in GA algorithm

4   Experiments

4.1   Data Sets

The performance of the NB classifier was evaluated using three different online phishing datasets. Table 1 contains descriptions of the datasets used. Data1 was obtained from [23]. Data2 came from the UCI machine learning repository [24], and Data3 came from [25]. These datasets have a wide range of properties, including URL- and content-based elements. Each dataset was divided into 80 percent training and 20 percent test sections.

Table 1. Phishing website datasets.

Dataset	Data1	Data2	Data3
Total number of websites	11430	11055	88647
Number of phishing websites	5715	4898	30647
Number of Legitimate websites	5715	6157	58000
Number of features	87	30	111

4.2   Parameters Settings

Table 2 shows the common parameter setting of GA algorithm. These parameters were set based on initial series of experiments as well as recommended values in previous studies.

Table 2. Parameters settings.

Parameter	Value
Number of runs	20
Number of Generations in GA	100
Number of chromosomes	10
Mutation probability in GA	0.01
Crossover probability in GA	0.9
Fitness function	$\alpha = 0.99, \beta = 0.01$

The goal of this study is to improve the NB classifier's classification accuracy in the detection of phishing websites. As a result, the fitness function parameter was set to 0.99 in order to prioritize classification accuracy over the number of selected features [28, 29].

4.3 Performance Evaluation

In general, evaluating the classification accuracy of machine learning classifiers is a crucial stage. When performing a classification task, a set of instances known as training is preserved in order to build the classifier. Another set of previously unseen instances is used to estimate the classification power of the created classifier. Two typical approaches, accuracy and F1-score, are used to estimate the capacity of the NB classifier to predict the correct class or category of unseen test examples. The classification accuracy of the NB classifier is computed as follows:

$$Accuracy = \frac{TP + TN}{TP + FP + TN + FN}$$

Assume the websites in the dataset's test section are of class C. The classification algorithm predicts a category label for each website, and these predictions will fall into four categories in relation to category C [4, 26].

TP (true positives): the group of websites that are in category C and were correctly forecasted to be in category C.
TN (negatives): a set of websites that are unrelated to category C and were allocated to a category other than C.
FP (false positives): a set of websites that were forecasted to be relevant to category C but are really from another category.
FN (false negatives): a set of websites that were predicted to be unrelated to category C but are, in reality, related to category C.

F1-Score is calculated based on two measures named precision and recall using the following equation [4, 27]:

$$F1 - Score = 2\frac{recall*precision}{recall + precision}$$

Precision and Recall are calculated using the following formulas:

$$Precisin = \frac{TP}{TP + FP}$$

$$Recall = \frac{TP}{TP + FN}$$

5 Results and Discussion

This section defines the experimental findings of the proposed model for detecting phishing websites. The model was built with the Python Scikit-learn ML toolkit. To provide fair and comparable comparisons, the proposed model was applied to all datasets using the same common parameters listed in Table 2. The initial portion of the tests involved applying a Naive Bayes classifier over the three datasets without feature selection. Table 3 shows that the NB classifier performed poorly on Data2, with a classification accuracy of 0.598 and an F1-score of 0.55. In the case of Data1, the performance of the NB classifier is superior to its performance on Data2, where the F1-Score and accuracy reached 0.74. As can be observed, the best performance of NB is on Data3. The differences in the performance of the NB classifier on the three datasets are related to differences of the features in these datasets. It is obvious that various dataset variables influence the effectiveness of the NB classifier in distinguishing between phishing and legitimate websites.

Table 3. Results of NB classifier without feature selection

Dataset	Precision	Recall	F1-Score	Accuracy
Data1	0.76	0.75	0.74	0.748
Data2	0.79	0.60	0.55	0.598
Data3	0.85	0.84	0.83	0.840

Table 4 displays the NB classifier's classification results after using the GA method to discover and eliminate noisy and uninformative features from feature space. It is clear that using GA for feature selection resulted in significant improvements in accuracy, F1-Score, and number of selected features. As illustrated in Data1, the accuracy and F1-Score rates increased from 0.74 to 0.92. Furthermore, the accuracy and F1-Score values on Data2 increased from 0.55 and 0.598, respectively, to 0.914 and 0.913. The accuracy and F1-Score of NB with GA on Data3 have also improved up to 91%.

Table 4. Results of NB classifier after applying feature selection using GA algorithm

Dataset	Metric	Precision	Recall	F1-Score	Accuracy	No. of selected features
Data1	Avr	0.927	0.927	0.927	0.926	28.2
	STD	0.005	0.005	0.005	0.003	1.989
Data2	Avr	0.913	0.913	0.913	0.914	11.7
	STD	0.005	0.005	0.005	0.002	2.406
Data3	Avr	0.918	0.918	0.918	0.915	42.6
	STD	0.004	0.004	0.004	0.003	4.477

Figure 3 clearly shows that there are significant differences in F1-Score rates between NB and NB with GA algorithms. Furthermore, Fig. 4 displays the discrepancies between the initial number of features in the applied datasets and the averages of selected feature subsets by the GA algorithm. The GA-based FS algorithm selected less than 40% of the features in the dataset for all datasets studied. Other features are labeled as noisy and uninformative and are thus removed from the feature space. It may be stated that GA is capable of detecting and eliminating unnecessary features without reducing the accuracy of the NB classifier in detecting phishing websites.

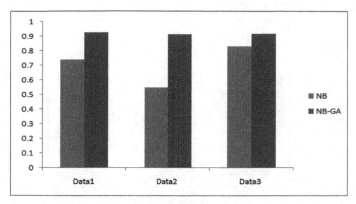

Fig. 3. Comparison between NB classifier and NB with GA in terms of F1-Score

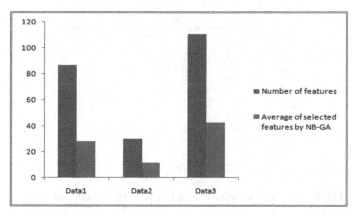

Fig.4. .Comparison between number of selected features by GA and the original sets of features in the phishing website datasets

Finally, Figs. 5, 6, and 7 depict the convergence behaviors of the GA algorithm over Data1, Data2, and Data3, respectively. These figures show that GA with NB classifier achieved fast and stable convergence towards the optimal solution (subset of features) on all evaluated phishing website datasets.

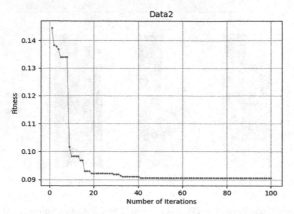

Fig. 5. Convergence behaviour of GA with NB classifier on Data1

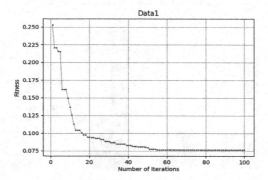

Fig. 6. Convergence behaviour of GA with NB classifier on Data2

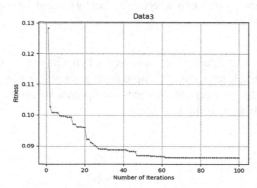

Fig. 7. Convergence behaviour of GA with NB classifier on Data3

6 Conclusion

This paper presented an effective machine learning-based phishing website detection model for avoiding internet users' personal information from being stolen through fraudulent websites. It is based on the Naive Bayes (NB) and the Genetic Algorithm (GA) classifiers. The NB classifier assesses subsets of characteristics provided by the GA algorithm in order to capture the most informative combination of attributes, resulting in the best classification accuracy between phishing and authentic websites. The NB-GA model's performance was evaluated using three phishing website datasets with varying types and numbers of features. The experiments have demonstrated that the NB classifier, when combined with the GA algorithm, could work effectively in the detection of phishing websites. In the future, the proposed approach in this work could be implemented to tackle other security problems such as intrusion detection in IoT networks and android malware detection.

References

1. Anti-Phishing Working Group (APWG). https://docs.apwg.org//reports/apwg_trends_report_q4_2019.Pdf. Accessed 20 Feb (2023)
2. Kalaharsha, P., Mehtre, B.M.: Detecting Phishing Sites - An Overview (2021)
3. Dutta, A.K.: Detecting phishing websites using machine learning technique. PLoS ONE **16**(10), e0258361 (2021)
4. Hannousse, A., Yahiouche, S.: Towards benchmark datasets for machine learning based website phishing detection: An experimental study. Eng. Appl. Artif. Intell. **104**, 104347 (2021)
5. Das, A., et al.: SoK: a comprehensive reexamination of phishing research from the security perspective. IEEE Commun. Surv. Tutorials **22**(1), 671–708 (2020)
6. Korkmaz, M., Ozgur, K.S., Banu, D.: Feature selections for the classification of webpages to detect phishing attacks: a survey. In: 2020 International Congress on Human-Computer Interaction, Optimization and Robotic Applications (HORA), pp. 1–9 (2020)
7. Chantar, H., Tubishat, M., Essgaer, M., Mirjalili, S.: Hybrid binary dragonfly algorithm with simulated annealing for feature selection. SN Comput. Sci. **2**(4), 1–11 (2021). https://doi.org/10.1007/s42979-021-00687-5
8. Mafarja, M.M., Eleyan, D., Jaber, I., Hammouri, A., Mirjalili, S.: Binary dragonfly algorithm for feature selection. In: 2017 International Conference on New Trends in Computing Sciences (ICTCS), pp.12–17 (2017)
9. Xue, B., Zhang ,M., Browne, W.N., Yao, X.: A survey on evolutionary computation approaches to feature selection. In: IEEE Transactions on Evolutionary Computation, vol. 20(4), pp. 606–626 (2016) https://doi.org/10.1109/TEVC.(2015)
10. Shirazi, H., Bezawada, B., Ray, I.: know thy domain name Unbiased Phishing Detection Using Domain Name Based Features. In: Proceedings of the 23nd ACM on Symposium on Access Control Models and Technologies SACMAT '18, pp. 69–75. New York, NY, USA: Association for Computing Machinery (2018)
11. Zaini, N., et al.: Phishing detection system using machine learning classifiers. Indonesian J. Electr. Eng. Comput. Sci. **17**, 1165–1171 (2020)
12. Rao, R.S., Vaishnavi, T., Pais, A.R.: Catchphish: detection of phishing websites by inspecting URLs. J. Ambient. Intell. Humaniz. Comput. **11**(2), 813–825 (2019). https://doi.org/10.1007/s12652-019-01311-4

13. Jain, A.K., Gupta, B.B.: A machine learning based approach for phishing detection using hyperlinks information. J. Ambient. Intell. Humaniz. Comput. **10**, 2015–2028 (2019)
14. Jain, A.K., Gupta, B.B.: Phish-safe: URL features-based phishing detection system using machine learning. In: M. U. Bokhari, N. Agrawal, and D. Saini (Eds.), Cyber Security, pp. 467–474. Singapore: Springer Singapore (2018). https://doi.org/10.1007/978-981-10-8536-9_44
15. Rajab, K.D.: New hybrid features selection method: a case study on websites phishing. Secur. Commun. Network. **2017**, 1–10 (2017). https://doi.org/10.1155/2017/9838169
16. Mitchell, T.: Machine Learning. McGraw-Hill (1997)
17. Rish, I.: An empirical study of the naive Bayes classifier. In: Proceedings of IJCAI-01 workshop on Empirical Methods in AI. pp. 41–46, Sicily, Italy (2001)
18. Holland, J.H.: Adaptation in Natural and Artificial Systems, University of Michigan Press, Ann Arbor, MI, 1975. Second edition (1992)
19. Yang, J., Honavar, V.: Feature subset selection using a genetic algorithm, intelligent systems and their applications. IEEE **13**, 44–49 (1998)
20. Ferri, F.J., Kadirkamanathan, V.: Feature subset search using genetic algorithms, IEE/IEEE Workshop on Natural Algorithms in Signal Processing, IEE, Press (1993)
21. Chaikla, N., Yulu, Qi.: Genetic algorithms in feature selection, IEEE SMC'99 Conference Proceedings. In: 1999 IEEE International Conference on Systems, Man, and Cybernetics (Cat. No.99CH37028), vol. 5, pp. 538–540 (1999)
22. Mafarja, M., Abdullah, S.: Investigating memetic algorithm in solving rough set attribute reduction. Int. J. Comput. Appl. Technol. **48**(3), 195 (2013). https://doi.org/10.1504/IJCAT. 2013.056915
23. Hannousse, A., Salima, Y.: Web page phishing detection, Mendeley Data, V2, https://doi.org/ 10.17632/c2gw7fy2j4.2.(2020)
24. Machine learning repository. https://archive.ics.uci.edu/ml/. Accessed 15 Feb (2023)
25. Vrbančič, G., Fister, I., Podgorelec, V.: Datasets for phishing websites detection. Data Brief **33**, 106438 (2020). https://doi.org/10.1016/j.dib.2020.106438
26. Chantar, H., Mafarja, M., Alsawalqah, H., Heidari, A.A., Aljarah, I., Faris, H.: Feature selection using binary grey wolf optimizer with elite-based crossover for Arabic text classification. Neural Comput. Appl. **32**(16), 12201–12220 (2019). https://doi.org/10.1007/s00521-019-043 68-6
27. Singh, G.A.P., Gupta, P.K.: Performance analysis of various machine learning-based approaches for detection and classification of lung cancer in humans. Neural Comput. Appl. **31**(10), 6863–6877 (2019)
28. Mafarja, M., Heidari, A.A., Habib, M., Faris, H., Thaher, T., Aljarah, I.: Augmented whale feature selection for IoT attacks: Structure, analysis and applications. Futur. Gener. Comput. Syst. **112**, 18–40 (2020)
29. Thaher, T., Chantar, H., Too, J., Mafarja, M., Turabieh, H., Houssein, E.H.: Boolean particle swarm optimization with various evolutionary population dynamics approaches for feature selection problems. Expert Syst. Appl. **195**, 116550 (2022). https://doi.org/10.1016/j.eswa. 2022.116550
30. Chantar, H., Mafarja, M., Alsawalqah, H., Heidari, A., Aljarah, I., Faris, H.: Feature selection using binary grey wolf optimizer with elite-based crossover for Arabic text classification. Neural Comput. Appl. **32**, 12201–12220 (2020)
31. Zuhair, H., Selamat, A., Salleh, M.: Feature selection for phishing detection: a review of research. Int. J. Intell. Syst. Technol. Appl. **15**(2), 147 (2016). https://doi.org/10.1504/IJI STA.2016.076495
32. Lininger, R., Vines, R.D.: Phishing: Cutting the identity theft line. John Wiley & Sons (2005)

Object-Relational Database Design Approaches: A Survey of Approaches and Techniques

Huda M. Bohalfaya, Abdelsalam M. Maatuk, and Esra A. Abdelnabi[✉]

Faculty of Information Technology, University of Benghazi, Benghazi, Libya
{huda.buhalfaya,abdelsalam.maatuk,esra.ali}@uob.edu.ly

Abstract. The primordial part of realizing a computer system is conceptual modelling, which has met with great success in relational database design using an ER model. Unfortunately, with the development of the computer field, relational databases confronted shortcomings in their applications and the object-relational model became used more and more. The tools of presenting conceptual modelling do not support all new concepts introduced by such models and the syntax of the SQL4 language. This paper aims to survey the previous works and various proposals on how to create rules for designing the object-relational (O-R) database to indicate their strengths and limitations. The paper provides a comprehensive explanation and evaluation of the existing approaches and the possibility of transferring all data semantics and relationships. This work demonstrates the importance and difficulty of these guidelines and discusses many previous works in this field. This paper confirms that modern technologies and new databases play an important role in the success of software design.

Keywords: Databases · Database Design · Object-Relational Database Design

1 Introduction

A successful database design should precisely specify the purpose of the expected database. Historically, organizations often used a manual system to come up with successful paper-and-pencil systems. As a rule, this is completed through the folder and file systems. Typically, such systems collect small data, and enterprise business users have few reporting needs. Computer files are like manual files. However, with large, computerized files developed, the problems became conspicuous [1].

Figure 1 illustrates the evolution of the process that databases went through from the late 1940s through and beyond the turn of the millennium.

Another important aspect of a successful database design is data modelling skills, which are also an essential part of the designing process; as concept modelling is the most important phase for database design. In terms of database design, the first step is data modelling, which indicates designing a particular model for determining a domain of a problem. Moreover, data models can be used to simplify the interaction between the designer, application programmer and end user. Additionally, the basic building blocks

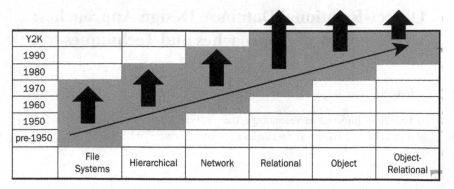

Fig. 1. The evolution of database modelling techniques

of data models must be known, i.e., entities, attributes, relationships, and constraints to create data models [2].

The most popular model in database design is the relational model. It represents the most used model for both users and designers. The strength of the relational model comes from its mathematical foundation, especially calculus. Furthermore, the abstraction and isolation of data are powerful improvements, which give the edge over the other systems and are considered a radical leap forward. Furthermore, the relational model has formalized how the data is stored and handled using query languages. Despite that, new and complex data types and system requirements for complex information systems are not suitable for traditional relational database systems. This is due to the difficulty to adapt modern data models and it slows the performance; as data is to be incorporated into relations and tuples, and the relationships among them are determined by data instances [3, 4].

Nowadays, databases encompass many data types, e.g., strings, images, etc. that are demanded by businesses. Consequently, the relational model has limited various applications, which require complex information from data. Although relational models occupy the market in the last decades, they have some restrictions to support the persistence of data needed by up-to-date applications [5].

Newer databases have emerged to resolve such obstacles, which are called the second generation of databases, i.e., object-oriented databases that permit entities to be exemplified in types that intimately fit the real-world correspondent using complex user-defined types and flexible relationships [5, 23]. Entities or objects are defined according to the methods which operate on that data, which are not united to individual applications but rather to the data. This supplies the benefit of an extra layer of abstraction amidst the data and applications. Moreover, three powerful forms of relationships are provided by object-oriented management systems such as inheritance, polymorphism and encapsulation. Thus, objects with these features can behave differently and access information efficiently [3–6].

Nevertheless, even the support for handling complex data types in the new breed of databases was not enough, as it became necessary to establish methodologies and techniques that guide designers in the design of object-based databases and relational databases [5, 24, 25]. Moreover, with the advantages of object-oriented database management systems, the traditional database still holds the market due to its simplicity, albeit limited.

Another cause of failure is the business factor and is due to the limitations of object-oriented database systems and their applications [3].

Some effort has been made to develop object-based database models that improve and support the relational model with object-oriented features. Enriched object-based data semantics (e.g., user-defined data types, inheritance, and encapsulation) that are advantageous for database design should be considered in the database conceptual model.

The perseverance of this study splits into two groups: the ones who believed the SQL was essential, and the others who say that the relational model was essential [3]. The first group prefers the extension of the relational database system by language extensions interpreted as their position in the "Third-Generation Database System Manifesto." While the second group chooses to extend the relational database as interpreted in "The Third Manifesto" [7]. As a result, object-oriented features and the relational model are conjunct and resulted in an object-relational database system. Therefore, an object-relational database is a solution that collects the advantages of the relational model's powerful language feature described in the third manifesto, and the object-oriented features originally proposed in the first manifesto. Figure 2 illustrates the concepts of object-oriented features and the relational model. The ANSI/ISO SQL99 standard is the mainly comprehensive definition of the object-relational model, i.e., SQL3 [3].

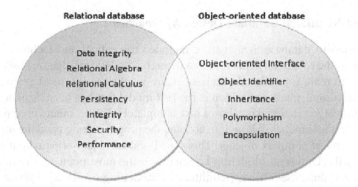

Fig. 2. Relational DB with Object-Oriented DB

The main reason for the object-relational database system's appearance is that both, relational data models and object-oriented data models, were lacking in some characteristics. Therefore, this work was initiated to create a model which represents a combination of both models [8]. The Object-Oriented model was generated to handle very particular requirements. The relational model focuses on effective data management based on an intact mathematical foundation [4]. Unfortunately, the object-relational database system has not formalized the phases of the design of object-relational schemas [9]. However, the appearance of new technology is not enough to uphold the representation of complex objects and applications [5]. Methodologies that guide designers for this technology in the same way in traditionally relational databases are needed.

Many factors have driven the investigation conducted in this study. This paper surveys the approaches to designing the object-relational (O-R) database and provides an analysis of their weaknesses and strengths. The previously proposed methods and generalize similar steps to develop more comprehensive steps to be used with any database management system that supports such types of databases were studied. Various techniques of database mapping including enhanced relationship types such as generalization, aggregation, composition and inheritance to an object-relational data model were discussed.

The paper is organized as follows: Sect. 2 summarizes the research on the relational database design approaches. Section 3 presents the results, and Sect. 4 concludes the paper.

2   Relational Database Design Approaches

This section provides state-of-the-art research on object-relational transformations and related aspects of object-relational database design. The section provides an investigation into the problems of O-RDB design. It reviews various techniques and proposals for this purpose, identifies their differences and assesses the impact of existing literature and shows how it has shaped current and future research in this area.

2.1   Object-Relational Database Design Approaches

Studies related to database design have included theoretical and technological solutions, whereas the relational database has a theoretical relational algebra basis only [10]. Moreover, to create a relational database many would use the most popular way of designing relational databases, which is the E/R model that has been designed to guide designers to design relational databases task completely. While, others used new object-oriented design techniques, taking into account the program design and the use of object features to support complex objects. This type is called object-oriented databases. For example, UML (Universal Modeling Language) is the most popular way of designing object-oriented databases. It has permitted the modelling of the full system including the database schema in a uniform way [5]. Whereas the object-relational design faces problems with the construction of the database regarding three factors which are the ambiguity of transformations of a conceptual model, multiplicity of criteria in quality assessment and a lack of a constructive model [10].

2.2   UML-Based Object-Relational Database Design Approaches

Eder and Kanzian [11] have focused on the generalization constructs of conceptual models and proposed a study that has explored the performance implications of the various design alternatives for mapping generalizations into the schema of an object-relational database system. Therefore, the study is an experimental analysis of design choices for mapping generalization to the logical schema of an object-relational database.

In addition, the study has provided a set of guides for a specific database management system, and detailed performance analysis for logical design to present high performance.

Concerning object-relational database design methodologies, several studies attempt to find a good standard for database design. The authors in [5] presented some guidelines for object-relational database design, in which the conceptual schema is represented in UML and target language. However, only two types of relationships were considered, which are simple and composite aggregations. Moreover, the composition aggregation had not transformed from a conceptual to a logical model. In addition, the transformation steps have not been clearly explained. This study was implemented on SQL Oracle 8i.

Another study has proposed a methodology for object-relational database design, which is based on an extended UML with required stereotypes. The methodology was based on the SQL:1999 object-relational model and Oracle8i DBMS [12].

Vara et al. [13] described a study that attempts to create and defines a transformation model, which transforms Platform Independent Models (PIM) to Platform Specific Models (PSM), with a set of formalized steps for the development of an object-relational database, in which the field of web information systems was only identified. It is worth mentioning that the work was described using UML in two phases. The first phase was regarding data PIM as the conceptual data model by SQL:2003 using an extended UML class diagram called profile UML. The second phase was regarding PSM level represented in extended UML same as the first phase, which tended in describing the specific model which was expressed and represented by Oracle10g.

Soumiya et al. [14] presented an approach for a comparative analysis of the migration to the relational database of the time object. The study attempts to create formalized steps, involved in the transformation from UML class diagrams into temporal Object-relational database (TORDB) handling a valid time at attributes.

Wang [15] highlights a set of problems encountered in relational databases and how to solve these problems using ORDB features. These problems are transitive dependency, multivalued attributes and aggregation of composition problems. Besides, Wang [15] was able to solve it using the advantages of the ORDB, suggested a set of solutions for it and applied these solutions to a case study using the UML class diagram.

2.3 Logical-Based Object-Relational Database Design Approaches

Awang et al. [16] debated a major concept in object-oriented technology, which is inheritance. Algorithms and rules are developed and described, based on which a simple tool is designed to help system developers convert inheritance structures into relational tables. However, the solution has not clearly stated how inheritance structure could be represented in a relational database.

Most of the studies of the ORDB in this area, which have made a lot of effort, can be classified into three types: one is used for building a conceptual model by using the UML class diagram to represent a persistent object. Another one is used for defining the mapping from conceptual objects to database objects using the new ORDB resources. The last one is used for extending the UML class diagram to represent new ORDB elements. Castro et al. [17] proposed a generation CASE tool to create logical models for ORDBMS. The goal of the study is to increase the use of ORDB. The ArgoUML is used with new modules. However, concerning the previously mentioned proposals to be used in a real project, it is requisite to make improvements. Worth mentioning here that two program modules have been developed to transform a conceptual model in SQL:2003 standard code and the Oracle11g data defining language from graphic logical schema.

2.4 Physical-Based Object-Relational Database Design Approaches

Some studies have focused only on how to maintain some semantics of relationships. Pardede et al. [18] have proposed a solution to preserve a collection of semantics in the ORDB using a collection of data types and implementing the proposed aggregation and association relationships. The proposed solution can be summarized in three main steps, in the case of whole-part relationships (simple and composite) aggregation. The first step is of mapping a whole class as a table. Secondly, the simple aggregation part class is mapped to a user-defined type, whereas the composition aggregation of the class is mapped to a row type. In the third step, when it is an association relationship, the One-to-Many relationship is mapped as a reference type, which is located as a collection on the "one" side. Therefore, the Many-to-Many relationship is mapped as a reference type inside one of the associated types. Eessaar [19] has proposed an approach that allows the designer to find a suitable design for whole-part relationships, which is based on the values of secondary characteristics of whole-part relationships.

Other studies have focused on defining some steps and guiding transformation from conceptual to implementation modelling on ORDBs. Golobisky and Vecchietti [9] succeeded to create a set of transformation definitions between UML classes and ORDBs. However, these definitions did not comprehend all the probability of design concepts for ORDBs. These definitions had been done only on Oracle 10g, where the other database management system support object-relational models have not been used.

Rombaldo et al. [20] highlighted an important problem when developers mapped classes to relational tables, which did not exploit the power of the object-relational model, and merely moved the class to a table. It suggested a working mechanism to move an object to an object within the database. One of the most important features of this work was that the steps were clear as any designer can convert the object to an object even if it did not have a background in the databases management system or a particular language. However, these steps are applied only to one type of database management system, which is Oracle11g.

2.5 Reverse-Engineering-Based Object-Relational Database Design Approaches

In the past few years, when new types of databases appeared, especially when object-oriented construct was merged into a relational database, there were some efforts of reverse engineering databases to analyze these types of databases and obtain new methods to re-design these databases. Reverse engineering techniques for ORDB constructs have not been yet supplied. In this sense, Cabot et al. [21] presented a method that considers new constructs in the reverse engineering of an existing ORDB. This method is divided into three stages. The first stage extracted the schema from an existing database by executing the convenient set of queries over its data dictionary. The second stage applied a set of rules to the scheme obtained to be UML compliant. Finally, the obtained conceptual schema is improved by the user. Finally, a prototype tool has been designed and implemented on the Oracle9i database management system.

Fouad and Mohamed [22] presented an approach of database reverse engineering, which covers the transformation of some object constructs. The approach focused on understanding how object construct was added in relational databases. The conceptual schema that was obtained has been expressed as a UML class diagram. This approach was tested in Oracle 11g. The class diagram was used to represent database tables, i.e., classes and table relationships, as associations. Business rules executed in the database as integrity constraints and triggers are transformed into Object Constraint Language (OCL) phrases. Each OCL phrase is transformed to a conceptual level of either one of the database constraints, e.g., (CHECK constraints, constraints enforced by triggers).

3   Discussions

Several studies have been proposed to design most of the features of object-oriented models that are suitable for relational databases. However, despite all the proposed solutions, object-relational still lacks the existence of standard rules at the logical design phase. In addition, the lack remains less focused on richer representations such as aggregations, inheritance and polymorphism relationships to be represented within database modelling.

Most of the approaches for ORDB design are focused on the features of object-oriented language within relational databases. Unfortunately, there is a lack of studies that focus on more enriched data semantic and relationship types e.g., aggregations, inheritance and polymorphism. A method that considers all these data features to be used to design an ORDB completely is needed. In addition, a solution to model and comprehend all the data semantics and relationships has not been developed yet. Furthermore, current models cannot adopt a recent standard for ORDB design. Therefore, this research gap motivates this study to establish a model for the defined problem. Table 1 shows a comparison of the ORDB design approaches and their limitations. Table 1 contains a set of abbreviations for the data types and relationships that are, in the conceptual model, created in the UML class diagram. These abbreviations are Simple Attribute (SA), Composed Attribute (CA), Multivalued Attribute (MA), Derived Attribute (DA), Relationship Attribute (RA), Binary Relationship (BR) 1:1, 1:N, N:M, Simple Aggregation Relationship (SAR), Composition Aggregation Relationship (CAR), Inheritance Relationship (InhR), Polymorphism Relationship (PolyR), Recursive Relationship (RR).

Table 1. A comparison of the ORDB design approaches.

No	Author	year	Conceptual level (UML class diagram)													Logical level (ORM using SQL standard)
			Attributes					Relationships								
			SA	CA	MA	DA	RA	BR 1:1	AR 1:N	AR N:N	SAR	CAR	InhR	PolyR	RR	
1	Marcos [5]	2001	√	√	√	√	×	√	√	√	√	√	×	×	×	SQL:1999
2	Marcos [12]	2003	√	√	√	√	×	√	√	√	√	√	√	×	×	SQL:1999
3	Eric [18]	2004	×	×	×	×	√	×	√	√	√	√	×	×	×	SQL:2003
4	Maria [9]	2005	√	√	√	×	×	√	√	√	√	√	√	×	×	SQL:2003
5	Juan [13]	2007	×	√	√	√	×	√	√	√	√	√	√	×	×	SQL:2003
6	Jordi [21]	2008	√	√	√	√	√	√	√	√	×	√	√	×	×	SQL:2003
7	Erki [19]	2009	–	–	–	–	–	–	–	–	–	–	–	–	–	SQL:2003
8	Wang [15]	2011	×	×	√	×	×	×	×	×	×	√	√	×	×	SQL:2008
9	Carlos [20]	2012	√	×	√	×	×	√	√	×	√	√	√	×	√	SQL:2008
10	Castro [17]	2012	√	√	√	×	×	√	√	×	√	√	√	×	√	SQL:2003
11	Toufik [22]	2018	√	√	×	√	×	×	√	×	√	√	√	×	√	–

4 Conclusion

This research studies the up-to-date literature on object-relational development conceptually and logically. Few research efforts have tried to create guidelines that help designers create an O-R database design, so the researcher had difficulty finding previous studies covering this area. This paper provides a comprehensive literature review of Object-Relational database design proposals. Some of the problems with relational databases and traditional approaches are covered as well.

The proposed methods and the rules to develop more comprehensive steps to be used with any database management system that supports such types of databases were studied. Various techniques of database mapping including enriched relationship types such as generalization, simple aggregation, composition aggregation and inheritance to an object-relational data model were discussed. These approaches use different techniques and rules to design an object-relational database. The paper deeply studied several works, compared them, and identified the strengths and weaknesses of each of them.

In brief, most ORDB design approaches focus on the advantages of an object-oriented language using the characteristics of traditional relational databases. Therefore, there is a lack of studies dealing with data semantics and more enriching types of relationships, such as aggregations, inheritance, polymorphism, and other composite and complex data definitions. There is a need for a method that takes all the features of these modern and enriched data types into account to use it to design a more specific and representative ORDB. In addition, no solution has been developed to model and understand all data semantics and relationships, yet the currently proposed models do not adopt a modern ORDB design standard. Therefore, this research area needs further study and analysis to develop a comprehensive method for designing databases according to the relational-oriented model.

References

1. Ireland, C.J.: Object-relational impedance mismatch: a framework-based approach. Dissertation, The Open University (2011)
2. Elmasri, R., Navathe, S.: Fundamentals of Database Systems, 6th edn. Pearson, Hoboken (2016)
3. Lord, C., Gupta, S.: The evolution of object-relational databases (2002)
4. Coronel,C., Morris, S.: Database Systems: Design, Implementation, and Management. Cengage Learning, Australia (2017)
5. Marcos, E., Vela, B., Cavero, J.M., Cáceres, P.: Aggregation and composition in object-relational database design. In: 5th Conference on Advances in Databases and Information Systems, pp. 195–209, September 2001
6. Keivani, N., Maatuk, A.M., Aljawarneh, S., Ali, M.A.: Towards the maturity of object-relational database technology: promises and reality. Int. J. Technol. Diffus. 6, 1–19 (2015). https://doi.org/10.4018/ijtd.2015100101
7. Dietrich, S.W., Urban, S.D.: An Advanced Course in Database Systems: Beyond Relational Databases. Pearson/Prentice Hall, Upper Saddle River (2005)
8. Castro, K.: Object-relational Data Model. https://www.tutori-alspoint.com/Object-relational-Data-Model. Accessed 25 Aug 2019
9. Golobisky, M.F., Vecchietti. A.: Mapping UML class diagrams into object-relational schemas. In: Proceedings of ASSE, vol. 1, pp. 65–79 (2005)
10. Auziņš, A., Eiduks, J., Vasiļevska, A., Dzenis, R.: Object-relational database structure model and structure optimisation. Appl. Comput. Syst. 23, 28–36 (2018). https://doi.org/10.2478/acss-2018-0004
11. Eder, J., Kanzian, S.: Logical design of generalizations in object-relational databases. In: ADBIS (Local Proceedings) (2004)
12. Marcos, E., Vela, B., Cavero, J.M.: A methodological approach for object-relational database design using UML. Informatik Forschung und Entwicklung 18, 152–164 (2004). https://doi.org/10.1007/s00450-004-0158-4
13. Vara, J.M., Vela, B., Cavero, J.M., Marcos, E.: Model transformation for object-relational database development. In: Proceedings of the 2007 ACM Symposium on Applied Computing (2007). https://doi.org/10.1145/1244002.1244222
14. Soumiya, A.E., Mohamed, B.: Converting UML class diagrams into temporal object relational database. Int. J. Electr. Comput. Eng. (IJECE) 7(5), 2823 (2017). https://doi.org/10.11591/ijece.v7i5.pp2823-2832
15. Wang, M.: Solving relational database problems with ORDBMS in an advanced database course. Inf. Syst. Educ. J. (ISEDJ) 9(4), 80–90 (2011)

16. Awang, M.K., Labadu, N.L., Campus, G.B.: Transforming object-oriented data model to relationaldata model. New Comput. Archit. Appl. **2**(3), 402–409 (2012)
17. de Castro, T.R., de Souza, S.N.A., de Souza, L.S.: CASE tool for object-relational databasedesigns. In: 7th Iberian Conference on Information Systems and Technologies (CISTI 2012), pp. 1–6. IEEE, New York (2001)
18. Pardede, E., Rahayu, J.W., Taniar, D.: Mapping methods and query for aggregation and association in object-relational database using collection. In: International Conference on Information Technology: Coding and Computing, 2004 Proceedings ITCC, pp. 539–543. IEEE, New York (2004). https://doi.org/10.1109/itcc.2004.1286513
19. Eessaar, E.: On finding suitable designs for whole-part relationships in object-relational databases. Inf. Syst. Dev., 951–962 (2008). https://doi.org/10.1007/978-0-387-78578-3_28
20. Rombaldo, C.A., Alves Souza, S.N., Souza, L.S.: O-ODM framework for object-relational databases. Int. J. Interact. Multimed. Artif. Intell. **1**(6), 29–35 (2012). https://doi.org/10.9781/ijimai.2012.164
21. Cabot, J., Gómez, C., Planas, E., Rodríguez, M.E.: Reverse engineering of OO constructsin object-relational database schemas. Jornadas de IngenierÃa del Software y Bases de Datos **20**(49), 134 (2008)
22. Fouad, T., Mohamed, B.: Reverse engineering of object relational database. In: Proceedings of the 2018 International Conference on Software Engineering and Information Management, pp. 73–76. ACM (2018). https://doi.org/10.1145/3178461.3178481
23. Maatuk, A.M., Akhtar Ali, M., Aljawarneh, S.: Translating relational database schemas into object-based schemas: university case study. Recent Pat. Comput. Sci. Innov. Educ. Technol. E-Learn. Soc. Netw. **8**(2), 122–132 (2015). https://doi.org/10.2174/221327590866615071 0174102
24. Maatuk, A., Akhtar Ali, M., Rossiter, N.: Converting relational databases into object-relational databases. J. Object Technol. (JOT) **9**(2), 145–161 (2010)
25. Maatuk, A.: Migrating relational databases into object-based and XML databases. Ph.D thesis, University of Northumbria, Newcastle, UK, September 2009
26. Maatuk, A., Akhtar Ali, M., Rossiter, N.: Semantic enrichment: the first phase of relational database migration. In: Proceedings of the 2008 International Conference on Systems, Computing Sciences and Software Engineering (SCSS), Bridgeport, USA, pp. 373–378 (2008)

Event Abstration in a Forensic Timeline

Hudan Studiawan[✉][iD]

Department of Informatics, Insitut Teknologi Sepuluh Nopember, Surabaya, Indonesia
hudan@its.ac.id

Abstract. Event abstraction is a process of extracting main events from a large set of data, allowing investigators to identify patterns, connections, and anomalies in event logs that may reveal further evidence of malicious activity. In this paper, we investigate the use of event abstraction in a forensic timeline. This work applies the Drain method, a tree-based abstraction approach, and demonstrates its efficiency in producing accurate event abstraction. It also discusses the challenges faced by investigators in event abstraction and its analysis in a forensic timeline. Finally, this paper presents case studies of web server attacks and creates their event abstraction from a forensic timeline.

Keywords: event abstraction · Drain method · forensic timeline · log parsing

1 Introduction

A forensic timeline is a sequence of timestamps and events extracted from digital evidence that helps investigators identify and examine the events that happened on a system [2]. A forensic timeline analysis is the process of analyzing the sequence of events that have occurred on a computer or network in order to reconstruct the history of the system and identify any potential security threats or other issues [12]. This can be done in order to determine whether or not the system was compromised. This analysis is often carried out as part of a digital forensic investigation, which is when a group of knowledgeable professionals investigates the digital evidence obtained from a computer or network in order to get information about what took place.

There are a few different approaches that may be used to get a digital forensic timeline analysis; these approaches vary according to the particular requirements of the inquiry as well as the tools and resources that are available. Utilizing specialized software tools, such as log2timeline Plaso [9], that have been developed for the purpose of doing digital forensic timeline analysis is a frequent strategy that may be used. These kinds of programs are often able to automatically parse and analyze massive amounts of digital data, enabling the investigator to search for certain patterns and signs that might assist in reconstructing the chain of activities that took place on a computer or network.

Reviewing events from the digital evidence by hand and looking at the many files and data sources on the system is yet another method that may be used

T. A. T. Benmusa et al. (Eds.): ILCICT 2023, CCIS 2097, pp. 119–129, 2024.
https://doi.org/10.1007/978-3-031-62624-1_10

to identify the order in which the events transpired [12]. It is possible for this approach to be a procedure that requires a lot of time and effort to complete, yet it is useful for some kinds of inquiries when the tools and resources are not available or restricted.

Datetime   **Message**
...
2016-10-05T10:39:01 [CRON pid: 1807] pam_unix(cron:session): session closed for user root
2016-10-05T10:39:01 [CRON pid: 1807] pam_unix(cron:session): session opened for user root by (uid=0)
2016-10-05T10:39:26 [sshd pid: 1822] pam_unix(sshd:auth): authentication failure; logname= uid=0 euid=0 ...
2016-10-05T10:39:27 [sshd pid: 1822] Failed password for root from 192.168.210.131 port 57190 ssh2
2016-10-05T10:39:33 [sshd pid: 1822] Connection closed by 192.168.210.131 [preauth]
2016-10-05T10:39:33 [sshd pid: 1822] Failed password for root from 192.168.210.131 port 57190 ssh2
2016-10-05T10:39:33 [sshd pid: 1822] PAM 1 more authentication failure; logname= uid=0 euid=0 tty=ssh ...
2016-10-05T10:42:33 [sshd pid: 1833] Received disconnect from 192.168.210.131: 11: Bye Bye [preauth]
2016-10-05T10:42:33 [sshd pid: 1836] pam_unix(sshd:auth): authentication failure; logname= uid=0 euid=0 ...
...
Other 397,839 lines of records

Fig. 1. An illustration of a simplified forensic timeline from the dataset [6].

Analysis of a forensic timeline is essential because it gives useful information about the history of a computer or network and also has the ability to assist in the detection of possible risks to network security as well as other problems [13]. This provides a thorough picture of what has been recorded over the course of time. This may be beneficial for a number of objectives, including understanding the origin of an event or issue, recognizing patterns of behavior, and detecting possible security concerns.

On the other hand, the process of simplifying the information that is included in event logs, which are recordings of events that take place inside a computer system or network, is referred to as event log abstraction [4]. This simplification is often accomplished by collecting important information from the event logs, such as the time and date that the event happened, the kind of event that occurred, as well as any other pertinent facts. An event log signature is another name given to the condensed information that was produced. In another literature, the technique of collecting these abstractions from event logs is referred to as event log signature extraction [15].

As shown in Fig. 1, a forensic timeline has a date, time, and event or message from a case study dataset [6]. Figure 1 only shows a portion of the timeline, where there are other 397,839 lines of log entries that need to be analyzed. An abstraction will provide a quick overview for all of these events.

In this paper, we propose to apply event abstraction to a forensic timeline generated from a forensic image. The information that is extracted in a forensic timeline is intended to be simplified via the use of event log abstraction in order to make it simpler to analyze and comprehend. We use Drain [7] to perform event abstraction and it processes logs in real-time using a unique tree structure, offering enhanced accuracy and speed over traditional methods. Event abstraction makes it possible to quickly and easily understand the most important details about the events that have occurred in a computer system or network by extracting the key information from the event logs and organizing it in a readable format. This may be helpful for seeing trends, fixing difficulties, and spotting possible risks to the system's security. The reduced event logs take up less space and need less processing power than the original event logs. This is one more way that event log abstraction may assist decrease the amount of data that has to be handled.

In the subsequent sections, we initially discuss the related research in forensic timeline analysis and event abstraction (Sect. 2). Following that, we provide a formal explanation of the proposed method (Sect. 3). Subsequently, we share the outcomes of our experiments on two case studies in Sect. 4, and draw our conclusion and future work in Sect. 5.

2 Related Work

2.1 Event Log Abstraction

Event log abstraction is a technique that encapsulates the most frequently occurring words that represent every entry within a group of event log entries [4,14]. Essentially, the purpose of event log abstraction is to derive a log template from a collection of log entries. There are several methods to perform event log abstraction as follows.

Thaler et al. [15] use a neural language model for signature extraction in forensic log analysis. The neural language model approach differs from rule-based systems and hand-crafted algorithms in that it is less error-prone and does not require high maintenance effort. The neural language model learns to identify mutable and non-mutable parts in a log message, which enables signature extraction. This approach is based on complex, probabilistic rules that help detect these parts.

An automatic method for event log abstraction works by using graph clustering to group similar events together [14]. The benefits of using graph clustering to group event logs are that it eliminates the need for manual input parameters and model training, making the process faster and more efficient. Graph clustering also groups similar events together, which helps identify the main activity from event logs more accurately. The method models event logs as a graph and uses a graph clustering approach to group log entries, which can be applied to any type of log file.

A recent study by Bhattacharya et al. [1] discuss the importance of analyzing semistructured IoT device logs in real-time to proactively manage systems and improve network stability. The authors propose a new log abstraction framework that uses information extraction and natural language processing models to extract valuable insights from streaming event log traces. They argue that this approach can significantly improve the accuracy of log mining models and minimize false positives.

Finally, the work by El Masri et al. [4] describes a systematic literature review of automated log abstraction techniques. The objective of the work is to build a quality model for evaluating automated log abstraction techniques. They built a quality model composed of seven desirable aspects, including coverage, delimiter independence, efficiency, system knowledge independence, mode, scalability, and parameter tuning effort [4].

2.2   Forensic Timeline Analysis

A forensic timeline refers to a chronological series of timestamps and events derived from a digital device, which assists investigators in pinpointing and scrutinizing the occurrences within a system [2]. Timeline analysis can be performed along with browser forensics. One such tool is the Web Browser Forensic Analyzer, which provides an integrated analysis function for all major web browsers in various time zones [10]. This tool can be used to construct a timeline array using the time information contained in each web browser's log file. NetAnalysis is another tool that can be used to analyze historical information. This tool can show the type of protocol used, the last visited timings, URL, and host name, which can be used to construct a timeline of the suspect's internet activity [10].

In another research, forensic timeline analysis in the WaybackVisor system involves proactive collection and preservation of I/O logs from ATA drives, which are then transferred to a Hadoop cluster [8]. The raw I/O logs are converted into key-value pairs, followed by the generation of MD5 hash values for each written 4 KiB sector using the MapReduce framework. The system can search for a specific file in the hash database by comparing the MD5 hashes of the file's sectors with those in the database. The results of the timeline analysis are visualized in bar charts and heatmaps, providing a clear overview of access patterns on the monitored ATA drives.

The work by Du et al. [3] notes that millions of low-level events cannot be easily understood by investigators without knowing the ground truth. Therefore, automated high-level digital event generation is proposed as a solution. File system traces, which also record an individual's actions on a device, are another important source of information for timeline analysis. For instance, in a file download action, the date and time of the file represent when the file was placed on the computer. File system metadata consists of a wealth of useful information for an investigation.

Timeline analysis can be conducted by investigating timestamp patterns resulting from common user operations in Windows' New Technology File System (NTFS) [5]. The researcher set up a controlled testing environment, developed a custom PowerShell script for timestamp extraction from the Master File Table (MFT), and performed a variety of file operations. They analyzed the resulting timestamp patterns to create a rule or fingerprint for each specific file operation scenario. Based on their findings, they derived a set of time rules that describe possible filesystem operations, providing a reference for forensic analysts to identify normal and suspicious timestamp patterns.

Forensic image   Forensic timeline   Preprocessing   The Drain3 method   Event abstraction
                                                                                          results

Fig. 2. The proposed method for generating abstractions from a forensic timeline.

3 Proposed Method

In this section, we describe the proposed method for generating abstraction in a forensic timeline as shown in Fig. 2. First, we generate a forensic timeline using log2timeline Plaso, which extracts time and events from a forensic image. Second, we perform event preprocessing to be ingested into the Drain method as the event abstraction technique. Finally, event abstraction involves producing higher-level representations or summaries of the raw event data, making it more digestible and analyzable.

3.1 Building a Forensic Timeline

The first step is to gather the necessary digital evidence in the form of a forensic image. Then, we build a forensic timeline using log2timeline Plaso [9], or Plaso in short. It is a great tool for digital forensic investigators, as it can help them quickly build an accurate timeline of events. With Plaso, forensic investigators can quickly and easily analyze a timeline extracted from digital artifacts and evidence, such as computer log files, file metadata, system and application configuration files, and user activity logs. This tool can help investigators determine the sequence of events in order to identify any malicious activity or suspicious behavior.

The command to generate a timeline is as follows: *psteal.py –source forensic-image.c01 -o dynamic -w forensic-image.csv*. The *psteal.py* command is a convenience script in the Plaso digital forensics platform that combines the functionalities of the *log2timeline.py* and *psort.py* commands. It extracts events from a source and then sorts and outputs them in a single step, rather than requiring the user to first generate a Plaso storage file and then process that file with a separate command.

psteal.py is the main command that invokes the *psteal* script. Option *–source* specifies the source from which to extract events. In this case, it's a forensic disk image file named *forensic-image.e01*. The next option, *-o dynamic*, sets the output module. The dynamic output module provides a flexible way of controlling which fields are included in the output and how they are formatted. Finally, *-w forensic-image.csv* specifies the output file where the sorted events will be written. In this case, it is a CSV file named *forensic-image.csv*. The -w flag stands for "write". In addition to a CSV file as the output, the tool creates a Plaso storage file that encapsulates the extracted events and associated metadata. Once we have reconstructed the timeline, we can proceed to the next step.

3.2   Event Preprocessing

After obtaining the forensic timeline, we obtain eight columns from the CSV file, namely datetime, timestamp_desc, source, source_long, message, parser, display_name, tag. To perform event abstraction, we need to extract two columns, specifically "datetime" and "message".

The datetime column represents the timestamp of the event. It is the specific date and time when the event occurred. The timestamp is one of the most critical pieces of information in a forensic timeline because it allows investigators to order events chronologically and correlate events across different sources. The datetime is typically displayed in ISO 8601 format (YYYY-MM-DDTHH:MM:SS), often with an additional microsecond component and timezone offset.

Furthermore, the message column provides a brief description or summary of the event. It is designed to give a human-readable overview of the event and might include information about the event's source (e.g., the name of the log that it came from), the type of event, and other relevant details. The exact content of the message column can vary widely depending on the type of event and the source of the data. These two columns are then supplied to the event abstraction method, but only the message column is abstracted.

3.3   Generating Event Abstraction

Event abstraction is the process of extracting the most salient and relevant aspects of a sequence of messages. This is done by breaking down the sequence into its individual components, recognizing patterns, and extracting the most important characteristics of each event.

To generate event abstraction from a sequence of events in a forensic timeline, we use the Drain method [7]. Drain is an online log parsing method designed to address the time-consuming nature of traditional, offline log parsing methods. Drain uses a fixed depth parse tree with specially designed parsing rules, allowing it to parse logs in real-time. Drain demonstrated high accuracy and significantly improved running time compared to the current leading online parser.

Drain initially processes the incoming raw log message before the parse tree is utilized. This process permits users to input basic regular expressions that are derived from their domain knowledge and correspond to frequently used variables like IP addresses and block IDs. Following this, Drain eliminates the tokens in the raw log message that align with these regular expressions.

The second step of the Drain commences at the initial node of the parse tree, using the preprocessed log message. The nodes in the first layer of the parse tree correspond to log groups, each with log messages of varying lengths. Drain determines a path to a node in the first layer, guided by the length of the preprocessed log message. This overall tree structure is illustrated in Fig. 3. The tree is generated from a public dataset [6] that will be discussed in Sect. 4.

In the third step, Drain navigates from a node in the first layer, identified in the second step, towards a leaf node. This action is grounded in the presumption that the initial tokens in a log message are more probable to be constants. Drain

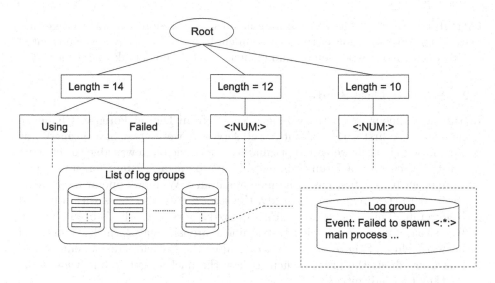

Fig. 3. An illustration of the Drain method for generating abstractions.

chooses the subsequent internal node based on the tokens found at the starting positions of the log message.

In the fourth step, Drain identifies the most appropriate log group from the list of log groups. It computes the similarity between the log message and the log event of every log group. Once it identifies the log group with the highest similarity, it contrasts this with a pre-established similarity threshold. If the similarity meets or exceeds this threshold, Drain designates this group as the most fitting log group. If not, it signals that there is not a suitable log group.

If a suitable log group is found, Drain incorporates the log ID of the present log message into the log IDs of the identified log group. The log event within this log group is then updated. If Drain is unable to locate a fitting log group, it forms a new log group using the current log message and refreshes the parse tree to include this new log group. Using the Drain method, we extract the abstraction from the timeline and then discuss the experimental results in the next section.

4 Experimental Results and Analyses

This section includes details about the experiment settings, the datasets used, the experiments performed, and the result analysis of the method utilized. It also discusses the results of the experiments and their implications.

4.1 Experiment Settings

For generating a timeline, we use log2timeline Plaso version 20230226. To implement the Drain technique, we use the implementation of the method from Ohana et al. [11] namely Drain3. Both Plaso and Drain3 are publicly available on

GitHub repositories. The Python language used is version 3.9. All packages are installed on an Anaconda virtual environment to make sure they have an isolated environment, have dependency management, and do not break each other.

4.2   Forensic Case Study

In this experiment, we used two case studies from Digital Forensic Challenge Images [6]. The first case is about a web server. A web server of a business was compromised via their website. Fortunately, a forensic team was able to get there promptly to capture a forensic image of the operating system for subsequent examination. In this first case, the image is from a Windows operating system.

Similar to the previous case study, the second case also deals with a hacked web server [6]. This time, though, it's a Linux-based system that's been affected. In this situation, we need to closely examine a forensic image, which is a detailed forensic timeline of the Linux web server after the breach. This timeline could tell us a lot about the breach, such as how the hackers got in and what weak spots they took advantage of.

4.3   Results and Discussion

The sample of the experiment is depicted in Fig. 4. When the Drain processes log messages, it groups similar messages together based on their structure and content, forming clusters. Each of these clusters is represented by a template and is assigned a unique identifier for easy reference and tracking. "ID" refers to the unique identifier assigned to each log template or cluster. In addition, the "size" value indicates how many log messages have been matched to that template.

As shown in Fig. 4, <:NUM:> is a placeholder or mask that represents a variable part of a log message. The method uses these placeholders to generalize log messages into templates. <:NUM:> is used to represent the variable part of the log message, which in this case is the number. This allows the method to group similar log messages together based on their structure and content, while still acknowledging the parts that can vary. This is a key part of how the Drain is able to effectively mine and cluster log messages.

Another placeholder is <:*:>, which is a mask that represents a variable part of a log message that does not match any specific mask such as <:NUM:> or <:IP:>. <:*:> is used to represent the variable part of the log message, which in this Fig. 4 is the EHCI platform driver (ID=243) or a user name (ID = 355 and ID = 357).

Other possible placeholders are <:IP:> and <:HEX:>. <:IP:> is used to represent an IP address in the log message. If the method identifies a part of the log message as an IP address, it replaces it with <:IP:> in the abstraction results. <:HEX:> is used to represent a hexadecimal number in the log message. If the method recognizes a part of the message as a hexadecimal number, it replaces it with this placeholder in the generated template.

As demonstrated in the experiment, event abstraction offers numerous benefits. First, it enhances efficiency by reducing the volume of data to be processed and stored, as raw logs can be quite extensive, with numerous records being generated every second. Furthermore, it improves usability by converting low-level, often difficult-to-understand logs, into a form that emphasizes key information, thereby facilitating troubleshooting and decision-making.

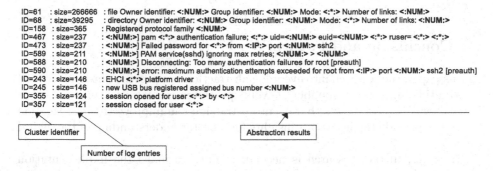

Fig. 4. An example of abstraction results.

In addition, log abstraction bolsters security by aiding in the identification of patterns and anomalies that may indicate potential threats, such as repeated failed login attempts (ID = 473 with 237 records). It also provides a scalable solution to handle the exponential increase in logs that comes with growing system complexity and scale. Related to scale, a forensic timeline can have hundreds of thousands of records, as shown in Fig. 1.

Event log abstraction, especially when applied to a forensic timeline, offers other advantages such as enhanced data analysis, troubleshooting, and reporting. The abstraction simplifies log data into event logs, enabling easier recognition of patterns and trends. As shown in Fig. 4, the simplified view aids in identifying issues and optimizing system performance, such as ID = 158 about *registering protocol family* during the boot process of the system. For troubleshooting, the detailed history provided by event logs facilitates quicker problem identification and resolution, such as ID = 590 about *error of maximum authentication attempts exceeded* for a particular user.

A further benefit of event log abstraction is that it may assist to decrease the quantity of data that has to be handled and kept. As demonstrated in Fig. 4, the repeated information is summarized using the ID and size fields. For example, cluster ID = 61 holds 266,666 records about *file owner identifier* and *group identifier*. This is an advantage that can help make event log abstraction more appealing. The original event logs take up less space and need more processing power than the simplified event log signatures, which makes it simpler to organize and analyze vast amounts of data.

Event abstraction, despite its benefits, comes with potential disadvantages, notably data loss and difficulty defining events. The abstraction process can result in some details from the original logs being lost or overlooked, delaying troubleshooting efforts or pattern identification. Defining meaningful events from raw events, particularly in complex systems generating diverse events, can pose a challenge. The quality of the abstraction is largely dependent on the efficacy of the event definition process. Hence, despite the numerous advantages of event log abstraction, one must consider these trade-offs and carefully design the abstraction process to cater to the specific requirements of the investigated timeline.

5   Conclusion and Future Work

In this paper, the research into event log abstraction has provided insights or brief information from a large number of events presented in a forensic timeline. It has been shown in experiments that event abstraction can improve the investigation as well as provide the necessary insights for a better understanding of the digital evidence.

However, further research is needed in order to make the implementation of abstraction more efficient and effective. Firstly, there is a need to refine the abstraction process, including efforts to reduce manual labor in preparing the event log model and enhance the process's accuracy. Secondly, research should focus on better methods for identifying correlations within event logs, potentially utilizing machine learning techniques for pattern detection and improved data visualization for understanding these correlations. Thirdly, the use of event log abstraction in predictive analytics could lead to models capable of detecting and predicting future problems. Lastly, it recommends studying the application of event log abstraction in various domains, such as IT security, enterprise resource planning, and project management, to develop strategies specific to each domain's requirements.

Acknowledgements. The author gratefully acknowledges financial support from the Institut Teknologi Sepuluh Nopember for this work under the project scheme of the Publication Writing and IPR Incentive Program (PPHKI).

References

1. Bhattacharya, S., Ray, B., Chugh, R., Gordon, S.: An online parsing framework for semistructured streaming system logs of internet of things systems. IEEE Open J. Instrum. Meas. **2**, 1–18 (2023)
2. Chabot, Y., Bertaux, A., Nicolle, C., Kechadi, M.T.: A complete formalized knowledge representation model for advanced digital forensics timeline analysis. Digit. Invest. **11**, S95–S105 (2014)
3. Du, X., Le, Q., Scanlon, M.: Automated artefact relevancy determination from artefact metadata and associated timeline events. In: 2020 International Conference on Cyber Security and Protection of Digital Services (Cyber Security), pp. 1–8 (2020)
4. El-Masri, D., Petrillo, F., Guéhéneuc, Y.G., Hamou-Lhadj, A., Bouziane, A.: A systematic literature review on automated log abstraction techniques. Inf. Softw. Technol. **122**, 106276 (2020)

5. Galhuber, M., Luh, R.: Time for truth: forensic analysis of NTFS timestamps. In: Proceedings of the 16th International Conference on Availability, Reliability and Security, pp. 1–10 (2021)
6. Hadi, A.: Digital Forensic Challenge Images (2023). https://www.ashemery.com/dfir.html
7. He, P., Zhu, J., Zheng, Z., Lyu, M.R.: Drain: an online log parsing approach with fixed depth tree. In: 2017 IEEE International Conference on Web Services (ICWS), pp. 33–40 (2017)
8. Hirano, M., Tsuzuki, T., Ikeda, S., Taka, N., Fujiwara, K., Kobayashi, R.: Waybackvisor: hypervisor-based scalable live forensic architecture for timeline analysis. In: International Conference on Security, Privacy, and Anonymity in Computation, Communication, and Storage, pp. 219–230 (2017)
9. Metz, J., et al.: log2timeline plaso: super timeline all the things (2023). https://github.com/log2timeline/plaso
10. Nalawade, A., Bharne, S., Mane, V.: Forensic analysis and evidence collection for web browser activity. In: 2016 International Conference on Automatic Control and Dynamic Optimization Techniques (ICACDOT), pp. 518–522 (2016)
11. Ohana, D., et al.: Drain3 (2023). https://github.com/logpai/Drain3
12. Studiawan, H., Firdaus, A., Pratomo, B.A., Ahmad, T.: Anomaly detection on drone forensic timeline with sigma rules. In: 2023 International Conference on Emerging Smart Computing and Informatics (ESCI), pp. 1–5 (2023)
13. Studiawan, H., Sohel, F.: Anomaly detection in a forensic timeline with deep autoencoders. J. Inf. Secur. Appl. **63**, 103002 (2021)
14. Studiawan, H., Sohel, F., Payne, C.: Automatic event log abstraction to support forensic investigation. In: Proceedings of the Australasian Computer Science Week Multiconference, pp. 1–9 (2020)
15. Thaler, S., Menkonvski, V., Petković, M.: Towards a neural language model for signature extraction from forensic logs. In: Proceedings of the 5th International Symposium on Digital Forensic and Security, pp. 1–6 (2017)

Innovative SQL Query Generator Using an Arabic Language Description

Salma Salah Ounifi, Mohamed Samir Elbuni, and Yousef Omran Gdura[✉]

Faculty of Engineering, Computer Engineering Department, University of Tripoli, Tripoli, Libya
{s.ounifi,m.elbuni,y.gdura}@uot.edu.ly

Abstract. This paper presents the development of an advanced system designed to efficiently process Arabic queries in today's data-driven landscape. By using the T5 sequence-to-sequence model developed by Google and fine-tuning it specifically for transforming textual and verbal input into SQL queries, the system becomes adept at accurately comprehending and interpreting Arabic queries.

The resulting system serves as a user-friendly tool that automates the generation of SQL queries. Users can input their queries in written or recorded Arabic utterances, eliminating the need for manual translation and query construction.

This involved fine-tuning T5 models on a SQL dataset, splitting the dataset, tokenizing it, and setting training parameters. The implementation phase included loading the fine-tuned model, which incorporated PICARD to generate valid queries effectively. This paper also explores the impact of Arabic translation on the performance and accuracy of the model.

The optimal testing on test set accuracy achieved was 63.11%, the real-world testing accuracy: T5-base without PICARD scored 56.96% and 51.36% on English and Arabic questions, respectively, while T5-large with PIARCD scored 77.74% and 70.34% on English and Arabic questions.

Keywords: databases · SQL · machine learning · T5 · Transfer learning · model training · fine tuning · spider dataset · Hugging Face Hub

1 Introduction

Retrieving information from databases can be a complex and challenging task, particularly when users should be familiar with the underlying data structure. Relational databases, which organize related data into tables linked by shared attributes, offer a common data structure. This structure enables users to search across multiple tables with a single query, facilitating comprehension of data relationships (PHILLIPS 2022).

However, non-experts or casual users often find themselves overwhelmed by the technical complexities of formal query languages (Stockinger, Affolter and Bernstein 21 June 2019). Even experts may face time constraints when constructing the necessary queries. Consequently, there is a pressing need for an automatic SQL query system that can map natural language utterances to SQL queries. This approach has attracted significant attention from both the database and natural language processing communities.

© The Author(s), under exclusive license to Springer Nature Switzerland AG 2024
T. A. T. Benmusa et al. (Eds.): ILCICT 2023, CCIS 2097, pp. 130–144, 2024.
https://doi.org/10.1007/978-3-031-62624-1_11

The current automatic SQL query systems or text-to-text transformers are based on the transfer learning technique that has emerged as a powerful technique in Natural Language Processing (NLP), which is a prominent field within Artificial Intelligence (AI) that plays a vital role in Human-Computer Interaction.

The transfer learning involves training a neural network on one task and subsequently adapting or fine-tuning it for a new task. This approach allows the network to leverage the knowledge acquired from the original task. The process of transfer learning consists of two primary steps. Initially, the models are trained on large-scale datasets, typically encompassing millions of features. This stage, known as pretraining, aims to impart the models with fundamental data features. Subsequently, the pretrained models can be fine-tuned on a downstream task using a comparatively smaller set of labeled examples. Notably, fine-tuned models frequently achieve higher accuracy levels compared to supervised models trained from scratch with an equivalent quantity of labeled data.

However, in the field of NLP, there are various sequence-to-sequence (seq2seq) models available, such as Bart and T5. For our proposed approach, we have chosen to implement T5 as our seq2seq model. T5, short for Text-To-Text Transfer Transformer, was introduced in a paper by (Shazeer, et al. n.d.). T5 is an encoder-decoder model that has been pre-trained on a mixture of unsupervised and supervised tasks, where each task is transformed into a text-to-text format.

Thus, the objective of this paper is to leverage machine-learning techniques and develop an AI model that assists both novice and expert Arabic-speaking users in working with and manipulating SQL databases through a natural language interface. By bridging the gap between human language and database queries, the system simplifies the interaction process and enhance usability for various users.

This research paper is structured into five sections that contribute to the comprehensive presentation of the study. Section 2 critically examines previous approaches undertaken to attain the primary objective of the paper, alongside a detailed analysis of their outcomes. In Sect. 3, the paper methodology is introduced, explaining the diverse strategies employed to accomplish the desired outcomes. Section 4 focuses on the implementation approach, encompassing a comprehensive discussion of the obtained results, the testing process, and the evaluation of the proposed approach. Lastly, Sect. 5 concludes the paper by offering concluding remarks on the research findings and initiates a discussion on potential avenues for future work.

2 Literature Review

This section provides an overview of the techniques introduced in recent years to accomplish the primary objective of this study, which is text-to-SQL conversion.

The LUNAR and LADDER systems were among the pioneering database NLP systems designed to cater to non-technical users, enabling them to pose natural language queries about moon rock samples and US Navy ships, respectively, during the 1970s (Kaur and Bali n.d.) (Baig, et al. 2022).

In 2008, the Arabic Query Analyzer (AQA) was introduced as a retrieval system for Arabic language queries, distinct from traditional SQL queries. AQA relies on a stem-based morphological analyzer that necessitates a lexicon encompassing all existing stems in Arabic. The effectiveness of AQA depends on the clarity of the user's query and the robustness of the database structure. Notably, AQA offers users flexibility by allowing the use of alternative words. For instance, an employee's address can be queried using different Arabic words. An advantage of the AQA system is its independence from the underlying database. Consequently, any modifications made to the database structure do not impact its performance. Furthermore, AQA is domain-agnostic, capable of implementation on any database schema (Otair, Al-Sardi and Al-Gialain 2008).

The paper titled "Formation of SQL from Natural Language Query using NLP" (Uma M 2019) published in 2019, presents an overview of how regular expressions and NLP techniques are employed to translate English language queries into SQL. In this proposed system, users submit English queries in text format, which are subsequently processed by multiple NLP modules. Following the NLP phase, a mapping process identifies the attributes in the English query, maps them to construct the final SQL query, and executes it against the database to retrieve the desired information for the user. However, a limitation of this system is that it was trained using only a single table (Uma M 2019).

Various Datasets were introduced in the field of text-to-SQL generation such as ATIS, GeoQuery and WikiSQL (Hemphill, Godfrey and Do n.d.) (Zelle and Mooney 1996) & (Zhong, Xiong and Socher 2019). These datasets have two shortcomings:

- First, datasets containing complex programs are often insufficient in terms of the number of programs required to train modern data-intensive models, and they typically consist of a single dataset where the same database is used for both training and testing the model.
- Second, Existing datasets with a high number of programs and databases, such as WikiSQL (Zhong, Xiong and Socher 2019), are mostly made up of basic SQL queries and single tables (Yu, et al. 2018).

To evaluate a model's semantic parsing performance on unseen complex programs and its generalizability across new domains, it is crucial to have a dataset encompassing several complex programs and databases with multiple tables. The Spider dataset, introduced in 2019, addresses this need by offering a large and intricate cross-domain dataset for semantic parsing, specifically for the text-to-SQL task. (Yu, et al. 2018).

In the published paper (Rajkumar, Li and Bahdanau 2022), an empirical evaluation of the Text-to-SQL capabilities of the Codex language model (Yu, et al. 2018) is conducted. Codex is a large neural network currently available through a private beta test, designed to translate natural language instructions into code (Trummer 2022). It serves as a strong baseline on the Spider benchmark (Rajkumar, Li and Bahdanau 2022). The paper compares the Codex model to recent advances in the broader field, which demonstrate that scaling training data and model size for generative language models can enable advanced capabilities such as few-shot learning (Paredes and Torr n.d.) without the need for fine-tuning, similar to Codex and GPT-3 (Yu, et al. 2018) (OpenAI n.d.). Additionally, the results of the two models are compared to fine-tuned versions of the Encoder-decoder model T5 (Shazeer, et al. n.d.) and BRIDGE v2 (Victoria, et al. 2020) a sequence-to-sequence model based on BERT (Devlin, et al. n.d.).

3 Methodology

The methodology employed in our work primarily focuses on fine-tuning a pre-trained model using transfer learning for text-to-SQL tasks, using a dataset that provides relevant Text-SQL examples to facilitate effective model training. Additionally, we developed a web application interface that enables users to provide their information through oral or written means, enhancing versatility and user-friendliness.

The methodology consists of the following steps, as depicted in the diagram shown in Fig. 1:

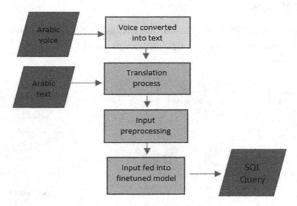

Fig. 1. Project methodology

3.1 Transcription and Translation Process

In the transcription process, a recorded audio is converted into text using the OpenAi whisper model that was introduced in the paper (Radford, et al. 2022). We chose the whisper model based on its superior characteristics including being open source, supporting multitask training, being multilingual, exhibiting excellent performance, and using diverse data for training.

For the translation process, we utilized a pretrained model specifically trained for machine translation tasks. We selected the model version that receives Arabic as the source language and English as the target language, aligning with our goals. The chosen model is named Helsinki-NLP/opus-mt-ar-en (Arabic Translation model Helsinki-NLP, available on hugging face hub n.d.), and is characterized by its small size, high accuracy, and the flexibility to accept English as the source language without compromising the translation process, thus enhancing its usability.

3.2 Input Preprocessing

Prior to feeding the translated text into the model, we performed preprocessing steps to prepare the input. These steps involve adding a prefix, tokenization, and setting model-specific features. The preprocessing phase significantly impacts the model's performance, as these hyperparameters influence the model's generation process and must be carefully chosen.

The prefix for our project is English-To-SQL, this prefix is prepended to the translated text before the tokenization step.

3.3 Finetuning Process

The selected model has undergone fine-tuning using the Spider Dataset (Yu, et al. 2018). Figure 2 shows the main steps of the fine-tuning process.

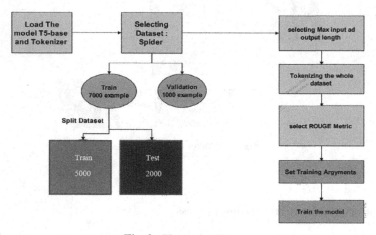

Fig. 2. Finetuning Process

3.3.1 Loading Model

Loading the model using hugging Face Hub is a much easier task since it requires only accessing model checkpoint (name) on the Hub. (T5 base model source on hugging face hub n.d.) Model checkpoint is T5-base.

3.3.2 Selecting Dataset

In this project, we selected Spider dataset. It is a large-scale, complex and cross-domain semantic parsing and text-to-SQL dataset annotated by 11 college students (Yu, et al. 2018). It consists of 8000 questions and SQL queries on 160 databases with multiple tables, covering different domains. Spider Dataset is divided into two sub sets:

1. A training subset that consists of 7000 samples on 140 different databases distributed randomly.

2. A validation subset contains 1034 samples on 20 databases

In our work, we chose an 8-batch size for our implementation. Testing size is 2000, validation size is 1000, and training size is 5000. Based on the size of the entire dataset: 25%, 12.5%, and 62.5% respectively.

3.3.3 Setting the Max. Input and Output Length

Since the length of dataset samples varies, it is important to determine the maximum question and query length as well as the ideal length that produces the best results. To achieve this, we utilized a statistical data visualization library; called Seaborn, to plot the number of tokens of inquiries and queries against their count as shown in Fig. 3. This finding led us to set the model's maximum input length at 512 tokens in order to give the user more freedom, and the model max input length is set to 256 tokens because the most.

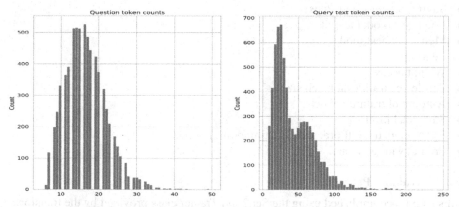

Fig. 3. Query and Question token length in the training set

3.3.4 Tokenizing the Dataset

Models do not accept regular data, so the input must be converted into a readable format by the model which is called tokenization. Datasets module provides a powerful function called *map*; this function supports processing batches of examples at once which speeds up tokenization.

3.3.5 Selecting Computing Metrics

To evaluate our model performance and results, we used ROUGE as a recall metric. ROUGE, which stands for Recall-Oriented Understudy for Gisting Evaluation, is a set of metrics and a software package used for evaluating automatic summarization and machine translation software in natural language processing. Thus, ROUGE fulfilled the goal of this paper because we wanted to put our model's ability to generate SQL queries as references to the test as much as possible. Our proposed program computing metrics are ROUGE-1/ROUGE-2/ROUGE-L's F1 score.

ROUGE-1, ROUGE-2, and ROUGE-L are metrics that compare an automatic summary or translation with a human reference by counting the number of matching words or phrases. ROUGE-1 counts each word, ROUGE-2 counts two consecutive words, and ROUGE-L counts the longest sequence of words in order. These metrics help evaluate the quality of automatic summarization and machine translation systems.

3.3.6 Set Training Arguments

To set the training arguments for our seq2seqmodel t5-base, we used the class Seq2SeqTrainingArguments provided by Transformers library. The parameters that were defined to control our training process are:

- Output Dir
- Evaluation strategy and steps
- Saving Strategy and steps
- Load best model at end
- Metric for best model
- Learning rate
- Weight decay
- Per device train/eval batch size
- Amount of training epochs
- Save total limit
- Fp16 refers to Half precision floating point Format
- Predict with generate.

3.3.7 Training Process

This step is accomplished using the Seq2Seq Trainer class provided by the transformer library, we pass all our prepared arguments to this class and train the model The necessary parameters to train any model are: model check point, training arguments training dataset, evaluation dataset, data collator and tokenizer.

3.4 The User Interface

Our user interface was developed using Gradio package, which allows researchers to generate a visual interface for their ML models (Abid, et al. n.d.) to improve accessibility and facilitate collaboration. Our interface consists of two main Markdowns: With PICARD, Without PICARD. PICARD is discussed in the next chapter.

4 Results and Discussion

This section presents and discusses the experimental results obtained by our proposed model. We begin by discussing fine-tuning of different versions of our model on the suggested dataset. Then we talk about the training and testing process and compare our results to the performance of other models.

4.1 Finetuning and Implementation

We used the transfer learning technique and adapted the T5 pre-trained model to be fine-tuned on our task; a text-to-SQL generation system.

The T5 model comes in various versions with variety of sizes and parameter counts. We ran our proposed fine-tuning process on the two versions of the T5 model, which are listed in Table 1, with 3, 8, and 12 epochs. Our test set was used to evaluate the model's performance and ability to generate new queries to previously unseen questions.

Table 1. T5 model

Model name	Size	Number of parameters
T5-Base	892 MB	220 million
T5-large	2.95 GB	770 million

The following two chapters present the results obtained in the finetuning and Testing process using the T5-Base and T5_large versions.

4.2 T5-Base

Finetuning T5-Base

Table 2 shows the results of passing the T5-Base model through the finetuning process stages to produce the finetuned model with a different number of epochs each time.

Table 2. T5-Base Finetuning results

Num of epochs	ROUGE-1	ROUGE-2	ROUGE-L
3	56.36%	36.85%	53.91%
8	58.29%	39.89%	55.92%
12	58.14%	40.24%	55.85%

Remark: These result shows that increasing the number of epochs has little effect on the model training accuracy. Training with 8 epochs yielded the best results.

Testing T5-Base

The results of testing the model T5-base with various numbers of epochs are shown in Table 3.

Remark: The results in Table 3 shows that increasing the number of epochs has had an effect on testing accuracy. The 12-epoch finetuned version produced the best test accuracy.

Table 3. T5-base Test Results

Num of epochs	ROUGE-1	ROUGE-2	ROUGE-L
3	55.58%	36.65%	53.176%
8	59.0205%	42.84%	55.924%
12	63.11%	50.52%	61.22%

4.3 T5-Large

The T5-large model is larger than the T5-Base, and therefore the training and testing took longer time. Due to this matter, the testing process of T5-Large version was not complete, and we tested only the 3-epoch version.

Finetuning T5-Large
Table 4 summarizes the T5-large finetuning results:

Table 4. T5-Large finetuning results

Num of epochs	ROUGE-1	ROUGE-2	ROUGE-L
3	58.96%	40.73%	56.62%
8	59.32%	41.76%	50.06%
12	59.72%	41.23%	56.91%

Remarks on T5-Large
As shown in Table 4, the increase in the number of epochs has little effect on model behavior. The optimal performance was again achieved using 8 epochs training, but the difference is so small that it can be ignored.

Testing T5-Large
Unfortunately, testing T5-Large was halted due to model size, which caused RAM to crash during the session. Thus, we tested only the 3-epoch version on the spider test set. ROUGE-1, ROUGE-2, and ROUGE-L, and their accuracy was 60.14%, 43.97%, and 58%, respectively.

4.4 Testing Other Models

We tested other models on our test set to compare their performance, and we also tested T5-base and T5-large checkpoints without any further finetuning to highlight the effect of the finetuning process on the spider dataset. Table 5 summarizes the testing results by each model. Note here that the T5-small model was fine-tuned using the spider dataset (t5-small-finetuned-spider model n.d.).

Table 5. Testing other models results

Model	ROUGE-1	ROUGE-2	ROUGE-L
Finetuned T5-Base	63.11%	50.52%	61.22%
Finetuned T5-Large	60.14%	43.97%	58%
T5-base	5.633%	0.679%	5.3817%
T5-Large	5.305%	0.5586%	5.09%
T5-small finetuned -spider	64.11%	52.17%	62.29%

Remark: Our baselines are the optimal versions achieved with T5-base finetuned with 12 Epochs and T5-large finetuned with 3 Epochs.

4.5 Finetuned Models with PICARD

In previous sections, we discussed model performance in the context of the Spider dataset; however, in real life, the model must generalize to different database schemas and questions. PICARD was first mentioned in a paper (Scholak, Schucher and Bahdanau 2021).PICARD, is an incremental parsing method for constraining auto-regressive decoders of language models. PICARD aids in the discovery of valid output sequences by rejecting invalid tokens at each decoding step. (Scholak, Schucher and Bahdanau 2021).

For real-world testing, we created a small database with the schema shown in Fig. 4 which was passed to the model and tested using 10 manually written queries. Then, compare the results to the correct queries.

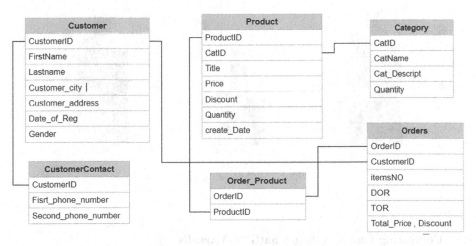

Fig. 4. User interface Database schema

4.6 User Interface Implementation

In the previous section, we discussed the proposed interface. In this section, we will put it into action using our baseline and PICARD model, and then present the results.

Using 10 questions, interacted with the interface. Each question was asked in both English and Arabic. To highlight the impact of the translation stage.

We calculated model accuracy using manually written queries as references, and we used the ROUGE metric that we had previously used in the testing step. Our implementation accuracy is summarized in Table 6.

Table 6. Models' accuracy

Metric	T5-base accuracy		T5-large WITH PICARD (Finetuned weights for PICARD based on T5 large model source n.d.)	
	English	Arabic	English	Arabic
ROUGE-1	57.37%	51.36%	77.74%	70.34%
ROUGE-2	27.59%	24.04%	63.74%	48.98%
ROUGE-L	55.04%	48.43%	76.39%	66.95%

The Arabic translation step impacted question clarity and information availability, lowering model performance and accuracy. Figure 5 illustrates the model comparison.

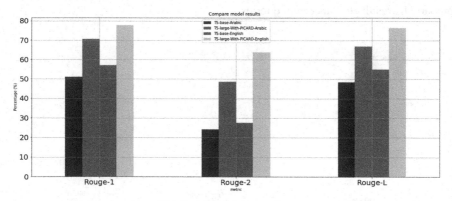

Fig. 5. Models' comparison

4.7 Comparing Our Results to ChatGPT-3 Results

Chat GPT is a trained model by OPENAI (ChatGPT-3: Optimizing Language Models for Dialogue n.d.) which interacts in a conversational way. The dialog format makes it possible for ChatGPT to answer follow-up questions, admit its mistakes, challenge incorrect premises, and reject inappropriate requests. ChatGPT is a sibling model of InstructGPT, which is trained to react to a prompt with a detailed response (ChatGPT-3: Optimizing Language Models for Dialog n.d.).

For our implementation, we used the prefix: Generate SQL query prepended to the question to specify the task to the ChatGPT-3 to generate a suitable answer. The testing process was accomplished using the Telegram API provided by open AI.

We tested this model on our real-world test database by asking the same 10 queries in both Languages English and Arabic and compared the results with our previously discussed results. Table 7 presents ChatGPT-3 results compared to T5-large with PICARD results.

Table 7. ChatGPT-3 results

Metric	ChatGPT-33		T5-large WITH PICARD (Finetuned weights for PICARD based on T5 large model source n.d.)	
	English	Arabic	English	Arabic
ROUGE-1	58.24%	57.58%	77.74%	70.34%
ROUGE-2	29.97%	33.95%	63.74%	48.98%
ROUGE-L	55.96%	54.88%	76.39%	66.95%

5   Conclusion

5.1 Summary

Interacting with databases is a critical ability that has grown in importance in recent years due to the rising need for different sorts of databases to store any form of data. SQL is a challenging language to master since it needs practice as well as knowledge of the database with which we are interacting. Because SQL is a schema-dependent language, the same query can be asked of two distinct databases, but the results will be different because the relationships between the database's entities are not the same.

The main goal of this research is to make it easier for casual database users to access any database and quickly retrieve the required information. We were able to create a user-friendly web app interface for accessing any database by utilizing machine learning technology. We tested our technique using a sample database that we developed for the sake of applying our work. By simply navigating the interface's tabs, we were able to connect with the information in our database via text input or recorded vocal input.

In summary, our work was divided into two parts: finetuning and testing the various T5 models on a SQL dataset, and implementing the finetuned model on a generalized database. The first part involved loading the model and tokenizer, selecting the spider dataset, and splitting it into three independent subsets: training, validation, and testing. After that, we set the maximum input and output lengths because they were important inputs to both the model and the tokenizer. Tokenizing the entire dataset, selecting the compute metric to be used in measuring model accuracy across all project steps, preparing the data loader, data collators, and optimizer, setting training arguments, and finally starting the training process with the train subset.

After fine-tuning the model, we tested it against the test-set to determine testing accuracy. T5-large with 8 epochs achieved an optimal training accuracy of 59.27%, while T5-base with 12 epochs achieved optimal testing accuracy of 63.11%.

The second step involved loading a model that had been fine-tuned on the spider dataset but had an important feature: its training process included PICARD, so the model's outputs are dependent on a schema that was passed to the model in addition to the user input. This step was completed to demonstrate the impact of PICARD on the generation of valid queries with valid attributes.

T5-base without PICARD scored 56.96% on English and 51.36% on Arabic questions, but T5-large with PICARD scored 77.74% and 70.34% on English and Arabic questions, respectively. The Arabic translation stage had an impact on question clarity and information availability, which resulted in worse model performance and accuracy.

5.2 Future Work

This field has grown tremendously in recent years, and many studies could be conducted to improve the accuracy and generalization of the model to any database schema. The emergence of advanced machine learning libraries and applications, on the other hand, provides improved toolkits that could be used to drive further research and development in NLI:

- Improving the training process in order to produce more generalized models.
- Connecting query execution to the NLI interface provides a more clear and direct visualization of database contents to the user.
- Greater flexibility by allowing other programming languages besides SQL to be generated based on user input.
- Instead of relying solely on T5 model, which is pre-trained exclusively on English text, our approach can be implemented using multilingual models. For instance, mT5 is a suitable alternative as it has been pre-trained on a diverse dataset encompassing 101 languages. This broader linguistic coverage enhances the model's capability to handle multilingual contexts effectively.

References

Kaur, S., Bali, R.S.: SQL generation and execution from natural language processing. Int. J. Comput. Bus. Res. (n.d.)

Zelle, J., Mooney, R.J.: Learning to Parse Database Queries Using Inductive Logic Programming. Department of Computer Sciences University of Texas, Department of Mathematics and Computer Science Drake University, 24 August (1996). https://www.semanticscholar.org/paper/Learning-to-Parse-Database-Queries-Using-Inductive-Zelle-Mooney/b7c0e47f8b76 8258b7d536c21b218e6c46ab8791?p2df

Abid, A., Abdalla, A., Abid, A., Khan, D., Alfozan, A., Zou, J.: Gradio: hassle-free sharing and testing of ML models in the wild (n.d.). https://arxiv.org/abs/1906.02569

Arabic Translation model Helsinki-NLP. Hugging face hub (n.d.). https://huggingface.co/Helsinki-NLP/opus-mt-ar-en

Baig, M.S., Imran, A., Yasin, A.U., Butt, A.H., Khan, M.I.: Natural language to SQL query: a review. Islamabad: Department of Creative Technologies Faculty of Computing & AI, Air University, Avai (2022)

ChatGPT-3: Optimizing Language Models for Dialogue. OpenAI (n.d.). https://openai.com/blog/chatgpt/

Devlin, J., Chang, M.-W., Lee, K., Toutanova, K.: BERT: pre-training of deep bidirectional transformers for language understanding (n.d.). https://arxiv.org/abs/1810.04805

Evaluating metric ROUGE (n.d.). https://huggingface.co/spaces/evaluate-metric/rouge

Finetuned weights for PICARD based on T5 large model source (n.d.). https://huggingface.co/tscholak/1wnr382e

Hemphill, C., Godfrey, J., Do, G.: The ATIS Spoken Language Systems Pilot Corpus. Texas Instruments Incorporated (n.d.). https://aclanthology.org/H90-1021.pdf

Hugging Face transformers community (n.d.). https://huggingface.co/

OpenAI. Language models are few-shot learners. OpenAI (n.d.). https://arxiv.org/pdf/2005.14165.pdf

Otair, M., Al-Sardi, R., Al-Gialain, S.: An Arabic retrieval system with native language rather than SQL queries. Arab Academy for Banking and Financial Sciences (2008)

Paredes, B.R., Torr, P.H.S.: An embarrassingly simple approach to zero-shot learning (n.d.)

PHILLIPS, ALEX: What is a Relational Database? Features & Uses, 5 January 2022. https://www.salesforce.com/uk/blog/2022/01/what-is-a-relational-database.html

Radford, A., Wook, K.J., Xu, T., Brockman, G., McLeavey, C., Sutskever, I.: Robust speech recognition via large-scale weak supervision, 6 December 2022. https://arxiv.org/pdf/2212.04356.pdf

Rajkumar, N., Li, R., Bahdanau, D.: Evaluating the text-to-SQL capabilities of large language models. University of Cambridge, ServiceNow, Mila, McGill University, Canada CIFAR AI Chair (2022)

Batista, D.S.: The Attention mechanism in natural language processing - seq2seq. The attention mechanism in natural language processing - seq2seq (davidsbatista.net), 25 January 2020

Scholak, T., Schucher, N., Bahdanau, D.: PICARD: parsing incrementally for constrained autoregressive decoding from language models. ElementAI, ServiceNow company, 10 September 2021. https://arxiv.org/pdf/2109.05093.pdf

Seaborn for statistical data visualization (n.d.). https://seaborn.pydata.org/

Shazeer, N., ct al.: Exploring the limits exploring the limits of transfer learning with a unified text-to-text transformer (n.d.)

Spider dataset documentation. Hugging Face hub (n.d.). https://huggingface.co/datasets/spider

Stockinger, K., Affolter, K., Bernstein, A.: A comparative survey of recent natural language interfaces for databases, 21 June 2019

T5 base model source on hugging face hub (n.d.). https://huggingface.co/t5-base

t5-small-finetuned-spider model. Hugging face hub (n.d.). https://huggingface.co/tomhavy/t5-small-finetuned-spider?text=hello

Trummer, I.: CodexDB: generating code for processing SQL queries using GPT-3Codex. Cornell University Ithaca, NewYork (2022)

Tunstall, L., von Werra, L., Wolf, T.: Natural language processing with transformers building language applications with hugging face, Chapter 1 (n.d.)

Uma, M., Sneha, V., Bhuvana, J., Bharati, B., Sneha, G.: Formation of SQL from natural language query using NLP. Computer Science and Engineering Sri Sivasubramaniya Nadar College of Engineering, Chennai, India (2019)

Vaswani, A., et al.: Attention is all you need. [1706.03762] (arxiv.org), 12 June 2017
Lin, X.V., Socher, R., Xiong, C.: Bridging textual and tabular data for cross-domain text-to-SQL semantic parsing. Salesforce research, 31 December 2020. https://arxiv.org/pdf/2012.12627. pdf
Yu, T., et al.: Spider: A Large-Scale Human-Labeled Dataset for Complex and Cross-Domain Semantic Parsing and Text-to-SQL Task (2018). https://paperswithcode.com/paper/spider-a-large-scale-human-labeled-dataset
Zhong, V., Xiong, C., Socher, R.: SEQ2SQL: generating structured queries from natural language using reinforcement learning. Salesforce research Palo Alto, CA, 9 November 2019. https://arxiv.org/pdf/1709.00103v7.pdf

Handling Imbalanced Datasets in Software Refactoring Prediction

Ali Aburas$^{(\boxtimes)}$

University of Tripoli, Al-Farnaj, Tripoli, Libya
al.aburas@uot.edu.ly

Abstract. Software refactoring modifies the internal structure of the software without changing its original functionality. Several studies used different machine learning classification algorithms to predict software refactoring opportunities for developers. However, the issue of an imbalanced dataset still needs to be addressed. An imbalanced dataset is a scenario that arises when we have unequal distribution of classes in a dataset. One way to balance a dataset is by adding instances to the minority class (Oversampling) or deleting instances from the majority class (Undersampling). In this paper, four popular techniques of both categories have been evaluated for their capability of improving the imbalanced ratio of highly imbalanced datasets belonging to software refactoring. We used eight publicly available datasets from Java open-source software systems. Four classification algorithms, Naive Bayes, SVM, Forest Trees, and Decision Tree, were applied to evaluate the results of each resampling technique. The experimental results show that oversampling techniques performed better than random undersampling. In particular, when the datasets were balanced with the synthetic minority oversampling technique (SMOTE), the random forest ML algorithm obtained higher scores in different evaluation metrics on all datasets.

Keywords: Imbalanced dataset · Resampling · Software Refactory

1 Motivation and Introduction

Software refactoring modifies the internal structure of the software without changing its original functionality [1]. Software refactoring is employed to improve the overall internal quality and reduce the complexity of the code [1]. However, identifying which code to be refactored represents a significant challenge to software developers. Researchers have applied different machine learning (ML) classification algorithms to predict refactoring opportunities to help developers apply refactoring techniques to improve software quality [1–3].

The results of a recent systematic literature review show an increase in the number of studies on automatic refactoring approaches [4]. Various ML classification algorithms, like Support Vector Machine (SVM), learn from datasets containing code metrics labeled with refactored and non-refactored instances.

© The Author(s), under exclusive license to Springer Nature Switzerland AG 2024
T. A. T. Benmusa et al. (Eds.): ILCICT 2023, CCIS 2097, pp. 145–158, 2024.
https://doi.org/10.1007/978-3-031-62624-1_12

Then, the resulting models predict the classes and methods that need refactoring. However, the issue of imbalanced datasets was not addressed, which is a known challenge in ML [5,6].

An ML classification algorithm learns from a large enough example input dataset or observation with the desired output or class. Then, the algorithm should find the patterns in the relevant input of each class and be able to predict or classify the unseen class considering their input [7]. The best example of a classification algorithm is spam email filtering, where the expected output is to classify an email as spam or not.

A training dataset (or training data) is the initial data used to train the classification algorithms. The training dataset consists of many examples from the problem domain with input data (e.g., features) and output data (e.g., class labels). However, imbalanced datasets are present in many real-world datasets, such as software refactoring, fraud detection, spam filtering, disease prediction, and hardware fault detection [8]. An imbalanced dataset is a scenario that arises when we have unequal distribution of class in a dataset, i.e., the number of samples in the negative class (majority class) is very large compared to that of the positive class (minority class). Imbalance datasets substantially compromise the learning process since most ML classification algorithms expect balanced class distribution [5]. Providing a balanced class distribution dataset to the classification algorithms will result in an optimal result [5].

To get a real feeling of the problem, we will use the Java-based antlr4 dataset containing method-level code metrics to predict whether a method is refactored. The antlr4 dataset was obtained from the PROMISE Repository [9]. The antlr4 dataset contains 96 columns and 3298 rows. Each column corresponds to a code metric (i.e., a feature), and every row represents the features of a method. The target column shows the refactored occurrence at the method level (indicated by '1') or not (indicated by '0'). The antlr4 dataset has 3258 rows, with a target of 0, and 40 rows have a target of 1. It means there were refactored occurrences in only 40 out of 3298 methods. As we can see, the degree of class imbalance for this dataset is very high, equal to 0.012. In other words, 98.8% of the samples belong to the majority class (non-refactored occurrence).

Let's build a model using a Support Vector Machine (SVM) [5] that learns from the antlr4 dataset and predicts whether a method was refactored or not. To this end, we split the antlr4 dataset into training data (80%) and testing data (20%). Then, we fit the SVM model on the training data. Finally, the SVM model uses the testing data to validate its prediction of whether a method was refactored or not.

If we measure the accuracy of the SVM model, we get 99%. However, if we compare it to the precision and recall, we will get 54 and 41, respectively. The recall metric shows that if there were only 100 methods that were refactored, the model only predicted 41 out of the 100 that needed refactored. Additionally, the precision metric shows that if there were only 100 methods that were not refactored, the model predicted 54 methods out of 100 that were refactored. For a developer, it is a waste of time and effort because the model predicts 54 methods that need to be refactored, and they are not. At the same time, the model misses 59 refactoring opportunities where the developer can apply the software refactoring.

This illustrates the SMV model does not perform well, even with high accuracy of 99%. We are getting very high accuracy because the model predicts mostly the majority class (non-refactored occurrence). Studies show that the model always predicts the majority class in a dataset with highly imbalanced classes but fails to predict the minority class [10–13]. As we can see, if the imbalanced data is not handled beforehand, this will impact the performance of the classifier model.

One popular approach to handling imbalanced datasets is resampling techniques. Resampling techniques modify the number of samples or instances in a dataset to balance the dataset [10, 14, 15]. Resampling techniques can be divided into two categories: undersampling and oversampling techniques. Undersampling reduces the data by removing samples from the majority class to balance the class distribution better. On the other hand, oversampling techniques involve adding new samples by randomly repeating some samples to the minority class to create a balance data distribution [8].

In this study, we use eight imbalanced datasets from software refactoring[1] (released in 2018) to investigate the impact of four resampling techniques (i.e., Random Undersampling, CNN, Random Oversampling, and SMOTE). Four ML classification algorithms: Naive Bayes, Support Vector Machine, Decision Tree, and Forest Trees, have been applied with different evaluation metrics to measure the effectiveness of the classification algorithms.

The paper is organized as follows: Section 2 discusses the relevant work to our study. Section 3 presents our methodology and evaluation metrics. Section 4 contains the experiment results. Finally, the conclusion and future work is provided in Sect. 5.

2 Related Work

In recent years, researchers have widely studied the challenges of imbalanced datasets. Authors in [16] studied various resampling techniques, including random undersampling, random oversampling, and SMOTE resampling technique. Their study used five imbalanced datasets from different application domains, including credit card fraud, bioassay, yeast bacteria, Satimage, and diabetes datasets. Their results show undersampling approaches give a better overall performance on all datasets. In [10], authors proposed a selective oversampling approach (SOA). They used an outlier detection technique to isolate the most representative data points from the minority class. Then, they used these data points for synthetic oversampling. To evaluate their approach SOA, four slightly different artificial datasets and four real-world datasets (Bankruptcy-manufacture, Bankruptcy-construction, Wine, and Bank marketing) were used for comparison.

---

[1] http://www.inf.u-szeged.hu/~ferenc/papers/RefactDataSet/.

Their results showed that SOA outperformed SMOTE resampling technique on four real-world datasets.

The authors in [13] conducted an experiment with oversampling and undersampling techniques on an imbalanced public dataset from the Kaggle website named *Santander Customer Transaction Prediction*. In addition, they measured different ML classification algorithms with varying evaluation metrics. Their results showed the oversampling technique outperformed the undersampling technique for different classifiers. Another study investigated the imbalanced datasets in educational data mining [17]. The study compared several resampling techniques, including random oversampling, random undersampling, and SMOTE, using the High School Longitudinal Study dataset. The Random Forest was used as a classification algorithm to evaluate the results of each resampling technique. Their results showed that random oversampling for highly imbalanced data worked best. Authors in [18] investigated the impact of different resampling methods on two datasets compromising network traffic. Their goal was to reduce the effect of dataset imbalance on developing effective supervisory control and data acquisition (SCADA) intrusion detection systems. They stated that both the dataset imbalance and the data quality affect the performance of the classifiers.

Our work differs from the previous studies because we use the datasets from the software refactoring domain to evaluate the performance of three resampling techniques: random oversampling, random undersampling, and SMOTE. To our knowledge, the study presented in this paper introduces a new research contribution. The results of the conducted experiments on real data in the software refactoring domain can serve the researchers who deal with imbalanced datasets in developing prediction algorithms in software refactoring.

3   Methodology

This paper aims to investigate the impact of imbalanced datasets on developing an effective ML classification algorithm in predicting software refactoring opportunities for developers. This section provides the steps needed to achieve the goal of this paper.

3.1   Datasets and Preprocessing

This study uses eight real-world datasets in the software refactoring field. These datasets were built from extracted OO metrics from four Java open-source software systems (i.e., antlr4, junit, mapdb, and mcMMO). The datasets were manually validated, and they only contain true positive refactoring instances attached to source code elements at the method and class levels [9]. These datasets were released in 2018 and are publicly available and provided by the PROMISE repository [9]. The datasets have been used in previous empirical studies [2,3]. Table 1 shows the attributes of the datasets, including the number of attributes, total number of instances, and number of instances belonging to the minority class, along with their imbalance Ratio. Minority class instances represent the refactored occurrence, while majority class instances represent the non-refactored occurrence.

Table 1. Detailed characteristic of datasets.

Dataset	Attributes	Instances	No. of Refactoring	Imbalance Ratio
DS1: antlr4-Class	137	436	23	5.28%
DS2: antlr4-Method	96	3298	40	1.21%
DS3: junit-Class	137	657	9	1.37%
DS4: junit-Method	96	2280	12	0.53%
DS5: mapdb-Class	137	439	4	0.91%
DS6: mapdb-Method	96	3501	3	0.09%
DS7: mcMMO-Class	137	301	4	1.33%
DS8: mcMMO-Method	96	2531	5	0.20%

The datasets contain different source code metrics like Code Complexity, Lines of Code, and Comment Lines Of Code. The code metrics were calculated at class and method levels [9]. Some unnecessary attributes, such as Long-Name, Parent, and Path, were removed during the dataset preprocessing. In addition, the attribute refact_sum, which represents the total number of refactoring occurrences, was replaced with 0 and 1, where refactored became 1 and non-refactored became 0 [1].

3.2 Resampling Methods

A widely adopted approach for dealing with highly imbalanced datasets is called resampling. It consists of removing samples (i.e., instances) from the majority class (undersampling) or adding more samples from the minority class (oversampling) to balance a dataset. Several undersampling techniques exist, such as random undersampling and condensed nearest neighbor. Examples of the oversampling technique are random oversampling and SMOTE [8]. We used the following resampling techniques that balance the class distribution in the imbalanced datasets [6,8].

1. **Random Undersampling (RUS).** It is one of the easiest undersampling methods to balance a dataset. In RUS, a few sampling from the majority class are randomly selected. Then, they are removed until the minority and majority classes have an equal distribution of data [8]. RUS could discard samples that could have important information.
2. **Condensed Nearest Neighbor (CNN).** CNN undersampling generates a subset of samples from the dataset such that for every sample in the subset nearest neighbor is of a different class. The goal of CNN is to eliminate the

redundant and noisy samples from the majority class [6]. The disadvantage of CNN is that it can be slower than other resampling techniques since it requires many iterates over the dataset [19].

3. **Random Oversampling (ROS).** Unlike undersampling, ROS randomly is a method that involves randomly adding samples from the minority class by replication [8]. However, ROS is prone to overfitting due to replicating the same samples.

4. **Synthetic Minority Oversampling Technique (SMOTE).** SMOTE oversampling generates synthetic samples of the minority class by choosing samples depending upon their nearest neighbors [20]. The SMOTE technique works in four steps. First, it identifies a random number of minority samples. Second, it calculates the distance between the chosen samples and their nearest neighbors (the number of neighbors is specified as an argument in the SMOTE() function as k). In the third step, it chooses one of the nearest neighbors to add new synthetic samples of the minority class. Finally, SMOTE repeats the steps until the dataset is balanced. The advantage of this approach is that it prevents the overfitting that ROS could cause [8,10].

3.3   Visualize the Distribution of Classes

To obtain some overview of class distribution after resampling methods discussed in the previous section (Sect. 3.2), we visualize the distribution of the antlr4-Method (D2) dataset before and after resampling (Fig. 1).

Figure 1(a) represents the visualization of the original imbalanced antlr4-Method (D2) dataset. We can see a large mass of samples (blue circles) for class 1 (non-refactored) and a small number of samples (orange circles) for class 1 (refactored). Figure 1(b) shows the dataset after RUS. The RUS decreased the majority class from 3298 to 40, the same as the minority class. Figure 1(c) shows the dataset after CNN undersampling. From the visualization, we can see that, as expected, only those samples in the majority class closest to the minority class examples in the overlapping area were retained.

Figure 1(d) illustrates the data distribution after ROS. After ROS, the minority class increased from 40 to 3298, the same as the majority class. Finally, Fig. 1 (e) illustrates the data distribution after SMOTE. Similar to random oversampling, the minority class increased from 40 to 3298 after SMOTE. Comparing the graph between ROS and SMOTE, we can see that the synthetic instances created by SMOTE are all along a line.

3.4   Classification Algorithms

To evaluate the effect of undersampling and oversampling methods reviewed in the previous section, we use four ML classification algorithms (i.e., classifiers): Naive Bayes [21], Support Vector Machine (SVM) [7], Random Forest (RF), and Decision Tree (DT) are discussed in [10, 22].

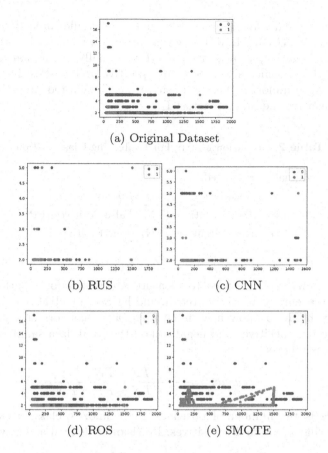

(a) Original Dataset

(b) RUS   (c) CNN

(d) ROS   (e) SMOTE

Fig. 1. Visualization of class distribution for antlr4-Method (D2) dataset (Color figure online)

3.5 Assessment Metrics

Choosing the evaluation metric is one of the most signification issues while working with imbalanced datasets [5]. This section explains the evaluation metrics we used to measure the prediction of classification algorithms' performance.

1. **Confusion Matrix** summarizes the performance of a classification algorithm and helps to understand what a classification algorithm predicts correctly and what errors it makes. The confusion matrix is a two-cross matrix detailed in Table 2. The rows represent the actual values of the outputs, whether or not the observations belong to a negative or a positive class. On the hand, the columns represent the predicted output of the classifier, whether the predicted value is in class negative or positive.

   The confusion matrix holds one of four outcomes. First, the actual value is negative, and the classifier also predicted a negative, a True Negative (TN).

Second, the actual value is a negative, but the classifier predicted a positive, a False Positive (FP). Third, the actual value is a positive, but the classifier predicted a negative, a False Negative (FN). Finally, the actual value is positive, and the classifier also predicted a positive, a True Positive (TP). This paper uses the minority class as positive (i.e., refactored) and the majority class as negative (i.e., non-refactored).

Table 2. Confusion Matrix For Evaluating Classification

Actual	Predicted	
	Negative	Positive
Negative	True Negatives (TN)	False Positives (FP)
Positive	False Negatives (FN)	True Positives (TP)

The confusion matrix is used to measure a classification's performance by calculating accuracy, precision, recall, and F1-Score metrics.

2. **Accuracy** helps to know how much a classifier has correctly predicted. It counts the true positives and negatives on the total data samples. Accuracy is defined as follows:

$$Accuracy = \frac{TP + TN}{TP + TN + FP + FN} \tag{1}$$

3. **Precision** is the number of positives (i.e., minority class) a classifier has predicted that are actually positives. Precision is defined as follows:

$$Precision = \frac{TP}{TP + FP} \tag{2}$$

4. **Recall** is the number of positives (i.e., minority class) a classifier has correctly predicted out of the total number of positives. Precision is defined as follows:

$$Recall = \frac{TP}{TP + FN} \tag{3}$$

5. **F1-Score** is the harmonic mean between precision and recall. It is better to optimize the F1-Score to achieve an optimal result.

$$F1 - Score = 2 * \frac{Precision * Recall}{Precision + Recall} \tag{4}$$

4   Experimental Results

This section presents the results of our experiment in predicting software refractories. The study used eight open-source imbalanced Java datasets to run through different sampling and classification algorithms.

The experiment was conducted on a computer with an i7-7700 CPU 3.60 GHz, 32 GB RAM, and a 64-bit Windows 10 Pro operating system. In addition, the classification algorithms have been applied using *scikits.learn* library in Python 3.11.3. The mean precision, recall, accuracy, and F1-Score have been computed using a five-fold stratified cross-validation with five repetitions. This means that 80% of the data is used for training, and 20% of the data is used for testing. The evaluation metrics and resampling methods in Python can be calculated and implemented using *scikits.learn* and *imbalanced-learn* libraries, respectively. Resampling methods are applied to the training dataset that can be used to train the classifiers. In addition, before training each classifier, a random search is performed for the best hyperparameters [23]. We used the randomized search algorithm provided by the *scikits.learn* library.

We conducted five experiments to evaluate the effect of imbalanced datasets. In the first experiment, we assessed the performance of classifiers using the imbalanced dataset without applying resampling techniques. The other four of our experiments were to sample the datasets using one of the resampling techniques as described in the previous Sect. 3.2. We discuss the evaluation of prediction performance and the results of each experiment in the following sections.

4.1   Results of the Imbalanced Datasets

In the first experiment, we run the classifiers before applying any resampling techniques to evaluate the impact of data imbalance on developing an effective classifier. A classifier without resampling techniques gives us a baseline to compare the classifier's performance.

Table 3. Evaluation metrics for the classifiers before applying resampling

Metrics	Classifier	Dataset							
		DS1	DS2	DS3	DS4	DS5	DS6	DS7	DS8
Accuracy	NB	0.88	0.95	0.88	0.47	0.90	1.00	0.87	0.66
	SVM	0.98	0.99	0.99	1.00	0.99	1.00	0.98	1.00
	RF	0.95	0.99	0.99	1.00	0.99	1.00	0.98	1.00
	DT	0.96	1.00	0.99	1.00	0.98	1.00	0.97	1.00
Precision	NB	0.36	0.21	0.21	0.00	0.18	0.00	0.00	0.00
	SVM	0.60	0.54	0.60	1.00	0.50	0.00	0.00	0.20
	RF	0.20	1.00	0.00	0.40	0.00	0.00	0.00	0.00
	DT	0.80	1.00	0.30	0.80	0.00	0.00	0.00	0.00
Recall	NB	0.98	0.95	0.80	1.00	0.80	0.00	0.20	0.50
	SVM	0.37	0.41	0.40	0.73	0.60	0.00	0.00	0.20
	RF	0.04	0.48	0.00	0.20	0.00	0.00	0.00	0.00
	DT	0.38	0.72	0.20	0.53	0.00	0.00	0.00	0.00
F1-Score	NB	0.50	0.32	0.32	0.00	0.26	0.00	0.00	0.00
	SVM	0.44	0.46	0.47	0.83	0.53	0.00	0.00	0.20
	RF	0.06	0.62	0.00	0.27	0.00	0.00	0.00	0.00
	DT	0.47	0.82	0.23	0.63	0.00	0.00	0.00	0.00

Table 3 shows the results of the performance ML classification algorithms before applying resampling methods to the datasets. It can be observed from the table that some models have high precision, but they are unable to predict any correct positive result. The accuracy of SVM, RF, and DT algorithms, in the case of highly imbalanced datasets, such as mapdb-Class (DS5), mapdb-Method (DS6), mcMMO-Class (DS7), and mcMMO-Method (DS8), are very high. But, the precision and recall scores are equal to 0. This was caused because few refactored occurrences exist in the mentioned datasets (less than ten instances). For example, the SVM classifier has a recall 0.20% on dataset D8. This means that around 20% of the minority class (i.e., refactored) is captured by the SVM classifier. This indicates that imbalanced datasets are problematic because they lead to inaccurate results [6, 8].

4.2   Results of the Undersampling

The imbalanced datasets were balanced in the second experiment using random undersampling (RUS). Table 4 showed the evaluation metrics of each classifier when we used the RUS technique. The results showed some improvement on the DS1, DS2, DS3, and DS4. We can notice that Naive Bayes (NB) got the highest score compared to the other classifiers. However, in the DS5, DS6, DS7, and DS8 datasets, the metrics score of the classifiers with RUS was equal to 0.00. The high ratio imbalance of those datasets probably caused this. ROS removes majority instances to make the majority class the same size as the minority class, which results in a significant data loss and yields an undersized dataset [13, 20].

Table 4. Evaluation metrics for the classifiers with RUS

Metrics	Classifier	Dataset							
		DS1	DS2	DS3	DS4	DS5	DS6	DS7	DS8
Accuracy	NB	0.83	0.91	0.46	0.80	0.00	0.00	0.00	0.00
	SVM	0.63	0.89	0.44	0.79	0.00	0.00	0.00	0.00
	RF	0.56	0.80	0.56	0.61	0.00	0.00	0.00	0.00
	DT	0.63	0.71	0.56	0.57	0.00	0.00	0.00	0.00
Precision	NB	0.83	0.89	0.43	0.83	0.00	0.00	0.00	0.00
	SVM	0.72	0.91	0.40	0.93	0.00	0.00	0.00	0.00
	RF	0.54	0.78	0.60	0.57	0.00	0.00	0.00	0.00
	DT	0.68	0.68	0.50	0.58	0.00	0.00	0.00	0.00
Recall	NB	0.89	0.92	0.43	0.80	0.00	0.00	0.00	0.00
	SVM	0.73	0.88	0.47	0.75	0.00	0.00	0.00	0.00
	RF	0.66	0.82	0.30	0.70	0.00	0.00	0.00	0.00
	DT	0.63	0.77	0.40	0.60	0.00	0.00	0.00	0.00
F1-Score	**NB**	**0.83**	**0.90**	**0.43**	**0.79**	**0.00**	**0.00**	**0.00**	**0.00**
	SVM	0.62	0.88	0.36	0.77	0.00	0.00	0.00	0.00
	RF	0.59	0.79	0.39	0.59	0.00	0.00	0.00	0.00
	DT	0.61	0.71	0.39	0.56	0.00	0.00	0.00	0.00

In our case, the DS5, DS6, DS7, and DS8 datasets contain a sample size that is way too small to represent the problem statistically.

In the third experiment, the datasets were balanced using the CNN technique. Table 5 shows the results of balancing datasets using the CNN technique. CNN obtained better results than the RUS in terms of accuracy. This was probably because the CNN technique removed the outliers to get minimal majority class samples. Although the CNN undersampling produced a better accuracy score than the RUS, the CNN technique produced a 0.00 F1-Score for datasets with high imbalance ratios, such as D5, D6, D7, and D8. This is because CNN produced datasets that are significantly smaller in size compared to the original dataset.

Table 5. Evaluation metrics for the classifiers with CNN

Metrics	Classifier	Dataset							
		DS1	DS2	DS3	DS4	DS5	DS6	DS7	DS8
Accuracy	NB	0.98	0.94	0.71	0.46	0.68	0.70	0.67	0.64
	SVM	0.82	0.98	0.78	0.95	0.68	0.87	0.64	0.86
	RF	0.76	0.91	0.75	0.86	0.60	0.87	0.64	0.82
	DT	0.68	0.94	0.76	0.41	0.62	0.95	0.47	0.82
Precision	NB	0.96	0.88	0.34	0.17	0.00	0.00	0.40	0.17
	SVM	0.63	1.00	0.40	0.80	0.00	0.00	0.00	0.20
	RF	0.77	0.77	0.00	0.20	0.00	0.00	0.00	0.00
	DT	0.46	0.98	0.13	0.58	0.00	0.40	0.00	0.00
Recall	NB	0.96	0.82	0.63	0.73	0.00	0.20	0.30	0.20
	SVM	0.53	0.89	0.17	0.53	0.00	0.00	0.00	0.10
	RF	0.27	0.49	0.00	0.10	0.00	0.00	0.00	0.00
	DT	0.45	0.65	0.20	0.41	0.00	0.40	0.00	0.00
F1-Score	**NB**	0.96	0.83	0.44	0.27	0.00	0.08	0.33	0.18
	SVM	0.57	0.94	0.23	0.61	0.00	0.00	0.00	0.13
	RF	0.37	0.59	0.00	0.13	0.00	0.00	0.00	0.00
	DT	0.37	0.77	0.16	0.38	0.00	0.40	0.00	0.00

4.3   Results of the Oversampling

In the third experiment, we applied the random oversampling technique (ROS), and the results improved dramatically for all the classifiers. We noticed that the evaluation metrics increased significantly to 1.00. However, the ROS technique may raise the likelihood of overfitting since it replicates exact copies of the minority class [13,20].

In our final experiment, we applied SMOTE technique to balance the datasets with the number of neighbors k = 3. The results obtained after performing the classifiers on the balanced datasets are shown in Table 6. It can be seen from the results SVM and DT provided similar results (accuracy, precision, recall, and F1 score). RF performed better in the F1-Score as compared to the other classifiers.

Table 6. Evaluation metrics for the classifiers with SMOTE

Metrics	Classifier	Dataset							
		DS1	DS2	DS3	DS4	DS5	DS6	DS7	DS8
Accuracy	NB	0.80	0.70	0.95	0.76	0.95	0.86	0.96	0.92
	SVM	0.98	0.98	0.99	0.99	1.00	1.00	0.99	1.00
	RF	0.98	1.00	1.00	1.00	1.00	1.00	0.99	1.00
	DT	0.95	0.98	0.98	0.99	0.99	1.00	0.98	0.86
Precision	NB	0.80	0.63	0.91	0.67	0.91	0.78	0.93	1.00
	SVM	0.99	0.98	1.00	0.98	1.00	1.00	0.99	1.00
	RF	0.97	0.99	1.00	1.00	1.00	1.00	1.00	1.00
	DT	0.92	0.98	0.97	0.99	0.99	1.00	0.97	1.00
Recall	NB	0.85	0.97	0.99	1.00	1.00	1.00	0.99	1.00
	SVM	0.98	0.99	0.99	1.00	1.00	1.00	0.99	1.00
	RF	0.99	1.00	1.00	1.00	1.00	1.00	0.99	1.00
	DT	0.98	0.99	1.00	0.99	0.99	1.00	0.99	1.00
F1-Score	NB	0.81	0.76	0.95	0.80	0.95	0.87	0.96	0.92
	SVM	0.98	0.98	0.99	0.99	1.00	1.00	0.99	1.00
	RF	**0.98**	**1.00**	**1.00**	**1.00**	**1.00**	**1.00**	**0.99**	**1.00**
	DT	0.95	0.98	0.98	0.99	0.99	1.00	0.98	1.00

This is because the RF classifier can handle large datasets and is less prone to overfitting [24].

5   Conclusions

This paper aimed to illustrate the impact of imbalanced datasets with different imbalance ratios on developing effective software refactoring prediction systems. To this end, we evaluated three resampling techniques (i.e., random undersampling, random oversampling, and SMOTE) in software refactoring classification tasks. We conducted four experiments by performing four ML classification algorithms (i.e., NB, SVM, DT, and RF) on eight publicly available datasets from the software refactoring domain. The experimental results show that oversampling techniques performed better than random undersampling. In particular, when the datasets were balanced with SMOTE, the random forest ML algorithm obtained higher scores in different evaluation metrics on all datasets. In addition, the results showed that if the original dataset has a small number of samples to represent the problem, then undersampling will increase the risk of overfitting. In particular, when the datasets were balanced with random undersampling, the evaluation metrics significantly dropped to zeros. This is because samples are removed from the majority class without knowing their usefulness in the dataset.

The results from this study could help researchers understand how the resampling methods work across datasets with different class imbalance ratios. Moreover, our results could help researchers apply the appropriate resampling techniques when creating software refactoring prediction systems. For future work, we plan to combine undersampling and oversampling methods and deep learning algorithms.

References

1. Kaur, S., Singh, P.: How does object-oriented code refactoring influence software quality? Research landscape and challenges. J. Syst. Softw. **157**, 110394 (2019)
2. Akour, M., Alenezi, M., Alsghaier, H.: Software refactoring prediction using SVM and optimization algorithms. Processes (8) 2022
3. Kataria, S., Subrahmanyam, V.V.: Software defects classification using RNN model. J. Algebraic Stat. **13**(3), 1208–1218 (2022)
4. Baqais, A., Alshayeb, M.: Automatic software refactoring: a systematic literature review. Software Qual. J. **28**, 06 (2020)
5. Zheng, M., Wang, F., Xiaowen, H., Miao, Y., Cao, H., Tang, M.: A method for analyzing the performance impact of imbalanced binary data on machine learning models. Axioms **11**(11), 607 (2022)
6. Fernández, A., García, S., Galar, M., Prati, R.C., Krawczyk, B., Herrera, F.: Learning from Imbalanced Data Sets. Springer, Cham (2018). https://doi.org/10.1007/978-3-319-98074-4
7. Cervantes, J., Garcia-Lamont, F., Rodríguez-Mazahua, L., Lopez, A.: A comprehensive survey on support vector machine classification: applications, challenges and trends. Neurocomputing **408**, 189–215 (2020)
8. Kulkarni, A., (Sondor) Chong, D., Batarseh, F.A.: Foundations of data imbalance and solutions for a data democracy. ArXiv, abs/2108.00071 (2021)
9. Hegedűs, P., Kádár, I., Ferenc, R., Gyimóthy, T.: Empirical evaluation of software maintainability based on a manually validated refactoring dataset. Inf. Softw. Technol. **95**, 313–327 (2018)
10. Gnip, P., Vokorokos, L., Drotár, P.: Selective oversampling approach for strongly imbalanced data. PeerJ Comput. Sci. **7**, e604 (2021)
11. Thabtah, F., Hammoud, S., Kamalov, F., Gonsalvesv, A.: Data imbalance in classification: experimental evaluation. Inf. Sci. **513**, 11 (2019)
12. Saini, M., Susan, S.: VGGIN-Net: deep transfer network for imbalanced breast cancer dataset. IEEE/ACM Trans. Comput. Biol. Bioinf. **20**(1), 752–762 (2023)
13. Mohammed, R., Rawashdeh, J., Abdullah, M.: Machine learning with oversampling and undersampling techniques: overview study and experimental results. In: 2020 11th International Conference on Information and Communication Systems (ICICS), pp. 243–248 (2020)

14. Kumar, P., Bhatnagar, R., Gaur, K., Bhatnagar, A.: Classification of imbalanced data: review of methods and applications. IOP Conf. Ser. Mater. Sci. Eng. **1099**(1), 012077 (2021)
15. Le, T., Vo, M.T., Vo, B., Lee, M.Y., Baik, S.W.: A hybrid approach using oversampling technique and cost-sensitive learning for bankruptcy prediction. Complexity **2019** (2019)
16. Tyagi, S., Mittal, S.: Sampling approaches for imbalanced data classification problem in machine learning. In: Singh, P.K., Kar, A.K., Singh, Y., Kolekar, M.H., Tanwar, S. (eds.) Proceedings of ICRIC 2019. LNEE, vol. 597, pp. 209–221. Springer, Cham (2020). https://doi.org/10.1007/978-3-030-29407-6_17
17. Wongvorachan, T., He, S., Bulut, O.: A comparison of undersampling, oversampling, and smote methods for dealing with imbalanced classification in educational data mining. Information **14**, 54 (2023)
18. Balla, A., Habaebi, M.H., Elsheikh, E.A.A., Islam, M.R., Suliman, F.M.: The effect of dataset imbalance on the performance of SCADA intrusion detection systems. Sensors **23**(2) (2023)
19. More, A.: Survey of resampling techniques for improving classification performance in unbalanced datasets. CoRR, abs/1608.06048 (2016)
20. Douzas, G., Bacao, F., Last, F.: Improving imbalanced learning through a heuristic oversampling method based on K-means and smote. Inf. Sci. **465**, 1–20 (2018)
21. Zhang, H.: The optimality of Naive Bayes, vol. 2 (2004)
22. Aniche, M., Maziero, E., Durelli, R., Durelli, V.H.S.: The effectiveness of supervised machine learning algorithms in predicting software refactoring. IEEE Trans. Softw. Eng. **48**(4), 1432–1450 (2020)
23. Bergstra, J., Bengio, Y.: Random search for hyper-parameter optimization. J. Mach. Learn. Res. **13**(2) (2012)
24. Wyner, A.J., Olson, M., Bleich, J., Mease, D.: Explaining the success of AdaBoost and random forests as interpolating classifiers. J. Mach. Learn. Res. **18**(1), 1558–1590 (2017)

KnowAir: A Low-Cost PM2.5 Sensor Citizen-Based Air Pollution Monitoring System for Real-Time

Eiman M. Saleh$^{(\boxtimes)}$ ⑩, Sarah Al-Werfalli, Tariq Imbarak, Salwa Elakeili, and Howayda Elmajpri

Benghazi University, Benghazi, Libya
{eiman.sahly,itstd.2929,tariq.ambark,Salwa.elakeili, howayda.elmajpri}@uob.edu.ly

Abstract. Air pollution poses the world's most significant environmental health risk to people everywhere. According to certain World Health Organization (WHO) estimates, air pollution exposure results in millions of premature deaths each year, with children under five making up a significant portion of these fatalities. While it is estimated that more than 90% of the world's population lives in areas of dangerously high levels of air pollution. In order to recognize and understand air quality trends, access to real-time air quality data is essential. Thus, there is an urgent need to fill the gaps in this data with more low-cost air quality monitoring stations. In this paper, a health-oriented air quality monitoring prototype was developed, as well as air quality data collection using low-cost PM2.5 sensors. The study aims to raise citizens' awareness of the dangers of pollution by giving them real-time readings. And providing community service to protect people with cardiovascular diseases and those directly affected by the COVID-19 crisis, by means of an effective tool that avoids exposure to high levels of outdoor air pollution. The study is designed according to the health organization's guidelines. This study describes the methodology used to develop this system along with some results of the primary data analysis. The city of Benghazi is taken as a case study.

Keywords: Air Quality Monitoring · Particulate Matters (PM) · Pollution Monitoring · PM2.5 Sensor · Public Health

1 Introduction

Air is an essential element of life, and air pollution poses a major threat to health and the climate. According to the World Health Organization (WHO) [1], an estimated 7 million people die annually due to stroke, heart disease, lung cancer, and acute and chronic respiratory diseases. Respiratory diseases are one of the leading causes of death worldwide and include conditions such as chronic obstructive pulmonary disease, asthma, and pneumonia. Recently, the number of cases of pneumonia caused by the coronavirus has increased in light of the outbreak of the COVID-19 pandemic. Exposure to air pollution causes, in children, reduced lung growth and function, respiratory infections, and

T. A. T. Benmusa et al. (Eds.): ILCICT 2023, CCIS 2097, pp. 159–172, 2024.
https://doi.org/10.1007/978-3-031-62624-1_13

exacerbation of asthma. According to WHO estimates [2], more than 80% of asthma deaths occur in developing countries. While ischemic heart disease, stroke, diabetes, and neurodegenerative conditions are among the most common causes of premature death in adults when exposed to outdoor air pollution [3].

The airborne matter particles may be categorized into three groups based on their micrometer diameter: PM10 (2.5 μm to 10 μm), PM2.5 (2.5 μm), and PM1.0 (1.0 μm). Figure 1 shows a comparison of the size between the average diameter of human hair (~70 μm) and fine beach sand (~90 μm) against PM2.5 and PM10.

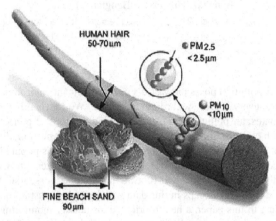

Fig. 1. Shows a comparison of the size of PM2.5 and PM10 against the average diameter of a human hair (~70 μm) and fine beach sand (~90 μm) [4].

The PM2.5 is considered the most harmful to human health and is one of the causes of early death, because it is able to penetrate the lungs and bloodstream, affecting the heart, blood vessels, and respiratory system, stroke and cause lung cancer [3, 5, 6]. The latest estimates from the WHO [1], indicate that about 99% of the world's population lives in places with air pollution above the recommended air quality guidelines. As confirmed by recent studies [7–10], air pollution is an important factor in increasing the infection rate and death rate with the COVID-19 virus. Recent years have seen the number of air quality monitoring stations grow, while a worrying number of cities still do not have air quality monitoring, these communities are expected to face high levels of pollution. According to WHO's database [11], Fig. 2 shows the location of PM2.5 pollution concentration monitoring stations in the world. The reasons for the uneven global distribution of PM2.5 air quality monitors to the world are due to the cost of a fixed air monitoring station being no less than $10,000 plus installation and maintenance costs.

Due to the lack of information on the spatial distribution of air pollution, most citizens are unaware of the amount of pollution in their area or the harm it causes. In order to close filling, the global air quality data gap, a significant number of air quality monitoring stations must be installed in cities that lack monitoring. Moreover, the issue of accurate estimation of the spatial distribution of pollutants in urban areas, where a large number of stations need to be spread over large geographical areas. In particular, in Libya, there

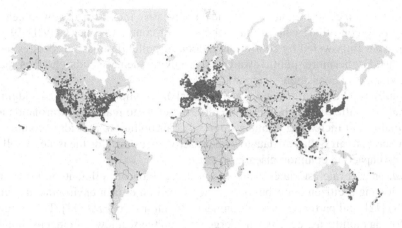

Fig. 2. Shows the Global distribution of air quality monitoring stations. The red dots denoting government stations and blue dots denoting data from air monitors operating independently, adapted from [11]. (Color figure online)

aren't any universal air quality monitoring stations. Additionally, considering the difficult conditions this country is currently in, there is a lack of environmental awareness among the populace, and pollution rates are rising as a result of continuous ignorance regarding air quality, summarized in the following:

- Rubbish burning: Where waste is incinerated between residential neighborhoods.
- Burning car tires: Tires are disposed of by burning.
- Fireworks: Excessive use of fireworks on all occasions.
- Weapons: Excessive use at weddings.
- Remnants of the war: The remnants of the wars that took place in recent years are widely spread in the country.
- Recklessness in dealing with chemicals: This includes the case of the disappearance of a cylinder of chlorine gas from a factory, and the procedures were not taken seriously in the search for it, which caused 30 cases of chlorine gas poisoning in the Qwarsha area in Benghazi.
- Dangerous emissions from automobile exhaust: due to the lack of public transportation, the number of cars has increased dramatically, consistent with a direct increase in pollution. In addition, the illegal trade has recently been active, in the sale of carbon contained in car exhaust, which has led to a dangerous increase in the levels of emissions of toxic gases from cars.

Here comes the importance of developing a system capable of monitoring external pollution to help citizens avoid exposure to pollution. While increasing access to public air quality data is a critical first step towards addressing the problem of air pollution and raising public awareness of the community. Our goal is to design and prototype a low-cost and energy-saving air pollution control system that contributes to the improvement of healthy buildings for citizens. Appropriate preventive measures can control respiratory diseases and enable individuals to enjoy a good quality of life. The main contribution of this paper is as follows:

- First, the main contribution is to provide a preventive tool for people with heart and respiratory conditions who are at higher risk of contracting the COVID-19 virus. People are empowered by controlling indoor air pollution to avoid seizures in their patients. Furthermore, public awareness of environmental conditions thus making behavioral decisions about outdoor activities.
- Secondly, providing information on the spatial distribution of air toward bridging the global air quality data gap. By giving citizens access to real-time information about air quality and increasing public awareness of air pollution. Providing communities with access to air pollution data to take proactive steps towards the issue of pollution and its impact on common diseases in society.
- Third, an accurate estimate of the spatial distribution of pollutants in urban areas, by adopting a citizen contribution strategy based on citizen environmental sensing (CES) [12], and participatory environmental monitoring (PEM) [13]. This is done by deploying monitoring devices on a large scale on the windows of citizens' buildings to cover the largest geographical area, to provide more data, and to obtain a clear picture of pollution levels and places of concentration in the city.

2 Air Quality Platforms

Recently, there has been an emerging trend of using low-cost air sensors as alternatives to the existing widespread and expensive stationary monitoring stations. Deploying low-cost sensors in large numbers could also help detect pollution hotspots and assess exposure in real-time. It should be noted that the idea of citizen sensing - associated with citizen science - has spread as a result of developments in information and communication technology and the availability of low-cost sensing capacity in urban areas. Citizen sensing uses inexpensive sensors to gather data on local environmental issues which is then uploaded online to a platform for data visualization and empowers citizens to use that data. There are numerous air monitoring systems that gather environmental data; nevertheless, when choosing the component parts, affordability, ease of assembly, and ease of use were the key criteria taken into consideration. Table 1 presents some of the existing air monitoring systems and they were compared with the proposed system (KnowAir) in terms of Cost, pollutant, data transfer method, and device type (It is stationary or wearable).

As with the above examples, most air monitoring systems tend to be expensive and unaffordable to most individuals due to their price. KnowAir is built with these characteristics and costs $56.71, making it much cheaper than the current alternatives.

3 Development of KnowAir System

Since low-cost PM2.5 sensors are easy to install and manage, they may provide a way to speed up access to air quality information for areas without real-time government monitoring of air quality. KnowAir has two primary strategies:

1. Citizen sensing-supported approach through the contributions of employees in bridging the air quality data gap by sharing their data.

Table 1. A shortlist of sensor systems by pollutant, Method for Data transmission, a data visualization web API or a mobile application, Device type, and cost

Model	Pollutant	Data transfer method	Web/App	Type	Cost
KnowAir	PM_{10}, $PM_{2.5}$	GSM, Wi-Fi	Yes/Yes	Stationary	$56.71
MoreAir AQ-N [14]	PM_{10}, $PM_{2.5}$	Wi-Fi	Yes/No	Stationary	$95
MoreAir AQ-N [14]	PM_{10}, $PM_{2.5}$	Wi-Fi	Yes/No	Wearable	$95
Atmosome [15]	CO_2, $PM_{2.5}$	GSM	Yes/No	Stationary	$108
Smart Citizen [16]	Smoke, $CO+NO_2$	Wi-Fi	Yes/Yes	Stationary	$119
Speck [17]	$PM_{2.5}$	Wi-Fi	Yes/No	Stationary	$150
AirQualityEgg [18]	CO, NO_2, O_3, SO_2 PM	Wi-Fi	Yes/No	Stationary	$195
AirBeam [19]	CO, NO_2, PM	Wi-Fi	Yes/Yes	Wearable	$249
LCS [20]	PM, CO, NO_2, O_3	Bluetooth	Yes/ No	Wearable	$250
AIRQino [21]	PM_{10}, $PM_{2.5}$, NO_2, O_3	GPRS	Yes/No	Stationary	$1000

2. A smart home approach to protecting people from exposure to excessive levels of pollution by following the instructions of the health organization.

The KnowAir system contains a PMs 7003 sensor that detects the suspended particulate matter in the air and sends it to the ESP8266, which estimates the amount of pollution based on Air Quality Index (AQI) levels (Table 2 lists the critical PM2.5 and PM10 scores). Based on the air pollution level, the microcontroller selects the appropriate procedure based on the sensor reading (see Fig. 3), as follows;

– The first stage: is preventative in nature. Although there are very minor percentages of air pollution, it is not hazardous and there is no danger in the air. This process involves numerous operations (alert the user and allow the window to open), as shown in Fig. 4. A visual alert on the screen and a message sent to the user's mobile phone are the two methods of notification.

– The second stage: Due to the high level of air pollution, this phase is risky. Closing the window, turning on the air purifier or adaption (if any), and sending warning messages in various ways are all actions that are taken (sound warning - turning on the red light - sending a warning message to the mobile phone - showing a warning message on the device screen), as shown in Fig. 5.

Table 2. The scale for the AQI levels of health concern ranges from 0 to 500. The level of air pollution and the resulting health risk increase with increasing AQI values. As an illustration, an AQI score of 50 or less indicates healthy air quality, whereas one of over 300 indicates hazardous air quality.

Air Quality Index levels (AQI)	$PM_{2.5}$ (μg/m³)	PM_{10} (μg/m³)	Air Pollution Level
0-50	0-12	0-50	Level 1: Good
51-100	13-35	51-150	Level 2: Moderate
101-150	36-56	151-250	Level 3: Unhealthy for Sensitive Groups
101-200	57-150	251-350	Level 4: Unhealthy
201-300	151-250	351-420	Level 5: Very Unhealthy
301-500	251-500	421-600	Level 6: Hazardous

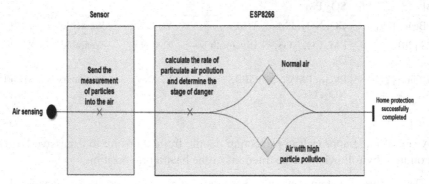

Fig. 3. Service of the KnowAir system UCM.

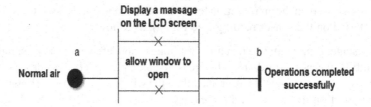

Fig. 4. Additional procedures in the case of normal air.

3.1 Prototype Components

The proposed system of components is all listed in Table 3, along with an estimation of their costs. And, Fig. 6 illustrates a diagram of the proposed system that shows the relationships between the primary components as blocks connected by lines.

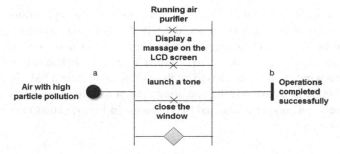

Fig. 5. Additional procedures in the case of air with high particle pollution.

Table 3. Components of the prototype.

Nr.	Components	Prices
1	ESP8266 NodeMCU V1.0 ESP-12E	$6.95
2	PMs 7003 sensor	$15
3	I2C 16 × 2 Character LCD	$1.9
4	Servo motor	$1.41
5	Buzzer	$0.10
6	LED	$2.92
7	Jumper Cable	$6.44
8	Breadboard	$2
9	Power bank 10000 mAh	$19.99
Total		**$56.71**

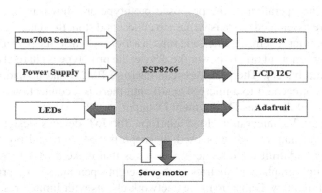

Fig. 6. Illustrates the prototype block diagram

The KnowAir system contains the main components; a) PMs 7003 is a kind of digital sensor to detect and measure the number of suspended particles in the air by laser scattering in real-time. b) The ESP8266 microcontroller chip has wireless transceivers meaning it is ideal for Internet of Things (IoT) operations and applications that require wireless connectivity. It enables to establish TCP/IP connections with ease and connect to Wi-Fi networks. c) LCD Display comes with a built-in potentiometer to display information about AQI levels. d) Servo motor is an electromechanical device that can open or close a window in a room based on the AQI reading from a PMs 7003 sensor. e) Power bank 10000 mAh extends the operating time of the proposed device without the need to charge via a charger connected to the mains. In Fig. 7, shows the simulation of the proposed system.

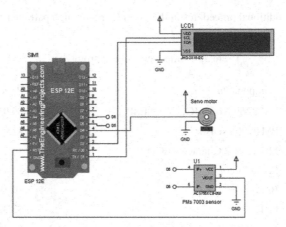

Fig. 7. Illustrates Connected LCDI2C/Sensor/Servo motor to ESP 12E.

3.2 Prototype Operation

The steps for the operation of the proposed prototype are shown in Fig. 8. Once the components are assembled, code is written to collect and store the data. After the code is uploaded to the microcontroller, the code runs in a loop as long as the power supply of the microcontroller is not cut off. To power the device, the prototype is charged continuously from an external battery. The prototype can measure PM2.5 and upload readings to a cloud platform or cache it to a microSD card until there is a connection with the cloud platform. In Fig. 9 illustrates Deployment Diagram.

The Adafruit IO integrated cloud platform for IoT devices designed primarily for data retrieval and storage was used. It supports ESP8266 and provides embedded UI support. Adafruit includes several features that make it easy to visualize real-time data through graphs and metrics. A lightweight open messaging protocol called MQTT (MQ Telemetry Transport) gives network clients with limited resources which is an easy method to share telemetry data in low-bandwidth settings. The protocol is used for machine-to-machine (M2M) communication and uses a publish/subscribe communication structure.

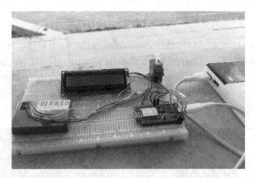

Fig. 8. Illustrates Prototype.

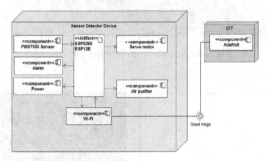

Fig. 9. Illustrates Deployment Diagram

3.3 Experiment

One of the first experimental procedures was to perform tests to verify that correct data was obtained from the PMs 7003 sensor after connecting all components of the system together.

- **Experiment 1:** The experiment was conducted in an outdoor environment for twelve days over a 24-h period, during the month of February of the year 2022, in Al-Hawari district of Benghazi. This environment is supposed to present a high concentration of particulate matter, due to the heavy traffic in the area, as well as the smoke from the cement plant and landfill.
- **Experiment 2:** This experiment was conducted for the purpose of measuring the large differences in the concentration of the pollutant during the month of June of the year 2023, due to the abundance of dust in this month of the year.

4 Results and Discussion

The section presents the results of the two experiments conducted in this paper, time series graphs showing PM2.5 concentrations over time will be presented. This type of graph is an important tool for showing trends and changes in data over time.

4.1   Experiment 1

The surrounding area is affected by the smoke from the factory and the intensive burning of rubbish throughout the day. Therefore, a sensor was installed to measure the percentage of pollution in this area. The sensor was placed on the window of the chamber, as shown in Fig. 10. The time series graphs for Experiment 1 are shown in Fig. 11.

Fig. 10. Smoke from burning garbage.

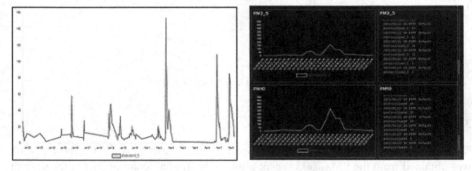

Fig. 11. Time series graphs for Experiment 1

From the images, it can be observed that the sensor responded to the large change in PM2.5 concentration when the wind started to spread the smoke from the cement plant around the window of the room. During the high pollution level, the servo motor was doing the required task of closing the window in time as well as giving warnings about the high percentage of pollution. The sudden air pollution reached extremely dangerous proportions for human health at 10:19 pm, and the value was about 166 $\mu g/m^3$ from the peak of the experiment. Figure 12 shows PM2.5 concentration data for February 2022.

- Add Data	⬇ Download All Data	▼ Filter

‹ Prev	First

Created at	Value
2022/02/22 10:20:11PM	7
2022/02/22 10:20:05PM	7
2022/02/22 10:20:00PM	11
2022/02/22 10:19:55PM	16
2022/02/22 10:19:49PM	21
2022/02/22 10:19:44PM	23
2022/02/22 10:19:38PM	26
2022/02/22 10:19:33PM	90
2022/02/22 10:19:28PM	89
2022/02/22 10:19:22PM	166
2022/02/22 10:19:17PM	95

Fig. 12. Measurements are shown to level 5, which is a level dangerous to human health

4.2 Experiment 2

In Fig. 13 and Fig. 14, presents the time series data of the Prototype in Experiment 2. From the graphs, it is possible to observe that the device showed a clearly responded to the high variation in pollutant concentration. This is due to the dust storms that occur frequently during this month. It can be seen that, at 10:6 am, the air pollution reached the fourth level. That is, the air is considered unhealthy for sensitive groups: the elderly, children, people with heart disease, and people with respiratory conditions, such as asthma. It is worth mentioning here that the device has taken safety measures such as closing the window and alerting the weather to avoid going out into the open air.

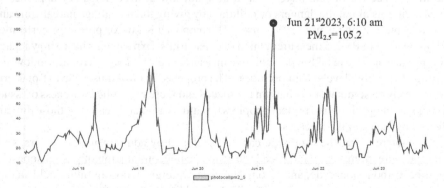

Fig. 13. $PM_{2.5}$ Time series graph for Experiment 2.

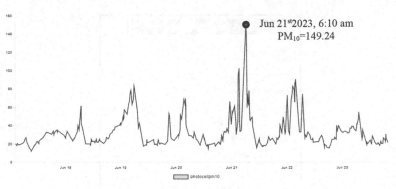

Fig. 14. PM_{10} Time series graph for Experiment 2.

Comparing data with official government air quality stations, which typically employ gravity samplers with filters to measure PM2.5 and PM10 and are subject to tight quality control procedures, is regarded to be the most effective technique to examine sensor performance [22]. Unfortunately, In Libya, these stations are not accessible. Therefore, without making any comparisons to these stations, this study is employed as an observer of PMs 7003's performance. The prototype Developed in this paper does not have sensors to measure temperature and humidity, due to a short budget, it was not possible to analyse the impact of those weather conditions on the performance of the prototypes, and thus remains an important issue for future work.

5 Conclusions

Many communities are expected to experience relatively high levels of pollution, and most of these communities lack air quality monitoring stations. Low-cost sensors may serve as primary indicators for measuring air pollution in many developing countries. The main objective of this paper was to design a low-cost participatory approach to educate citizens about the dangers of pollution by giving them readings in real-time and as well as preventing respiratory diseases. The proposed KnowAir prototype performed well in measuring PM2.5 measurement in two field trials. Experiments have shown quick response in real-time in taking preventative measures such as closing a room window and alerting at very high levels of air pollution. The proposed KnowAir uses the IoT platform to effectively disseminate information to citizens and increase public awareness of issues arising from air pollution to protect people with cardiovascular disease and those directly affected by the COVID-19 crisis.

As a future work, the prototype can be developed by adding various sensors, such as temperature, humidity, wind speed, direction, and a combination of gas sensors such as ozone, carbon monoxide, and so on. The use of reference tools in future field studies in performance evaluation, such as DustTrak. In addition, many of the proposed models can be installed to collect large air pollution data at multiple locations. Thus, an analysis of this data can be done using AI methods to predict pollution levels in order to take necessary prevention measures.

References

1. World Health Organization (WHO). https://www.who.int/health-topics/air-pollution#tab= tab_1. Accessed 15 Apr 2022
2. World-Health-Organization. http://www.emro.who.int/health-topics/asthma/index.html. Accessed 15 Apr 2022
3. World Health Organization (WHO). https://www.who.int/news/item/22-09-2021-new-who-global-air-quality-guidelines-aim-to-save-millions-of-lives-from-air-pollution. Accessed 15 Nov 2022
4. Guaita, R., Pichiule, M., Maté, T., Linares, C., Díaz, J.: Short-term impact of particulate matter (PM2. 5) on respiratory mortality in Madrid. Int. J. Environ. Health Res. **21**, 260–274 (2011)
5. Air, I.: 2020 World Air Quality Report. Region & City PM2. 5 Ranking. IQ Air, 25 February 2020
6. Shrestha, S.L.: Analysis of ambient particulate air pollution and health in Nepal. J. Global Ecol. Environ. 14–29 (2021)
7. Pozzer, A., Dominici, F., Haines, A., Witt, C., Münzel, T., Lelieveld, J.: Regional and global contributions of air pollution to risk of death from COVID-19. Cardiovasc. Res. **116**, 2247–2253 (2020)
8. Travaglio, M., Yu, Y., Popovic, R., Selley, L., Leal, N.S., Martins, L.M.: Links between air pollution and COVID-19 in England. Environ. Pollut. **268**, 115859 (2021)
9. Magazzino, C., Mele, M., Sarkodie, S.A.: The nexus between COVID-19 deaths, air pollution and economic growth in New York state: evidence from deep machine learning. J. Environ. Manage. **286**, 112241 (2021)
10. Vasquez-Apestegui, B.V., et al.: Association between air pollution in Lima and the high incidence of COVID-19: findings from a post hoc analysis. BMC Public Health **21**, 1–13 (2021)
11. WHO Organization: WHO ambient (outdoor) air quality database: summary results, update 2018. Retrieved (2018)
12. Angelidou, M., Psaltoglou, A.: Enhancing urban sustainability through social innovation: citizen environmental sensing for air quality monitoring. In: Sixth International Conference on Environmental Management, Engineering, Planning and Economics (CEMEPE) and SECOTOX Conference, Thessaloniki, Greece (2017)
13. Jalbert, K., Kinchy, A.J., Perry, S.L.: Civil society research and Marcellus Shale natural gas development: results of a survey of volunteer water monitoring organizations. J. Environ. Stud. Sci. **4**, 78–86 (2014)
14. Gryech, I., Ben-Aboud, Y., Guermah, B., Sbihi, N., Ghogho, M., Kobbane, A.: MoreAir: a low-cost urban air pollution monitoring system. Sensors **20**, 998 (2020)
15. Bhimaraju, H., Pandey, V., Nag, N., Jain, R.: Atmosome: the Personal Atmospheric Exposome. medRxiv, pp. 2020.2007. 2002.20145433 (2020)
16. https://smartcitizen.me/. Accessed 25 May 2023
17. Williams, R., Kaufman, A., Hanley, T., Rice, J., Garvey, S.: Evaluation of elm and speck sensors. US Environmental Protection Agency: Washington, DC, USA (2015)
18. https://airqualityegg.com/home. Accessed 13 May 2023
19. https://www.habitatmap.org/airbeam. Accessed 15 Feb 2023

20. Kortoçi, P., et al.: Air pollution exposure monitoring using portable low-cost air quality sensors. Smart Health **23**, 100241 (2022)
21. Cavaliere, A., et al.: Development of low–cost air quality stations for next generation monitoring networks: calibration and validation of NO2 and O3 sensors. In: EGUsphere 2023, pp. 1–27 (2023)
22. Brauer, M., Casadei, B., Harrington, R.A., Kovacs, R., Sliwa, K., Group, W.A.P.E.: Taking a stand against air pollution—the impact on cardiovascular disease: a joint opinion from the World Heart Federation, American College of Cardiology, American Heart Association, and the European Society of Cardiology. Circulation **143**, e800–e804 (2021)

Implementation of Qur'anic Question Answering System Based on the BERT Model

Ebtihal Alarabi[✉] and Issmail Ellabib

Computer Engineering Department, University of Tripoli, Tripoli, Libya
{e.alarabi,i.elabib}@uot.edu.ly

Abstract. The Holy Qur'an is the oldest comprehensive Arabic book of recommendation for Muslims worldwide. Provide knowledge and information used in various ways. People often utilize the Holy Qur'an, considered a reliable and trustful legislated text, for education and to meet their needs and inquiries of the Muslim community. Like extracting an answer span from the provided passage, The Qur'an has the potential to captivate the curiosity of non-Muslims and propel them towards exploring a vast array of topics and pursuing answers. Over the past few years, Question Answering (Q.A.) has drawn much attention from the NLP community. Researchers and experts have developed various Qur'anic Question Answering (QAA) systems. Nevertheless, the main challenge in the Arabic language is the need for more resources, making it difficult to provide highly accurate Arabic QA systems.

The first Qur'an Question Answering shared task workshop, "Qur'an QA 2022," aims to promote state-of-the-art research on Qur'anic question answering QA in general and machine reading comprehension MRC in particular. It aims to develop models to extract questions answering the holy Qur'an passages.

This research paper motivated by this task, suggests an ensemble learning model based on Arabic-supported versions of BERT, which will be implemented using the KNIME platform. We aim to use this model for Arabic Question Answering.; as a result, we get 0.488 for the AUC and 0.946 for accuracy.

Keywords: BERT · Arabic language · KNIME platform · Question Answering model

1 Introduction

The Holy Quran is the main reference point for the global Muslim population of approximately 1.9 billion. The Holy Quran contains 114 chapters, 6,236 verses, and 80,000 words, encompassing instructional and narrative elements. Researchers have thoroughly explored the potential of the Quran to create datasets, perform automatic text classification, answer questions, and conduct semantic searches based on ontology [2].

The comprehension reading process involves reading the text and then answering a question about it. One area where machine reading comprehension (MRC) has become

© The Author(s), under exclusive license to Springer Nature Switzerland AG 2024
T. A. T. Benmusa et al. (Eds.): ILCICT 2023, CCIS 2097, pp. 173–183, 2024.
https://doi.org/10.1007/978-3-031-62624-1_14

popular is natural language processing (NLP), as it provides a helpful benchmark for evaluating machines' abilities to understand natural language. A key advantage of MRC is the availability of numerous datasets, often in multiple languages, which enable researchers to test and improve machines' reading comprehension skills. MRC requires devices to read text passages and answer questions about them [3].

To put it differently, NLP (Natural Language Processing) extracts information from various types of content to perform the task of Question Answering, such as structured and unstructured data, using queries [4]. The United Nations Educational Scientific and Cultural Organization (UNESCO) reported. Arabic has over 400 million speakers worldwide [16]. Language is an essential and integral part of the world's cultural diversity.

The Qur'an QA task may be more challenging due to its small dataset of 1,337 questions and passages [1]. The mixture of Modern Standard Arabic (M.S.A) for the questions and Classical Arabic (C.A.) for passages further contributes to its complexity. [5]. We analyzed the model using the KNIME Analytics Platform (introduced in [17]), open-source software allowing users to access, blend, research, and visualize their data without coding is one of the most excellent tools for the future of Machine learning, Deep learning, and Natural language processing.

2   Related Work

Over time, researchers have utilized various machine learning techniques, including traditional algorithms like support vector machines, string matching, and probabilistic models. [6]. Implementing Natural Language Processing techniques to extract information from the Holy Quran successfully removed the answers. These techniques, however, give inaccurate results, such as in [7] and [8]. A survey highlighted efforts to address the main challenges of answering questions in Arabic [9]. They describe the methods and tools used, including the early classification of the questions into name, date, and quantity to determine the question type. Alqahtani [2] developed a model for answering Arabic Quranic questions. This model enhances the user's query by incorporating semantic features through the word2Vec Algorithm. There is a growing demand for a Question Answering System (QAS) that can provide more accurate results than other techniques mentioned earlier. Researchers may use a Quranic dataset to delve deeper into the Holy Quran [18].

In recent years, the NLP community created various datasets to evaluate machine reading comprehension (MRC) systems. Among these, the Stanford Question Answering Dataset (SQuAD) is widely used, which includes over 100,000 annotated examples for research purposes. [3]. Rajpurkar presented the SQuAD 1.0 dataset, which has become a prominent benchmark for answering questions in the English language. To address the need for more data in Arabic natural language processing, Mozannar presented the Arabic Reading Comprehension Dataset (ARCD), which consists of 1,395 questions posed by crowd workers [10].

An advanced method in natural language processing involves utilizing transformer-based models to drive question-answering systems. This method involves extracting relevant information from a text in response to a specific inquiry or question [3] and [11].

It would be challenging to incorporate the texts from the Qur'an into modern embedding models because of the dataset's complications (Malhas and Elsayed, 2020) developed the AyaTEC first fully reusable test collection for Arabic question and answers on the Holy Qur'an.

The workshop on shared tasks focuses on tackling the difficulty of answering Modern Standard Arabic questions using insights from the verses of the Holy Quran [1]. Team Star suggested a new Arabic Question Answers dataset based on the Holy Qur'an, which contains around 625 questions and answers. The best E.M. score of 0.269 was achieved by team TCE [12]. All participating teams leveraged transformer-based models that support Arabic while constructing their systems. The successful teams utilized AraBERT and AraElectra models, showcasing their superior performance.

After prior investigations, we have implemented ARABI workflow on the KNIME platform, including two approaches that help analyze the dataset and answer the specific question correctly.

3 Methodology

Implementing computer-based techniques and tools has led to significant advancements in extracting accurate information from text. In this section, we will explain the essential components and concepts we have utilized in developing our approach, which we will further elaborate on in the following section.

As mentioned earlier, the proposed QQA system will use the KNIME platform to provide accurate and reliable answers to user queries; KNIME is an open-source platform designed for data analysis, offering a robust suite of tools for data mining and machine learning. The system will consist of two main parts, and we will discuss them in the

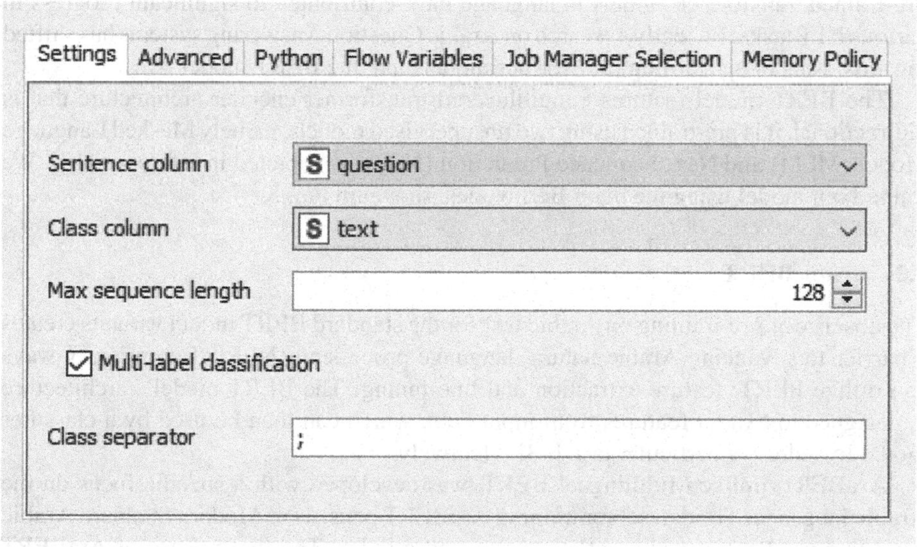

Fig. 1. The main settings

experimental work section. Figure 1 and Fig. 2 demonstrate the setting of optimization hyperparameters. In this setting, we consider the maximum sequence length, number of epochs, and training batch size. Choose Adam as Optimizer for improving the model accuracy and speed, Fine-Tuning as the advanced settings for the BERT model.

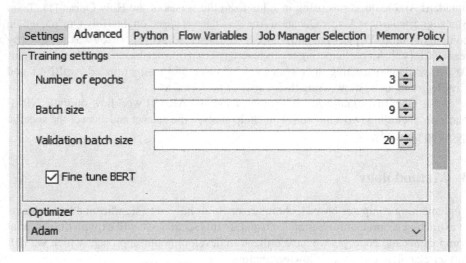

Fig. 2. The advanced Training settings

3.1 Bert

Pre-trained transformer models in language have contributed to significant progress in various NLP tasks. Recently, research on Arabic Question Answering systems has shifted towards using deep learning transformer models like the BERT model.

The BERT model features a multilayered transformer encoder architecture that is bidirectional. It is pre-trained using two unsupervised models, namely Masked Language Model (MLM) and Next Sequence Prediction (NSP), as depicted in reference [13]. We trained our model using the main Bert Nodes, shown in Fig. 3.

3.2 ArabicBERT

The absence of pre-training on Arabic text for the standard BERT model variants creates a barrier to advancing Arabic natural language processing (NLP). Two primary ways can utilize BERT: feature extraction and fine-tuning. The BERT model's architecture is designed to extract features from input data, which can then be used by a classifier model to address a particular task [13] effectively.

AraBERT, unlike Multilingual BERT, was developed with a specific focus on the Arabic language. The dataset for training AraBERT consists of Modern Standard Arabic from various Arabic media outlets, news, and articles. The first release of AraBERT contains 77 million sentences and 2.7 billion tokens, around 23 gigabytes of text. This

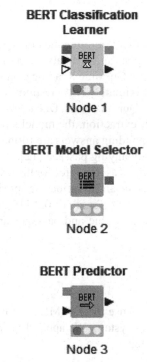

BERT Classification Learner

Node 1

BERT Model Selector

Node 2

BERT Predictor

Node 3

Fig. 3. The primary BERT model nodes.

dataset is 17 times bigger than the Arabic pre-training dataset that Multilingual BERT was trained on [15].

In our model, we utilized the pre-trained BERT models, specifically Bert-base-multilingual-un-case, as shown in Fig. 4. This model can support 102 languages.

It has been specifically trained in Arabic using 12 hidden layers, 768 sizes, 12 attention heads, and 0.1 dropouts on each layer. In total, it has 110 parameters [15].

| Settings | Advanced | Python | Flow Variables | Job Manager Selection |

○ TensorFlow Hub   ● Hugging Face

Display models: | All

Select model: | asafaya/bert-base-arabic

Fig. 4. Model Selection.

3.3 Dataset

Three Islamic specialists, experts in interpreting the holy Qur'an (tafsir), collaborated to create the AyaTEC dataset. Specialists and ordinary people on Islamic websites gathered the questions in this dataset [1]. The Qur'anic Reading Comprehension Dataset (QRCD) is a small dataset comprising approximately 700 questions, with many repeated questions related to different passages from Qur'an verses. Due to the limited number of questions available for training and answer extraction, the model's performance was affected. A question-passage pair and corresponding answers are formatted as JSON Lines (JSONL file) and extracted from the accompanying passage [12].

The QRCD uses the Tanzil project as its source for the text of the Qur'an, as described in [1]. This project contains the Qur'an in various script styles, but we have used the straightforward and clear text style of Tanzil v1.0.2 [19]. It is essential to know that Questions are in Modern Standard Arabic and passages are from the Holy Qur'an in Classical Arabic [1].

4 Experimental Work

In this section, we illustrate how to use the KNIME to provide easy implementation of the Qur'anic Question Answering system. We applied the JSONL data reading nodes, as described in Fig. 5, as a first step.

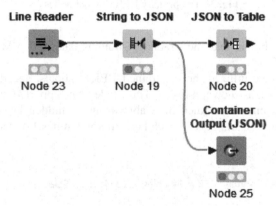

Fig. 5. The JSONL format read nodes.

Then, the data will be transformed from JSON format to table format with 274 rows, including the passage number and its related Question and answers. Figure 6 shows the Line reader, which reads the data as separate lines and Fig. 7 displays the JSON format. Figure 8 illustrates the next steps for reading the data set and transforming it to table form and the data ready to be implemented.

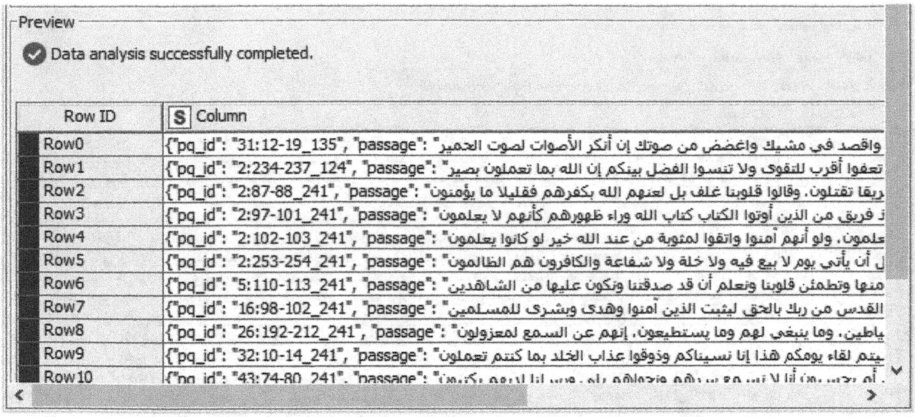

Fig. 6. Line Reader.

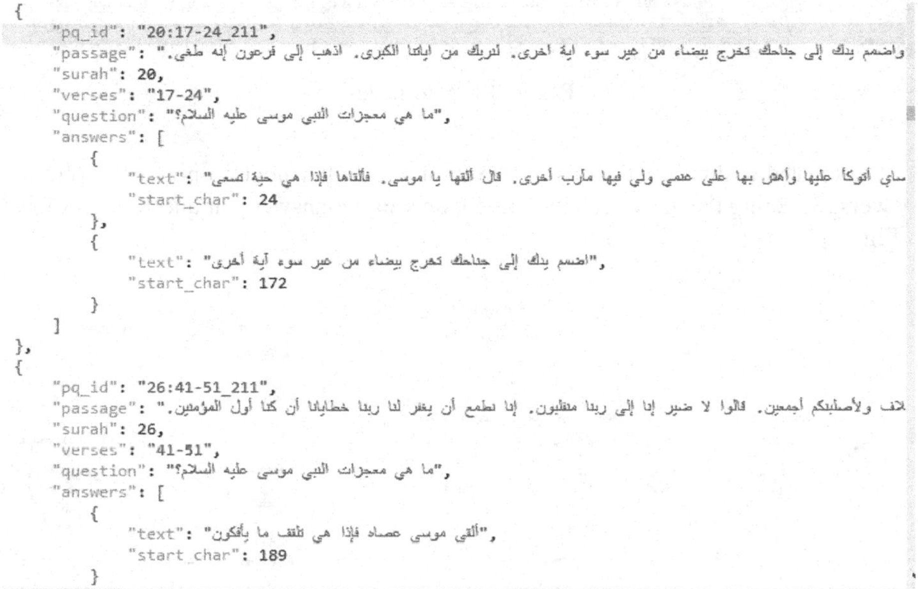

```
{
    "pq_id": "20:17-24_211",
    "passage": ".واضمم يدك إلى جناحك تخرج بيضاء من غير سوء اية أخرى. لنريك من اياتنا الكبرى. اذهب إلى فرعون إنه طغى. "
    "surah": 20,
    "verses": "17-24",
    "question": ",ما هي معجزات النبي موسى عليه السلام؟"
    "answers": [
        {
            "text": "ساي أتوكأ عليها وأهش بها على غنمي ولي فيها مآرب أخرى. قال ألقها يا موسى. فألقاها فإذا هي حية تسعى"
            "start_char": 24
        },
        {
            "text": ",اضمم يدك إلى جناحك تخرج بيضاء من غير سوء آية أخرى"
            "start_char": 172
        }
    ]
},
{
    "pq_id": "26:41-51_211",
    "passage": ".لنف ولأصلبنكم أجمعين. قالوا لا ضير إنا إلى ربنا منقلبون. إنا نطمع أن يغفر لنا ربنا خطايانا أن كنا أول المؤمنين."
    "surah": 26,
    "verses": "41-51",
    "question": ",ما هي معجزات النبي موسى عليه السلام؟"
    "answers": [
        {
            "text": ",ألقى موسى عصاد فإذا هي تلقف ما يأفكون"
            "start_char": 189
        }
```

Fig. 7. JSON OUTPUT.

During the implementation phase, we configured the BERT model selector and opted for the asafaya/bert-base available in Hugging Face. However, we encountered some systematic errors that led to suboptimal predictions. We also discovered that many of the answer spans had a high overlap. Despite several attempts with the available data and trying various methods, we ultimately decided to use only the data consisting of 274 tuples comprising both questions and answers. We used the development data with 238 tuples as test data for the BERT predictor.

Extracted values - 3:20 - JSON to Table			

File Edit Hilite Navigation View

Table "default" - Rows: 274   Spec - Columns: 18   Properties   Flow Variables

Row ID	S Column
Row0	إن الله لا يحب كل مختال فخور. واقصد في مشيك واغضض من صوتك إن أنكر الأصوات لصوت الحمير" :"passage" ,"135_19-12:31" :"pq_id"}
Row1	يعفو الذي بيده عقدة النكاح وأن تعفوا أقرب للتقوى ولا تنسوا الفضل بينكم إن الله بما تعملون بصير" :"passage" ,"124_237-234:2" :"pq_id"}
Row2	سكم استكبرتم ففريقا كذبتم وفريقا تقتلون. وقالوا قلوبنا غلف بل لعنهم الله بكفرهم فقليلا ما يؤمنون" :"passage" ,"241_88-87:2" :"pq_id"}
Row3	عن عند الله مصدق لما معهم نبذ فريق من الذين أوتوا الكتاب كتاب الله وراء ظهورهم كأنهم لا يعلمون" :"passage" ,"241_101-97:2" :"pq_id"}
Row4	بي ما شروا به أنفسهم لو كانوا يعلمون. ولو أنهم آمنوا واتقوا لمثوبة من عند الله خير لو كانوا يعلمون" :"passage" ,"241_103-102:2" :"pq_id"}
Row5	، آمنوا أنفقوا مما رزقناكم من قبل أن يأتي يوم لا بيع فيه ولا خلة ولا شفاعة والكافرون هم الظالمون" :"passage" ,"241_254-253:2" :"pq_id"}
Row6	كتم مؤمنين. قالوا نريد أن نأكل منها وتطمئن قلوبنا ونعلم أن قد صدقتنا ونكون عليها من الشاهدين" :"passage" ,"241_113-110:5" :"pq_id"}
Row7	أكثرهم لا يعلمون. قل نزله روح القدس من ربك بالحق ليثبت الذين آمنوا وهدى وبشرى للمسلمين" :"passage" ,"241_102-98:16" :"pq_id"}
Row8	ما كنا ظالمين. وما تنزلت به الشياطين. وما ينبغي لهم وما يستطيعون. إنهم عن السمع لمعزولون" :"passage" ,"241_212-192:26" :"pq_id"}
Row9	، والناس أجمعين. فذوقوا بما نسيتم لقاء يومكم هذا إنا نسيناكم وذوقوا عذاب الخلد بما كنتم تعملون" :"passage" ,"241_14-10:32" :"pq_id"}
Row10	هون. أم أبرموا أمرا فإنا مبرمون. أم يحسبون أنا لا نسمع سرهم ونجواهم بلى ورسلنا لديهم يكتبون" :"passage" ,"241_80-74:43" :"pq_id"}
Row11	ي ربه إن طلقكن أن يبدله أزواجا خيرا منكن مسلمات مؤمنات قانتات تائبات عابدات سائحات ثيبات وأبكارا" :"passage" ,"241_5-1:66" :"pq_id"}
Row12	هية. والملك على أرجائها ويحمل عرش ربك فوقهم يومئذ ثمانية. يومئذ تعرضون لا تخفى منكم خافية" :"passage" ,"241_18-13:69" :"pq_id"}
Row13	لكة والروح إليه في يوم كان مقداره خمسين ألف سنة. فاصبر صبرا جميلا. إنهم يرونه بعيدا. ونراه قريبا" :"passage" ,"241_7-1:70" :"pq_id"}
Row14	اتخذ إلى ربه مآبا. إنا أنذرناكم عذابا قريبا يوم ينظر المرء ما قدمت يداه ويقول الكافر يا ليتني كنت ترابا" :"passage" ,"241_40-38:78" :"pq_id"}
Row15	ن لم ينته لنسفعا بالناصية. ناصية كاذبة خاطئة. فليدع ناديه. سندع الزبانية. كلا لا تطعه واسجد واقترب" :"passage" ,"241_19-9:96" :"pq_id"}
Row16	القدر خير من ألف شهر. تنزل الملائكة والروح فيها بإذن ربهم من كل أمر. سلام هي حتى مطلع الفجر" :"passage" ,"241_5-1:97" :"pq_id"}
Row17	جدا ونحن له مسلمون. تلك أمة قد خلت لها ما كسبت ولكم ما كسبتم ولا تسألون عما كانوا يعملون" :"passage" ,"201_134-130:2" :"pq_id"}
Row18	إن الله سميع عليم. فمن خاف من موص جنفا أو إثما فأصلح بينهم فلا إثم عليه إن الله غفور رحيم" :"passage" ,"201_182-180:2" :"pq_id"}
Row19	ه عزيز حكيم. وللمطلقات متاع بالمعروف حقا على المتقين. كذلك يبين الله لكم آياته لعلكم تعقلون" :"passage" ,"201_242-240:2" :"pq_id"}
Row20	ن ذلك فهم شركاء في الثلث من بعد وصية يوصى بها أو دين غير مضار وصية من الله والله عليم حليم" :"passage" ,"201_12-11:4" :"pq_id"}
Row21	ي مما ترك الوالدان والأقربون والذين عقدت أيمانكم فآتوهم نصيبهم إن الله كان على كل شيء شهيدا" :"passage" ,"201_33-32:4" :"pq_id"}

Fig. 8. JSON to Table.

We created a simple model using the duplicated filter node to prevent duplicated answers. Selecting the question button to obtain a single-answer pair question, as shown in Fig. 9 [20].

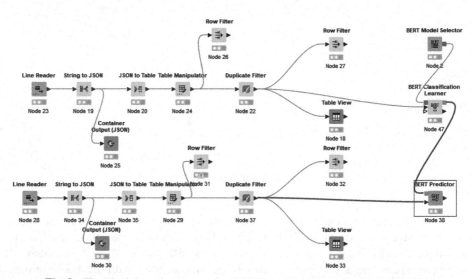

Fig. 9. The Final Question Answering BERT model (*ARABI QA WORKFLOW*).

Using the BERT-fine-tuned technique, a small batch size of 9, and running 3 epochs with a maximum sequence length of 128 worked best for our model. KNIME packages have installed Text Processing preferences, including Tokenization. The Tokenizer can use a pool size of up to 10 concurrently. We preprocess the data by using some nodes like Row Filter by selecting a specific question, and after execution, we get all the possible answers for the question. After that, we filtered the duplicated question, as shown in Fig. 11. We get one answer called the Golden one. If we choose a question like: What are the miracles of Prophet Moses, peace be upon him?

ما هي معجزات النبي موسي عليي السلام ؟. All possible answers before the duplicated filter as shown in Fig. 10.

Figure 11. Shows the Golden answer: ﴿وَإِذِ اسْتَسْقَىٰ مُوسَىٰ لِقَوْمِهِ فَقُلْنَا اضْرِب بِّعَصَاكَ الْحَجَرَ ۖ فَانفَجَرَتْ مِنْهُ اثْنَتَا عَشْرَةَ عَيْنًا﴾. (And when Moses prayed for water for his people, We said 'Strike the rock with your staff.' So twelve springs gushed forth from it). Surah 2.

ALBAQARA (THE COW) - Juz' 1-AYA (60) after removing the duplicated question.

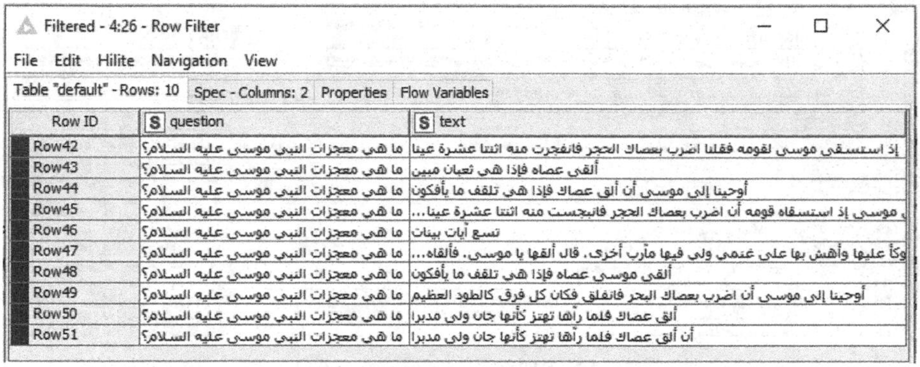

Filtered - 4:26 - Row Filter

File Edit Hilite Navigation View

Table "default" - Rows: 10 | Spec - Columns: 2 | Properties | Flow Variables

Row ID	question	text
Row42	ما هي معجزات النبي موسى عليه السلام؟	إذ استسقى موسى لقومه فقلنا اضرب بعصاك الحجر فانفجرت منه اثنتا عشرة عينا
Row43	ما هي معجزات النبي موسى عليه السلام؟	ألقى عصاه فإذا هي ثعبان مبين
Row44	ما هي معجزات النبي موسى عليه السلام؟	أوحينا إلى موسى أن ألق عصاك فإذا هي تلقف ما يأفكون
Row45	ما هي معجزات النبي موسى عليه السلام؟	موسى إذ استسقاه قومه أن اضرب بعصاك الحجر فانبجست منه اثنتا عشرة عينا...
Row46	ما هي معجزات النبي موسى عليه السلام؟	تسع آيات بينات
Row47	ما هي معجزات النبي موسى عليه السلام؟	وكأ عليها وأهش بها على غنمي ولي فيها مآرب أخرى. قال ألقها يا موسى. فألقاه...
Row48	ما هي معجزات النبي موسى عليه السلام؟	ألقى موسى عصاه فإذا هي تلقف ما يأفكون
Row49	ما هي معجزات النبي موسى عليه السلام؟	أوحينا إلى موسى أن اضرب بعصاك البحر فانفلق فكان كل فرق كالطود العظيم
Row50	ما هي معجزات النبي موسى عليه السلام؟	ألق عصاك فلما رآها تهتز كأنها جان ولى مدبرا
Row51	ما هي معجزات النبي موسى عليه السلام؟	أن ألق عصاك فلما رآها تهتز كأنها جان ولى مدبرا

Fig. 10. Answers of miracles of Prophet Moses verse.

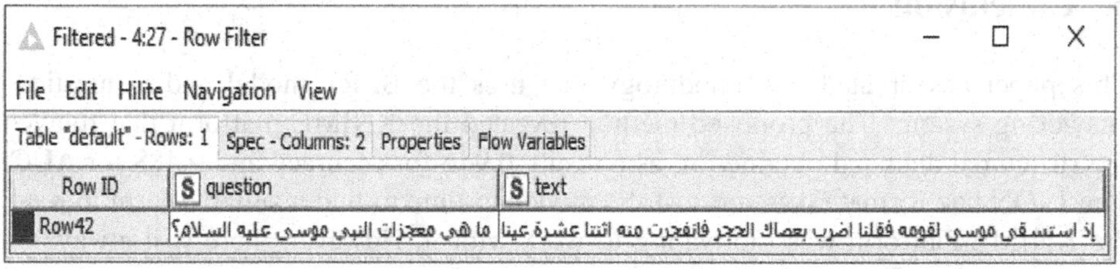

Filtered - 4:27 - Row Filter

File Edit Hilite Navigation View

Table "default" - Rows: 1 | Spec - Columns: 2 | Properties | Flow Variables

Row ID	question	text
Row42	ما هي معجزات النبي موسى عليه السلام؟	إذ استسقى موسى لقومه فقلنا اضرب بعصاك الحجر فانفجرت منه اثنتا عشرة عينا

Fig. 11. Golden answer of miracles of Prophet Moses verse.

5 Results

The long-standing goal of Question Answering (Q.A.) in Natural Language Processing is to provide a clear and accurate answer to a specific question based on a given text. In this paper, we employ the KNIME platform to solve the task by adopting the following steps: trained the model using BERT classification learner and tested with BERT predictor—the prediction results of this model as shown in Fig. 12, and the output table in Fig. 13.

Training statistics - 4:47 - BERT Classifica...

File Edit Hilite Navigation View

Table "default" - Rows: 3 | Spec - Columns: 3 | Properties | Flow Variables

Row ID	D loss	D accuracy	D AUC
Row0	367,426,515,073,236,...	0.743	0.419
Row1	700,403,337,983,426,...	0.946	0.488
Row2	1,001,276,998,342,93...	0.903	0.522

Fig. 12. Training statistics

Output Table - 4:38 - BERT Predictor

File Edit Hilite Navigation View

Table "default" - Rows: 17 | Spec - Columns: 37 | Properties | Flow Variables

Row ID	S question	S text	S Prediction
Table_0_Row0	ما هي مصارف الزكاة؟	للفقراء والمساكين والعاملين عليها والمؤلفة قلوبهم وفي الرقاب والغارمين وفي سبيل الله وابن السبيل	اصطفى لكم الدين فلا تموتن إلا وأنتم مسلمون
Table_0_Row1	حل الإسلام دم الش...	كتب عليكم القصاص في القتلى الحر بالحر والعبد بالعبد والأنثى بالأنثى	اصطفى لكم الدين فلا تموتن إلا وأنتم مسلمون
Table_0_Row20	و سبب نزول سيدنا ...	لا تقربا هذه الشجرة فتكونا من الظالمين. فأزلهما الشيطان عنها	اصطفى لكم الدين فلا تموتن إلا وأنتم مسلمون
Table_0_Row23	ماذا يشمل الإحسان؟	بالوالدين إحسانا وذي القربى واليتامى والمساكين	اصطفى لكم الدين فلا تموتن إلا وأنتم مسلمون
Table_0_Row47	من بنى الكعبة؟	إبراهيم	اصطفى لكم الدين فلا تموتن إلا وأنتم مسلمون
Table_0_Row48	هو جزاء من يقول إن ...	على الله الكذب لا يفلحون. متاع في الدنيا ثم إلينا مرجعهم ثم نذيقهم العذاب الشديد بما كانوا يكفرون...	اصطفى لكم الدين فلا تموتن إلا وأنتم مسلمون
Table_0_Row49	الذي صنع عجلا من ...	السامري	اصطفى لكم الدين فلا تموتن إلا وأنتم مسلمون
Table_0_Row51	سيدنا محمد (ص) ه...	أنا أول المسلمين	اصطفى لكم الدين فلا تموتن إلا وأنتم مسلمون
Table_0_Row53	ما معنى الحطمة؟	نار الله الموقدة. التي تطلع على الأفئدة	اصطفى لكم الدين فلا تموتن إلا وأنتم مسلمون
Table_0_Row54	، اهلك الله قوم عاد؟...	أرسلنا عليهم ريحا صرصرا في أيام نحسات	اصطفى لكم الدين فلا تموتن إلا وأنتم مسلمون
Table_0_Row59	هناك علاقة بين الخو...	كيف تتقون إن كفرتم يوما يجعل الولدان شيبا	اصطفى لكم الدين فلا تموتن إلا وأنتم مسلمون
Table_0_Row60	، فترة رضاعة المولود...	الوالدات يرضعن أولادهن حولين كاملين لمن أراد أن يتم الرضاعة	اصطفى لكم الدين فلا تموتن إلا وأنتم مسلمون
Table_0_Row63	س المرأة المسلمة ...	لا يبدين زينتهن إلا ما ظهر منها	اصطفى لكم الدين فلا تموتن إلا وأنتم مسلمون
Table_0_Row67	ضد من فُرض الجهاد؟	قاتلوا في سبيل الله الذين يقاتلونكم	اصطفى لكم الدين فلا تموتن إلا وأنتم مسلمون
Table_0_Row75	ناك إسلام بدون الح...	أرسلنا فيكم رسولا منكم يتلو عليكم آياتنا ويزكيكم ويعلمكم الكتاب والحكمة	اصطفى لكم الدين فلا تموتن إلا وأنتم مسلمون
Table_0_Row...	سمح الإسلام بحرية ...	لا إكراه في الدين	اصطفى لكم الدين فلا تموتن إلا وأنتم مسلمون
Table_0_Row...	ثم الحاكم الذي لا ي...	من لم يحكم بما أنزل الله فأولئك هم الكافرون	اصطفى لكم الدين فلا تموتن إلا وأنتم مسلمون

Fig. 13. BERT predictor output table

6 Conclusion

This paper has created a methodology that uses the BERT model and a question-answering system. The proposed method revealed the KNIME platform that relayed the structured data and obtained it; as a result, 0.946 for accuracy and 0.488 for AUC. The JSON line format takes most of the modeling time to find a suitable form to read; the KNIME Platform was motivating to work with it. However, there will always be suggestions for improvements, like adding a model comparison node to compare two models, which as future work to build a model with excellent potential for creating extensive that comparing various machine learning techniques and visualizing the statistics, reliable Qur'anic data is needed to make more effective models to better understanding and interpreting answers Qur'anic question and Arabic text.

References

1. Malhas, R., Mansour, W.: Qur'an QA 2022: Overview of The First Shared Task on Question Answering over the Holy Qur'an (2022). https://gitlab.com/big-irqu/quranqa
2. Alqahtani, M., Atwell, E.: Arabic quranic search tool based on ontology. In: Métais, E., Meziane, F., Saraee, M., Sugumaran, V., Vadera, S. (eds.) Natural Language Processing and Information Systems. LNCS, vol. 9612, pp. 478–485. Springer, Cham (2016). https://doi.org/10.1007/978-3-319-41754-7_52
3. Rajpurkar, P., Zhang, J., Lopyrev, K., Liang, P.: SQuAD: 100,000+ Questions for Machine Comprehension of Text. https://stanford-qa.com
4. Bouziane, A., Bouchiha, D., Doumi, N., Malki, M.: Question answering systems: survey and trends. Proc. Comput. Sci. **73**, 366–375 (2015). https://doi.org/10.1016/j.procs.2015.12.005
5. Keleg, A., Magdy, W.: SMASH at Qur'an QA 2022: Creating Better Faithful Data Splits for Low-resourced Question Answering Scenarios (2022). https://smash.inf.ed.ac.uk/
6. Suzuki, J., Sasaki, Y., Maeda, E.: SVM answer selection for open-domain question answering. Association for Computational Linguistics (ACL), pp. 1–7 (2002). https://doi.org/10.3115/1072228.1072347
7. Singh, N.: niksss at Qur'an QA 2022: A Heavily Optimized BERT Based Model for Answering Questions from the Holy Qu'ran (2022). https://docs.wandb.ai/guides/sweeps
8. Baradaran, R., Amirkhani, H.: Ensemble learning-based approach for improving generalization capability of machine reading comprehension systems. Neurocomputing **466**, 229–242 (2021). https://doi.org/10.1016/J.NEUCOM.2021.08.095
9. Magdy Ezzeldin, A., Shaheen, M.: A Survey of Arabic Question Answering: Challenges, Tasks, Approaches, Tools, and Future Trends (2012). https://doi.org/10.13140/2.1.2607.5205.2012
10. Mozannar, H., El Hajal, K., Maamary, E., Hajj, H.: Neural Arabic Question Answering (2019). https://github.com/ "2021.nsurl-1.6"
11. Wasfey, A., Elrefai, E., Muhammad, M., Nawaz, H.: Stars at Qur'an QA 2022: Building Automatic Extractive Question Answering Systems for the Holy Qur'an with Transformer Models and Releasing a New Dataset (2022)
12. Devlin, J., Chang, M.-W., Lee, K., Toutanova, K.: BERT: Pre-training of Deep Bidirectional Transformers for Language Understanding, October 2018. http://arxiv.org/abs/1810.04805
13. Elkomy, M., Sarhan, A.M.: TCE * at Qur'an QA 2022: Arabic Language Question Answering Over Holy Qur'an Using a Post-Processed Ensemble of BERT-based Models (2022). https://github.com/mohammed-elkomy/quran-qa
14. Alammary, A.S.: BERT models for Arabic text classification: a systematic review. Appl. Sci. **12**(11), 5720 (2022). https://doi.org/10.3390/app12115720
15. Safaya, A., Abdullatif, M., Yuret, D.: KUISAIL at SemEval-2020 Task 12: BERT-CNN for Offensive Speech Identification in Social Media (2020). https://github.com/nlpaueb/greek-bert
16. https://www.unesco.org/. Accessed 19 May 2023
17. https://www.Knime.com/knime-analytics-platform. Accessed 23 June 2023
18. https://link.springer.com/article/https://doi.org/10.1007/s10579-011-91677/. Accessed 9 Apr 2023
19. https://tanzil.net/docs/tanzil_project. Accessed 26 Apr 2023
20. https://hub.knime.com/ebtiarabi/ARABI_Qustion_Answering_Workflow. Accessed 23 June 2023

IT Security Office: The Way Forward for IT Governance for Libyan Organizations

Ibrahim E. Lahmer[✉]

NOC, Tripoli, Libya
i.lahmer210@gmail.com, ilahmer@noc.ly

Abstract. IT governance (ITG) is the processes that ensure the effective and efficient use of IT in enabling an organization to achieve its goals. ITG ensures the organization, its data, and its people are protected, while reducing risk and syncing with business objectives. This is achieved through the appropriate IT policies, processes, and procedures, that must be applied consistently across the organization. This paper presents the way forward for adopting the ITG. It introduces the IT Security Office proposal that helps any Libyan organization or institution planning to deploy IT Governance. The proposal is based on the need for any organization to secure; according to the international IT policy and standards, (1) the current use, operation, and implementation of its Information Technology (IT) systems, and (2) the vision of the organization to adopt for example electronic administrative and financial systems and starting its digital transformation journey. This document is organized as follows. First, the proposal introduces IT and its Security Office function and adoption. Then, the proposal specifies the administrative hierarchy of the office in the organization chart and why we need it. Third, it defines the working conditions of the office in such an organizational chart. Fourth, the office duties and responsibilities are described. Finally, the proposal gives recommendations of how an organization could start working in this office and highlights some benefits of implementing such approach.

Keywords: IT Security · IT Governance · Security Office · Function · Organization · IT Operation · Standards and Procedures

1 Introduction

Information Technology (IT) and its role have become a vital and integral part of every organization's function. IT leads the organizations' businesses, and it must be aligned with the organization strategies. For example, IT systems are responsible for organizing the administrative and financial processes of any organization or institution. IT systems should be implemented in a way that meets the needs of the organization, so that these systems contribute (and not limited) to the following benefits:

– Saving time and effort for both administrators and workers in any organization.

PhD in Distributed Computing Security & MSc in Computer Network Security.
National Oil Corporation.

- Improving the production process and raising the quality.
- Getting rid of administrative and financial corruption.
- Assisting decision makers.

However, these benefits or the effectiveness use of the IT rely on the accuracy of the managed systems and information. The IT Security Office assures such accuracy. It provides support for creating policies and standards of implementing and using the Information Technology (IT), and it monitors and follows up the implementation, operation, and use of IT systems. This is to ensure (1) the protection and the continuity of the function of the information systems and infrastructure according to the international standards of information security, and (2) the protection of the Confidentiality, Integrity, and Availability (CIA) of the information and the data used and stored in the IT resources[4].

2   Literature Review

The presence of IT Security office has become a major support for large institutions, companies, and international organizations, whether governmental, commercial or voluntary. There is a noticeable adoption of this office in these bodies. In 2011, the PricewaterhouseCoopers conducted a global study/survey to determine that to what extent the IT Security Office was adopted and used in these bodies. In their annual Information Security Report of the same year, the study showed that in 2006, 43% of about 200 of these bodies had an information security office, and in 2008 it reached to 56%. This percentage was doubled to reach 85% in 2009. The increase in the adoption and use of such office gives a significant sign of its importance[1–3].

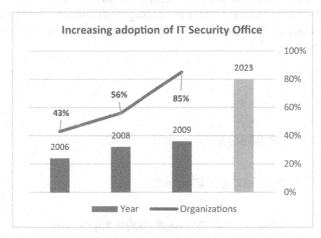

Fig. 1. Increasing adoption of IT Security Office.

We note that the increase in the adoption of this office doubled in three years between 2006 and 2009. In the time of writing this paper, it is more than ten years! If the same study is conducted now (i.e. 2023) the ratio could be larger and may reach 95% or more.

Libyan organizations: public and/or private sectors, should not be among those may fail to adopt this office or administration. This is because of the importance of its duties (Fig. 1).

As mentioned by Raymond a cybersecurity expert from an IT and cybersecurity firm [22], organizations should at least apply the basic cybersecurity measures to mitigate the information security risks and meet the compliance requirements. Organizations that neglect these cybersecurity measures and regulations can find themselves in a high risk; technically and legally. Based on all of this, the essential practice that most organizations adopted, is designating someone in charge of cybersecurity Office; Chief of Information (IT) Security Office (CISO).

2.1 Administrative Hierarchy of the IT Security Office

According to the Global State of Information Security Survey (GSISS), companies are increasingly recognizing the importance of having a top-level manager or executive dedicated to security issues. Based on IDG's 2021 Security Priorities study, among more than 600 organizations surveyed in this study, almost two third of security managers/chiefs have a direct connection to the top management. As shown in Fig. 2, 40% of them, the top security executive reporting to the CEO, and 27% reporting to the Board of Directors (BoD). The study also showed the fact that more businesses are adding security executives to their leadership teams– 67% in 2021 versus 61% in 2020 [5].

In order to ensure the performance of this office in any organization, it should be directly associated with the top management (e.g. Chairman of the Board of Directors) to achieve the following: (1) coordinating efforts between all the organization departments that use and implement the IT; (2) directly meet the needs of this office without delay; (3) submitting reports related to the IT security status of the organization to both the top management (Board of Directors) and the managers of the Information and Communication Technology (ICT) departments to take the appropriate action/implementation plan without any delay.

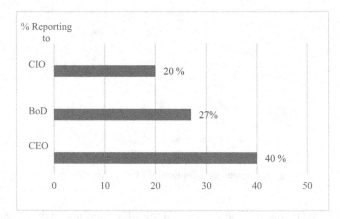

Fig. 2. IT Security Office Reporting to Top Management.

The important existence of such office with this administrative hierarchy in the orga-nizational chart supports the need to (1) be more proactive in managing their information risk, and (2) face the greatest challenges, namely, the protection of their information sys-tems and data. This protection has multiple aspects, and they include all the information resources of the organization that are distributed between different IT sectors and other organization departments. The presence of this office with this administrative hierarchy obligates and imposes on these departments the implementation and application of IT security regulations and standards that are needed for the protection of the data and its IT resources. However, the question raises is that what are the essential requirements or working conditions of such office to achieve its duties successfully?

2.2 Working Conditions (Requirements)

- Firstly; Working alongside with the ICT managers who manage the implementation and operation of the information and communication systems in the organization. This is to ensure that the ICT systems are implemented according to the ICT security policies, standards and procedures, so that reducing the vulnerabilities and preventing an ease of penetration of the ICT infrastructure and systems by their implementation.
- Secondly; Working alongside with other managers of the organization, where their employees use the IT resources to facilitate the tasks assigned to them. This is to ensure that the use of the IT is according to an acceptable use policy (AUP), educat-ing the organization employees, and reducing the feasibility for penetrating the IT infrastructure and systems by their use.
- Thirdly; Knowing and following up of any decision or plan related to IT and commu-nication projects, whether small or large projects, from IT departments or from other departments, in order to provide support from a standpoint of the IT security and its requirements. Here are two simple examples. First, when an organization decides to use a new IT technology or system which is based on the use of various web develop-ment tools (frontend development tool, e.g. Angular.js) and internet browsers. These might pose security risks or threats [6]. When the IT Security Office is aware of the software developers needs to satisfy the business goals, the office can factor that into the decisions regarding the security policy and technologies such as implementing firewalls, network and database security mechanisms, or even assessing the security of the developed code, and enforcing other security mechanisms as needed. Second example is that when the organization decides to make a new data center for disaster recovery, the office can examine the IT security requirements of such data center. This includes, but not limited to, the IT physical security, the organization data and IT resources availability, and access monitoring and control standards of such data center [7].

3   Generic IT Security Office Duties – Mandatory Function

This section describes in brief the main functions of the IT Security office which are presented in:

- Overseeing all the IT security policies, standards, and procedures for the organization. This includes the IT policy and standards for both implementing and using the IT systems and infrastructure.
- Following up the software and technical solutions that are related to the performance and the implementation of IT security procedures.
- Following up the applications and software solutions that are designed and developed by the IT department team of the organization, if any, or by a third party company and provided to organization departments to facilitate their functions (i.e. daily tasks). This is to ensure the use of system development standards and information security mechanisms in these applications and software solutions, protecting their availability, and protecting them against an easy penetration by reducing the weak points in these software solutions. This is because weak points allow misuse of these solutions and hackers to easily access sensitive information and the data of the organization [20].
- Following up the latest technology trends in the IT security, including new security software and tools as well as the best knowledge of how the IT hackers and intruders are behaving.

4 Detailed IT Security Office Duties & Responsibilities

In details, the office duties can be categorized in five main components; IT Policy and Standards, Management Support, IT Monitoring and Testing, IT Incident and Risk Management, IT Audit and Follow up Management [9–14].

4.1 IT Policy and Standards

This office provides direction and practical setting for IT Organization security policies and procedures to protect the IT critical resources and services which includes data, information and IT appliances. This could be achieved according to the following:

- Creating the IT usage policy to avoid the misuse of the IT in the organization.
- Creating the IT policy of the security standards and procedures. This is to reduce the weaknesses and prevent the ease of penetration of the IT infrastructure as a result of setting and implementing the IT for the organization.
- Reviewing, from time to another, the standards and procedures used in setting up and implementing the IT, and developing a vision to improve these standards and procedures when necessary as the used IT is evolved.
- Working with the organization legal affairs department to review and document the IT policy and regulations in term of legal aspects.
- Working with the top management, e.g. Board of Directors, to ratify these IT policies and regulations and to enforce their implementations.
- Working with other organization departments and managements to support the implementation of these IT policy and regulations.
- Working with the organization legal affairs department to study and review the General Data Protection Regulation (GDPR). This is to include the necessary terms in the IT usage policy and security standards regulations that protect the user and the implementer of the IT in the organization.
- Working with the organization legal affairs department to evaluate the existing and emerging IT-security related laws, regulations, and policies to be complied with.

4.2 Management Support

This office assists the ICT managers and supervisors with ICT security administration, implementation, and management. This includes:

- Implementing the IT security policy, standards and procedures.
- Ensuring the existence of the IT security tools from appliances and software in all of the IT infrastructure and data centers. This is to enforce the implementation of the IT policy, standards and procedures that are ratified.
- Looking and studying the latest technology trends in the IT security to specify what is needed to improve the safety and security of the organization's IT resources and data.
- Testing and evaluating the chosen IT security technologies, advising on security related technology projects, and aiding in the management of security technology, with special emphasis on mission critical IT resources.
- Raising the awareness and the culture of information security for the employees of the organization.

4.3 IT Monitoring and Testing

This office conducts the IT Health Check and IT security testing and monitoring for the organization. This is to support the implementation and the optimal operations for the IT policies and practices and to identify any IT security threats or risks. This includes:

- Monitoring computers and network resources for any suspicious activity through the IT infrastructure.
- Testing/assessing information resources, internally and externally, for any security breaches or vulnerabilities in the IT infrastructure.
- Conducting security scanning of the computers and servers that host and run the organization data and applications. This is to reveal any foreign programs that cause direct or indirect harm to the application and the data of the organization.
- Testing the IT windows and web-enabled services of the organization to discover any weakness in the developed applications of such services.
- Monitoring and logging events from various IT resources used and record theses logs in Data Logs.
- Conducting IT security analysis on the Data logs which are recorded to specify the performance of the IT resources and to identify any IT security threats.

4.4 IT Incident and Risk Management

This office manages and oversees the incident response, investigation, and reporting regarding the IT security incidence and events. It also, maintains an information security risk management program to evaluate threats and vulnerabilities that have been identified via monitoring and testing functions, and it assures creation of appropriate remediation plans. This includes the following:

- Performing network intrusion detection and conducting forensic and administrative investigations related to such incidence and events.

- Receiving and processing IT security incident complaints, and overseeing recovery, and restoration for IT security-related events.
- Taking the permitted and required actions to protect the IT resources of the organization in coordination with the related departments such as ICT and service departments.
- Providing support in assessing IT security risks, creating and monitoring IT security plans, and aiding IT disaster and cyber recovery planning.

4.5   IT Audit and Follow up Management

The office audits (i.e. examines and evaluates) the IT procedures and operations to ensure that they are complied with both the IT security policy and standards and the needs of the organization. This includes the audit and the follow-up of the following:

- Controls of the IT implementation.
- Controls of the maintenance and analysis for the entire security audit logs.
- Controls of the use and monitor of the administrative privileged IT accounts.
- Controls of application software security.
- Controls of data back-up operations.
- Controls of security of wireless communication.
- Controls of limitation and monitor of ports and protocols.
- Controls of continuous vulnerability testing and remediation.
- Controls of secure configurations of network devices such as firewalls, routers and switches.
- Controls of IT physical security.

IT security auditing determines whether the IT security controls mentioned above ensuring the following:

- Protecting the confidentiality, integrity and availability (CIA) of the organization data and the IT resources; such as software applications, servers and PCs resources.
- Aligned with the organization's business overall goals.

5   Recommendations on Security Office Establishment

This office should be established due to both the importance and the size of its duties. Carrying out the tasks of this office, while the existence of ICT departments and other departments that use (and may implement) the IT, is a complex task. However, it is not difficult to accomplish. In order to avoid the failure of the work of this office when it is established, and to start its main tasks/duties smoothly and working in steady pace and effectively, the Office should start by doing the following preliminary tasks.

5.1   Preliminary Task: Documented Technical Study and Proposals

Conducting a comprehensive technical study to document the existing IT standards used by the ICT departments that implement the ICT systems in the organization. The results of this study are to identify any problems facing these departments in implementing their work according to the international standards for information security.

- Throughout this study, the existing criteria (standards) used in implementing the IT is/are defined, and evaluated from the IT security standpoint. Based on the outcome of this evaluation, the existing (used) standards are categorized into two types: (i) standards that are consistent with international standards of information security, and this type can be maintained, and (ii) standards that are inconsistent with international standards of information security which may lead to (1) compromise the confidentiality and the integrity of the organization data and its sensitive information, and (2) affect the functionality of the organization when using the IT to run its business; specially when there is a potential to implement electronic administrative and financial system.
- Providing practical and technical proposals for implementing solutions to solve the problems facing ICT departments in implementing and applying the IT according to the international standards of information security.
- To typically implement these proposals, they are formulated into two types:

  - The first type of proposals deals with the problems/issues that can be resolved directly without pre-requirements or needs to apply the solutions of these problems. In this type of proposals, the solutions are written in the form of scripts and then interpreted into executive regulations (standards) for their application.
  - The second type of proposals is concerned with problems/issues that cannot be resolved directly, but needs to be solved using small projects supported by regulations. This is because of the requirements that must be provided before implementing these solutions. In this type of proposals, the solutions are written in the form of texts and then interpreted into executive regulations for their application. These projects identify the requirements, the stages of each project, the estimated budget for each one and its completion as well as the aspects of budget expenditure.

- Periodic reports shall be submitted to the one who is entitled[1] to follow up the work of this study, i.e. the one who is responsible to follow up the preliminary work of this office.
- Whenever the regulations that are related to the duties of the IT Security Office are implemented, the performance of these regulations MUST be evaluated regularly, and periodic reports are presented.

5.2 The Benefits of This Study

International IT security frameworks and standards [9][20] can be used to direct this study to ensure that the study aligns with the information system auditing mechanisms and its realization of the following potential and promised benefits:

1. Start working quickly in the duties of the office, as some of the tasks achieved during this study are part of the office main tasks.
2. Providing support to improve the performance of the IT department. This is done via defining the current duties/roles of IT managers, engineers, and technicians, and

---

[1] Entitled person is the one who is in full authority to follow up and approve the needs of the IT Security Office.

determining the shortages in the IT roles that are needed according to the IT security standards. A list of recommendations and suggestions are advised to both the one who is entitled to follow up the work of this office and the IT departments. This is to establish and reassure the IT roles according to the international standards of information security, so that the organization can implement the IT technologies to facilitate its function according to the international standards. This list of recommendations and suggestions is part of IT change management process. In other words, this study can contribute in defining the chains of responsibility and authority.

3. Start working with the IT governance process. This is because defining the chains of responsibility in term of IT security is one of the main key components of IT governance process. As described by COBIT framework and IBM IT Governance Approach, it "is used to define the chains of responsibility, authority, and communication to empower people, as well as to define the measurement and control mechanisms to enable people to carry out their roles and responsibilities" [17]-[20].

4. Identifying the first component of a systematic approach used in Information Security Management System (ISO 27001) which consists of three main components; People, Processes, and Technology that help to protect and manage all the organization Data and IT resources through IT Incident and Risk Management.

5. By defining the current condition of the IT policy and standards used in the implementation of the IT projects in the organization, the study could find out the reasons and issues that hinder the best practice of implementing and using IT in the organization. Thus, the study could support a detailed plan/s for the digital transformation project in term of IT Security need based on the organization vision.

6. Last but not least, the study can identify the priorities/preferences that must be achieved from the functions of this office (in Sect. 4) and not included in the work of this study. This relies on the needs, the importance of the work to be done, and the budget available to the office and the ICT departments, as well as the top management approvals. Note that the implementation of the duties of this office will also rely on (i) identifying the components and the requirements of this office; and (ii) developing plans that must be documented and reviewed before implementing them in coordination with the related departments.

5.3   The Study Needs (Requirements/Working Conditions)

1. The consent and collaboration of the IT and ICT managers is required to conduct this study.
2. The office chooses capable and skilled people who are needed from the IT or other organization departments in coordination with the managers of these departments, to assist in accomplishing this study.
3. Collaboration of IT engineers, developers and technicians to complete this study, so that first block or component of the IT security office could be made, i.e. roles and responsibilities and we start work according to the IT standard.
4. Non-intervention of others in the work of this study is essential, except when it is needed.
5. Transparency in the study is important, so as to be able to maximize the performance in implementing and using the IT at the organization.

6. Confidentiality of some of the outcomes of this study is also important, the result or the outcomes that may affect the privacy and the security of the organization data or some of the staff of the IT or other departments in the organization.
7. Collaborate with some international organizations of IT security and standards when needed.

5.4 Additional Requirements to Run the Office

The following additional requirements may be needed to get use of the outcomes of the study in achieving the office duties successfully.

- Select the consultants from the competent companies, and sign supporting service agreements when necessary. This is to carry out the duties of this office according with the international IT security policy and standards.
- The office chooses competent engineers and technicians, if any, from the IT departments to implement and follow up the work of this office in coordination with ICT managers, and from outside to perform some other duties as needed and described above.
- Assign budget to this office to perform its duties and to attend both training courses and workshops that are related to its duties.
- Non-intervention of others in the work of this office unless it is requested.
- The office needs to be independently represented in the IT security's needs, goals and vision for the organization and not be buried too deep into an operational capacity of the IT security.

5.5 The Study Implementation Tasks and Schedule

In any organization, the scheme of the implementation tasks includes questionnaire to be answered, observation on IT operations and interview of the IT admins and supervisors. This scheme should be supported by Information System Auditing guidance and procedures. This section presents the study implementation tasks and schedule. The study implementation schedule presented with a part time job IT system auditor. Note that the starting date of such study is not specified, as it is based on the approval of this proposal in any organization. The period assigned to this study is subjected to increase and decrease depending on the existing working condition of the IT team of the organization. However, during this study period, it is feasible to start the implementation of some proposals that solve the existing issues of not implementing and using the IT according to the international standards of information security management (Table 1) (Fig. 3).

Table 1. Tasks Details

Tasks	Description
Task-1	Preparing for the study by understanding the existing of the organization ICT departments and identifying a strategy to conduct the study
Task-2	Collecting the data and information regarding the used IT policy and standards
Task-3	Documenting the collected data and information
Task-4	Evaluating the collected and documented data/information of the used IT policy and standards based on the international IT policy and standards for information security
Task-5	Identifying the problems and issues that hinder the typical use of IT policy and standards
Task-6	Categorizing the existing IT policy and standards used in the IT department
Task-7	Creating and classifying technical and documented proposals for solutions to address the existing issues of using IT policy and standards
Task-8	Reviewing the proposals to be implemented

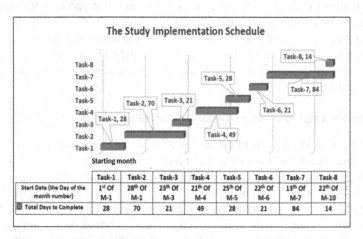

Fig. 3. The study implementation schedule.

6   Discussion and Future Work

This paper has defined the IT Security office and why it is needed. It has also proposed a method of how any Libyan organization could start its implementation. The IT Security Office focuses exclusively on delivering the highest levels of IT security and assurance that could be implemented in five functions; IT Policy and Standards, Management Support, IT Monitoring and Testing, IT Incident and Risk Management, IT Audit and Follow up Management. These five functions present the basis of the four domains of the IT governance, named Value Delivery, Performance Management, Resource Management, and Risk Management. Studying the AS-IS of the existing IT service management can identify any problems and gabs in the IT implementation and use. The IT standards, policies, and procedures are the measurements in such study. The expected output of the study is to assess and measure the performance of IT processes within the organization. For the best performing organization, the output of the study should divide the management and operational responsibilities between IT operations and the information security and assurance functions. However, there is a need to define the IT Security Office organizational chart/team and the roles and responsibilities of the information security personnel. This need varies from an organization to another. It can be determined once the proposed study is completed, and the cybersecurity roadmap is crafted.

References

1. Vaynberg, B.: How has the CISO function changed through the years? https://www.mimecast.com/blog/ciso-at-25/. Accessed Dec 2022
2. PwC Global: Annual Information Security Survey. PricewaterhouseCoopers pwc (2012). https://www.pwc.com/gx/en/issues/cybersecurity.html
3. Maali, M., Skidmore, T.: Real-time compliance management Report. PricewaterhouseCoopers pwc (2021). https://www.pwc.com/us/en/risk-assurance/state-of-compliance-study/assets/pwc-2018-state-of-compliance.pdf
4. ISO/IEC 27000:2018: Information technology and Security techniques, ISMS-Overview and vocabulary, 2018 2018-02, 5th edn. 27p. Technical Committee: ISO/IEC JTC 1/SC 27, Information security, cybersecurity and privacy protection (2018). https://www.iso.org/standard/73906.html. Accessed 21 Apr 2023
5. International Data Group (IDG) Research Team: A Crisis Of Confidence Pushes New Security Initiatives", Executive Summary, IDG Security Priorities Study IDG Communications, INC (2021). https://www.idg.com/tools-for-marketers/research-security-priorities. Accessed 2022
6. Barker, W.C., et al.: Securing Web Transactions, TLS Server Certificate Management. NIST SPECIAL PUBLICATION 1800-16, June 2020. https://nvlpubs.nist.gov/nistpubs/SpecialPublications/NIST.SP.1800-16.pdf. Accessed May 2023
7. Security Policy, NISSA Publication, National Information Security & Safety Authority. https://nissa.gov.ly/en/main-services/policies/. Accessed Feb 2023
8. Simos, M.: How to organize your security team: The evolution of cybersecurity roles and responsibilities, August 2020. https://www.microsoft.com/security/blog/2020/08/06/organize-security-team-evolution-cybersecurity-roles-responsibilities/. Accessed Feb 2023
9. ISACA Publication, Certified Information Security Auditor (CISA): Review Manual 27th Edn. updated 2019 Job Practice, ISBN 978-1-60420-767-5, CISA® Review Manual 27th Edition (2019)
10. CISA Publication: Cybersecurity and Infrastructure Security Agency (CISA)", National Cybersecurity and Communications Integration Center's (NCCIC), Computer Emergency Response/Readiness Team of United Sate (US-CERT) (2021). https://www.us-cert.gov/about-us, https://www.cisa.gov/about-cisa. Accessed Dec 2022
11. SANS Publications: IT security recommendations and models, SANS Institute of advanced technologies for information management and security. https://www.sans.org/. Accessed Feb 2022
12. NIST Publications and Resources: The National Institute of Standards & Technology (NIST), and "National Volunerabilty Database (NVD). https://nvd.nist.gov/general, https://www.nist.gov/. Accessed My 2023
13. IT Security Office Duties, Guides and Policies of Standford Univerosity and Northwestern University. https://uit.stanford.edu/security, https://www.it.northwestern.edu/about/policies/

14. Allen, J.H., et al.: Structuring the Chief Information Security Officer Organization, September 2015, SEI Technical Report for roles and duties of the IT Security Office, Carnegie Mellon® and CERT. https://resources.sei.cmu.edu/asset_files/TechnicalNote/2015_004_001_446198. pdf. Accessed May 2023

15. US Department of HomeLand Security (DHS) Publication, September 2013, Information System Security Officer Guide. https://www.dhs.gov/sites/default/files/publications/Inform ation%20System%20Security%20Officer%20%28ISSO%29%20Guide.pdf. Accessed Feb 2023

16. InfoSec Publications, Online Repository for Information Security (InfoSec) Reports. https:// informationsecurity.report/. Accessed Feb 2022

17. ITPC, IT Policy Compliance Group, February 2010. Best Practice for Managing Information Security Report. http://eval.symantec.com/mktginfo/enterprise/other_resources/b-best_practices_for_managing_information_security-february_2010_OR_2876547.en-us. pdf. Accessed Oct 2022

18. LOGIIC Group: LOGIIC public reports "Improving cybersecurity in the oil and gas sector, LOGIIC: Linking the Oil and Gas Industry to Improve Cybersecurity. https://www.automa tionfederation.org/Logiic/LogiicProjects. Accessed Aug 2022

19. Mueller, L., et. al.: IBM IT Governance Approach, Business Performance through IT Execution. 1st Edn. (2008). https://www.redbooks.ibm.com/abstracts/sg247517.html. Accessed May 2023

20. Lainhart, J., et al.: Cobit® 2019 Framework: Introduction & Methodology. COBIT: Control Objectives for Information and Related Technology, ISACA Publication. http://www.isaca. org/. Accessed May 2023

21. ISO/IEC Publication: 27001Standards,Information Security Management System (ISMS). https://www.iso.org/. Accessed June 2023

22. Raymond Pompon: The Five Cybersecurity Practices Every Organization Should Adopt (2020). https://www.f5.com/labs/articles/cisotociso/the-five-cybersecurity-practices-every-organization-should-adopt. Accessed Aug 2023

Sentiment Analysis of Libyan Middle Region Using Machine Learning with TF-IDF and N-grams

Abdullah Habberrih🆔 and Mustafa Ali Abuzaraida$^{(\boxtimes)}$ 🆔

Computer Science Department, Faculty of Information Technology, Misurata University, Misurata, Libya
{m09181037,abuzaraida}@it.misuratau.edu.ly

Abstract. Arabic dialects are commonly used on social media platforms by Arabic speakers to express their opinions and connect with each other. However, due to the lack of standardized rules or grammars, analyzing Arabic dialects with NLP tools can be more challenging than standard Arabic. Moreover, the poems domain within Arabic dialects is considered to be more challenging than other domains due to structural differences between poems and regular expressions. This study investigates the use of TF-IDF and N-grams with Lemmatization techniques to develop machine learning classifiers for sentiment analysis in the domain of poems within the Libyan dialect, specifically the Libyan Middle Region dialect. Three experiments were conducted using ML classifiers, namely, SVM, NB, and LR. The first experiment explored classifiers' performance using .TF-IDF with Unigrams, whereas the second experiment investigated the use of TF-IDF with Trigrams, and the third experiment examined the impact of combining Unigrams and Trigrams on the classifiers' performance. The experimental results indicate that utilizing Unigrams with TF-IDF can enhance classifier performance, whereas Trigrams with TF-IDF can have a negative effect on the classifiers' performance. Notably, SVM achieved the highest accuracy of 69.04% in the first experiment, while LR achieved the highest accuracy of 58.60% in the second experiment, and SVM achieved an accuracy of 68.92% in the third experiment. Furthermore, in terms of precision, LR in the first experiment outperformed the other classifiers across all experiments with 70.49%.

Keywords: Sentiment Analysis · Libyan Dialect · Machine Learning

1 Introduction

Individual behavior is heavily influenced by abstract sentiments and convictions, including attitude, emotion, opinion, and bias. The ability to convey the opinions of others is intrinsic to every human being, serving as a hallmark of their status as social creatures [3]. The widespread usage of social communication channels, such as Twitter, Facebook, and YouTube, has escalated due to the increasing expression of opinions on various products and topics [1]. This has necessitated the analysis of textual data, leading

T. A. T. Benmusa et al. (Eds.): ILCICT 2023, CCIS 2097, pp. 197–209, 2024.
https://doi.org/10.1007/978-3-031-62624-1_16

many researchers to employ Natural Language Processing (NLP) techniques to study people's opinions and attitudes [2]. Sentiment Analysis is one of NLP tasks that aims to discern the sentiment conveyed in a given text. In contemporary times, this area of research has gained significant popularity due to its utilization of opinionated data that provides users with reviews of various services that are pertinent to their everyday lives [3].

In contemporary times, SA has emerged as a crucial field owing to its diverse applications across multiple domains, most notably in providing decision-making support. SA can aid individuals in their day-to-day activities, such as purchasing a new car, or selecting a suitable restaurant. In the business realm, SA is widely utilized to collect customer feedback and streamline product efficiency in accordance with user requirements. Furthermore, SA finds extensive use in the field of predictions and trend analysis, where it can help track public sentiment via sentiment scrutiny, thus enabling individuals to predict market scenarios and make informed trading and polling decisions. SA is also utilized in finance, politics, and election prediction, and can assist in garnering citizens' responses regarding crucial issues [3, 4, 16].

According to [5], the Arabic language holds the fifth position among the most widely spoken languages globally. Arabic is characterized by three main variations, namely Classical Arabic (CA), Modern Standard Arabic (MSA), and Dialectal Arabic (DA) [2]. CA is the language utilized for writing the holy book of Islam, Quran, while MSA is employed in politics, journalism, books, and education. DA, on the other hand, is an informal version of Arabic, widely used for daily communication. It varies from country to country and even from city to city, but there are six popular types of DA, including Maghrebi (spoken in Northern Africa), Khaliji (spoken in the Arab Gulf region), Shami (Levantine), spoken in Jordan, Lebanon, Palestine, and Syria, Egyptian (spoken in Egypt), Sudanese, and Iraqi, spoken in Sudan and Iraq [7].

The objective of this study is to perform sentiment analysis on the poems domain of middle region of the Libyan Dialect by comparing three Machine Learning classifiers, namely Support Vector Machine (SVM), Naive Bayes (NB), and Logistic Regression (LR). Additionally, the study will employ various preprocessing techniques and TF-IDF with N-grams as the feature extraction techniques.

The remainder of this paper is organized as follows: Sect. 2 provides a brief overview of the literature review and Sect. 3 outlines the methodology. Section 4 presents the experimental results and associated discussion and finally Sect. 5 concludes the study.

2 Literature Review

This section provides a summary of various studies, with a focus on those that employed sentiment analysis in the poem's domain.

Alsharif et al. (2013) [8] used four machine learning techniques (NB, SVM, VFI, and Hyper-pipes) to extract emotions from Arabic poetry in their study. Four classes of poetry were used, and a dataset of 1,231 Arabic poems from an online database was employed. Preprocessing techniques, such as error scraping, diacritics, stop words, stemming, and rooting techniques, were applied using the POS tag. The study used a bag-of-words approach as a feature vector in two different ways, with two non-linear functions applied for feature selection. The study evaluated the classifiers using 416 poems, with 10-fold cross-validation during training and precision, recall, and f-measure techniques utilized for evaluation. The feature vectors ranged from 400 to 2000 unigrams, with each vector having a size of 400. The Hyper-pipes algorithm achieved the highest precision at 79% with feature vectors of length 800 and 2000, while the VFI algorithm achieved the highest f-measure at 73% with a feature vector of length 2000.

On the other hand, Ahmed et al. (2019) [9] conducted a study to classify modern Arabic poems into four categories - Love, Islamic, Social, and Political poems - using machine learning techniques, including SVM, NB, and LSVC. The datasets were collected from an unspecified website, consisting of four groups and multiple files with varying numbers of verses. Preprocessing steps such as Tokenization, Stop-words removal, and Stemming were used to reduce the size of the datasets. For feature selection, the authors used an equation that calculates the number of any feature that appears in a category deducted from the number of the same feature that appears in all other categories. The evaluation of the classifiers was performed using precision, recall, and f-measure techniques. The LSVC classifier achieved the best performance, with a precision of 72%, recall of 47%, and f-measure of 51%, followed by the NB classifier with a precision of 64%, recall of 47%, and f-measure of 49%, while the SVM classifier recorded the lowest precision of 17.75%, recall of 14%, and f-measure of 18%.

Therefore, in 2021, Abugharsa [1] conducted a study to compare the performance of Machine Learning (ML) and Deep Learning (DL) techniques on Misurata sub-dialect poems. Four ML classification algorithms were used, including Logistic Regression, Random Forest, Naïve Bayes, and Support Vector Machine, while Mazajak, a tool designed to detect sentiment from Modern Standard Arabic (MSA) using a CNN algorithm, was used for DL. The study's results indicated that the ML classifiers outperformed the Mazajak classifiers in terms of accuracy, with the ML classifiers achieving a score of 68.0%, while the Mazajak model scored 60.66%.

3   Methodology

In the previous section, some of the previous studies were presented and discussed. However, this section will highlight the proposed methodology of this study. Moreover, the methodology of this study is shown in Fig. 1.

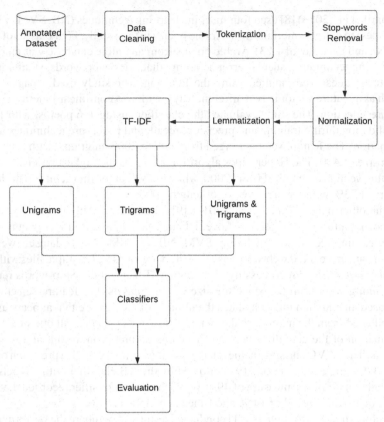

Fig. 1. Study Methodology.

3.1 Dataset

In this study, a secondary dataset is used, which was collected and annotated by the author in [1]. The dataset focuses on Libyan middle region poems and consisted of 22,762 records that were annotated as positive, or negative. Table 1 presents the description of the dataset.

Table 1. Dataset Description.

Columns	Sentiment	Sentence
Count	22,762	22,762
unique	2	21,387
top	positive	حاجة غريبة
freq	13,216	20

Moreover, Table 2 shows the number of samples for each class.

Table 2. Number of Samples in the Dataset.

Class	Number of Samples
Positive	13,216
Negative	9,546
Total	22,762

Additionally, Table 3 highlights some of the samples of the positive class and the negative class.

Table 3. Examples of the Dataset.

Sentiment	Sentence
Positive	ضحكت ضحك قلبي ورفرف طاير
Positive	اللي شوفها نحلف اتقول بشاير
Positive	ضحكت الله ايعينها
Positive	روحي و كلي صرت دوم سجينها
Negative	و عارف و اني عارف كلها تغبى
Negative	بحالك و حالي يا عزيز عليا
Negative	غالب عليا الشوق هيج شغبه
Negative	إلهامي و خبر عن أمور خفية

3.2 Data Preprocessing

The pre-processing phase plays a crucial role in SA as it enhances the quality of data and improves the overall performance of the analysis. This phase can be carried out through various stages that depend on the language's nature and the analysis objectives. The majority of social media text is considered to be unstructured or noisy due to a lack of standardization, spelling mistakes, missing punctuation, non-standard words, and repetitions. Therefore, pre-processing the text has gained increasing importance, particularly with the proliferation of websites producing noisy text. However, the pre-processing phase encounters numerous challenges and obstacles, particularly when dealing with sentiments expressed in unstructured languages such as Arabic dialects [11]. The preprocessing techniques that utilized in this study as following:

Data cleaning: It involves eliminating any extraneous data in a dataset that could potentially interfere with classification accuracy [10]. This process typically entails removing duplicate rows, non-Arabic characters, punctuation marks such as #, !, @, (), numerical values, missing values, and superfluous spacing. Table 1 indicates that there are 1,375 duplicate rows present in the dataset that should be removed, leaving only the first occurrence of each duplicated row.

Tokenization: This phase constitutes the second step of the preprocessing process, entailing the segmentation of the text stream into words or tokens using a delimiter, which can be a whitespace or any punctuation character. The output of this process is a collection of individual words that can be subjected to further analysis [12].

Stop-words Removal: The process of removing stop-words involves eliminating natural language words that carry little meaning [13]. These words, such as pronouns, articles, and prepositions, are typically irrelevant to the categorization task in text mining. Stop words are common words that frequently appear in a text but have no significant semantic relation to the context in which they exist. Examples of such words include " إلى" (to), " حتى" (until), " أنت" (you), " من" (of), and similar words.

Normalization: It is a crucial step in the preprocessing process, which involves transforming text to achieve consistency and standardize its form [13]. For instance, the letter [ة] appearing at the end of a word is replaced with [ه], and the letters [أ إ آ] are substituted with [ا].

Lemmatization: It is a linguistic method that involves the analysis of a word's morphology and the removal of its inflectional suffix, resulting in the generation of its base form or lemma, which corresponds to its dictionary entry [14].

3.3 Feature Extraction

After the data has been preprocessed, the next step is the feature extraction and selection, which involves identifying the most effective features for the sentiment analysis process and removing irrelevant, redundant, and noisy data. This step results in reducing both the dimensionality of the feature space and the processing time, ultimately improving the efficiency and effectiveness of the analysis [12]. The feature extraction techniques that utilized in this study as following:

TF-IDF: It is a technique that consists of two main components: Term Frequency (TF) and Inverse Document Frequency (IDF). The TF component calculates how frequently a given word appears within a text, while the IDF component adjusts for words that appear too frequently in texts [15]. This approach has been shown to outperform using TF or IDF separately [6].

N-grams: It consists of Unigrams, Bigrams, and Trigrams. Unigrams which are known as Bag of Words (BOW) are the simplest features to extract and provide good coverage of the data, while bigrams and trigrams allow for capturing negation or sentiment expression patterns [13].

4   Experiments and Results

This study employed three experiments to extract sentiment from the Libyan middle region dialect. The first experiment utilized TF-IDF with Unigrams, the second experiment utilized TF-IDF with Trigrams, and the third experiment employed a combination of Unigrams and Trigrams. These experiments were conducted using three ML classifiers, namely SVM, NB, and LR, and evaluated using Accuracy, Precision, Recall, and F1-score metrics.

In the first experiment, each word was treated as a feature and assigned a weight based on its significance in the dataset. The second experiment, on the other hand, considered each set of three adjacent words as features. The third experiment combined the first and second experiments. In terms of feature count, the first experiment had 15,549 features, the second experiment had 18,490 features, and the third experiment had 69,818 features.

Moreover, Table 4 shows the results of the classifiers for the first experiment: TF-IDF with Unigrams.

Table 4. First Experiment Results.

Classifier	Accuracy (%)	Precision (%)	Recall (%)	F1-Score (%)
SVM	**69.04**	**70.10**	**81.85**	**75.51**
NB	68.61	68.83	84.44	75.83
LR	68.30	70.49	78.53	74.29

In all evaluation metrics, SVM outperforms NB and LR as shown in Table 4 with an accuracy of 69.04%, while NB and LR achieve accuracies of 68.61% and 68.30%,

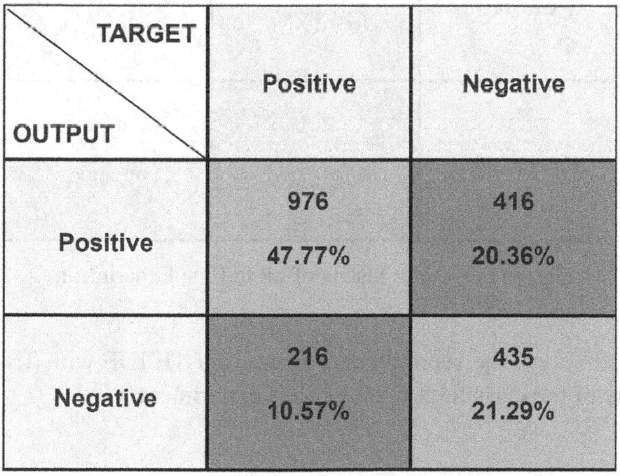

TARGET \\ OUTPUT	Positive	Negative
Positive	976 47.77%	416 20.36%
Negative	216 10.57%	435 21.29%

Fig. 2. Confusion Matrix of SVM in First Experiment.

respectively. Additionally, the first experiment's confusion matrix for the classifiers is depicted in Figs. 2, 3, and 4.

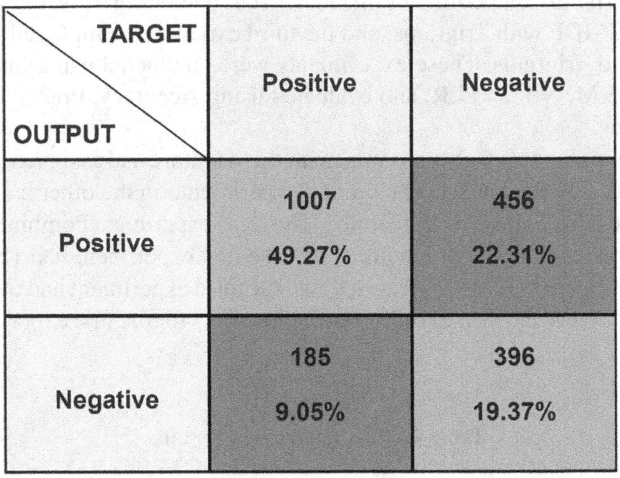

TARGET OUTPUT	Positive	Negative
Positive	1007 49.27%	456 22.31%
Negative	185 9.05%	396 19.37%

Fig. 3. Confusion Matrix of NB in First Experiment.

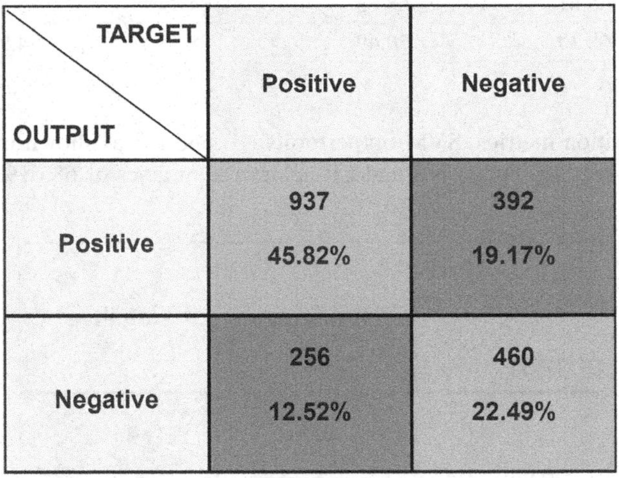

TARGET OUTPUT	Positive	Negative
Positive	937 45.82%	392 19.17%
Negative	256 12.52%	460 22.49%

Fig. 4. Confusion Matrix of LR in First Experiment.

As mentioned above, the second experiment used TF-IDF with Trigrams, Table 5 shows the results of the classifiers in the second experiment.

Table 5. Second Experiment Results.

Classifier	Accuracy (%)	Precision (%)	Recall (%)	F1-Score (%)
SVM	58.55	58.46	99.97	73.78
NB	58.58	58.48	99.95	73.79
LR	**58.60**	**58.49**	**99.94**	**73.79**

According to Table 5, LR achieves the highest precision of 58.49%, followed by NB with 58.48%, while SVM has the lowest precision of 58.46%. Notably, all classifiers have low accuracy at 58%, which may be attributed to the Trigrams' nature of using three consecutive words as features, leading to unfavorable feature dependencies. Moreover, the second experiment's confusion matrix for the classifiers is depicted in Figs. 5, 6, and 7.

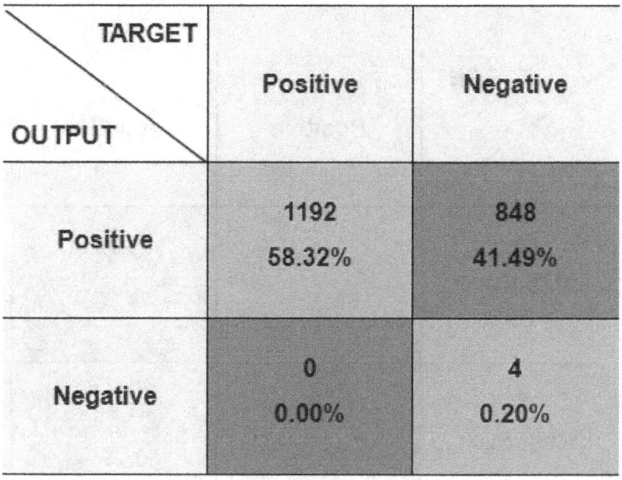

TARGET OUTPUT	Positive	Negative
Positive	1192 58.32%	848 41.49%
Negative	0 0.00%	4 0.20%

Fig. 5. Confusion Matrix of SVM in Second Experiment.

Furthermore, Table 6 presents the outcomes of the third experiment, which combines the first and second experiments.

As shown in Table 6, SVM achieved the highest accuracy of 68.92%, followed by LR with 68.83%, while NB had the lowest accuracy with 66.93. On the other hand, LR had the highest precision of 69.43%, followed by SVM and NB with 69.15% and 65.55%, respectively. Figures 8, 9, and 10 displays the confusion matrix of the classifiers used in the third experiment.

TARGET / OUTPUT	Positive	Negative
Positive	1192 58.35%	846 41.41%
Negative	0 0.00%	5 0.24%

Fig. 6. Confusion Matrix of NB in Second Experiment.

TARGET / OUTPUT	Positive	Negative
Positive	1192 58.32%	846 41.39%
Negative	0 0.00%	6 0.29%

Fig. 7. Confusion Matrix of LR in Second Experiment.

Table 6. Third Experiment Results.

Classifier	Accuracy (%)	Precision (%)	Recall (%)	F1-Score (%)
SVM	**68.92**	**69.15**	**84.35**	**75.99**
NB	66.93	65.55	89.71	75.75
LR	68.83	69.43	83.20	75.69

TARGET / OUTPUT	Positive	Negative
Positive	1006 49.22%	449 21.97%
Negative	186 9.10%	403 19.72%

Fig. 8. Confusion Matrix of SVM in Third Experiment.

TARGET / OUTPUT	Positive	Negative
Positive	1037 51.64%	545 27.14%
Negative	119 5.93%	307 15.29%

Fig. 9. Confusion Matrix of NB in Third Experiment.

Upon comparing the experiments, it can be observed that the first experiment out-performs the others, possibly due to the suitability of Unigrams for the dataset, which considers short sentences in each record. This is further supported by the second experiment, where the use of Trigrams results in low accuracy scores of 58% for all classifiers. However, the combination of Unigrams and Trigrams may be a viable option, as seen in the converged accuracy between the first and third experiments. The third experiment also highlights the potential of this combination to enhance classifier performance, evident in LR highest precision score of 69.43% across all classifiers.

In addition, it is worth noting that the domain of poems presents more challenges than other domains, such as movies, reviews, politics, and sports. This is supported by

TARGET OUTPUT	Positive	Negative
Positive	992 48.53%	437 21.38%
Negative	200 9.78%	415 20.30%

Fig. 10. Confusion Matrix of LR in Third Experiment.

the literature reviews conducted in this study and is reflected in the experimental results, which are consistent with those reported in [1]. Notably, the study in [9] achieved the best precision of 72%, possibly due to the use of Stemming in the preprocessing stage rather than Lemmatization. Conversely, the study in [8] obtained the highest accuracy of 79%, supporting the use of Unigrams as a feature extraction method to enhance classifier performance.

5 Conclusion

Sentiment analysis is a crucial application of NLP that leverages the wealth of information offered by textual data. However, developing NLP models and tools for Arabic dialects poses a formidable challenge, given the limited written resources available for many of these dialects. In this study, three ML classifiers were investigated for extracting sentiment from the Libyan middle region dialect, using TF-IDF with Unigrams, Trigrams, and a combination of both. The results indicate that using Unigrams as a feature extraction technique can significantly enhance classifier performance, while the use of Trigrams can lead to inferior performance. For future work, the authors aim to explore the impact of the Stemming step in the preprocessing phase and the use of bigrams with unigrams as feature extraction on the classifiers' performance.

References

1. Abugharsa, A.: Sentiment Analysis in Poems in Misurata Sub-dialect--A Senti-ment Detection in an Arabic Sub-dialect. arXiv Prepr. arXiv:2109.07203 (2021)
2. Alyami, S., Alhothali, A., Jamal, A.: Systematic literature review of arabic aspect-based sentiment analysis. J. King Saud Univ. Inf. Sci. **34**(9), 6524–6551 (2022)

3. Mehta, P., Pandya, S.: A review on sentiment analysis methodologies, practices and applications. Int. J. Sci. Technol. Res. 9(2), 601–609 (2020)
4. Duwairi, R.M., Marji, R., Sha'ban, N., Rushaidat, S.:Sentiment analysis in Arabic tweets. In: 2014 5th International Conference on Information and Communication Systems (ICICS), pp. 1–6 (2014)
5. Alshutayri, A.O.O., Atwell, E.: Exploring Twitter as a source of an Arabic dialect corpus. Int. J. Comput. Linguist. 8(2), 37–44 (2017)
6. Elouardighi, A., Maghfour, M., Hammia, H., Aazi, F.: A machine Learning approach for sentiment analysis in the standard or dialectal Arabic Facebook comments. In: 2017 3rd International Conference of Cloud Computing Technologies and Applications (CloudTech), pp. 1–8 (2017)
7. Elnagar, A., Yagi, S., Nassif, A.B., Shahin, I., Salloum, S.A.: Sentiment analysis in dialectal Arabic: a systematic review. Adv. Mach. Learn. Technol. Appl. Proc. AMLTA 2021, 407–417 (2021)
8. Alsharif, O., Alshamaa, D., Ghneim, N.: Emotion classification in Arabic poetry using machine learning. Int. J. Comput. Appl. 65(16), 1–6 (2013)
9. Ahmed, M.A., Hasan, R.A., Ali, A.H., Mohammed, M.A.: The classification of the modern Arabic poetry using machine learning. TELEKOMNIKA (Telecommun. Electron. Control. 17(5), 2667–2674 (2019)
10. Al-Harbi, W.A., Emam, A.: Effect of Saudi dialect preprocessing on Arabic sen-timent analysis. Int. J. Adv. Comput. Technol. 4(6), 91–99 (2015)
11. Nassr, Z., Sael, N., Benabbou, F.: Preprocessing Arabic dialect for sentiment mining: state of art. Int. Arch. Photogram. Remote Sens. Spatial Inf. Sci. 44, 323–330 (2020). https://doi.org/10.5194/isprs-archives-XLIV-4-W3-2020-323-2020
12. Sayed, A., Elgeldawi, E., Zaki, A.M., Galal, A.R.: Sentiment analysis for Arabic reviews using machine learning classification algorithms. In: 2020 International Con-ference on Innovative Trends in Communication and Computer Engineering (ITCE), 2020, pp. 56–63 (2020)
13. Shoukry, A., Rafea, A.: Preprocessing Egyptian dialect tweets for sentiment min-ing. In: Fourth Workshop on Computational Approaches to Arabic-Script-based Languages, 2012, pp. 47–56 (2012)
14. Symeonidis, S., Effrosynidis, D., Arampatzis, A.: A comparative evaluation of pre-processing techniques and their interactions for twitter sentiment analysis. Expert Syst. Appl. 110, 298–310 (2018)
15. Al, A.A., Shamsi, S.A.: Sentiment analysis of Emirati dialect. Big Data Cogn. Comput. 6(2), 57 (2022). https://doi.org/10.3390/bdcc6020057
16. Habberrih, A., Abuzaraida, M.A.: Sentiment analysis of arabic dialects: a review study BT - computing and informatics. In: Zakaria, N.H., Mansor, N.S., Husni, H., Mohammed, F. (eds.), pp. 137–153. Springer Nature, Singapore (2024). https://doi.org/10.1007/978-981-99-9589-9_11

Data Quality Considerations for ERP Implementation: Techniques for Effective Data Management

Mohamed Elbadri[1], Ahmed Altaher[2,3](✉) (iD), and Sharafedeen Alkawan[2]

[1] University of Grenoble Alpes, Grenoble, France
[2] S2A2I-Lab, Saint Martin d'Hères, France
ahmed.ah.altaher@gmail.com
[3] College of Electronic Technology, Tripoli, Libya

Abstract. Most industrial companies implement enterprise resource planning systems to enrich their digital transformation. ERP systems are databased technologies that employee big data, machine learning, data science and automation. Data is important to deploy such centralized systems, and to improve business decisions. ERP system can merge data from warehouse, sales orders, marketing commands, finance, human resources and management offices. It helps enterprises to get advantages of digital ecosystems and competitive rank in the market. Data quality issues in ERP implementation can have significant consequences for businesses success and their competitive positions. To mitigate these consequences, enterprises must prioritize data quality during ERP implementation. Implementing robust data governance practices, conducting data cleansing and validation, ensuring data accuracy and completeness, and establishing data quality monitoring mechanisms are crucial steps to enhance data quality and minimize the negative impact on business operations.

This paper focuses on some data issues that may face implementers during data migration phase, in addition, it proposes some solutions. The work reviews current related studies that help companies to overcome lack of quality data and related problems that may cause delay, budget deficit and collapse of ERP projects. It discusses three concepts namely, data integration, ETL process and data integrity in order to help ERP project managers distinguish these activities. Additionally it provides technical recommendations to manage data quality for success of ERP implementations.

Keywords: Data Migration · ERP Integrity · Quality Data

1 Introduction

During ERP implementation, old data migration, from old distributed resources to a novel centralized system, shapes an important step toward good execution of ERP projects. This phase requires suitable arrangements such as finding skilled developers, allocating data resources and preparing data backups. ERP developers, implementers and project

T. A. T. Benmusa et al. (Eds.): ILCICT 2023, CCIS 2097, pp. 210–220, 2024.
https://doi.org/10.1007/978-3-031-62624-1_17

managers can name many difficulties, although data migration is not appropriately covered. Some risks may occur such as extending project duration, exceeding a dedicated budget due to hiring outsourcing skills, and getting rough opinions from stakeholders. In this case, implementers face difficulties to avoid data quality issues, e.g. missed, repeated or altered data.

Large enterprises own distributed data in several places that can be in different data store formats such as database records or digital spreadsheets. This data cannot be migrated into the new ERP system without prior processing and handling. Low quality of data may therefore delay the project schedule due to the required processing and handling. Preparing or hiring effective data force implementers is important as well as taking data issues in their minds, i.e. data needs collecting, cleansing, and evaluating of its integrity, i.e. to be ready for the ERP system. For instance, as soon as the project staff start to collect the required ERP data, duplicate data can be found in several places. In this case, data should be processed and tuned through deleting, altering and reediting of this data. The ERP users shall notice data formats, adjustable fields size and meaningful values, i.e. according to their use with ERP data and business records.

In small and medium enterprises (SME), ERPs are integrative systems that involve centralized version of the SME transactional operations. Today, all identified data redundancies and inconsistencies that can guarantee the transactional operation, and often the success of the company, although in the future can lead to the failure of the ERP implementation. Consultants should strive to understand, standardize and integrate deficient business processes before large-scale ERP implementation. Thus, no crucial aspect of the SME operation is forgotten or disregarded [1].

Consultants that are hired, to carry out the ERP system, have an important role at early stages of the implementation and ongoing-live phases. In addition, the attention, from the top management and experts, is a significant element in the ERP project success [2]. ERP implementers may append timetable to have quality data besides hiring experts, in result, allocating more budget because special skills and knowledge are important to do so. To mention some skills, data dashboards require data science expertise at manufacturing and managements levels in order to track production capacity and quality. Companies normally hire dedicated personnel or train their adjacent IT staff to have these add-on skills. Many companies (around 20%) just starting to figure that data science and AI are among major skills gap and around 40% of these companies decided to enrich their staff skills [3].

In this paper, data quality is defined and related data issues are clarified. Additionally, authors survey some recent solutions that automate the process of data cleansing and help to reach data integrity. The paper defines the notion of the data quality issues and their characterization in the context of ERP implementation. The main goal is to provide concise recommendations, which help ERP project managers and implementers avoid data quality issues. The paper contributes to the data management of ERP projects by highlighting the differences between data integration, ETL process, and data integrity to help ERP project managers distinguish these activities. By presenting technical recommendations, the paper also contributes to the management of data quality in ERP projects to ensure successful implementations.

2   The Process of Data Migration

For business applications, data migration process aims to transfer/convert data originally founded in the old system into formats that are suitably conform to the new system purpose. This data can be in hard, e.g. catalogues or booklets, or soft records, e.g. databases. In modern systems, data is in digital formats, although it is distributed among enterprises departments or branches. In further complexity, modern enterprises switch on premise infrastructure and applications to cloud-computing models, i.e. cloud-based storage and apps, to allow users to store, access, and modify their data on the internet through a cloud service provider. Service providers are responsible for managing and operating this data storage as a service (SaaS). Enterprises subscribe to a specific data storage capacity, usually in a pay-as-you-go model [3]. In this model, data synchronization and downloading are necessary. Hence, data migration consist converting hard records and soft data into required digital formats in order to be ready for manipulation by computer software. The process also could be to convert from old distributed databases to new centralized ERP database as depicted by Fig. 1.

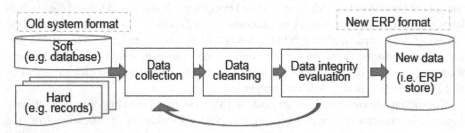

Fig. 1. Data Migration principal steps with integrity after collecting and cleansing of data.

3   Importance of Data Quality

Poor data quality occurs when stakeholders discover inaccuracies and inconsistencies in a data collection or when data extraction is not as intended [4]. Incorrectly entered, duplicate, incomplete or irrelevant data cause poor quality. Hence, the use of poor quality data in an ERP can degrade the quality of transactional, master, analytical data resources. As a result, use of this data, for business analysis, shall lead to harmful, difficult, and unwise decisions.

Due to existence of non-proper data, the process of migrating data from physical catalogs or records, a single data resource (i.e. database), or distributed databases to an ERP database shall encounter some issues that lead to migration delays. In this case, data integrity is needed to increase the quality of data resources before bringing the ERP online. If the data resources are accurate, complete, and logically consistent, then one can said that these resources have data integrity (i.e. to guarantee quality data). The later therefore requires systematic inspection to verify storage, processing, reporting and analysis of data. Additionally, checking the data integrity require good participation of the enterprise workforce to eliminate any information gaps between the implemented ERP system and reality. This participation facilities the communication from/to top management and enhances the integrity and efficiency of the system in order to increase data quality [2].

Indeed, the company's information system shall be improved by adopting good quality practices to ensure the data integrity. Moreover, through such practice improvements, enterprises can identify and overcome many barriers, e.g. inefficient cross-functional collaboration, and potential risks, e.g. users enter incorrect data into the ERP system, which can affect the success of the ERP project [1].

Quality issues could be related to data sources, data transfer or/and data entry. During data migration, i.e. to the ERP system, data transfer quality should be guaranteed through integrity inspection, e.g. incomplete migrated data, repeated, non-clean; entry mistakes, mismatch data and bad data mapping are the common factors that contribute to bad quality. Errors can happen throughout migration of a huge data transfer. Mismatch data usually is exist when dealing with big databases of tables from legacy systems. Indeed, testing is important step to evaluate the data integrity. This step lets the developers identify the scale of success. A good plan is to migrate a small sample of data individually first, to make sure everything in the system is working normally, then a larger dedicated sample of data is migrated afterwards, and so on.

To sum up, data quality means data integrity from a data analysis perspective and good decisions from a business perspective. In other words, having high quality and integrity data at the operational and tactical levels shall feed useful information for decision-making processes at the executive and strategic levels.

4 Consequences of Poor Quality Data

In practice, the use of poor quality data leads to tangible penalties for any company. The industry 1-10-100 rule means; data entry verification costs $1, while $10 to clean this data once records are infected with impure data, and $100 if the business does nothing [3]. Poor-quality data can lead to weak customers' relationships, imprecise data analytics, wrong decisions, and low business performance. Poor data quality may seem like a minor source of problems, but they can easily escalate as repeated data errors grow and accumulate [5, 6]. Hence, any use/entry of poor quality data can lead to unsatisfied results that may include:

1. Imprecise reporting and decision-making: if users enter incorrect, incomplete or inconsistent data in the ERP system, results can be inaccurate financial statements, inventory records, customer or critical business information. This can lead to weak decisions based on unreliable information.
2. Process inefficiencies: ERP systems are planned to improve efficiency of business processes. However, poor quality data can disrupt these processes. Incorrect data, related to inventory/supply chain management, can increase orders delays or cause stock outs. This might lead to operational inefficiencies, increased costs and dissatisfied customers.

3. Increased time and effort: poor quality data needs more time and effort than expected. During ERP implementation, data cleansing and data migration activities become complex and time-consuming while dealing with inaccurate data that leads to delay of implementation, rise of project cost and set a strain on resources.

4. User resistance challenges: users may resist adopting the ERP system if they face data quality issues. If employees experienced data related issues in the past, they may lack confidence in the system accuracy and resist using it. This resistance can hinder and undermine the overall success of the ERP project.

5. Customer dissatisfaction: poor quality data can have direct impact on customer satisfaction, e.g. incorrect billing, shipping errors or failed deliveries due to inaccurate customer records. Such issues can lead to customer dissatisfaction, trust loss, company's reputation damage.

6. Regulatory compliance issues: poor quality data can cause non-compliance with regulatory requirements, e.g. The ERP system fails to summarize and report accurate information required for regulatory purpose, leading to legal and financial consequences, i.e. fines, penalties or legal actions.

To mitigate these consequences, enterprises and stakeholders should prioritize data quality management as a crucial aspect.

5   Techniques to Handle Data Quality Issues

Many techniques, that can support ERP implementers, are exist since long time, although they are used for data warehousing and data management. ETL (Extracting, Transforming and Loading) and data integration are renovated tools in terms of ERP data management, i.e. managing data for ERP implementations. More insights on these techniques are followed.

5.1   Extraction, Transforming and Loading

Many reasons justify the need for ETL as a data integration tool phase within the ERP systems implementation, this step therefore is needed to handle data issues such as existence of heterogeneous data formats (e.g. data formats might be ambiguous or difficult to interpret/transform), outdated databases in legacy systems, and structural changes of the data sources over time. These issues make decisions uncertain. Indeed, ETL is a crucial element in data warehousing process where most of the data cleaning and curation is done [7].

Maintaining compatibility of data formats is necessary process to have data integrity. Now, technology is more precise in data compatibility. In fact, ETL provides a solution of data sourcing (from original data), then transforming the data into a compatible format, finally loading the data, which is the part that solves the data migration issues [8]. This methodology enables implementers to use smart solutions regarding data warehouse management. Some applications, e.g. the Talend software, are capable tools that can automatically manage this envisaged solution.

Intelligent platforms can centralize data processing and gives more automated, secured and smooth data migration. To name a method, ETL is one of the approaches that corresponds to data management (Fig. 2).

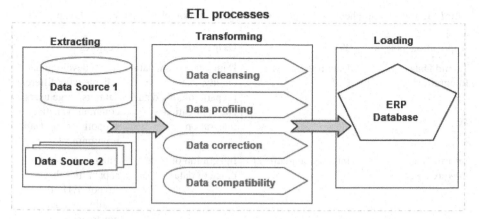

Fig. 2. Extracting, Transforming and Loading (ETL) of data to new ERP central database

5.2 Data Integration

Data integration share some ETL commonalities as they both deal with the process of combining data from various sources and making it accessible and usable in a unified manner. Although, data integration is more comprehensive process [9]. While ETL is a specific type of data integration process that focuses on the extraction, transformation, and loading of data into a target system, data integration is a broader concept that encompasses various techniques and approaches for integrating data from different sources and systems. ETL is a crucial part of data integration, and both are essential components in modern data management and analytics workflows [7–9]. Data integration ensures that data from different departments, systems, and sources are brought together and consolidated within the final ERP system. Additionally, Data integration enables many business functions (e.g. finance, inventory management, sales, procurement, human resources, and more) to seamlessly share and exchange data, facilitating cross-functional processes and ensuring consistency and accuracy across different areas of the enterprise [10]. Data integration in ERP systems often involves real-time or near-real-time data synchronization. This means that all changes are automatically propagated to other relevant modules or components. This real-time data integration allows for accurate and up-to-date information throughout the organization [11]. In this manner, integrating data within the ERP system eliminates data divisions, i.e. data silos. Enterprises can break down these silos and create a unified view of data, enabling better decision-making and analysis [12]. Finally, ERP systems also require data integration to interact with external systems, such as suppliers, customers, banks, or third-party applications. Integration interfaces or APIs (Application Programming Interfaces) are often used to exchange data between the ERP system and these external entities, ensuring seamless data flow and process automation [13]. Generally, data integration is a critical aspect of ERP systems, enabling enterprises to streamline operations, improve data accuracy, and gain comprehensive insights into their business processes [14, 15]. Table 1 depicts some well-known integration software that have data ETL feature to assist ERP implementers to extract, transform and load quality data.

Table 1. Non-comprehensive list of well-known integration platforms with ETL capabilities

Application tool	Type	Usage	Features
Talend Data Integration	Data Integration & ETL	Data integration, data quality, data preparation, big data, and application integration	Rapid development, reliable with different datasets, large users community, native support for Big Data Environment
Informatica PowerCenter	Integration platform	Integration of wide range of data	Integration capabilities that support ETL, data quality, and data governance
Microsoft SQL Server Integration Services	Integration and ETL tool	Development environment to solve complex business problems by copying or downloading files, loading data warehouses, cleansing and mining data	Powerful visual development with Management Studio It integrates well with other Microsoft products
IBM InfoSphere DataStage	Integration and ETL tool	Designing, developing, and running jobs that move and transform data	Visual interface for designing, developing, and managing ETL processes Extensive connectivity options and supports large-scale data integration projects
SAP Data Services	Integration services	Data integration, data quality, data profiling and data processing	Integration capabilities, transform trusted data-to-data warehouse system for analytical reporting
Oracle Data Integrator	Integration platform	Data transformation, movement, and synchronization capabilities	Declarative design approach and tight integration with Oracle databases

(continued)

Table 1. (*continued*)

Application tool	Type	Usage	Features
Pentaho Data Integration	open-source integration & ETL	Data integration, ETL processes	Visual interface, supports a wide range of data sources, and offers features like data profiling and cleansing
Apache NiFi	open-source data integration	Data flow management	Web-based interface and allows users to design and execute data integration workflows with a focus on data routing, transformation, and system mediation
Matillion ETL	cloud-native ETL platform	Modern data integration in cloud environments	Support for popular cloud services such as Amazon Web Services (AWS), Google Cloud Platform (GCP), and Microsoft Azure
Mage	open-source ETL	Integration and transforming data	Integration and synchronization of data from third-party sources. Supports building real-time and batch pipelines
Airbyte	open-source ELT and integration platform	Integration and synchronization of data sources	Offers pre-built data connectors from an API or User Interfaces

ERP project managers and implementers can choose an integration or ETL tool. However, better to have team skills and to decide with their teammates. The applications that are mentioned in Table 1 can assist teams to migrate data and to manage its quality.

6 Discussions

Considering data quality, when it comes to ERP implementations, all the three aspects ETL, Data Integration, and Data Integrity—are important and play different roles in ensuring high-quality data. Focusing on data quality in new ERP projects, all these three aspects are interconnected and essential for success. ETL ensures that data is appropriately extracted, transformed, and loaded into the ERP system, addressing quality issues along the way. Data integration establishes a unified view and consistent data flow, reducing data discrepancies and enhancing quality, while data integrity ensures the overall accuracy, completeness, and reliability of data within the ERP system.

By addressing data quality issues during the extraction and transformation stages, ETL helps maintain accurate and reliable data within the ERP system. Data integration supports data quality by ensuring consistency, coherence, and completeness of data across the ERP system. It helps prevent redundancy, data inconsistencies, and conflicting information, ultimately improving the overall data quality and reliability. Data integrity measures, such as data validation rules, referential integrity constraints, and data governance policies, help enforce data quality standards and prevent issues like duplicate records, missing values, or incorrect data. Maintaining data integrity is crucial for ERP implementations as it safeguards the reliability of information and supports effective decision-making processes.

Technically, to achieve optimal data quality in ERP implementations, it is crucial to select one or to combine all these three aspects as they work together to ensure accurate, consistent, and reliable data within the system.

7 Conclusions

Data quality plays a crucial role in ERP implementations, especially with the advancements in business analytics and artificial intelligence. When migrating data from diverse sources, whether they are outdated or modern systems, it is essential to prioritize integration, ETL processes, and data integrity. This approach ensures that the data maintains a high level of quality and becomes a fundamental factor in the success of the ERP project. In this regard, the present work aims to provide practical recommendations specifically tailored for ERP project managers and implementers. Data quality can be improved, and potential risks during the migration phase can be mitigated, ultimately resulting in a successful ERP implementation, by following these recommendations:

- **Develop a Data Strategy:** Create a comprehensive plan that outlines the standards and processes for data quality throughout the project. Define data quality metrics, establish data cleansing and validation procedures, and identify responsibilities for data quality management.
- **Engage Data Stewards and Data Governance:** Assign dedicated data stewards or a data governance team responsible for overseeing data quality, resolving data-related issues, and ensuring adherence to data management policies and practices.
- **Foster Collaboration and Communication:** Encourage collaboration and open communication among project stakeholders, including business users, IT teams, and data experts. Regularly review and discuss data quality metrics, address concerns, and incorporate feedback to improve the overall success of the ERP project.
- **Perform Data Profiling and Analysis:** Achieve a thorough analysis of the data to be migrated, including identifying inconsistencies, duplicates, missing values, and data quality issues. This analysis will help in determining the scope and complexity of the migration process and identify appropriate correction actions.

- **Define Data Migration Requirements:** Clearly define the data migration requirements and objectives, including data mapping, transformation rules, and data validation criteria. Collaborate with stakeholders to ensure that all necessary data elements are captured and migrated accurately.
- **Implement Data Cleansing and Transformation:** Prior to the migration, cleanse and transform the data to ensure consistency, accuracy, and completeness. Remove duplicate records, standardize formats, and resolve any data anomalies or errors to improve data quality.
- **Ensure Data Integrity and Validation:** Establish data integrity checks and validation mechanisms to ensure the accuracy and reliability of the migrated data. Implement data validation rules and perform thorough testing to identify and rectify any discrepancies or inconsistencies.
- **Conduct Thorough Testing:** Perform comprehensive testing of the ERP system and the migrated data to validate functionality, performance, and data integrity. Test various scenarios and perform end-to-end testing to ensure that the system operates as intended and that data is accurately processed and displayed.
- **Train Users and Provide Documentation:** Educate and train users on the importance of data quality and the correct usage of the ERP system. Provide detailed documentation and resources that explain the data migration processes, data entry guidelines, and best practices to maintain data quality.
- **Monitor and Maintain Data Quality:** Establish ongoing monitoring and maintenance processes to continually assess and improve data quality within the ERP system. Implement data governance practices, regular data audits, and data quality checks to address any issues that may arise post-migration.

References

1. Christofi, M., Nunes, M., Chao Peng, G., Lin, A.: Towards ERP success in SMEs through business process review prior to implementation. J. Syst. Inf. Technol. **15**(4), 304–323 (2013)
2. Mahar, F., Ali, S.I., Jumani, A.K., Khan, M.O.: ERP system implementation: planning, management, and administrative issues. Indian J. Sci. Technol. **13**(01), 1–22 (2020)
3. David, J.: The AI talent shortage is not over yet. Wall Str. J. (2020). Accessed 20 June 2023
4. Vosburg, J., Kumar, A.: Managing dirty data in organizations using ERP: lessons from a case study. Ind. Manag. Data Syst. **101**(1), 21–31 (2001)
5. Keith, D.: The impact of poor data quality (and how to fix it). Dataversity (2023). Accessed 23 June 2023
6. Gudivada, V., Apon, A., Ding, J.: Data quality considerations for big data and machine learning: going beyond data cleaning and transformations. Int. J. Adv. Softw. **10**(1), 1–20 (2017)
7. Souibgui, M., Atigui, F., Zammali, S., Cherfi, S., Yahia, S.B.: Data quality in ETL process: a preliminary study. Procedia Comput. Sci. **159**, 676–687 (2019)
8. Nguyen, T.: Improving the ETL process for a case company. Thesis of Master in IT. Metropolia University of Applied Science, Finland (2023). Accessed 20 June 2023
9. Jovanovic, P., Nadal, S., Romero, O., Abelló, A., Bilalli, B.: Quarry: a user-centered big data integration platform. Inf. Syst. Front. **23**, 9–33 (2021)
10. Chopra, R., Sawant, L., Kodi, D., Terkar, R.: Utilization of ERP systems in manufacturing industry for productivity improvement. Mater. Today Proc. **62**, 1238–1245 (2022)

11. Sarferaz, S.: Compendium on Enterprise Resource Planning: Market, Functional and Conceptual View Based on SAP S/4HANA, pp. 29–50. Springer, Cham (2022). https://doi.org/10.1007/978-3-030-93856-7

12. Muniswamaiah, M., Agerwala, T., Tappert, C.: Data virtualization for decision making in big data. Int. J. Softw. Eng. Appl 10(5), 45–53 (2019)

13. Budiman, K., Putra, A.T., Sugiharti, E., Muslim, M.A., Arifudin, R.: Implementation of ERP system functionalities for data acquisition based on API at the study program of universities. J. Phys. Conf. Ser. 1918(4), 042151 (2021)

14. Beheshti, H.M., Blaylock, B. K., Henderson, D.A., Lollar, J.G.: Selection and critical success factors in successful ERP implementation. Compet. Rev. 24(4), 357–375 (2014)

15. Watson III, E.F., Schwarz, A.H.: Enterprise and business process automation. In: Nof, S.Y. (ed.) Springer Handbook of Automation. Springer Handbooks, pp. 1385–1400 . Springer, Cham (2023). https://doi.org/10.1007/978-3-030-96729-1_65

Fractional Calculus Application for PID Controller of a Nuclear Power Plant

Hala Elhabrush[1]($\boxtimes$), Mohamed Samir Elbuni[1], and Abdullah Ezzedin[2]

[1] Computer Engineering Department, University of Tripoli, Tripoli, Libya
{h.elhabrush,m.elbuni}@uot.edu.ly
[2] Nuclear Engineering Department, University of Tripoli, Tripoli, Libya
a.ezzedin@uot.edu.ly

Abstract. A fractional order PID (FOPID) controller was designed to control a pressurized water reactor (PWR) nuclear power plant. The reactor was represented by a simplified model using point kinetic equations with one group of delayed neutrons and the associated thermal hydraulic equation. The FOPID design was based on minimizing the sum of integral of squared error (ISE) and integral of squared controller output (ISCO) using particle swarm optimization (PSO) algorithm. Compared with other optimization methods, the PSO is faster, simpler and needs fewer parameters to be adjusted. The simulation of the reactor power response to a reactivity insertion using the FOPID controller showed better performance with respect to the power increase overshoot compared to those of the PID controller. In addition, the settling and steady state times were shorter.

Keywords: fractional order PID (FOPID) · pressurized water reactor (PWR) · particle swarm optimization (PSO) algorithm

1 Introduction

Most of process plants controllers are based on the use of PID controllers due to their design simplicity and good performance in terms of short settling time and small percentage overshoot. A survey made by Yamamoto and Hashimoto in 1991 [1], showed that more than 90 percent of the control loops were of the PID type. The evolution use of fractional calculus in recent years contributed to the improvements of PID quality and robustness through the use of FOPID controllers with non-integer differentiation and integration parts.

In ordinary calculus, the order of differentiation and integration *n* is always an integer. Fractional calculus extends the order of differentiation and integration *n* to non-integer values. At present time, due to the availability of calculation tools and fast computers, the number of applications of fractional calculus has been growing rapidly [2].

The use of FOPID controllers for nuclear power plant control has been investigated in a number of recent studies [3–8]. The results of these studies suggest that FOPID controllers can be a promising alternative to traditional PID controllers for nuclear power plant control.

T. A. T. Benmusa et al. (Eds.): ILCICT 2023, CCIS 2097, pp. 221–236, 2024.
https://doi.org/10.1007/978-3-031-62624-1_18

In this paper, a FOPID controller was designed to control a PWR power plant. The FOPID parameters were tuned using PSO algorithm to get optimum time domain specifications. PSO possesses several distinguishing features that set it apart from other optimization algorithms, including its ease of implementation, strong performance, and efficient utilization of computational resources, making it a highly promising optimization algorithm [9]. The simulation results showed that the FOPID controller outperforms the PID controller.

2 Fractional Calculus

The question of validity of non-integer order of derivatives was first raised by L'Hopital on September 30th, 1695. He posed a question about the result of $\frac{D^n x}{Dx^n}$, if $n = \frac{1}{2}$ [10].

The generalized fundamental operator, which includes the differentiation and integration is given as:

$$aD_t^\alpha = f(x) = \begin{cases} \frac{d^\alpha}{dt^\alpha}, \Re(\alpha) > 0 \\ 1, \Re(\alpha) = 0 \\ \int\limits_a^t (dt)^{-\alpha}, \Re(\alpha) < 0 \end{cases} \tag{1}$$

where a and t denote the limits of the operation and α denotes the fractional order and generally it is assumed that $\alpha \in R$, but it may also be a complex number [2].

The popular definitions of fractional derivatives and integrals in fractional calculus are listed in [11].

3 Mathematical Model for a Nuclear Power Plant

The reactor is modeled using the point kinetic equations with one group of delayed neutrons and the associated thermal-hydraulic equations taking into account the reactivity feedback due to the fuel and coolant temperatures [12].

3.1 Neutron Point Kinetic Model

Neutrons are produced in a nuclear reactor from the fission process of uranium atoms. Most of the neutrons are emitted promptly. A small fraction of the fission neutron, delayed neutrons, are emitted after a certain time due to the disintegration of produced radioactive materials called precursors.

The neutron density in an operating nuclear reactor are presented by the following equations

$$\frac{dn}{dt} = \frac{\rho - \beta}{\Lambda} n + \lambda c \tag{2}$$

and

$$\frac{dc}{dt} = \frac{\beta}{\Lambda} n - \lambda c \tag{3}$$

where, n is a neutron density, c is a delayed neutron precursor concentration, ρ is a total core reactivity, β is an effective precursor yield per fission, Λ is a prompt neutron generation time[sec] and λ is a precursor decay constant $[sec^{-1}]$.

3.2   Total Reactivity Model

The reactivity, which is a measure of the reactor deviation from the critical state may change due to the effect of control rod movement or the temperature changes of the fuel and the moderator is given by

$$\rho = \rho_{rod} + \rho_f + \rho_m \tag{4}$$

If
$\rho > 0$ the reactor is super critical (power increases)
$\rho = 0$ the reactor is critical (steady power)
$\rho < 0$ the reactor is sub-critical (power decreases)
where ρ_{rod} is a reactivity due to a control rod movement, ρ_f is a reactivity of the fuel temperature change and ρ_m is a reactivity of the moderator temperature change.

3.3   The Core Thermal Hydraulic Model

The rate of energy stored in the fuel is expressed by

$$c_{pf}M_f \frac{dT_f(t)}{dt} = An(t) - H\big[T_f(t) - T_m(t)\big] \tag{5}$$

where, A is a conversion constant from neutron density to power $(Btu/sec.n/cm^3)$, $n(t)$ is a neutron density or reactor power $(\#n/cm^3)$, H is an overall heat transfer coefficient $(w/^{o}C)$, c_{pf} is a specific heat of fuel $(w - sec/gm-^{0}C)$, M_f is a mass of fuel (gm), T_f is a fuel temperature (^{o}C) and T_m is an average moderator temperature (^{o}C)

The rate of energy stored in the coolant (moderator) is expressed by:

$$c_{pm}M_m \frac{dT_m}{dt} = H\big[T_f(t) - T_m(t)\big] - Wc_{pm}[T_o(t) - T_i(t)] \tag{6}$$

where, T_i is the reactor coolant inlet temperature (^{o}C), T_o is the reactor coolant outlet temperature (^{o}C), W is a coolant mass flow rate (gm/sec), c_{pm} is a specific heat of moderator $(w - sec/gm^{o}C)$ and M_m is a mass of coolant in the reactor(gm).

3.4   Steam Generator Model

An energy balance applied to the primary side of steam generator yields the equation:

$$c_p M_G \frac{dT_{Gav}(t)}{dt} = Wc_p[T_{Gi}(t) - T_{Go}(t)] - H_G[T_{Gav}(t) - T_s(t)] \tag{7}$$

where, M_G is a mass of primary water in tubes, H_G is the total heat transfer coefficient $(W/^{o}C)$, T_s is a steam temperature, T_{Gi} is an inlet primary coolant temperature, T_{Go} is an outlet primary coolant temperature, c_p is a specific heat of primary coolant, W is a water mass flow rate and T_{Gav} is an average primary coolant temperature in steam generator

The energy balance applied to the secondary side of the steam generator yields:

$$\big(M_T c_{pT} + M_s c_{ps}\big) \frac{dT_s(t)}{dt} = H_G[T_{Gav}(t) - T_s(t)] - P_G(s) \tag{8}$$

where

$$P_G = w_s(H_s - H_{sF}) = w_s\Delta H \tag{9}$$

$$w_s = PK_vO \tag{10}$$

where, M_T is a mass of tube metal, c_{pT} is a specific heat of tube metal, M_s is a mass of steam and water mixture, c_{ps} is a specific heat of steam and water mixture, P_G is a power extracted from the steam generator, w_s is a steam flow rate, ΔH is an enthalpy difference of the saturated steam and feed water, P is the saturated steam pressure, K_V is the throttle constant and O is the fractional valve opening ($0 < O < 1$).

After carrying out the linearization, and by taking the Laplace transform, the Simulink diagram for this mathematical model is implemented as shown in Fig. 1. The reactor and steam generator data are listed in Table 1 and Table 2 respectively.

Table 1. Reactor Data

Parameters	Symbol	Value	Parameters	Symbol	Value
Reactor power level	n_0	3.6×10^8 w	Moderator mass	M_m	2.579×10^6 gm
Neutron generation time	Λ	5×10^{-5} sec	Fuel mass	M_f	2.372×10^7 gm
Decay constant	λ	0.1/sec	Over all heat transfer coefficient	H	4.936×10^7 w/^{0}c
Delayed neutron fraction	β	0.0071	Moderator mass flow rate	W	4.291×10^6 gm/^{0}c
Fuel specific heat	c_{pf}	0.334 w-sec/gm^{0}c	Moderator coefficient of reactivity	α_m	-2.88×10^{-4} ρ/^{0}c
Moderator specific heat	c_{pm}	4.97 w-ses/gm^{0}c	Fuel coefficient of reactivity	α_f	-9.0×10^{-5}

4 Fractional Order PID Controller

FOPID controller, denoted as $PI^\lambda D^\mu$, introduces additional flexibility by enabling the adjustment of integral (λ) and derivative (μ) orders, in addition to the proportional, integral and derivative constants. The control action of the $PI^\lambda D^\mu$ controller can be mathematically expressed as follows [1]:

$$u(t) = K_p e(t) + K_i D^{-\lambda} e(t) + K_d D^\mu e(t) \tag{11}$$

Table 2. Steam Generator Data

Parameters	Symbol	Value	Parameters	Symbol	Value
Mass of primary water in tubes	M_G	4.291×10^6 gm	Specific heat of tube metal	C_{PT}	0,456 w-sec/gm^{0}c
Total heat transfer coefficient	H_G	5.0×10^7 w/^{0}c	Mass of tube metal	M_T	8×10^6
Specific heat primary coolant	C_P	4.97 w-ses/gm^{0}c	Enthalpy difference	Δ_H	1250 kJ/Kg
Specific heat of steam and water mixture	C_{PS}	1921 w-sec/gm^{0}c	Time delay of hot leg	Δ_1	5 sec
Mass of water and steam mixture	M_S	2×10^6	Time delay of cold leg	Δ_2	5 sec

where e(t) is the error signal, D is a derivative operator when its power is positive and an integral operator when its power is negative, λ and μ are positive real numbers, K_p is a proportional constant, K_i is an integral constant, K_d is a derivative constant.

After applying the Laplace transform to the Eq. (11) assuming zero initial conditions, the following equation is obtained:

$$G_c(s) = K_p + K_i s^{-\lambda} + K_d s^{\mu} \qquad (12)$$

Clearly, choosing $\lambda = 1$ and $\mu = 1$, a classical PID controller is obtained. The FOPID controller plane is shown in Fig. 2.

5   Tuning Methods

Numerous methods have been suggested for the tuning of FOPID controllers in both frequency domain and time domain. Researchers have discovered that the frequency domain design approach necessitates a simplified representation of the higher order process. Conversely, the controller parameters can be determined in time domain design approach by employing an optimization technique using the higher order process model [13]. Several objective functions can be minimized to determine the optimal parameters for FOPID [13, 14]. The following functions are used in our study:

- The weighted sum of Integral of Absolute Error (IAE) and Integral of Squared Control Signal (ISCO)

$$J = w_1 \int_0^\infty |e(t)|dt + w_2 \int_0^\infty u^2(t)dt \qquad (13)$$

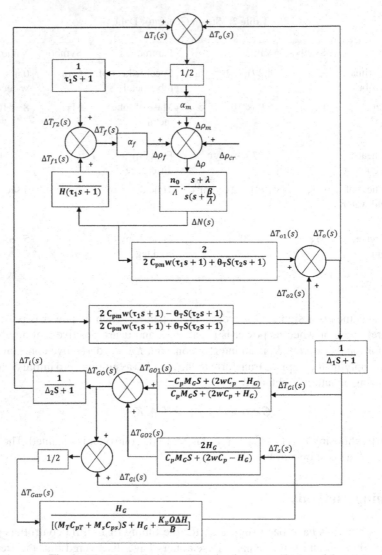

Fig. 1. The block diagram of the simple power plant model

- The weighted sum of Integral of Squared Error (ISE) and ISCO

$$J = w_1 \int_0^\infty e^2(t)dt + w_2 \int_0^\infty u^2(t)dt \tag{14}$$

- The weighted sum of Integral of Time multiplied Absolute Error (ITAE) and ISCO

$$J = w_1 \int_0^\infty t|e(t)|dt + w_2 \int_0^\infty u^2(t)dt \tag{15}$$

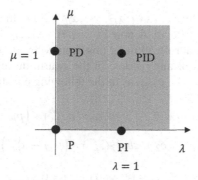

Fig. 2. The FOPID controller plane

- The weighted sum of Integral of Time multiplied Squared Error (ITSE) and ISCO

$$J = w_1 \int_0^\infty te^2(t)dt + w_2 \int_0^\infty u^2(t)dt \tag{16}$$

- The weighted sum of Integral of Squared Time multiplied Error whole Squared (ISTES) and ISCO

$$J = w_1 \int_0^\infty \left(t^2 e(t)\right)^2 dt + w_2 \int_0^\infty u^2(t)dt \tag{17}$$

- The weighted sum of Integral of Squared Time multiplied Squared Error (ISTSE) and ISCO

$$J = w_1 \int_0^\infty t^2 e^2(t)dt + w_2 \int_0^\infty u^2(t)dt \tag{18}$$

where $e(t) = r(t) - y(t)$, r(t) is the input signal, u(t) is the control signal, y(t) is the output signal and w_1, w_2 are weights.

6 Particle Swarm Optimization Algorithm

In the year 1995, PSO was presented by Dr. Kennedy and Dr. Eberhart. The idea behind the PSO was inspired by the way animals follow in searching for food or when migrating from one place to another. For example, birds and insects at first do not know what the appropriate destination is. But once one of them reaches the appropriate destination, it is shared with the rest. PSO is distinguished from other optimization techniques by its efficiency, simplicity, ease of application, and its need for a small number of parameters [15].

6.1 Standard PSO

In the standard PSO, we assume that we have a swarm consisting of N particles, and each particle has D dimensions. Each particle starts from a random position. Then the position of the ith particle denoted by $X_i = (x_{i1}, x_{i2}, \ldots, x_{iD})$, is modified in the current iteration based on its position and velocity denoted by $V_i = (v_{i1}, v_{i2}, \ldots, v_{iD})$, in the previous iteration, its best position during all iterations denoted by $P_i = (p_{i1}, p_{i2}, p_{i3}, \ldots, p_{iD})$, and also the best position of any particle in the swarm during all iterations, which is denoted by $P_g = (p_{g1}, p_{g2}, \ldots, p_{gD})$, as in the following equations

$$v_{id}^{(k+1)} = \omega * v_{id}^{(k)} + c_1 * rand_1(\ldots) * \left(p_{id} - x_{id}^{(k)} \right)$$

$$+ c_2 * rand_2(\ldots) * \left(p_{gd} - x_{id}^{(k)} \right) \tag{19}$$

$$x_{id}^{(k+1)} = x_{id}^{(k)} + v_{id}^{(k+1)} \tag{20}$$

where, N is a number of particles in the population (population size), D is a dimension of problem, k is a pointer of iterations (generations), $v_{id}^{(k)}$ is a velocity of particle i at iteration k, ω is an inertia weight factor, c_1, c_2 are the two positive constants, called acceleration coefficients, $rand_1, rand_2$ are the uniformly distributed random numbers between 0 and 1, $x_{id}^{(k)}$ is a current position of particle i at iterations k, p_{id} is the best position of particle i and p_{gd} is the best position of the swarm.

In each iteration, the particle's velocity is limited by $[V_{min}, V_{max}]$, where $V_{min} = X_{min}$, $V_{max} = X_{max}$.

6.2 Improved PSO

One of the disadvantages of the standard PSO is the possibility of particles flying to locations outside the specified research space. This problem can be solved by adding some modifications to the code, such as checking the position in each iteration to make sure that it is in the specified range. If the position $X_i < X_{min}$ then X_i is set at X_{min} and if $X_i > X_{max}$ then X_i is set at X_{max} as in the case of the velocity. Another method used is to recalculate the velocity and then the position. The recalculation is repeated until the position is confined to the specified range.

Although the previous methods found a solution to this defect, the computation cost increased. The equation for calculating the position was modified by adding the momentum factor to force the particles to fly within the specified research space [9]. The PSO equations become as follows

$$v_{id}^{(k+1)} = \omega * v_{id}^{(k)} + c_1 * rand_1(\ldots) * \left(p_{id} - x_{id}^{(k)} \right)$$

$$+ c_2 rand_2(\ldots) * \left(p_{gd} - x_{id}^{(k)} \right) \tag{21}$$

$$x_{id}^{(k+1)} = (1 - mc) * x_{id}^{(k)} + mc * v_{id}^{(k+1)} \tag{22}$$

where mc is momentum factor $(0 < mc < 1)$, and the particle's velocity is limited by $[V_{min}, V_{max}]$ where $V_{min} = X_{min}$, $V_{max} = X_{max}$. The suggested value of mc is 0.3 for better performance of PSO.

7   Implementation of FOPID for a Nuclear Power Plant Using PSO

In this paper, a PSO was used to find the optimal parameters for the FOPID controller which is used to control the power of the nuclear power reactor.

In an operating nuclear power plant, to raise the reactor power, the operator sets the desired power level to be reached on the control panel power instrument. The automatic control rod is raised to a certain distance to introduce a positive reactivity. The control and safety systems which incorporates a power comparison unit that compares the reached power and the preset power level send signals to raise the control rod till the desired power level is reached.

The FOPID is designed to determine the reactivity needed to make the difference in power between the calculated and the preset value the least. The closed loop system is shown in Fig. 3.

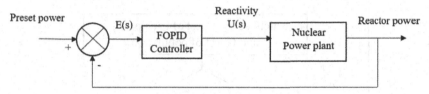

Fig. 3. FOPID control system

The PSO algorithm, which has been implemented as M file, is interconnected to SIMULINK model where the FOPID controller parameters are computed in the M file and then fed to The SIMULINK. The optimization was performed with this initial parameters:

- number of particles 100
- number of dimensions 5
- maximum iteration 100
- c1 = c2 = 2
- mc = 0.3
- the inertia factor ω with a maximum value of 0.9 and a minimum value of 0.4
- Range of FOPID parameters $K_p \in [0, 3 \times 10^{-6}]$, $K_i \in [0, 3 \times 10^{-4}]$, $K_d \in [0, 4 \times 10^{-4}]$, $\lambda \in [0, 1]$, and $\mu \in [0, 1]$.

A PSO program was written to generate the values of five parameters K_p, K_i, K_d, λ, and μ controller which are then submitted to the Simulink model. The Simulink model then computes the error and control signal which are sent back to the PSO program to compute the objective function and improve the value of K_p, K_i, K_d, λ, and μ, and so on. The algorithm iteration process is stopped when there is no significant improvement between current and previous global best position or the maximum iteration number is reached. The five parameters of the FOPID K_p, K_i, K_d, λ, and μ are obtained according to the minimum value of objective function. The flow chart of PSO-FOPID controller design is shown in Fig. 4.

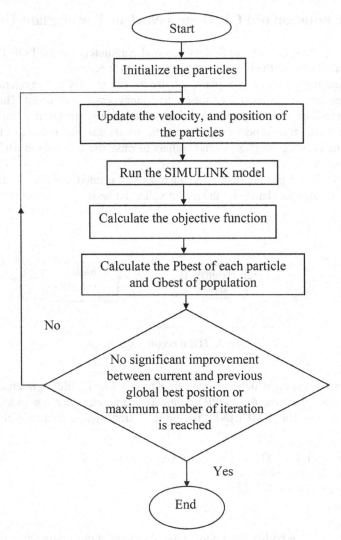

Fig. 4. The flow chart of PSO-FOPID controller design

8 Results and Discussions

8.1 Reactor Model Response to a Positive Reactivity Insertion

The model was run to see its response to a positive step reactivity insertion of 0.001 (raising the reactor power) while the reactor is operating at 360 MW. As can be seen from Fig. 5, the new steady state power increase of about 11.84 MW higher than the operating power was reached. Figure 5 shows a power overshoot of about 17.66% and a long time to reach the new steady state. The new steady state was reached when the negative reactivity resulted from the fuel and moderator temperature feedbacks compensated the reactivity inserted as shown in Fig. 6.

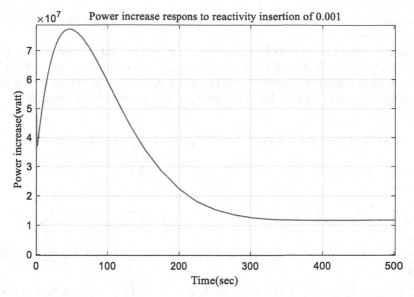

Fig. 5. Power increase response to reactivity insertion of 0.001

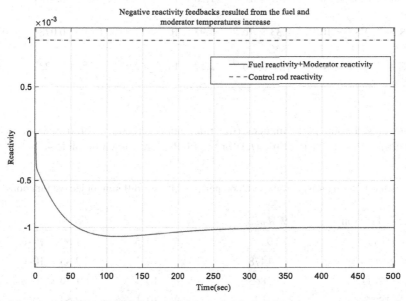

Fig. 6. Negative reactivity feedbacks resulted from the fuel and moderator temperatures increase

8.2 FOPID and PID Controller Design Results

As explained earlier, during the raising of the reactor power, the operator sets the power to be reached and allow the reactor control and safety system to control the automatic control rod movement till the desired new power level is achieved. Similarly, the FOPID was designed to calculate the amount of reactivity inserted in the reactor core to reach the preset power level.

The parameters of FOPID controller are tuned with PSO for the nuclear power plant model using each objective function (13)- (18). The weights w_1 and w_2 have been considered to be equal because the error index and the control signal are considered to be equally important. Table 3 shows the tuning results for the FOPID controllers.

Table 3. Tuning results for nuclear power plant with different objective function

Objective Function	The value of the objective function	K_p	K_i	K_d	λ	μ
IAE + ISCO	5.11×10^{-6}	1.27×10^{-7}	2.35×10^{-4}	9.96×10^{-5}	0.3208	0.1978
ISE + ISCO	2.90×10^{-6}	8.30×10^{-8}	8.76×10^{-6}	1.24×10^{-5}	0.1225	0.0279
ITAE + ISCO	5.13×10^{-6}	2.05×10^{-7}	9.33×10^{-5}	7.13×10^{-5}	0.7243	0.1852
ITSE + ISCO	1.34×10^{-6}	4.41×10^{-9}	1.66×10^{-6}	3.36×10^{-7}	0.0141	0.0043
ISTES + ISCO	1.83×10^{-6}	2.33×10^{-8}	4.97×10^{-5}	7.89×10^{-6}	0.0784	0.0220
ISTSE + ISCO	1.41×10^{-6}	7.57×10^{-9}	2.17×10^{-6}	2.95×10^{-6}	0.1237	0.0180

The closed loop performances (the maximum percentage of overshoot ($\%M_p$), settling time (t_s) and rising time (t_r))for the FOPID are shown in Table 4.

Table 4. Comparison of closed loop performance for different objective functions

Objective function	$\%M_p$	t_s	t_r
IAE + ISCO	13.9	$1.15 \times 10{-}5$	$1.59 \times 10{-}6$
ISE + ISCO	3.1478	3.21×10^{-5}	$3.35 \times 10{-}6$
ITAE + ISCO	4.3863	$1.38 \times 10{-}5$	$1.30 \times 10{-}6$
ITSE + ISCO	33.4872	2.09×10^{-4}	2.64×10^{-5}
ISTES + ISCO	31.3797	4.30×10^{-5}	5.40×10^{-6}
ISTSE + ISCO	30.5022	1.34×10^{-4}	1.69×10^{-5}

The corresponding closed loop responses are shown in Fig. 7.

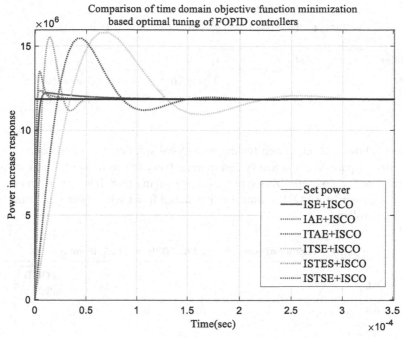

Fig. 7. Comparison of time domain objective functions minimization based optimal tuning of FOPID controllers for nuclear power plant

From Fig. 7 and Table 4, it can be concluded that the ISE + ISCO criteria for FOPID controller tuning is capable of providing closed loop response with low overshoot and fast response. Consequently, the ISE + ISCO criteria has been selected for the PID and FOPID controller tuning.

The parameters of PID controller are also tuned with PSO for the nuclear power plant model using ISE + ISCO objective function with the integro-differential operators as unity ($\lambda = \mu = 1$) to get a fair comparison. The tuning results for the FOPID and PID controllers using ISE + ISCO objective function are presented in Table 5.

Table 5. Tuning results for the FOPID and PID controllers

Controller	J_{min}	K_p	K_i	K_d	λ	μ
$PI^{\lambda}D^{\mu}$	2.8969×10^{-6}	8.25×10^{-8}	7.07×10^{-6}	9.23×10^{-7}	0.3667	0.1989
PID	3.0038×10^{-6}	6.80×10^{-8}	6.19×10^{-5}	4.66×10^{-7}	-	-

The closed loop performances (the maximum percentage of overshoot ($\%M_p$), settling time (t_s) and rising time (t_r) for FOPID and PID are presented in Table 6.

Table 6. The closed loop performances for FOPID and PID

Controller	$\%M_p$	t_s	t_r
$PI^\lambda D^\mu$	2.62	2.84×10^{-5}	3.40×10^{-6}
PID	8.95	3.07×10^{-5}	3.41×10^{-6}

The PSO method can search for the best global solution for FOPID controller and PID controller parameters in a very fast manner (very few iterations). The variation of objective function J of optimization process is shown in Fig. 8. It is clear from Fig. 8 that the best objective J for FOPID controller is reached faster with lower value than that of the PID controller.

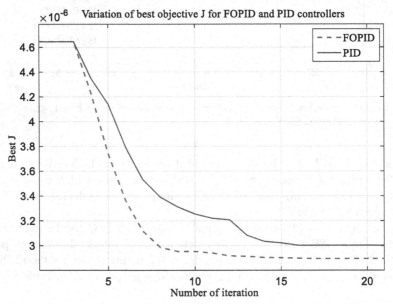

Fig. 8. The variation of best objective function J of optimization process for FOPID controller and PID controller

8.3 Simulation Results for FOPID and PID Controller

The simulation of the response of the reactor model to a preset power increase of 11.84 MW using the designed FOPID and the PID controllers is shown in Fig. 9.

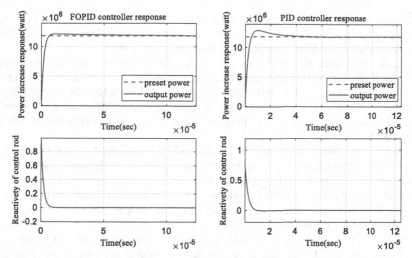

Fig. 9. Comparison close loop response for FOPID Controller and PID controller

It is evident from Fig. 9 that the set-point tracking performance of the FOPID controller is smoother with smaller overshoot (2.62%) than the performance of the conventional PID controller.

The power increase of 11.84 MW was reached within a very short time when the reactivity estimated by the FOPID was about 2.3287×10^{-4}. However due to the negative temperature feedbacks the positive reactivity insertion continued to increase till reached the expected reactivity of 0.001 needed to compensate the negative temperature reactivity feedbacks due to the increase in the fuel and moderator temperature when the thermal steady state is reached.

9   Conclusion

Fractional order PID controllers have been tuned for optimal power tracking of a PWR nuclear power plant which is presented by a simplified reactor model developed from the basic point-kinetics equations, thermal-hydraulic correlations and temperature reactivity feedbacks. PSO based optimization is used to tune the FOPID controller parameters to achieve efficient control performance. The five parameters K_p, K_i, K_d, λ, and μ are found directly without spreading in steps. The system with FOPID controller exhibits better time domain response in comparison with the integer order PID controller.

References

1. Chen, Y.: Ubiquitous fractional order controls? IFAC Proceedings Volumes **39**(11), 481–492 (2006). https://doi.org/10.3182/20060719-3-PT-4902.00081
2. Chen, Y., Petras, I., Xue, D.: Fractional order control - A tutorial. In: 2009 American Control Conference, 10–12 June 2009 2009, pp. 1397–1411 (2009)

3. Santhiya, M., Abraham, A., Pappa, N., Chitra, M.: Reduced order model based optimally tuned fractional order PID controller for pressurized water nuclear reactor. IFAC-PapersOnLine **51**(4), 669–674 (2018). https://doi.org/10.1016/j.ifacol.2018.06.177

4. Zare, N., Jahanfarnia, G., Khorshidi, A., Soltani, J.: Robustness of optimized FPID controller against uncertainty and disturbance by fractional nonlinear model for research nuclear reactor. Nuclear Eng. Technol. **52**(9), 2017–2024 (2020). https://doi.org/10.1016/j.net.2020.03.002

5. Gupta, D., Goyal, V., Kumar, J.: Design of fractional-order NPID controller for the NPK model of advanced nuclear reactor. Progress Nuclear Energy **150**, 104319 (2022). https://doi.org/10.1016/j.pnucene.2022.104319

6. Safarzadeh, O., Noori-kalkhoran, O.: A fractional PID controller based on fractional point kinetic model and particle swarm optimization for power regulation of SMART reactor. Nuclear Eng. Design **377**, 111137 (2021). https://doi.org/10.1016/j.nucengdes.2021.111137

7. Puchalski, B., Rutkowski, T.A., Duzinkiewicz, K.: Fuzzy multi-regional fractional PID controller for pressurized water nuclear reactor. ISA Trans. **103**, 86–102 (2020). https://doi.org/10.1016/j.isatra.2020.04.003

8. Das, S., Pan, I., Das, S.: Fractional order fuzzy control of nuclear reactor power with thermal-hydraulic effects in the presence of random network induced delay and sensor noise having long range dependence. Energy Conversion Manage. **68**, 200–218 (2013). https://doi.org/10.1016/j.enconman.2013.01.003

9. Cao, J.Y., Cao, B.G.: Design of fractional order controllers based on particle swarm optimization. In: 2006 1ST IEEE Conference on Industrial Electronics and Applications, 24–26 May 2006, pp. 1–6 (2006)

10. Ross, B.: A brief history and exposition of the fundamental theory of fractional calculus. In:, pp. 1–36. Springer (2006)

11. Joseph, M.K.: Fractional Calculus: Definitions and Applications. Western Kentucky University (2009)

12. Hetrick, D.L.: Dynamics of Nuclear Reactors. University of Chicago Press (1971)

13. Das, S., Saha, S., Das, S., Gupta, A.: On the selection of tuning methodology of FOPID controllers for the control of higher order processes. ISA Trans. **50**(3), 376–388 (2011). https://doi.org/10.1016/j.isatra.2011.02.003

14. Das, S., Pan, I., Das, S., Gupta, A.: A novel fractional order fuzzy PID controller and its optimal time domain tuning based on integral performance indices. Eng. Appl. Artif. Intell. **25**(2), 430–442 (2012). https://doi.org/10.1016/j.engappai.2011.10.004

15. Talukder, S.: Mathematical Modelling and Applications of Particle Swarm Optimization (2011)

Image Processing, Computer Vision and Internet of Things

Palm Print Recognition Based on a Fusion of Feature Selection Techniques

Bothaina F. Gargoum[1]([⊠]) [iD], Ahmed Lawgali[1] [iD], Mohamed A. E. Abdalla[1] [iD], and Amina A. Abdo[2] [iD]

[1] University of Benghazi, Benghazi, Libya
{bothaina.gargoum,ahmed.lawgali,mohamed.abdalla}@uob.edu.ly
[2] Collage of Computer Technology, Benghazi, Libya
amina.abdo@uob.edu.ly

Abstract. Automatic recognition of biometrics has been considered the best way for identifying and authenticating individuals. Palm-print recognition is one of the newest techniques in this field. This paper presents an approach to the automatic recognition of Palm-prints based on 2D images. The proposed approach adopts a combination of three different techniques of feature selection: histograms of oriented gradients, local binary patterns, and principal component analysis to increase the classification performance. For the classification, linear discriminant analysis is applied. The proposed approach was tested using palm-print datasets from PolyU-II and IIT-Delhi. Both datasets produced results that were more than 99% accurate. These findings outperform those of previous studies.

Keywords: Biometrics · Palm-print Recognition · Linear Discrimination Analysis · Principal Component Analysis · Local Binary Pattern · Histograms of Oriented Gradients

1 Introduction

In several cases, verification and identification are very important issues. It is commonly done using usernames and passwords, but there are numerous limitations; as it can be stolen or easily forgotten. Therefore, researchers try to establish new ways to avoid such limitations [1]. This has recently drawn a lot of attention from researchers in the field of biometrics. Furthermore, all features of fingerprints, such as palm prints, have discrete points and ridges. In addition, palm prints also contain other salient features, such as main lines and folds, which can be cheaply used for detection by various filters such as ordinal filters [4] and wavelet filters [5].

Several algorithms have been proposed to exploit many features. In most cases, fingerprint images for enrollment and identification were captured using the same type of equipment, i.e. They are detected in the same spectrum. Images of palm prints taken in various spectra are very contrasted. Blue and green light images only display surface roughness, whereas red and near-infrared light images reveal subsurface veins. The

T. A. T. Benmusa et al. (Eds.): ILCICT 2023, CCIS 2097, pp. 239–247, 2024.
https://doi.org/10.1007/978-3-031-62624-1_19

aforementioned performance loss may occur if the enrollment and verification images are in two distinct domains. Convolutional neural network (CNN) researchers have recently demonstrated interest in the subject include [13].

With a dual-path architecture, the researchers developed a new CNN model, with the first path processing the full input image and the second path extracting local information from more focused regions of the input image.

Others, however, have used Deep Segmentation Network (DHN) for recognition and CycleGAN for translating palm images [10]. One of the successful applications of pattern recognition for personal identification is palm-print recognition based on texture analysis.

For this reason, the researchers investigated an in-depth texture analysis to represent palm-print texture patterns based on the mixture of different texture information extracted through different descriptors such as "HOG and Gabor filters," "fractal dimensions," and "GLCM," that is, the characteristics of frequency, pattern, or statistical texture, based on methods [12].

Others, like [14], propose line feature local tridirectionally patterns (LFLTriDP), a texture descriptor-modified form of LTriDP that takes into mind the texture features of the palm print. A new palm-print verification model incorporating Sobel Edge Detection, 2D Gabor Filter, and Principal Component Analysis was proposed by researchers in [16]. Previous studies have demonstrated that when more than one item type is classified, classification accuracy is frequently higher. As a result, the works given in this paper propose an approach for palm-print recognition in which information extraction is used to address the fundamental challenge of palm-print recognition.

This article combines LBP and HOG feature extraction algorithms. PCA is then used to minimize the size of the retrieved features. An LDA classifier is employed to fit the dataset. The organization of the paper is as follows: the palm-print recognition system's approach is covered in Sect. 2. Section 3 presents the outcomes of the experiments on the studied datasets. Finally, Sect. 4 discusses the work's conclusions.

2   Method and Material

The Palm-print identification methodology given here delivers high levels of security and accuracy while making no predictions about how lighting, poses, or security breaches may change [15]. The next stage in this procedure is always the evaluation of the classification model. The methodology diagram for the palm-print recognition system disclosed in this paper is shown in Fig. 1.

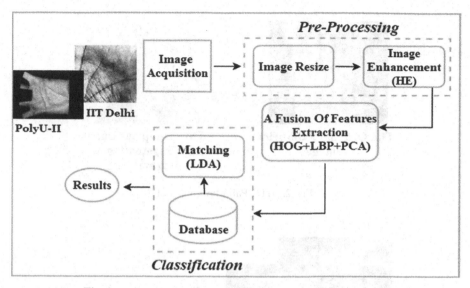

Fig. 1. Palm-print Recognition System Methodology Diagram

2.1 Image Acquisition

IITD [17] and PolyU-II [18] are two publicly available databases that are utilized to assess the suggested approach. Countless recognition systems have been evaluated using these datasets in biometrics.

IIT Delhi Database Touchless Palm-Print Database (Version 1.0)

The IITD palm-print dataset includes 2,601 contactless palm-print images gathered from 460 palms representing 230 subjects with both left and right palms. For each palm, five to six samples were collected. For each palm, five to six samples were taken. Particularly, the seventh subject's left palm produced seven images of palm prints. The matching ROIs have been provided with sizes of 150 × 150 pixels by the IITD palm-print database. Figure 2 depicts the automatic segmentation and normalization of the original image. In this study, a segmented grayscale image with dimensions of 150 × 150 pixels was employed.

The (PolyU-II) Palm-Print Database (The Second Version)

PolyU-II has 7,752 images of palm prints acquired from 386 palms of 193 subjects. The images were obtained from 386 palms of 193 subjects throughout two sessions. Each subject gave approximately 10 samples from both the left and right hands. In Fig. 3 each image was captured remotely under various indoor lighting settings, with no notable occlusions. Each palm was utilized to gather 20 samples throughout the period of two sessions.

There are ten distinct images in each session. The description of the user databases is given in Table 1.

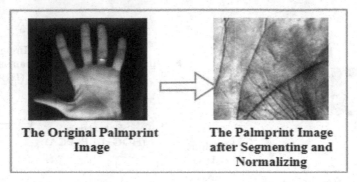

The Original Palmprint Image   **The Palmprint Image after Segmenting and Normalizing**

Fig. 2. IITD Palm-print Dataset

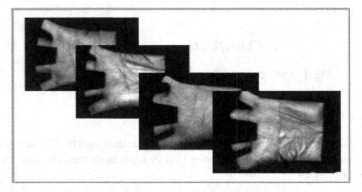

Fig. 3. PolyU-II Palm-print Dataset Examples

Table 1. The Datasets Used for the Experiment

Database	PolyU-II	IITD
Subjects	386	230
Images per subject	10	7
Image size	384 × 284	800 × 600
Total images	7,752	2601

2.2 Pre-processing

Pre-processing palm-print images is a crucial step in the biometric system as a whole.

- Image Resizing: The images in the databases were resized with the purpose of normalizing image sizes. Thus, the resolution of each image will be 64 × 64. This factor will reduce the training period [19].

- Image Enhancement: The histogram equalization technique is used to equalize the palm images, reducing the impact of irregular lighting and producing a texture image with evenly dispersed texture.

The histogram equalization method makes use of a cumulative distribution transformation function [3].

2.3 Features Extraction

The identification and verification of images rely primarily on the feature extraction stage. Flexing the hand and wrist causes lines to appear in the palm that has three primary features: The lifeline, the headline, and the heart line [7].

As depicted in Fig. 4, the palm print has other features, such as ridges and wrinkles, in addition to the principal lines and datum points.

The relevant line layouts and these features are listed below highly essential physiological traits that can be used to identify distinct individuals. Principal lines are distinct from thin, wavy, and curved lines. These features are listed below:

- Geometry features: The geometry features of a palm include width, length, and area.
- Principal line features vital physiological traits that, because of their constancy and individuality, separate individuals.
- The features of wrinkles: principal lines are different from thin, wavy, and curved lines.
- The features of wrinkles: principal lines are different from thin, wavy, and curved lines

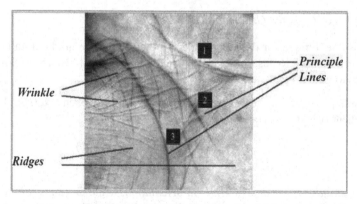

Fig. 4. The line patterns of a palm-print

In this work, a fusion of local features extraction named (HOG and LBP) is adopted to use in the features extraction stage. This work assumes that the classification model with the LDA classifier will perform better if HOG and LBP are combined. Combining these two techniques of features is essential because doing so previously provided successful results [13].

1) *Local Binary Pattern (LBP):*

LBP is a texture analysis coefficient that evolved by [8]. Each pixel in the palm image is labeled with this two-line pattern operator, which uses the gray value of the central pixel to identify eight nearby pixels. The feature vector shown in Fig. 5 is produced after the eight threshold binary bits are combined counterclockwise. A continuous change in pixel value won't break the local binary pattern coding. Because of this, it is very possible to show palms that are illuminated from a specific angle but with varying levels of light intensity.

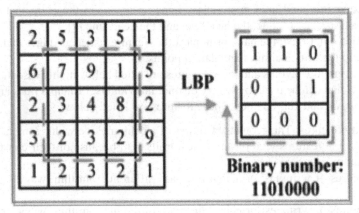

Fig. 5. Computation of Local binary pattern (LBPs).

2) *Histogram of Oriented Gradients (HOG):*

HOG is a technique for detecting objects. The size of the gradient and the edges' directions can be used to describe how the local item appears [12]. The following steps can be used to gather details about these features:

- The first step is to divide the image into a group of cells. For each pixel, Eq. 1 computes the gradient orientation (i.e., k,r, r, r).

$$\theta_{k,r} = tan^{-1}\frac{G(k, r + 1) - G(k, r - 1)}{G(k + 1, r) - G(k - 1, r)} \tag{1}$$

Where $\theta k,r$, *stands for the pixel's gradient orientation*, while G stands for the grayscale function. $\theta ij = 1...$ N2 represents the different cell orientations, and j represents the quantized M-bins histogram.

- The gradient orientation processes are shown in steps 2 and.
- Steps 4 and 5 demonstrate how to aggregate and decrease the orientations ij $= 1...$ N2 in an M-bins histogram for the same cell j.
- In step 6, the full set of generated histograms is organized and concatenated into a HOG histogram.

3) Principal Component Analysis (PCA)

Is one of the best and most reliable methods for dimensionality reduction. In computer vision has commonly incorporated PCA. The results showed that PCA is also capable of performing various recognition tasks [15]. Therefore, the entire feature vector that was retrieved by HOG and LBP is used in the PCA implementation. The classifier is expected to produce better results with the reduced feature vector.

2.4 Classification

In this phase, the subject is validated by matching the feature vectors, or the subject is found by scanning a database [6]. In our proposed methodology, classification was performed using the LDA classifier. The LDA was chosen as a metric for recognition since this classifier is trained and tested by features extracted from the Palm-print pattern. The LDA classifier is trained several times with the set of Palm-print images and then tested with other sets of Palm-print images.

The LDA technique has been employed in biometrics, agriculture, and medical applications due to its huge number of features. To complete the LDA approach, three phases must be accomplished:

- The first phase involves calculating the reparability of numerous classes (i.e., the difference between their means), often known as the "between-class variance" or "between-class matrix".
- The second step, the within-class variance or within-class matrix, is generated using the separation between the mean and the samples of each class.
- Finally, create the lower-dimensional space that increases variance across classes while limiting variance within classes in the third phase.

3 Discussion and Results

To determine the efficacy of the proposed approach, the yielded results were compared with previous studies, using the same databases and the same amount of images in the training and testing sets, and comparing the previous methodologies with the proposed methodologies.

As an illustration, in the first experiment, the PolyU-II database was divided into two experiments. In the first session set (F-S-set) experiment, the first 8 images were taken for each participant as a training set and the second 2 images as a testing set, respectively. The accuracy reached 99.80%. In the second session set (S-S-set) experiment, the first eight images were taken for training sets and two images for testing sets. The accuracy increased to 99.87%. The proposed experiments, as shown in Table 2, indicate that there is little performance difference when utilizing images within different sessions.

The IITD database was divided into two experiments and two sets: Left-hand and right-hand sets. In the first experiment (Left-hand), the dataset is imbalanced, so the first 4 images for each subject were used in the training, and the remaining images were used in the testing set. The performance reached 97.63%. Likewise, in the second experiment (Right-hand), the first four images were used for training and the rest for testing. The performance raised even further to 98.42%.

Table 3 shows a comparison of the results of previous studies from the PolyU-II dataset as it can be seen that the yielded results in this paper are the highest compared in both sets (First Session Set and Second Session Set).

Moreover, shows the accuracy of the proposed method from the IITD dataset compared with the already existing methods in Palm-print identification experiments. It can be noticed that the accuracy level of this paper seems to be the greatest in the Left and Right Sets.

Table 2. The Accuracy of the Proposed Approach from PolyU-II Dataset Compared with Other Studies

| Authors | Technique | PolyU-II | |
		F-S-set	S-S-set
Jumma Almaghtuf [2]	DBM	99.40%	99.20%
Qian Zheng [11]	DoN	99.60%	99.60%
Lunke Fei [3]	NDI	95.93%	94.73%
Qian Zheng [7]	FAST-RLOC	94.20%	94.53%
This paper	**LBP+HOG+PCA**	**99.80%**	**99.87%**

Table 3. The Accuracy of the Proposed Approach from IITD Dataset Compared with Other Studies

| Authors | Technique | IITD | |
		Left-hand	Right-hand
Marjan Stoimchev[15]	CNN	95.57%	92.82%
Anca Ignata [9]	FKINK	96.08%	97.08%
Jumma Almaghtuf [2]	DBM	96.01%	93.55%
Qian Zheng [11]	DoN	88.12%	90.51%
This paper	**LBP + HOG + PCA**	**97.63%**	**98.42%**

4 Conclusion

This paper has presented an effective and efficient approach that is a fusion of feature extraction from LBP, HOG, and PCA with an LDA classifier to recognize the automatic 2D Palm-print images. The proposed approach has presented different experiments on the two datasets. The dataset has been divided into two parts, the first is named left-hand; whilst, the second set is right-hand. The accuracy of the proposed approach on the first set was 97.63%. The second set was 98.42%. The fusion of the features extraction helped the classifier to yield 99.80% from the PolyU-II first set (F-S-set) and increased more to

99.87% of the accuracy rate. From the IITD dataset, the proposed approach has yielded 97.63% and 98.42% from the left and right hand palm images, respectively. Compared with previous studies, these results are the best.

References

1. Shen, W., Tan, T.: Automated biometrics-based personal identification. Proc. Natl. Acad. Sci. **96**(20), 11065–11066 (1999)
2. Almaghtuf, J., Khelifi, F., Bouridane: Fast and efficient difference of block means code for Palm-print recognition. Mach. Vis. Appl. **31**(6), 1–10 (2020)
3. Fei, L., Zhang, B., Xu, Y., Yan, L.: Palmprint recognition using neighboring direction indicator. IEEE Trans. Hum. Mach. Syst. **46**(6), 787–798 (2016)
4. Sun, Z., Tan, T., Wang, Y., Li, S.: Ordinal palm-print representation for personal identification. In: Proceedings of the International Conference on Computer Vision and Pattern Recognition, pp. 279–284 (2005)
5. Wu, X.Q., Wang, K.Q., Zhang, D.: Wavelet based palm-print recognition. IEEE Conference Publication. IEEE Xplore (2002). 7803-7508-4/02/$17.00
6. Lu, X., Jain, A.K.: Ethnicity identification from face images. In: Proceedings of SPIE, vol. 5404, pp. 114–123 (2002)
7. Zheng, Q., Kumar, A., Pan, G.: Suspecting less and doing better: new insights on palmprint identification for faster and more accurate matching. IEEE Trans. Inf. Forensics Secur. **11**(3), 633–641 (2015)
8. Ojala, T., Pietikainen, M., Maenpaa, T.: Multiresolution gray-scale and rotation invariant texture classification with local binary patterns. IEEE Trans. Pattern Anal. Mach. Intell. **24**(7), 971–987 (2002)
9. Ignat, A., Păvăloi, I.: Keypoint selection algorithm for palmprint recognition with SURF. Procedia Comput. Sci. **192**, 270–280 (2021)
10. Zhu, J.Y., Park, T., Isola, P., Efros, A.A.: Unpaired image-to-image translation using cycle-consistent adversarial networks. In: Proceedings of the IEEE International Conference on Computer Vision, pp. 2223–2232 (2017)
11. Zheng, Q., Kumar, A., Pan, G.: A 3D feature descriptor recovered from a single 2D palmprint image. IEEE Trans. Pattern Anal. Mach. Intell. **38**(6), 1272–1279 (2016)
12. Mutar, M.H., Ahmed, E.H., ALsemawi, M.R.M., Hanoosh, H.O., Abbas, A.H.: Ear recognition system using random forest and histograms of oriented gradients techniques. Indones. J. Electr. Eng. Comput. Sci. **27**(1), 181–188 (2022)
13. Stoimchev, M., Ivanovska, M., Štruc, V.: Learning to combine local and global image information for contactless palm-print recognition. MDPI (2021)
14. Li, M., Wang, H., Liu, H., Meng, Q.: Palmprint recognition based on the line feature local tri-directional patterns. IET Biom. **11**(6), 570–580 (2022)
15. Stoimchev, M., Ivanovska, M., Štruc, V.: Learning to combine local and global image information for contactless palmprint recognition. Sensors **22**(1), 73 (2021)
16. Verma, S., Chandran, S.: Contactless palmprint verification system using 2-D gabor filter and principal component analysis. Int. Arab J. Inf. Technol. **16**(1), 23–29 (2019)
17. IIT Delhi Touchless Palm-print Database version 1.0. http://www4.comp.polyu.edu.hk/~csa jaykr/IITD/Database_Palm.htm. Accessed 06 Aug 2018
18. The Hong Kong Polytechnic University Contactless 3D Palm-print Images Database. http://www4.comp.polyu.edu.hk/~csajaykr/myhome/database_request/3dhand/Hand3D. htm. Accessed 06 Aug 2018
19. Matkowski, W.M., Chai, T., Kong, A.W.K.: 20: Palmprint recognition in uncontrolled and uncooperative environment. IEEE Trans. Inf. Forensics Secur.Secur. **15**, 1601–1615 (2019)

Predictive Analytics Based on AutoML Email Spam Detection

Tarek A. M. Nagem[1]([✉]), Entesar H. Alfsai[1], Ebitisam K. Elberkawi[1], Fatma El-Deeb[2], and Salma Albar-Athe[3]

[1] University of Benghazi, Benghazi, Libya
{Tarek.Nagem,Entesar.Alfsai,Basma.Elberkawi}@uob.edu.ly
[2] College of Computer Technology Benghazi, Benghazi, Libya
[3] Derna University, Derna, Libya

Abstract. The dissemination of digital content through unsolicited, mass distribution is known as "spamming," with email being a common method of transmission, sending unwanted messages that cybercriminals can utilize to trick victims and get confidential credentials from the casualty. Spammers use many forms of communication to bulk-send their unwanted messages. Some of these are marketing messages peddling unsolicited goods. Other types of spam messages can spread malware, scam messages divulging personal information, or scary messages. Spam can exist for many reasons, but it can be used for malicious purposes such as Passwords and other sensitive data about intended Users. To overcome the security breach, the classification of spam emails for comprehending spam has been done using a variety of techniques, such as machine learning and natural language processing. This paper proposes a novel technique for email spam detection, the spam email is classified for the understanding of spam has been done using the H2O which is the name of the entire machine learning platform developed by H2O.ai, that includes the neural network algorithm as one of many algorithms available for building predictive models. The focus of the experiments is on email messages dataset. The data were divided into a training group and a test group, where the results showed that our approach outperformed.

Keywords: Spamming · AutoML · H2O · Email Spam · Deep Learning · Neural Network

1 Introduction

Spam is broadly defined as unsolicited messages sent to recipients by groups or individuals. Spam has been around for years and is now primarily used for advertising, marketing, and other promotional activities, and collecting confidential sensitive information from legitimate users such as bank account information, credit card information, passwords, and other private information about the intended user recently to carry out various cybersecurity attacks. Spamming comes through email, SMS, social networks, phone calls to victims, etc. Examples of spam include sending multiple messages about a product

T. A. T. Benmusa et al. (Eds.): ILCICT 2023, CCIS 2097, pp. 248–256, 2024.
https://doi.org/10.1007/978-3-031-62624-1_20

to entice the victim to purchase the product, or clicking on an ad to collect information about the user. Spamming exists to generate fake reviews in e-commerce applications, which can bring significant financial benefits to organizations and potentially hurt their competitors [1].

Spam in emails irritates users, which degrades the service's functionality [2]. Nevertheless, there are different solutions for combating spamming techniques, such as email spam filtering and classification strategies [3]. Also, different problems are faced by researcher analysts of spam discovery such as the restriction of the openly accessible dataset, However, on the other hand, not all email spam filtering techniques are effective at detecting spam [4].

Wherefore spam filtering is required, this includes using software techniques to distinguish between spam and non-spam emails, which prevents spam emails from reaching users' inboxes [5]. While numerous methods have been implemented to eliminate the spam threat or significantly reduce the amount of spam targeted to Internet users worldwide. Indicates that additional work is required. Several techniques were utilized for spam detection, such as using support vector machines (SVM), Naive Bayes (NB), Artificial Neural Networks (ANNs), K-Nearest Neighbors (KNN), Decision Trees (DTs), Random Forests, Convolutional Neural Networks (CNNs), and Hybrid methods [5]. Even though techniques like logistic regression, decision trees, and Bayesian classification were available, they still required a significant amount of time.

In recent times, deep learning neural networks, an advanced class of machine learning algorithms, have gained importance. It can learn the feature dynamically and act as a feature extractor, and on the other hand, it can represent a classifier that classifies the data based on the features learned autonomously from the data [7].

"Spam Email Detection Using Machine Learning Techniques" proposes the use of machine learning algorithms to detect spam emails. The authors compare three different techniques: Decision Trees, Random Forest, and Naive Bayes. The paper concludes that machine learning algorithms are an effective way to detect spam emails [8].

"Email Spam Detection using Machine Learning and Natural Language Processing Techniques" proposes a combination of machine learning and natural language processing techniques to detect spam emails. The authors used Support Vector Machines, Naive Bayes, and Logistic Regression for their experiments. The paper concludes that combining machine learning and natural language processing techniques can improve the accuracy of spam email detection [9].

"Top Spam Detection Techniques Used By Email Service Providers" discusses the various techniques used by email service providers to detect spam emails. The post explains that content-based filtering looks for keywords and phrases commonly used in spam emails, while reputation-based filtering checks the sender's reputation. The post also discusses the use of machine learning algorithms to detect patterns in email data. The post concludes that a combination of these techniques is most effective for detecting spam emails [7].

"How to Detect and Stop Email Spam" provides tips and best practices for detecting and stopping email spam. The article explains that spam filters should be used to automatically filter out known spam emails. The article also suggests keeping email lists clean by removing inactive subscribers and avoiding certain practices that can trigger spam filters, such as using all caps in the subject line or including too many links. The article concludes that by following these best practices, email marketers can improve their email deliverability and avoid being marked as spam [9].

This study proposes a new method to detect email spam. All experiments are performed via the neural network algorithm in H2O is designed to be highly scalable and easy to use. The name "H2O" was chosen because it represents the fluidity, clarity, and power of the machine learning tools provided by the platform. For the experiment, the dataset used was the Email spam dataset, which had been selected from Kaggle. The rest of the paper is organized as follows. Section 2 provides data sources. Details of the implementation are discussed in Sect. 3. The discussion of the final findings is presented in Sect. 4, Finally, Sect. 5 presents the conclusions of the study.

2 H2O Neural Network

Automated Machine Learning, also known as AutoML, is a process that automates the selection and tuning of machine learning models, making it easier to implement machine learning solutions. AutoML algorithms can automatically perform tasks Tasks such as data pre-processing, feature engineering, model selection, and hyperparameter tuning are part of the process. By automating these tasks, AutoML can save time, while delivering better results than manually designed models [10].

H2O is one of AutoML algorithms. The H2O Neural Network is a deep learning framework that supports a variety of machine learning algorithms, including neural networks, gradient boosting, and generalized linear models. The H2O framework is designed to make it easy for data scientists and developers to build and deploy machine learning models at scale. H2O is particularly well-suited for deep learning applications, thanks to its support for large-scale neural networks and distributed training. With H2O, data scientists can quickly build and test deep learning models, allowing them to make better predictions and insights from their data [10].

3 Data Acquisition

3.1 Datasets Description

Creating a dataset of the terms is the first step, for this purpose, the CSV database was chosen where experiments are executed using the Kaggle dataset. The most common words utilized in all of the emails are included in the database. 5172 rows, one for each email, make up the total number of emails. On the other hand, 3002, the name of the email is shown in the first column, it has been provided with numbers rather than the receivers' names in terms of protecting privacy, and the last column has the labels for prediction 1 for spam, and 0 for not spam. Although the remaining 3,000 columns contain the 3,000 terms that appear most common across all emails after excluding the non-alphabetical characters/words.

Table 1. Prevalent Words

The words						
the	number	account	and	for	of	.. etc.
confirm	you	pin	in	on	is	.. etc.
have	with	your	pass	we	send	.. etc.

The fact is that only about 3672 of the emails are spam and the rest are not. Emails are either categorized as spam or non-spam based on the words that exist the most frequently across the entire dataset of emails. The classification of emails and specifics of these words are presented in Tables 1, 2.

Table 2. Email Classification

Email No.	Number of Word $i1$	Number of Word i_2	Number of Word i_3	Number of Word i_n	Class
E$i1$	Ect (24)	For (6)	You (1)	...... (K)	0
Ei_2	Ect (17)	For (5)	You (2)	...... (L)	1
Ei_n	......	......	......	......	0 or 1

3.2 Datasets Partitioning

The data is divided into training data (70%) and testing data (30%) before providing it to the H2O classifier. The training data is fed into the H2O classifier and the network is trained in order to detect spam and non-spam email. The trained H2O classifier is used to predict the Email in the testing data. H2O performs a binary classification to identify whether the email is spam or non-spam. 3,620 emails were assigned to training, whereas 1,551 were assigned to testing, as shown in Fig. 1.

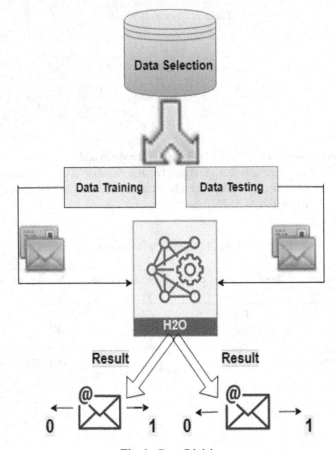

Fig. 1. Data Division

4 Implementation

H2O follows the model of multi-layer, feedforward neural networks for predictive modeling it uses a purely supervised training protocol.

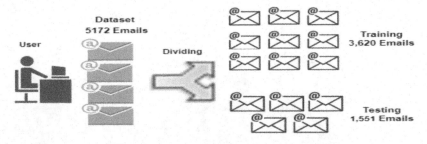

Fig. 2. Main Architecture of Proposed Approach

4.1 Training and Testing

The data utilized for training and testing purposes were separated into training and test sets, with the majority of the data being used for training (70%) and the rest being used for testing (30%), Figs. 2 and 3 show the division percentage for the two types of data. H2O randomly samples the data to help ensure that the testing and training sets are not similar.

4.2 Email Spam Prediction

The used the H2O have been into to predict Email spam detection. As Fig. 2 shows the system starting from the selection of the dataset. After that, the data has been split into two parts, part for the training, and part for testing. This work predictions, whether the Email is spam or not, was trained base on of the most common words in all the emails.

5 Results and Discussion

In this section, we have discussed the results obtained from our experiment. This system generates a prediction in binary form 0 means no spam and 1 means a spam in other words Event and No-event. In fact. Nevertheless, accuracy prediction system is high as we will see in this section. Various measures are used to evaluate the predictions of the system. The following three criteria are used to investigate the results that are generated by the system (Table 3).

Table 3. Confusion Matrix

Actual label	Predicted label	
	Spam	Non-Spam
Spam	True Positive (TP)	False Negative (FN)
Non-Spam	False Positive (FP)	True Negative (TN)

Four categories of binary classification, as shown in Fig. 3.

- True Positive (TP): email is correctly categorized as spam.
- False Positive (FP): email is non-spam, but it is classified as spam.
- True Negative (TN): email is correctly categorized as non-spam.
- False Negative (FN): email is spam, but it is classified as non-spam.

To evaluate these results we used various prediction. The measures that are used are the Accuracy, Precision (P), and Recall (R).

Classification accuracy is a basic evaluation metric. Accuracy is determined by calculating the percentage of correctly classified emails out of the total number of messages, as per the equation: [5].

$$\text{Accuracy} = \frac{TP + TN}{T_P + T_N + F_P + F_N} \tag{1}$$

Classified as

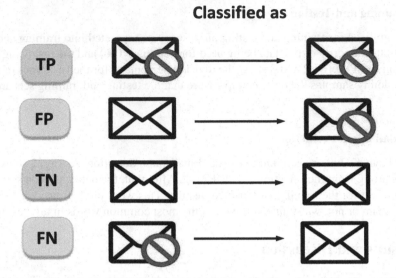

Fig. 3. Categories of Binary Classification

The precision measures the number of correct classifications penalized by the number of incorrect classifications. Calculating precision (P) involves determining the number of correctly classified spam emails out of the total classified emails, as per the equation: Eq. (2)

$$\text{Precision} = \frac{TP}{TP + FP} \tag{2}$$

The recall measures the number of correct classifications penalized by the number of missed entries. Recall (R): Eq. (3) calculates the number of correctly classified spam emails out of the total number of spam emails.

$$\text{Recall} = \frac{TP}{TP + FN} \tag{3}$$

Achieving high accuracy values is crucial for improving classification, which requires finding a balance between the three measures (Table 4).

Table 4. The Prediction's Findings

Class	n(truth)	n(classified)	Accuracy	Precision	Recall
1	479	475	96.71%	0.95	0.94
0	1102	1106	96.71%	0.97	0.98

6 Conclusions

One of the most significant forms of interpersonal communication is email. Spam and non-spam email messages fall into two categories. While not spam communications are the desired ones, spam messages are the unwanted ones that the user does not want to receive and must be removed or filtered beforehand, there are already many SMS spam detection classifiers, but there is no guarantee that they are totally effective.

The proposed work indicates that the detection and classification of email spam using deep learning techniques and H2O may be achieved perfectly.

On the email messages dataset, the experiment is conducted. The data were divided into two groups, a training group, and a test group, and the findings demonstrated that H2O can develop a more effective generative model and successfully complete the Email Spam recognition task, and the proposed approach achieved better prediction, and precision results.

References

1. Anshumaanmishra, Pandi, V.: Classifications of E-MAIL SPAM using deep learning approaches, 414–421 (2022). https://doi.org/10.3233/apc220058
2. Cormack, G.V.: Email spam filtering: a systematic review. Found. Trends Inf. Retr. **1**(4), 335–455 (2008)
3. Ji, H., Zhang, H.: Analysis on the content features and their correlation of web pages for spam detection. Commun. China (2015)
4. Almeida, T.A., Hidalgo, J.M.G., Yamakami, A.: Contributions to the study of SMS spam filtering. In: Proceedings of the 11th ACM Symposium on Document Engineering - DocEng 2011 (2011)
5. Zavrak, S., Yilmaz, S.: Email spam detection using hierarchical attention hybrid deep learning method. SSRN Electron. J. **90**(380) (2022). https://doi.org/10.2139/ssrn.4177036
6. Caudhari, N., Jayvala, Vinitashah: Survey on spam SMS filtering using data mining techniques. Int. J. Adv. Res. Comput. Commun. Eng. **5**(11) (2016)
7. Mathematics, A., Nivaashini, M., Athyamangalam, T.: SMS spam detection using deep neural network. Int. J. Pure Appl. Math. **119**(18), 2425–2436 (2018)
8. AbdulNabi, I., Yaseen, Q.: Spam email detection using deep learning techniques. Procedia Comput. Sci. **184**(2019), 853–858 (2021). https://doi.org/10.1016/j.procs.2021.03.107
9. Jáñez-Martino, F., Alaiz-Rodríguez, R., González-Castro, V., Fidalgo, E., Alegre, E.: A review of spam email detection: analysis of spammer strategies and the dataset shift problem. Artif. Intell. Rev. **56**(2), 1145–1173 (2023). https://doi.org/10.1007/s10462-022-10195-4
10. Sasaki, M., Shinnou, H.: Spam detection using text clustering. In: 2005 International Conference on Cyberworlds (CW 2005). IEEE (2005)
11. Xu, Q., et al.: SMS spam detection using noncontent features. IEEE Intell. Syst. **27**(6), 44–51 (2012)
12. Candel, A., LeDell, E.: Deep learning with H2O, H2O. AI Inc., pp. 1–21, February 2021. https://www.h2o.ai/resources/booklet/deep-learning-with-h2o/
13. Suleiman, D., Al-naymat, G., Itriq, M.: Deep SMS spam detection using H2O platform. Int. J. Adv. Trends Comput. Sci. Eng. **9**(5), 9179–9188 (2020). https://doi.org/10.30534/ijatcse/2020/326952020
14. Ahmed, N., Amin, R., Aldabbas, H., Koundal, D., Alouffi, B., Shah, T.: Machine learning techniques for spam detection in email and IoT platforms: analysis and research challenges. Secur. Commun. Netw. **2022** (2022). https://doi.org/10.1155/2022/1862888

15. Ostapowicz, G., et al.: Changes in hepatitis C-related liver disease in a large clinic population. Int. Med. J. **31**(2), 90–96 (2001). https://doi.org/10.1046/j.1445-5994.2001.00018.x
16. Abayomi-Alli, O., Misra, S., Abayomi-Alli, A.: A deep learning method for automatic SMS spam classification: performance of learning algorithms on indigenous dataset. Concurr. Comput. Pract. Exp. **34**(17) (2022). https://doi.org/10.1002/cpe.6989
17. Marwaha, M., Singla, N.: Email spam filtering techniques review, December 2021
18. Paul, P.M., Ravi, D.R.: A novel email spam detection protocol for next generation networks. Taga J. Graph. Tech. Tech. Assoc. (2018). https://www.researchgate.net/profile/R-RaviRa maraj/publication/362013052_A_Novel_Email_Spam_Detection_Protocol_for_Next_Gene ration_Networks/links/62d0e2ae9b8b7d1f6f711e7e/A-Novel-Email-Spam-Detection-Pro tocol-for-Next-Generation-Networks.pdf
19. Srinivasan, S., Ravi, V., Alazab, M., Ketha, S., Al-Zoubi, A.M., Kotti Padannayil, S.: Spam emails detection based on distributed word embedding with deep learning. Stud. Comput. Intell. **919**, 161–189 (2021). https://doi.org/10.1007/978-3-030-57024-8_7
20. Dada, E.G., Bassi, J.S., Chiroma, H., Abdulhamid, S.M., Adetunmbi, A.O., Ajibuwa, O.E.: Machine learning for email spam filtering: review, approaches and open research problems. Heliyon **5**(6), e01802 (2019). https://doi.org/10.1016/j.heliyon.2019.e01802

Enhancing a System for Predicting Diabetes Utilizing Conventional Machine Learning Approaches

Qusay Karghli[1] , Amina A. Abdo[1](✉) , Abdelhafid Ali Mohamed[1] ,
and Fatma Banini[2]

[1] College of Computer Technology-Benghazi, Benghazi, Libya
amina.abdo@uob.edu.ly
[2] University of Zawia, Zawia, Libya

Abstract. Diabetes is a prevalent sickness that involves millions of people world-wide. Despite several attempts to develop a precise model for predicting diabetes, there are still substantial unresolved research challenges. These challenges arise from the absence of suitable datasets and effective prediction methods. This has led scientists to employ machine learning-based methods to conquer these problems. This work aimed to explore how analyzing features and algorithms of machine learning might be employed in diabetes by applying five different machine-learning methods. The process of classifying may encounter obstacles due to certain features that may lead to difficulties. To overcome this issue, Logistic Regression (LR) has been utilized to determine the degree of effect of these attributes on predicting diabetes mellitus. In order to classify, the proposed diabetes prediction model applies various classifiers such as Adaptive Boosting (AdaBoost), k-nearest neighbor (KNN), linear discriminant analysis (LDA), NaïveBayes (NB), and Support vector machine (SVM) to the Pima Indian Diabetes (PID) database. Furthermore, the performance of each algorithm is scrutinized to determine the one with the highest accuracy, specificity, and recall. It was discovered that the NB model is more effective for binary classification with a refined selection of attributes, whereas random forest is more proficient in handling more features.

Keywords: Predicting Diabetes · Logistic Regression · SVM · KNN · AdaBoost · PID

1 Introduction

Chronic diabetes has an impact on how the body converts food into energy with over one million deaths per year attributed to diabetes alone, it is one of the top causes of death in developing nations [1]. The condition develops when the pancreas fails to create enough insulin or when the body has trouble using the insulin that is generated. Insulin is a type of hormone that controls blood glucose, without insulin, blood sugar levels keep rising and blood sugar metabolism is affected. Diabetes patients' inability to efficiently convert the carbs that consume into glucose sugar causes a steady rise in blood sugar levels [2].

T. A. T. Benmusa et al. (Eds.): ILCICT 2023, CCIS 2097, pp. 257–268, 2024.
https://doi.org/10.1007/978-3-031-62624-1_21

This implies that glucose stays in the blood instead of being delivered to all cells in the body. Prolonged elevated blood glucose levels can harm various organs, such as the heart, blood vessels, kidneys, eyes, feet, and nerves. This damage can potentially result in conditions like heart attacks and strokes [3]. To find a solution to this crucial disease, Organizations, and private citizens are funding research projects. The use of machine learning techniques for pattern discovery in historical data has become increasingly popular in the field of medicine, particularly in the diagnosis and prevention of diabetes [4]. Machine learning accelerates data analysis, allowing analysts to identify patterns and trends in diabetes. The ultimate aim is to simplify the process of identifying diabetes and ultimately improve patient care, whereas the medical community is highly interested in discovering guidelines that enhance our understanding of diabetes and facilitate early diagnosis [5, 6]. Recent studies have shown that machine learning-based models can predict inverse results caused by diabetes complications using administration medical data, demonstrating the potential of machine learning to assist with resource allocation and health organization [7]. By improving the speed and accuracy of physicians' work, machine learning has become a significant tool in the area of medicine.

This research attempts to predict and categorize the state of diabetes prediction and identify appropriate factors that affect diabetes conditions. Additionally, this study intends to design a system that can predict diabetes performance based on pre-defined data for a specific health condition by using AdaBoost, KNN, LDA, NB, and SVM classifiers. This research requires reliable data, information, and analytical tools to forecast specific health conditions or situations; for this reason, the PID dataset has been used.

The remainder of this work is divided into four parts. Section 2 explores the relationship between machine learning and medicine. Section 3 provides a thorough explanation of the methodology and dataset utilized in this study, with a focus on AI applications in diabetes prediction. Section 4 presents the results of the experiments followed by Sect. 5, which is presented discussions and analysis, while Sect. 6 summarizes the paper with a general summary of the findings and future work.

2 Related Work

Numerous diabetes prediction algorithms have been suggested by researchers to predict the types of diabetes accurately [8]. Machine learning approaches, such as SVM, decision tree (DT), and neural networks have been used to predict diabetes with varying degrees of accuracy.

Sanghyuck and Kang [9] conducted an experiment to predict pima Indian diabetes patients using two-class SVM and two-class boosted decision tree. The experiment showed that when classifying pima Indian diabetes patients, checking only the potential patient's glucose, BMI, and age is more efficient than conducting all medical checkouts, which can be time-consuming.

Similarly, the problem of detecting diabetes using machine learning algorithms was dealt by Selvaraj et al. [10]. The Naive Bayes Theorem, SVM, and Gradient Boosting Algorithm have been used for the prediction and detection of diabetes. The experiment showed that Gradient Boosting Algorithm is better than other algorithms.

The clinical dataset is used to predict diabetes in females of pima Indian heritage by Bhoj et al. [11]. The problem is approached as a binary classification problem, and supervised learning algorithms such as classification tree (CT), SVM, k-NN, Naïve Bayes, Random Forest (RF), Neural Network, AdaBoost (AB) and Logistic Regression (LR) are used to solve it. LR has been observed to perform better than other algorithms in various studies.

In the same context, Llaha and Rista [12] developed a decision-making structure for diagnosing diabetes by studying classification data mining approaches like NB, DT, SVM, and LR. They evaluated these methods to determine the highest performing one on the dataset. The decision tree as a classifier in data mining has shown promising results to be effective in predicting diabetes.

Chang et al. [13] presented an electronic diagnostic system that utilized machine-learning algorithms. The system is designed to be deployed within the Internet of Medical Things (IoMT) framework, specifically for the purpose of diagnosing type 2 diabetes. The authors utilized three comprehensible machine learning models, namely NB, RF, and J48 decision tree models. The authors indicated that the Naïve Bayes classifier was performing effectively.

Yakut [14] proposed a system to estimate whether individuals have diabetes or not using machine learning methods such as R, Extra Tree, and Gaussian Process. The machine learning techniques were applied using Colab Notebook. The study used the PID database to forecast diabetes. Other studies have also found RF Classifier to be an effective algorithm for predicting diabetes.

To sum up, the PID has been utilized in many works to forecast diabetes using machine learning methods. However, the task includes determining the most fitting attributes, classifiers, and methods for data mining is crucial for accurate predictions. While some studies have achieved high accuracy rates, others have not been as successful. This research aims to predict the type of diabetes and explore the proportion of each indicator to improve prediction accuracy.

3 The Design of the Proposed System

The suggested structure of our suggested system is separated into a variety of stages, as shown in Fig. 1. The entire implementation was carried out using Python Jupyter Note. Analyzing the data involved utilizing various packages like NumPy, pandas, Matplotlib. The functions associated with the Python tool kits that were explored for each phase and task performed are detailed below.

3.1 Dataset

The data gathered for this study is sourced from the National Institute of Diabetes and Digestive and Kidney Diseases (NIDDK) and is accessible in both Kaggle and UCI data repositories [15]. The dataset is specifically designed to predict the likelihood of diabetes in Pima Indian females aged 21 years or older. All the patients included in the dataset are females of Pima Indian heritage. To identify diabetic females in a given dataset, certain attributes are taken into account as shown in Table 1. These include age, pregnancies, glucose levels, blood pressure, skin thickness, insulin levels, BMI, diabetes pedigree function, and outcome. The dataset contains 768 records of women. It consists of two classes: non-diabetic patients labeled as 0, with a count of 500, and diabetic patients labeled as 1, with a count of 268. The dataset has no missing or null values.

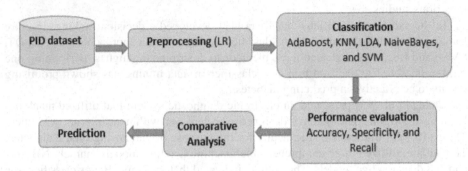

Fig. 1. Proposed system for predicting diabetes.

Table 1. The list of features of the PID database.

No	Name	Type	Description
1	Pregnancies	Numeric	The number of pregnancies
2	Glucose	Numeric	PGC 2 h in an OGTT
3	Blood Pressure	Numeric	Diastolic blood pressure
4	Skin Thickness	Numeric	Triceps skinfold thickness
5	Insulin	Numeric	2 h serum insulin
6	BMI	Numeric	Body mass index
7	Diabetes Pedigree Function	Numeric	Diabetes pedigree function
8	Age	Numeric	Age
9	Outcome	Numeric	0 or 1 (class label)

3.2 Data Preprocessing

Data preprocessing [16] is a crucial stage in data mining that involves various processes, including cleaning, transformation, integration, normalization, feature selection, and instance selection. Data preprocessing incorporates multiple steps to organize and prepare data effectively before applying classifiers. The preprocessing involves the removal of outliers as the primary step to ensure data standardization, followed by scaling the data for a uniform scale, thereby enhancing classifier performance. Additionally, it may include up sampling to balance the data and feature selection to choose only relevant features to reduce data dimensionality and enhance classifier performance. Once data preprocessing is complete, the resultant dataset can be relied upon for any subsequent data mining algorithm. This paper discussed focused on utilizing logistic regression in order to identify crucial features that contribute to the precise prediction of the model. Moreover, the SPSS program was utilized to obtain the best analysis of the dataset.

3.3 Machine Learning Methods

The study employs several classifiers, including AdaBoost, K_NN, LDA, NB, and SVM to forecast whether individuals are afflicted with diabetes or not.

Adaptive Boosting(AdaBoost). AdaBoost [17] is a method of boosting that merges several ineffective classifiers to create a powerful classifier. It is a technique in ensemble learning that was originally developed to enhance the effectiveness of binary classifiers. AdaBoost employs an iterative process to learn from the errors made by powerless classifiers and transform them into robust ones. This is achieved by assigning weights to each instance, with greater weights assigned to instances that are classified incorrectly. In simpler terms, AdaBoost converts weak learners into strong ones.

K-Nearest Neighbor Classification Approach. The KNN algorithm is a category of automatic learning algorithm that is considered to be an instance-based methodology. It is widely used in the field of example acknowledgment, particularly in the classification of text. The KNN algorithm is effective in adapting to large applications and is commonly used for mining purposes. It is favored in classes with multiple models because it can have multiple classifiers and class labels. KNN is a non-parametric method that saves all available data and classifies new data points based on resemblance. It can be used for both regression and classification, but it is mostly used for classification problems. Choosing the right K for the data is crucial in the case of classification and regression. The K-NN algorithm uses input data as training data sets [18].

Linear Discriminant Analysis (LDA). The LDA [19] is a classification approach that relies on the principles of Bayes' Theorem. However, instead of computing the posterior probability directly, LDA estimates the multivariate distribution of its distribution. The algorithm trains by establishing the linear combination of predictors that is useful in separating different classes. LDA classifies the predicted class by identifying the training samples that fall into linear decision boundaries. LDA has the advantage of always producing an explicit solution and being feasible due to its low dimensionality.

The Naive Bayes. The NB [20] is a probabilistic classifier that is based on probability models incorporating strong independence assumptions. These assumptions assume the assumption that the value of a specific feature is unrelated to the value of any other feature, given the class variable, is a key aspect. Although this assumption of independence is frequently violated, the NB classifier continues to exhibit strong performance even in the presence of this unrealistic assumption.

Support Vector Machines (SVM). SVM [21] is a supervised machine learning technique utilized for both classification and regression analysis tasks. It turns on by creating a boundary or hyperplane between different classes of data points, maximizing the distance between the separations between each class's nearest data points and the hyperplane. SVM is effective in cases where the data is not linearly separable, as it can transform the data using different kernels to map it into a higher dimensional space where it separates into two parts. SVM has been applied in various fields, consisting of image classification, text analysis, and bioinformatics.

3.4 Performance Metrics

Machine learning models can be evaluated using various metrics. Some of the most common metrics include classification accuracy, recall or sensitivity, and specificity [22]. Classification accuracy is measured by dividing the number of the model's accurate predictions by the overall predictions. Recall or sensitivity is a measure of how many of the actual positive cases the model accurately categorized, while specificity is a measure of how many of the actual negative cases the model correctly identified. In this work, the efficacy of a model was evaluated using classification accuracy, recall or sensitivity, and specificity. The formulas used to calculate these metrics are displayed in Eqs. 1, 2, and 3.

$$\text{Specificity} = \frac{TN}{TN + FP} * 100 \tag{1}$$

$$\text{Recall} = \frac{TP}{TP + FN} * 100 \tag{2}$$

$$\text{Accuracy} = \frac{TP + TN}{TP + FP + TN + FN} * 100 \tag{3}$$

Where TP denotes a positive prediction for the value and true, while TN indicates that the predicted value is negative and true. FP indicates that the predicted value is positive and false, and FN denotes that the predicted value is negative and false. These values are used to create a confusion matrix.

4 Experiments Results and Analysis

In this work, our primary goal is to examine and analyze the PID Dataset with modern algorithms to work with machine learning methods efficiently. The dataset includes 768 records of female patients, with 500 non-diabetic patients labeled as 0 and 268 diabetic patients labeled as 1. The dataset has nine columns and eight causal characteristics as illustrated in Sect. 3.1 (Table 1), and Table 2 illustrates a sample of the dataset. Furthermore, the experiments were carried out using this dataset and the train-test split procedure was used in two different stages (80:20 and 90:10) to estimate the performance of machine-learning techniques. This work discovered that machine learning models are impacted by the selection of significant features, which is why the regression coefficient was used to obtain important features in the database. The greater the coefficient of an attribute, the more it contributes to the overall value of the cost function.

Table 2. Sample of the PID database.

1	2	3	4	5	6	7	8	9
6	148	72	35	0	33.6	0.627	50	1
1	85	66	29	0	26.6	0.351	31	0
8	183	64	0	0	23.3	0.672	32	1
1	89	66	23	94	28.1	0.167	21	0
0	137	40	35	168	43.1	2.288	33	1
5	116	74	0	0	25.6	0.201	30	0
3	78	50	32	88	31	0.248	26	1
10	115	0	0	0	35.3	0.134	29	0
2	197	70	45	543	30.5	0.158	53	1
8	125	96	0	0	0	0.232	54	1

4.1 Feature Selection

A data preparation technique called feature selection [23] is used to cut down on the number of input variables while creating a predictive model. Statistically based feature selection techniques pick the input variables with the strongest correlation to the target variable after statistically assessing the relationships between each input variable and the target variable.

To ensure transparency and clarity in our model, we explain to end-users how we determine the importance of features. To select the most relevant features for our machine learning experiments, we utilize Logistic Regression Analysis Using SPSS and importance ranking on the dataset. This involves ranking features based on their importance for clustering and selecting a subset of important features. Additionally, In order to determine the features that have the strongest correlation with the output variable, we use statistical tests.

From Table 3 can be noted that the Diabetes pedigree Function, BMI, Blood pressure, pregnancies, and glucose (DPF) are statistically significant variables (P-value < 0.05), meaning that there is a relationship between Diabetes pedigree Function, BMI, Blood pressure, pregnancies, and glucose (DPF) in this sample, where we find The total effect of this variable is significant. While the incidence of diabetes is not affected by age, skin thickness, and insulin.

The results were assessed using three metrics: accuracy, specificity, and recall. These metrics were calculated utilizing the confusion matrix, which displays the actual and predicted outcome classes for the testing set. Accuracy measures the overall accuracy of the model, while specificity and recall measure the performance of the model on positive and negative classes, respectively. The confusion matrix is a useful tool for evaluating the performance of a multi-class machine learning model.

Table 3. Variables in the Equation.

Variable	Sig.	Exp (B)
Pregnancies	0.000	1.131
Glucose	0.000	1.036
Blood Pressure	0.011	0.987
Skin Thickness	0.929	1.001
Insulin	0.186	0.999
BMI	0.000	1.094
Diabetes Pedigree Function	0.002	2.573
Age	0.111	1.015
Variable	Sig.	Exp(B)

4.2 Experiment I

The first experiment was with five features including diabetes pedigree function, BMI, blood pressure, pregnancies, and glucose features using RF, KNN, LR, SVM, LDA, and AadBoost. The results were evaluated on the basis of correctly classified instances of specificity, recall, and accuracy. The performance indicators can be found in the provided Table 4.

Table 4. Results of feature-selection models (5 features)

Model	Training: Testing	Specificity%	Recall%	Accuracy%
AdaBoost	80:20	50.00	92.45	79
	90:10	66.67	89.00	81
KNN	80:20	54.17	75.47	69
	90:10	53.70	82.00	72
LDA	80:20	58.33	86.79	78
	90:10	62.96	89.00	80
NB	80:20	58.33	83.20	75
	90:10	62.96	85.00	77
SVM	80:20	54.17	86.79	77
	90:10	50.00	91.00	77

4.3 Experiment II

In the second experiment, all features in the dataset including age, pregnancies, glucose, blood pressure, skin thickness, insulin, BMI, and diabetes pedigree function have been used. In the same context, we applied five models to achieve efficient results. The evaluation of the results was based on the correct classification of specificity, recall, and accuracy. Table 5 provides performance indicators.

Table 5. Results of feature-selection models (8 features)

Model	Training: Testing	Specificity%	Recall%	Accuracy%
AdaBoost	80:20	82.61	61.26	74
	90:10	85.57	57.89	75
KNN	80:20	84.54	47.37	71
	90:10	84.78	54.84	73
LDA	80:20	91.75	57.89	79
	90:10	93.48	61.29	81
NaiveBayes	80:20	81.44	68.42	77
	90:10	86.96	74.19	82
SVM	80:20	93.81	49.12	77
	90:10	95.65	54.84	79

5 Discussion and Analysis

The study discusses the development of classification models for electronic diagnostic systems to predict diabetes. Figures 2 and 3 illustrate the models' achievement across different datasets, showcasing the evaluation metrics from various perspectives. The training process involved utilizing five different machine learning algorithms to train the models. These models were then assessed to determine their ability to predict whether a person has a positive diagnosis of diabetes mellitus. The evaluation was based on eight attributes in one case and five attributes in another. The first experimental outcomes show that the AdaBoost classifier outperformed the NB, KNN, SVM, and LDA with an accuracy metric of 81%, re-call of 92%, and specificity of 66.67%. However, the SVM had the best specificity of 93.81% of the four in the second experimental results. The variation in sensitivity and specificity can be attributed to the unequal distribution of samples between class 0 and class 1. The study used the Pima Indian Diabetes dataset for the experiment, which is a benchmark for diabetes classification research. Based on the analysis, it can be inferred that the aAdaBoost model performs effectively when a more precise selection of features is used for binary classification. However, it may not be as effective when there are many correlated features. On the other hand, the KNN model performs better when more features are used.

Table 6 presents a comparison between the accuracy of diabetes prediction studies using the PID database and the accuracy of the one of proposed methods in our system (NB classifier). After analyzing the results, it was found that the proposed method outperforms the previously studied models in terms of prediction accuracy.

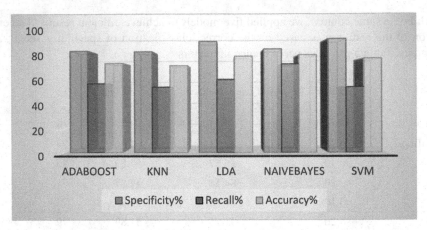

Fig. 2. Comparing performance metrics across models and with 5 values of PID.

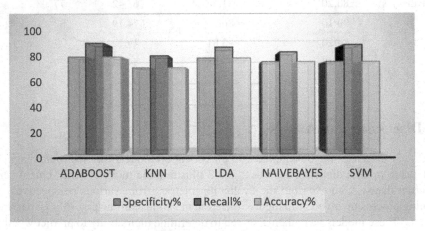

Fig. 3. Comparing performance metrics across models with 8 values of PID.

Table 6. A comparison between the proposed method and previous studies

Model	Accuracy%
Proposed Method (NaiveBayes classifier)	82
RF classifier [15]	81.7
C4.5 classifier [13]	79
SVM classifier [10]	70
AdaBoost [24]	78

6 Conclusion

This article discussed the development of classification models that are appropriate for Diabetes Prediction systems. The models were created by utilizing five different machine-learning algorithms and were tested to determine their ability to predict whether a person's diabetes mellitus diagnosis is positive based on eight or five specific attributes. Moreover, this work created a simple desktop app for diabetes prediction. The Experiments were carried out on PID database to predict diabetes. Furthermore, The models have been evaluated against existing techniques by using machine learning metrics and the suggested methods have yielded outstanding outcomes. The study discovered that machine learning models are impacted by the selection of significant features, which is why the logistic regression coefficient was used to obtain important features in the database. The higher the coefficient of a feature, the higher the value of the cost function. The future work plan involves developing innovative methods such as deep learning and utilizing them for various forms of medical examination.

References

1. Danholt, P.: Factish relations: affective bodies in diabetes treatment. Health **17**, 375–390 (2013)
2. Szablewski, L.: Glucose homeostasis–mechanism and defects. Diabetes Damages Treat. **2** (2011)
3. Sonksen, P., Sonksen, J.: Insulin: understanding its action in health and disease. Br. J. Anaesth. **85**, 69–79 (2000)
4. El_Jerjawi, N.S., Abu-Naser, S.S.: Diabetes prediction using artificial neural network (2018)
5. Akila1, A., Parameswari, R., Jayakumari, C.: Big data in healthcare: management, analysis, and future prospects. In: Handbook of Intelligent Healthcare Analytics: Knowledge Engineering with Big Data Analytics, pp. 309–326 (2022)
6. Agliata, A., Giordano, D., Bardozzo, F., Bottiglieri, S., Facchiano, A., Tagliaferri, R.: Machine learning as a support for the diagnosis of type 2 diabetes. Int. J. Mol. Sci. **24**, 6775 (2023)
7. Longato, E., Fadini, G.P., Sparacino, G., Avogaro, A., Tramontan, L., Di Camillo, B.: A deep learning approach to predict diabetes' cardiovascular complications from administrative claims. IEEE J. Biomed. Health Inform. **25**, 3608–3617 (2021)
8. Juneja, A., Juneja, S., Kaur, S., Kumar, V.: Predicting diabetes mellitus with machine learning techniques using multi-criteria decision making. Int. J. Inf. Retr. Res. (IJIRR) **11**, 38–52 (2021)
9. You, S., Kang, M.S.: A study on methods to prevent pima Indians diabetes using SVM. 인공지능연구**8**, 7–10 (2020)
10. (14) (PDF) Prediction and Detection of Diabetes using Machine Learning. https://www.researchgate.net/publication/359384363_Prediction_and_Detection_of_Diabetes_using_Machine_Learning. Accessed 08 June 2023
11. Bhoi, S.K.: Prediction of diabetes in females of pima Indian heritage: a complete supervised learning approach. Turk. J. Comput. Math. Educ. (TURCOMAT) **12**, 3074–3084 (2021)
12. Ahmed, N., et al.: Machine learning based diabetes prediction and development of smart web application. Int. J. Cogn. Comput. Eng. **2**, 229–241 (2021)
13. Chang, V., Bailey, J., Xu, Q.A., Sun, Z.: Pima Indians diabetes mellitus classification based on machine learning (ML) algorithms. Neural Comput. Appl., 1–17 (2022)
14. Yakut, Ö.: Diabetes prediction using colab notebook based machine learning methods. Int. J. Comput. Exp. Sci. Eng. **9**, 36–41 (2023)

15. Pima Indians Diabetes Database. https://www.kaggle.com/datasets/uciml/pima-indians-diabetes-database. Accessed 08 June 2023
16. Zelaya, C.V.G.: Towards explaining the effects of data preprocessing on machine learning. In: 2019 IEEE 35th International Conference on Data Engineering (ICDE), pp. 2086–2090. IEEE (2019)
17. Feng, D.-C., et al.: Machine learning-based compressive strength prediction for concrete: an adaptive boosting approach. Constr. Build. Mater. **230**, 117000 (2020)
18. Abdo, A., El-Tarhouni, W., Younus, W., Abraheem, A.: Iris recognition system based on fuzzy local binary pattern histogram and multiple classifiers. In: 2022 IEEE 2nd International Maghreb Meeting of the Conference on Sciences and Techniques of Automatic Control and Computer Engineering (MI-STA), pp. 452–457. IEEE (2022)
19. Park, C.H., Park, H.: A comparison of generalized linear discriminant analysis algorithms. Pattern Recognit. **41**, 1083–1097 (2008)
20. Rish, I.: An empirical study of the naive Bayes classifier. In: IJCAI 2001 Workshop on Empirical Methods in Artificial Intelligence, pp. 41–46 (2001)
21. Kumari, V.A., Chitra, R.: Classification of diabetes disease using support vector machine. Int. J. Eng. Res. Appl. **3**, 1797–1801 (2013)
22. Düntsch, I., Gediga, G.: Confusion matrices and rough set data analysis. J. Phys. Conf. Ser., 012055 (2019)
23. Brownlee, J.: How to choose a feature selection method for machine learning. Mach. Learn. Mastery **10** (2019)
24. AlZu'bi, S., et al.: Diabetes monitoring system in smart health cities based on big data intelligence. Future Internet **15**, 85 (2023)

Enhanced Facial Expression Recognition Using Pre-trained Models and Image Processing Techniques

Rayhan S. Alshwihde$^{(\boxtimes)}$ ⓘ and Wafa I. Eltarhouni ⓘ

University of Benghazi, Benghazi, Libya
itstd.4085@uob.edu.ly

Abstract. Facial expressions are a type of nonverbal communication and one of the most important activities in effective human-computer interaction. In recent years, facial expression recognition has been a hot topic for researchers particularly for smart applications. However, Facial Expression Recognition (FER) still faces many challenges, such as non-uniform illumination, aging, pose variations, etc. The proposed methodology is based on deep learning technique for extracting and classifying the features from images. Four datasets are utilized to evaluate the effectiveness of the suggested methodology which are CK+, JAFFE, RAFDB, and FER2013. The facial part is detached, cropped, and a CLAHE filter is applied to improve contrast in images. We use pre-trained models of VGG16, Inception V3, MobileNet, and DenseNet but replace their fully connected layers with our own suitable ones. The accuracy achieved on FER3013, RAFDB, CK+, and JAFFE datasets were 90.72%, 93.12%, 97.50%, and 93.55% respectively.

Keywords: Facial expressions recognition · Deep learning · Transfer learning

1 Introduction

The advancements in computer technology have led to the development of various fields, including pattern recognition and artificial intelligence, with the goal of facilitating natural communication between humans and computers. Nonverbal communication, such as body language and facial expressions, plays a significant role in this communication. Recognizing facial expressions has become an active research area with applications in medicine, security, and e-learning, among others. However, there is confusion between recognizing emotions and recognizing facial expressions in the realm of computer vision. Emotion recognition involves features such as facial expression, text, EEG, speech, etc., while recognizing facial expressions is determined by the movements of the muscles and wrinkles on the face. Ekman's [1] Facial Action Coding System (FACS) is used to classify facial movements into 44 regions called Action Units (AU) to help determine people's emotions. His theory also proposes seven primary expressions that appear in all people which are happy, sad, angry, fear, surprise, neutral, and disgusted. Therefore, understanding facial expressions is vital for natural communication between humans and computers.

T. A. T. Benmusa et al. (Eds.): ILCICT 2023, CCIS 2097, pp. 269–283, 2024.
https://doi.org/10.1007/978-3-031-62624-1_22

Facial expression recognition faces numerous challenges due to age, gender, cultural differences, and image quality. Older people may appear sad due to wrinkles and loose facial muscles, while women tend to show more expression than men. Different cultures also display expressions differently. Image quality can affect recognition, with factors such as environment, lighting conditions, and posture contributing to variations in expressions.

Traditional algorithms detect faces in images, extract features using methods like Local Binary Pattern (LBP) [2], Principal Component Analysis (PCA) [3], and Scale-Invariant Feature Transform (SIFT) [4], and classify them using Decision Tree [5], K-nearest neighbors (k-NN) [6], Support Vector Machines (SVM) [7], etc. However, the separation of feature extraction and classification limits performance enhancement. Overcoming these challenges requires developing more advanced algorithms that can account for individual differences in facial expressions and improve accuracy in recognizing emotions across diverse populations.

In order to overcome the limitations of conventional systems, numerous research studies have opted to utilize Convolutional Neural Network (CNN) models. This is because these models rely on a single network that can extract and categorize features. Nevertheless, due to the lengthy training period required for these models, they are not adequate for recognizing facial expressions. To circumvent this issue in our work, we utilized four pre-trained models: DenceNet 121, InceptionV3, VGG16, and MobileNet. By using pre-trained models and transfer learning, we were able to overcome the long training time required for facial expression recognition and achieve high accuracy in our classification task.

This paper proposes a multi-step approach to facial expression recognition. The system uses four established datasets of facial expression images to evaluate its performance and employs transfer learning-based feature models to extract features from all datasets. Each pre-training model used for feature extraction is combined with new classification layers to function as a single network during the classification stage, resulting in high accuracy in facial expression recognition. The proposed techniques have distinct performance levels, indicating the effectiveness of the system in accurately recognizing facial expressions.

2 Related Work

With the advancement of technology, numerous methods for recognizing facial expressions have emerged. This paragraph summarizes a number of experiments that have been done utilizing Machine and Deep learning to recognize the expressions in recognizing the facial images. The following is a quick list of works in this field:

Y. Nan et al. [8] enhanced model for facial expression identification is a breakthrough in the field. They have developed a system that is extremely accurate and effective by fusing deep learning approaches with cutting-edge dropout technology. The model performed better than other lightweight models like the MobileNet series and other cutting-edge techniques. Both the RAF-DB and FERPlus datasets' recognition accuracy scores 84.49% and 88.11%, respectively are impressive. These outcomes showed the model's potential for usage in practical applications like mental health monitoring or emotion recognition in human-computer interaction. The model was more resilient and dependable because dropout technology prevented it from overfitting to the training data.

In [9] suggested a deep learning technique based on attentional convolutional networks that can concentrate on main facial features. They also offer a thorough experimental analysis of their work on four popular facial expression recognition databases, including Japanese Female Facial Expression (JAFFE), FER2013, the extended Cohn-Kanade (CK+), and Facial Expression Research Group Database (FERG). The accuracy of the model was 99.3%, 98.0%, 92.8%, and 70.02% for FERG, CK+, JAFFE, and FER2013 datasets respectively.

The [10] paper proposed a facial emotion recognition system using textural images and a deep learning model CNN. The benchmark datasets CK+, JAFEE, and FER2013 are transformed into textural images such as LBP, LTP, and CLBP and labeled with emotions. The CNN model performs better when trained with CLBP images compared to other approaches for detecting emotion. Lower-level information in textural images is preferred over higher-level information in normal grayscale images for training the CNN model to achieve improved emotion detection accuracy. The study found that training a CNN model with textural images resulted in better efficiency. The accuracy of the CLBP model was 91.0%, 82.2%, and 64.5% for CK+, JAFFE, and FER2013 datasets respectively.

Zhu, J et al. [11] introduced a new method called ECAN, which uses contrastive learning to learn discriminative features in wild facial expression recognition scenes. ECAN includes two new metric loss functions to optimize feature output and improve inter-class separation and intra-class compactness. The proposed method outperforms other methods on two widely used wild FER datasets, achieving 89.77% accuracy on the RAFDB dataset and 73.73% accuracy on the FER2013 dataset.

Kola D and Samayamantula S.K [12] suggested a novel feature extraction approach to improve the FER's performance. They used a Modified Local Binary Pattern (LBP) calculated by taking 4-neighbors and diagonal neighbors into account separately, using (SVM) for classification. In this study, the face datasets JAFFE, CK, FERG, and FEI were used. The adaptive window approach has the highest recognition rate of 92.9% and 88.3% for 6-class and 7-class recognition on the JAFFE database, and a recognition rate of 96% and 93.9% for 6-class and 7-class recognition on the CK database.

3   Methodology

The proposed facial expression recognition methodology based on using four pre-trained models are VGG16, IncaptionV3, MobileNet, and DenceNet121. These models are modified by adding the same classification layers to them, and the performance of each model was evaluated by four facial expressions datasets which are RAF-DB, FER2013, CK+, and JAFFE. Before the feature extraction stage different techniques of pre-processing were applied to the images of CK+ and JAFFE. In the end, the results of the experiments are evaluated by a confusion matrix. The suggested model is shown in Fig. 1.

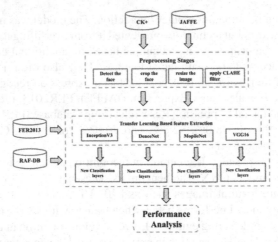

Fig. 1. The proposed methodology

3.1 Datasets

The performance of the models is strongly dependent on data because the quality of the data can determine how dependable and accurate the research results are. The proposed approaches have been implemented and tested on challenging datasets which are RAF-DB, FER2013, CK+, and JAFFE, as well as to compare them to some state-of-the-art approaches in order to examine and evaluate the performance of the various feature extraction and classification techniques we used.

Real-World Affective Faces (RAF-DB). The dataset called RAF-DB [13] contains a vast collection of 29672 facial images that are colored and distinct from each other. These images have a size of 349 × 349 and were obtained from the Internet, resulting in a comprehensive dataset for facial expressions Fig. 2 (A) presents the sample of the face images dataset.

Facial Expression Recognition 2013 (FER-2013). The FER-2013 standard dataset for recognizing facial expressions was presented in the ICML 2013 Challenges in Representation Learning [14]. In this study, we utilized the FER-2013 dataset, which comprises 35,887 grayscale images with a resolution of 48 × 48 pixels. The dataset encompasses seven emotions: anger, disgust, fear, happiness, sadness, surprise, and neutral. Figure 2 (B) displays four sample images.

Extended Cohn-Kaneda Dataset (CK+). The study used CK+ images [15] gathered from 123 people in 593 sequences, each with 8 different facial expressions. The image resolution is 640 × 490 pixels or 640 × 490 pixels. The dataset contains eight types of emotions which are anger, disgust, fear, happiness, sadness, contempt, surprise, and neutral because all datasets have 7 classes except CK+ has an additional class called "contempt" over the preceding class, which we deleted in order to make the classes equal. Figure 2 (C) depicts various sample images.

Japanese Female Facial Expression (JAFFE). The JAFFE dataset [16] contains 213 high-resolution facial expression images of ten Japanese women, each expressing seven main emotions. This dataset contains 3–4 images per subject, providing a comprehensive view of emotions displayed under controlled lighting conditions. It's reliable for research on facial expressions and emotions in humans. Figure 2 (D) provides examples of the different facial expression images.

Fig. 2. Four sample images from each dataset (A) RAFDB, (B) FER2013, (C) CK+, (D) JAFFE.

3.2 Images Pre-processing

All Datasets images are converted to grayscale to minimize complexity and remove irrelevant data such as environment and background. The Haar cascade frontal face based on the Viola-Jones detection algorithm is used [17] to locate the face in the image, returning four values: x-coordinate, y-coordinate, height, and width. However, only the eyes, nose, and mouth are needed. To obtain these features, a constant value c is added to both x and y points and subtracted from both height and width values of the square that determines the location of the face. The face is then cropped in the new indexes. This process is illustrated in Fig. 3.

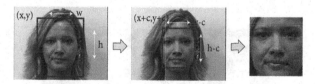

Fig. 3. Face detection and crop step.

We performed face detection and cropping only on CK+ and JAFFE datasets, while FER2013 and RAF-DB were not processed as their faces are already cropped. We apply Contrast Limited Adaptive Histogram Equalization (CLAHE) filter to enhance the details in an image by increasing contrast and brightness, producing an image that is clearer and more detailed at the end of this stage, the images are resized according to the default input size of the pre-training model that has been used All pre-processing steps are shown in Fig. 4.

Fig. 4. The steps of pre-processing phase.

3.3 Data Augmentation

Class imbalance is a problem when real-world datasets frequently only contain a small number of target class examples. When one class dominates a dataset but the samples from another class are few, the model may be misled about how relevant the target task is, to solve this problem "data augmentation" is applied. During the augmentation process, each sample image was read, and random transformations (zooming, rotation, flipping, and displacement) were applied to create new sample images by using the ImageDataGenerator function of TensorFlow, Table 1 shows the function parameters and the results of it in Fig. 5.

Table 1. ImageDataGeneraters parameters for data augmentation.

Parameter	Value
zca_epsilon	0.000001
rotation_range	0.5
width_shift_range	−0.1
zoom_range	0.3
channel_shift_range	1.05
vertical_flip	True
horizontal_flip	True

Fig. 5. Data augmentation results on JAFFE dataset.

3.4 Feature Extraction Based on the Transfer Learning Technique

Deep learning algorithms are designed to work with specific feature-space distributions, requiring complete redesigns when the distribution changes. Obtaining sufficient labeled data for training is also time-consuming, making it difficult to develop deep learning models for domains with limited labeled data. Transfer learning can improve learning effectiveness in such cases by using labeled data or information from related domains to aid deep learning algorithms in the target domain. This principle allows for better performance without requiring extensive training data collection [18]. One of the primaries uses for transfer learning is pre-trained models that were built on the ImageNet dataset can be utilized for real-world image-based classification. Large CNN are the foundation of several pre-trained models used in transfer learning such as VGG-16, VGG-19, and XCeption problems. In this research, four pre-training models (VGG16, Inception-V3, MobileNet, and DenseNet-121) are proposed for extracting face features in the initial recognition phase.

VGG16 Model. Simonyan and Zisserman [19] were the initial ones to propose the VGG network architecture. Their ImageNet challenge 2014 submission was based on VGG models with 16 layers (VGG16) and 19 layers (VGG19). The network is based on the AlexNet network but is deeper. When detecting and classifying images, it can more accurately express the features of the data set. It performs better when dealing with complicated background recognition tasks and big data sets.

Inception-V3 Model. Inception-V3 was developed in 2015 as an upgrade to its predecessor, Inception-V2 [20]. This model employs a combination of convolutional layers with varying kernel sizes and pooling layers to extract features from images. With 50 convolutional layers, Inception-V3 is a deep neural network that was built and trained by Google. The pre-trained version of Inception-V3 is capable of categorizing up to 1000 objects using ImageNet weights. The input size for images in the InceptionV3 network is 299×299 pixels, which is larger than the VGG-16 network. Due to its kernel size of 5×5, it has better performance in extracting features from images.

MobileNet Model. Google engineers presented MobileNets, a lightweight deep neural network with 28 layers, at CVPR 2017 [21]. It uses depthwise separable convolutions to reduce model size and processing, making it suitable for mobile and embedded vision applications. Batch normalization and ReLU non-linearity are implemented after each layer, with SoftMax receiving input from the final fully connected layer. The first layer is a complete convolutional layer, while the rest are depthwise separable convolutions.

DenseNet-121. The dense convolutional neural network (DenseNet) [22] is a feed-forward fully connected neural network, it directly connects all the layers that produce feature maps, allowing each convolution layer to know the feature maps produced by the previous convolution layer and revealing the dense connections between layers. Additionally, DenseNet employs a variety of methods to solve the gradient vanishing problem. In addition to this, DenseNet decreases the chance of model overfitting due to the small size training data set by applying regularization (Table 2).

Table 2. Displays the default input and output size of the feature extractor models.

The pre-trained model	Input size	Output size
VGG16	(224,224,3)	(7,7,512)
Inception V3	(299,299,3)	(8,8,2048)
MobileNet	(224,224,3)	(7,7,1024)
DenceNet	(224,224,3)	(7,7,1024)

3.5 Classification

To ensure that the pre-trained models remain unchanged, Their weights were kept frozen, but their classification layers were replaced with new ones and merged into a single model. This new model includes Fully Connected Neural Networks (Dense) as its new layers. This technology has proven to be highly effective in supervised learning, particularly for pattern recognition and classification problems. Its exceptional computing capabilities enable it to produce an output that precisely matches the target output. The structure of the classifications layers is shown in Table 3. By incorporating these new layers into pre-trained models, we can improve their performance and accuracy in recognizing and classifying facial expressions.

Table 3. The classifications layers.

Layers	Output
Flatten ()	Depends on the feature extractor output
Dropout (0.25)	Depends on the feature extractor output
Dense (1024)	(none, 1024)
Batchnormalization ()	(none, 1024)
Activation ('relu')	(none, 1024)
Dropout (0.25)	(none, 1024)
Dense (14)	(none, 14)
Batchnormalization ()	(none, 14)
Activation ('relu')	(none, 14)
Dropout (0.25)	(none, 14)
Dense (7)	(none, 7)

4 Implementation

To perform the experiments, Google Colaboratory Pro with T4 GPU and 32 GB RAM were utilized, along with the Tensorflow and Keras libraries, to implement VGG16, InceptionV3, MobileNet, and DenseNet121. Four datasets, namely CK+, FER2013,

RAF-DB, and JAFFE, were utilized. CK+ and JAFFE were split into 70% training, 20% validation, and 10% testing sets. The FER2013 and RAFDB datasets were further divided into training and testing sets. FER2013 has 28,709 training, 3,589 for validation, and 3,589 for testing, and RAFDB has 12271 images used for training and 3068 used for testing. We used different values for epochs and batch size with different datasets. In experiments with the CK+ and JAFFE datasets, we set the batch size to 32 and the epoch value to 100 On the other hand, for the FER2013 and RAFDB datasets, we used a batch size of 128 and 50 epochs, respectively. The optimizer was Adam; the learning rate that we used was the default learning rate for Adam in Keras which is 0.001, also the learning rate was reduced by 1e-10 every ten times when the validation set loss value cannot improve. Table 4 shows the other implementation parameters for the experiments.

Table 4. Implementation parameters.

Parameter	VGG16	InceptionV3	MobileNet	DenceNet121
Input shape	(224,224,3)	(299,299,3)	(224,224,3)	(224,224,3)
Trainable param	25,759,955	134,287,571	51,450,067	51,397,779
Optimizer	Adam	Adam	Adam	Adam
Weights	Imagenet	Imagenet	Imagenet	Imagenet
Loss function	Categorical cross entropy	Categorical cross entropy	Categorical cross entropy	Categorical cross entropy

5 Experiment Results and Discussions

The following are the results of each model on the four datasets. In all the experiments, the model that showed the best performance in the validation set was selected. To evaluate how well a classification method works, the confusion matrix is a useful tool. In this research, Confusion Matrix, Accuracy, and F-Score are used as evaluation metrics.

5.1 Results for CK+ dataset

The proposed methodology in this experiment was implemented and evaluated using the CK+ dataset. The best result was using MobileNet the recognition rate that was achieved is 97.50% after 99 training epochs, and the lowest one was 93.77% by the Inception V3+ANN model. The result of the different feature extraction Models are shown in Table 5. Figure 6 visualization of the learning rate, data loss rate, and F1-score of the best result.

5.2 Results for JAFFE Dataset

This experiment replicated the setup of the CK+ experiment and utilized the JAFFE dataset for performance evaluation of the proposed approach. MobileNet achieved the

Table 5. The results of CK+ dataset experiment

Methods	Accuracy	Loss value	F1-score
VGG16 + New layers	95.64%	0.5365	0.8112
InceptionV3 + New layers	93.77%	0.6082	0.7905
MobileNet + New layers	97.50%	0.3213	0.8906
DenceNet + New layers	94.90%	0.5792	0.8025

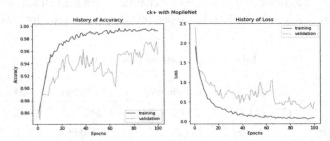

Fig. 6. Visualization of accuracy and data loss rate for MobileNet experiment using CK+.

highest recognition rate of 93.55%, followed by Inception V3 with 88.25%. VGG16 and DenseNet had identical results of 88.02% and ranked last. These findings are presented in Table 6, while Fig. 7 displays a visualization of learning rate, data loss rate, and F1-Score results solely for the best outcome.

Table 6. The results of JAFFE dataset experiments

Mothods	Accuracy	Loss value	F1-score
VGG16 + New layers	88.02%	1.3554	0.6636
InceptionV3 + New layers	88.25%	1.4462	0.7062
MobileNet + New layers	93.55%	0.8528	0.7196
DenceNet + New layers	88.02%	1.2750	0.6653

5.3 Results for RAF Dataset

The proposed approach was put to the test on the RAFDB dataset, and the results were impressive. In fact, the MobileNet model proved to be the top performer, boasting an accuracy rate of 93.12% and a loss value of 0.7982. The other models also performed

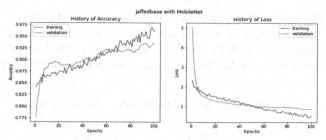

Fig. 7. Visualization of accuracy and data loss rate for MobileNet experiment using JAFFE dataset.

well, with accuracy rates ranging from 92% to 93%, as shown in Table 7. To further illustrate these findings, Fig. 8 depicts the learning rate and data loss rate for this dataset. Overall, these results demonstrate the effectiveness of our approach in accurately classifying facial expressions in real-world scenarios.

Table 7. The results of RAF dataset experiments

Mothods	Accuracy	Loss value	F1-score
VGG16 + New layers	92.46%	0.8609	0.6996
Inception V3 + New layers	92.25%	0.8764	0.7096
MobileNet + New layers	93.12%	0.7982	0.8780
DenceNet + New layers	92.90%	0.7708	0.6831

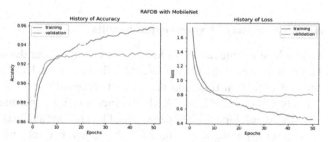

Fig. 8. Visualization of accuracy and data loss rate for MobileNet experiment using RAF dataset.

5.4 Results for FER2013 Dataset

The effectiveness of the proposed methodology was evaluated using the publicly available FER 2013 dataset, as previously described. For this experiment, a batch size of 128 and 50 epochs were employed, similar to the previous experiment. The recognition rates obtained for DenseNet, MobileNet, VGG16, and Inception V3 models were 90.37%,

90.51%, 90.72%, and 90.22%, respectively. It is noteworthy that the VGG16 model produced the best results with an improvement of 0.11% compared to other models. Table 8 presents the output of various feature extraction methods used in this study, while Fig. 9 illustrates the visualization of learning rate and data loss rate using this dataset.

Table 8. The results of FER2013 dataset experiments

Methods	Accuracy	Loss value	F1-score
VGG16 + New layers	90.72%	1.0145	0.8553
Inception V3 + New layers	90.22%	1.0451	0.8242
MobileNet + New layers	90.51%	1.0205	0.8394
DenceNet + New layers	90.37%	1.0451	0.8082

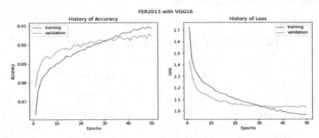

Fig. 9. Visualization of accuracy and data loss rate for MobileNet experiment using FER2013 dataset.

5.5   Discussion and Analysis of Experimental Results

In this study, we employed identical algorithm structures for all four datasets, with the sole variation being in the epoch and batch size. Our findings revealed that MobileNet exhibited the shortest execution time and the highest recognition rate in three out of four datasets, namely CK+, JAFFE, and RAFDB. InceptionV3 experiments took the longest time due to its default input size and number of layers. Our analysis of confusion matrices on CK+ dataset experiment demonstrated that anger, neutral, and sad were the best-performing classes with a recognition rate of approximately 100%. For experiment 2 using JAFFE dataset, we evaluated each class's accuracy, which ranged from 44.4% to 88.9%. In the REFDB dataset experiment, neutral had the highest performance with an 83.6% recognition rate while fear had the lowest recognition rate at 36.2%. Finally, for FER2013 dataset experiment, we observed accuracies of 45.3%, 56.4%, 33.2%, 88.9%, 64.1%, 85.4%, and 69.2% over angry, surprise, fear, neutral, sad, happy, and disgust respectively.

It is noteworthy that the confusion matrix for each experiment's model with the highest accuracy was previously described in our analysis. The confusion matrices of best result for each dataset are presented in Fig. 10 and Fig. 11 below.

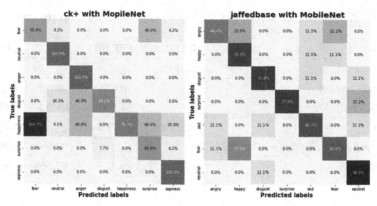

Fig. 10. The confusion matrices of best result for CK+ and JAFFE datasets.

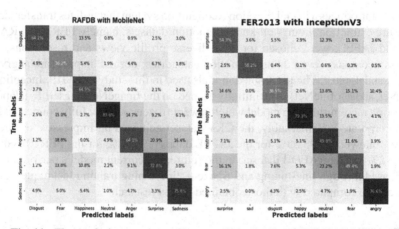

Fig. 11. The confusion matrices of best result for RAF and FER2013 datasets.

5.6 Comparison with Previous Approaches

Experimental comparisons between the suggested technique and a number of state-of-art, the proposed approach with CK+ achieve 97.5% which is higher than Modified CLBP-CNN [10] but 0.5% lower than Attentional-CNN [9], and compared to other existing approaches, our results in JAFFE dataset increased performance of 0.75%, 11.35%, and 5.25% over Attentional CNN [9], CLBP-CNN [10], and local binary pattern-adaptive window [12]. For FER2013 dataset the VGG16 and the additional layers approach achieves a recognition rate of 90.72% which is higher than all the other reported algorithms by a range of (16.99 −26.22%). The MobileNet as feature extractor achieves a 90.72% recognition rate on RAF-DB which is higher than A-MobileNet [8], and ECAN [11]. Table 9 compares the prior approaches to the proper approach. It includes various studies that make use of the same databases that we used in our research.

Table 9. Discussion and compares the existing approaches the proposed approach

MOD3EL	RAF-DB	FER2013	CK+	JAFFE
A-MobileNet [8]	84.49%	—	—	—
Attentional CNN [9]	—	70.02%	98.0%	92.8%
CLBP-CNN [10]	—	64.5%	91.0%	82.2%
ECAN [11]	89.77%	73.73%	—	—
local binary pattern-adaptive window [12]	—	—	93.9%	88.3%
OUR RESULTS	93.12%	90.72%	97.50%	93.55%

6 Conclusion and Future Work

This study introduces a Facial Emotion Recognition system that utilizes transfer learning for feature extraction. Four well-known emotion datasets, namely FER3013, RAFDB, CK+, and JAFFE, were chosen for their diverse profile views and resolutions. These datasets encompass seven distinct emotion categories: normal, happy, sad, angry, fear, surprise, and disgust. The pre-trained models used in this study (VGG19, Inception V3, DenseNet, and MobileNet) were initially trained on the ImageNet dataset. To adapt them for emotion recognition, the model weights were frozen and new fully connected layers were incorporated. Remarkably, the CK+ dataset achieved an impressive accuracy of 97.55%, followed by 93.55% for the JAFFE dataset, 90.72% for the FER2013 dataset, and 93.12% for the RAFDB dataset. In the future, the current model's performance can be improved through fine-tuning and freeze + fine-tuning training techniques, and the results can be compared with those obtained in this research.

References

1. Ekman, P., Friesen, W.V.: Facial action coding system (1978). https://doi.org/10.1037/t27 734-000
2. Shan, C., Gong, S., McOwan, P.W.: Facial expression recognition based on local binary patterns: a comprehensive study. Image Vis. Comput. **27**, 803–816 (2009). https://doi.org/10. 1016/j.imavis.2008.08.005
3. Gosavi, A.P., Khot, S.R.: Facial expression recognition using principal component analysis. Int. J. Soft Comput. Eng. (IJSCE) **3**(4), 258–262 (2013)
4. Lowe, D.G.: Distinctive image features from scale-invariant keypoints. Int. J. Comput. Vis. **60**, 91–110 (2004). https://doi.org/10.1023/B:VISI.0000029664.99615.94
5. Salmam, F.Z., Madani, A., Kissi, M.: Facial expression recognition using decision trees. In: 2016 13th International Conference on Computer Graphics, Imaging and Visualization (CGiV), pp. 125–130 (2016). https://doi.org/10.1109/CGiV.2016.33
6. Wang, X.-H., Liu, A., Zhang, S.-Q.: New facial expression recognition based on FSVM and KNN. Optik **126**, 3132–3134 (2015). https://doi.org/10.1016/j.ijleo.2015.07.073
7. Chen, L., Zhou, C., Shen, L.: Facial expression recognition based on SVM in E-learning. IERI Procedia **2**, 781–787 (2012). https://doi.org/10.1016/j.ieri.2012.06.171
8. Nan, Y., Ju, J., Hua, Q., Zhang, H., Wang, B.: A-MobileNet: an approach of facial expression recognition. Alex. Eng. J. **61**, 4435–4444 (2022). https://doi.org/10.1016/j.aej.2021.09.066

9. Minaee, S., Minaei, M., Abdolrashidi, A.: Deep-emotion: facial expression recognition using attentional convolutional network. Sensors **21**, 3046 (2021). https://doi.org/10.3390/s21093046

10. Mukhopadhyay, M., Dey, A., Kahali, S.: A deep-learning-based facial expression recognition method using textural features. Neural Comput. Appl. **35**, 6499–6514 (2023). https://doi.org/10.1007/s00521-022-08005-7

11. Zhu, J., Liu, S., Yu, S., Song, Y.: An extra-contrast affinity network for facial expression recognition in the wild. Electronics **11**, 2288 (2022). https://doi.org/10.3390/electronics11152288

12. Kola, D.G.R., Samayamantula, S.K.: A novel approach for facial expression recognition using local binary pattern with adaptive window. Multimed Tools Appl. **80**, 2243–2262 (2021). https://doi.org/10.1007/s11042-020-09663-2

13. Li, S., Deng, W., Du, J.: Reliable crowdsourcing and deep locality-preserving learning for expression recognition in the wild. Presented at the Proceedings of the IEEE Conference on Computer Vision and Pattern Recognition (2017)

14. Courville, P.L.C., Goodfellow, A., Mirza, I.J.M., Bengio, Y.: FER-2013 face database (2013)

15. Lucey, P., Cohn, J.F., Kanade, T., Saragih, J., Ambadar, Z., Matthews, I.: The extended Cohn-Kanade dataset (CK+): a complete dataset for action unit and emotion-specified expression. In: 2010 IEEE Computer Society Conference on Computer Vision and Pattern Recognition – Workshops, pp. 94–101 (2010). https://doi.org/10.1109/CVPRW.2010.5543262

16. Lyons, M., Akamatsu, S., Kamachi, M., Gyoba, J.: Coding facial expressions with Gabor wavelets. In: Proceedings Third IEEE International Conference on Automatic Face and Gesture Recognition, pp. 200–205 (1998). https://doi.org/10.1109/AFGR.1998.670949

17. Viola, P., Jones, M.: Rapid object detection using a boosted cascade of simple features. In: Proceedings of the 2001 IEEE Computer Society Conference on Computer Vision and Pattern Recognition, CVPR 2001, pp. I–I (2001). https://doi.org/10.1109/CVPR.2001.990517

18. Perkins, D., Salomon, G.: Transfer of learning, 11 (1999)

19. Simonyan, K., Zisserman, A.: Very deep convolutional networks for large-scale image recognition. http://arxiv.org/abs/1409.1556 (2015). https://doi.org/10.48550/arXiv.1409.1556

20. Szegedy, C., Vanhoucke, V., Ioffe, S., Shlens, J., Wojna, Z.: Rethinking the inception architecture for computer vision. Presented at the Proceedings of the IEEE Conference on Computer Vision and Pattern Recognition (2016)

21. Howard, A.G., et al.: MobileNets: efficient convolutional neural networks for mobile vision applications. http://arxiv.org/abs/1704.04861 (2017). https://doi.org/10.48550/arXiv.1704.04861

22. Huang, G., Liu, Z., van der Maaten, L., Weinberger, K.Q.: Densely connected convolutional networks. Presented at the Proceedings of the IEEE Conference on Computer Vision and Pattern Recognition (2017)

Identifying Bird Calls in Soundscapes Using Convolutional Neural Networks

Azer M. Eldukali and Amna Elhawil(✉)

University of Tripoli, Tripoli, Libya
`a.elhawil@uot.edu.ly`

Abstract. Birds are crucial for maintaining ecosystem balance and detecting environmental threats. Therefore, monitoring bird populations is essential for understanding ecosystem health. However, many birds are isolated in high-elevation habitats, making it challenging for researchers to study and monitor their populations. As a result, detecting birds based on their sounds can provide a passive, low-labor approach to monitoring bird populations.

This research aims to develop a deep-learning model that accepts an audio waveform of arbitrary length and then acoustically recognizes the species. Toward this end, a subset of the BirdCLEF 2022 dataset was used. This dataset covers 152 bird species. However, four species were selected based on their ecological significance and data availability, allowing comparison and evaluation of different strategies and techniques.

The developed model achieved an 89.66% macro F1 score on the test set. This promising result suggests that the techniques utilized in the model development process were effective and could be applied in similar contexts.

Keywords: Bird call recognition · BirdCLEF 2022 · Log-Mel-Spectrogram · Convolutional Neural Networks · Deep Learning

1 Introduction

Birds' sounds play a significant role in the natural world. They produce a wide variety of sounds, including calls, songs, and alarm calls. These sounds help birds establish and maintain social relationships. Monitoring bird species diversity and migration are essential for researchers and conservation practitioners in that they can accurately survey population trends. Working with audio data, on the other hand, may present unique challenges. First, the noisy environment audio data requires an intensive preprocessing procedure for noise reduction. The second problem stems from the style of the birdcalls. Some birds, for example, have many different calls, each serving a particular purpose. However, extensive research has been conducted in this area. Different audio visualization techniques have also been investigated, including Log-Mel-Spectrograms and Mel-Frequency Cepstral Coefficients (MFCC). According to research published in 2015 [1], the Log-Mel-Spectrograms outperform MFCCs as a sound visualization technique in the case of CNN. Recently, bird identification using Convolutional Neural Networks

T. A. T. Benmusa et al. (Eds.): ILCICT 2023, CCIS 2097, pp. 284–297, 2024.
https://doi.org/10.1007/978-3-031-62624-1_23

(CNN) has demonstrated encouraging results. [2, 3]. CNN is now the preferred deep learning model for classifications, according to the study's findings, this may greatly reduce network complexity and training parameters. [4].

Some methods mix recurrent neural networks (RNN) and convolutional neural networks, resulting in the convolutional recurrent neural network (CRNN), which is essentially CNN followed by RNN. The proposed network generates better, especially towards audio signal processing [5]. Recently, transfer learning for identifying bird sounds was proposed, asserting that tweaking a previously trained network may even outperform one without prior training [6].

Some approaches implemented a simple rule based on signal-to-noise ratio estimation to decide whether an audio segment contains bird sounds or background noise only [2, 5] and [7]. Although this process is not perfect, but fast and results in a good overall ranking of the training sample.

With the use of novel data augmentation and preprocessing techniques, a convolutional neural network with five convolutional layers and one dense layer predicted the primary species of each sound file with a mean average precision (MAP) score of 0.686 and a score of 0.555 when background species were used as additional prediction targets in addition to the primary species of each sound file [2].

ResNet-50, a common architecture that was pre-trained on the ImageNet [8] dataset and fine-tuned for the birdcall dataset, was utilized to identify 46 bird species with a validation accuracy of 65% [9].

An attention method was employed in conjunction with a pre-trained deep-CNN, the Inception-v4 [10], the state-of-the-art in image classification, to achieve great accuracy in bird call detection, reaching a 0.714 Mean Average Precision on 1500 bird species [11].

Several different convolutional neural network types (including standard CNNs, residual nets, and densely connected nets) were investigated for the Bird Audio Detection challenge in 2018; DenseNets were found to be the most effective and compact models, producing an area under the receiver operator curve score of 88.22% on the test set [12].

Modern models complicate the design by utilizing very large ensembles of PANN models. Pretrained Audio Neural Networks (PANNs) give a multi-task state-of-the-art baseline for audio-related tasks [13].

Sound Event Detection (SED) based model [14] was used for birdcall identification. The attention head serves as the decoder in SED models, whereas Noisy Student EfficientNet-b0 (EfficientNet-b0-ns) serves as the encoder. Bagging five SED-EfficientNet-b0-ns using various augmentation techniques resulted in an F1-score of 0.69 on the private leadership board, putting this model 69th out of 807 teams in the BirdCLEF 2022 competition hosted in Kaggle.

CNNs are a type of deep learning neural network that have been used extensively in image recognition tasks. However, they can also be used for audio recognition tasks, including identifying bird calls. CNNs are particularly useful for this task because they can learn to recognize patterns in the spectrogram of bird calls, which is a visual representation of the sound wave.

This research attempts to study and implement different approaches and strategies for bird sound identification using convolutional neural networks.

This paper is organized as follows: Sect. 1 contains the introduction. In contrast, Sect. 2 gives a brief overview of convolutional neural networks. The performance measurements are described in Sect. 3. In Sects. 4, the research technique is covered. The achieved results are discussed and analyzed in Sect. 5. The key findings of the present work are highlighted in Sect. 6 as a final point.

2   Convolutional Neural Networks

Convolutional Neural Networks (CNNs) are one of the popular categories of deep learning neural network designs. CNNs are especially useful for processing visual input, such as pictures and videos. Typical CNN design consists of a few convolutional layers. A ReLU layer follows each layer. In addition to a pooling layer, a few more convolutional layers (+ReLU), another pooling layer, and so on [15]. The convolutional layers cause the image to get smaller and smaller as it moves through the network, but they also cause it to get deeper and deeper (i.e., with more feature maps), as shown in Fig. 1. The final layer outputs the prediction, and a normal feedforward neural network made up of a few fully connected layers (+ReLUs) is added to the top of the linked layers.

The most widely known CNN architectures: VGGNet (2014) [16], ResNet (2015), and Xception (2016).

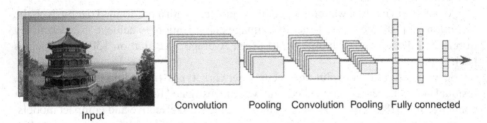

Fig. 1. Typical CNN architecture [17]

The architecture of the VGGNet is simple and traditional, consisting of two or three convolutional layers, a pooling layer, and so on (depending on the type of VGG, resulting in a total of 16 or 19 convolutional layers), plus a final dense network with two hidden layers and the output layer. There were numerous filters, but it only used three of them.

Kaiming He et al. [18] won the ILSVRC 2015 challenge with a Residual Network (or ResNet) that produced a remarkable top-five error rate of less than 3.6%. ResNet have been widely employed for bird vocalization recognition [4]. ResNet, as shown in Fig. 2, is nothing more than an extremely deep stack of simple residual units. Each residual unit is constructed from two convolutional layers (there is no pooling layer used!), Batch Normalization (BN), ReLU activation, 3×3 kernels, and padding that maintains spatial dimensions (stride 1, "same" padding).

It should be observed that (using a convolutional layer with stride 2), the number of feature maps doubles every few residual units, but their height and width are reduced by half. When this occurs, the inputs and outputs of the residual unit do not have the same

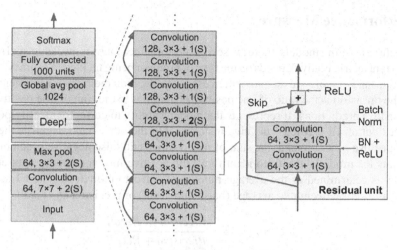

Fig. 2. ResNet architecture [17].

form, therefore they cannot be added together directly (for example, the skip connection is influenced by this problem; the dashed arrow in Fig. 2). Thus, inputs are processed via a 1 × 1 convolutional layer with stride two and the appropriate number of output feature maps to solve this problem as shown in Fig. 3.

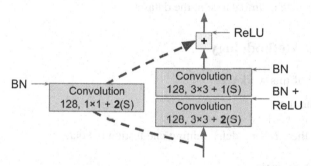

Fig. 3. Skip connection when changing feature map size and depth [17].

The Xception (which stands for Extreme Inception) architecture was proposed in 2016 by François Chollet (the author of Keras) [19]. Xception uses a layer known as a depth-wise separable convolution layer (or separable convolution layer for short). These layers had been used in various CNN systems but were not as essential as in the Xception architecture. Beginning with two typical convolutional layers, the Xception design only employs separable convolutions (a total of 34), along with a couple max pooling layers and the customary final layers (a dense output layer and another layer that pools global averages).

3   Performance Measure

For machine learning models, there are several performance metrics available, and selecting the right metric really depends on the type of problem being tackled. Accuracy, recall, precision, and F1-score are the most often used classification metrics for sentiment analysis. The precision is the ratio of true positive predictions to the sum of true positive and false positive predictions. It represents the model's ability to correctly identify positive instances out of all predicted positive instances. On the other hand, recall is the ratio of true positive predictions to the sum of true positive and false negative predictions. It represents the model's ability to identify all the positive instances in the dataset. The accuracy is determined as the average number of correct predictions. The F1-score is defined as a simple weighted average (harmonic mean) of precision and recall,

$$F1\ score = 2 \times \frac{Precision \times Recall}{Precision + Recall} \tag{1}$$

F1-score spans from 0 to 1, with a value closer to 1 being better [20].

In general, accuracy is not the recommended performance metric for classifiers, especially when working with skewed datasets [21]. Consequently, Marco F1-score is used in this paper because it considers both classifier's precision and recall. This provides more comprehensive view of its performance. Macro F1-score is calculated by computing the F1-score for each class separately, and then taking the average of these scores across all classes. This means that each class contributes equally to the final score, regardless of its size or imbalance in the dataset.

4   Research Methodology

The main steps of this work are:

1. Exploring the data
2. Preprocessing the data
3. Developing the CNN models, training and testing the dataset

4.1   Dataset Description

In this paper, BirdCLEF 2022 dataset hosted on Kaggle is used [22]. This dataset was derived from an open website called Xeno-canto [23]. It is dedicated to exchanging bird sounds; users upload their own recordings and label them by genus, species, subspecies, location, type, quality (from A to E, where A is the best quality of the sound) etc. The dataset consists of two folders:

1. *train_metadata*.csv – The training data's metadata cover a wide range of topics. The fields most immediately pertinent are:

   – *primary_label* - the bird species' code.
   – *secondary_labels*: Species in the background that the recordist has annotated. The absence of a field does not mean that no background birds are audible.
   – *filename*: the associated audio file.

- *rating*: a floating number representing the number of background species and the Xenocanto quality rating, ranging from 0.0 to 5.0, with 5.0 being the highest and 1.0 being the lowest. A score of 0.0 means that this recording has not yet received any reviews.

2. *train_audio* - The majority of the training data is made up of sparse recordings of individual bird calls that users of xenocanto.org have kindly submitted. Where necessary, these files have been converted to the *ogg* format and down-sampled to 32 kHz in order to match the test set audio.

The audio files are processed by dividing the number of samples in each audio waveform by the sample-rate to obtain the length of audio clip in seconds.

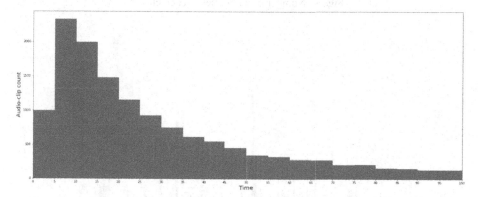

Fig. 4. Number of audio clips within five second interval

Figure 4 shows the length distribution of audio files. It is notable that the recordings vary in length, some are less than one second, and others are more than an hour. Approximately (1000) audio files have a length of fewer than five seconds, and most audio files (2500) have a length of five to ten seconds. Figure 5 shows the number of audio files in each class.

Figure 6 depicts that the dataset has a massive class imbalance; some classes contain only one audio file while others contain 500. Because the model requires all inputs to be in the same shape, all the audio clips that are less than five seconds are zero-padded to five seconds segments whereas the audio clips that are longer than five seconds are splitted into sliding windows of lengths five and hop three seconds. In addition, we notice that some audio files have only one segment (the audio files that are less than five seconds) while others have more than 1000 segments. Moreover, there is a massive difference in the number of audio segments in each class; some classes have only seven audio segments, while others have 17270.

To summarize, the main challenges that make this task extremely difficult to tackle. The most prominent difficulties are:

1. The dataset consists of 14852 audio files in the Ogg compressed file format covering 152 different species, so loading and parsing the data can be a bottleneck during the training process.

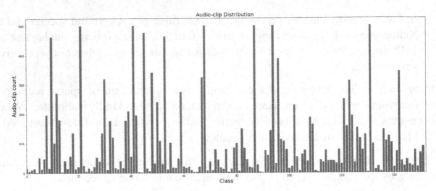

Fig. 5. Number of audio files in each class

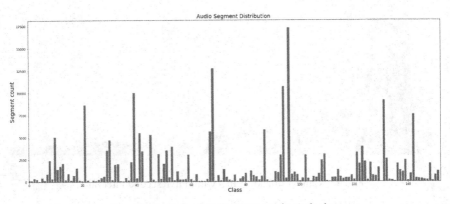

Fig. 6. Number of audio segments in each class

2. The dataset has a massive class imbalance; while some classes have many samples, others have very few. This can lead to biased models that perform poorly on the underrepresented classes.
3. The duration of recordings varies significantly; while some are less than one second, others can last for several hours. This variability in duration can pose a challenge for data analysis and processing.
4. Some of the recordings have environmental noise overlapping with bird calls. This can make distinguishing the bird calls from other sounds in the environment difficult.
5. Some bird species have many types of calls; each serves a specific purpose, from warning signals to territorial defense or attracting mates.
6. Some of the recordings in the dataset contain multiple species singing simultaneously, making this task a multilabel classification problem.

These challenges were thoroughly studied and analyzed in this work.

4.2 Preprocessing the Data

Data preprocessing is the process of converting raw data into a suitable format for deep learning algorithm. Currently, the data sits on a drive as *ogg* files, so the steps for getting it into the model are roughly as follows:

1. Splitting the available data into three sets: training, validation, and test.
2. Standardizing the audio files.
3. Removing the background noise.
4. Generate audio waveforms of equal length.
5. Extracting Log-Mel-Spectrogram from each audio segment.
6. Saving the preprocessed data into TFRecord files.

Here is a brief description of each step. The available data is divided into three sets: training, validation, and test. The model is trained on the training set whereas the validation set is used to tune hyperparameters and prevent overfitting, and the test set is used for testing the model's performance on unseen data.

Data is split into ten equal folds, each exclusive of the others, using the stratified sampling technique to maintain a constant class ratio in each fold, as shown in Fig. 7. Finally, eight folds were selected as the "training set," with the remaining two folds serving as the "validation set" and "test set," respectively.

All audio files were resampled at the same rate (32,000) and then converted to mono-channel format to ensure consistency.

Some of the recordings contain environmental noise that overlaps with birdcalls, which can make it difficult for the model to distinguish the birdcalls from the background noise. To address this issue, a background noise filter that relies on a method called "spectral gating" was be applied to the recordings before they are fed into the model, as shown in Fig. 8. This filter can help to remove the unwanted environmental noise and isolate the birdcalls, allowing the model to more accurately identify and classify the different bird species present in the recordings.

The model expects inputs of the same length. However, the recordings are of different duration. This issue was resolved by padding the recordings that are shorter than five seconds with zeros and cutting the long recordings using the sliding window technique into segments of five seconds with a three-second overlap between adjacent segments.

The last step is to generate the Log-Mel-Spectrograms with following parameters:

- Sample rate 32,000
- Number of Mels is 120
- Minimum frequency is 100 Hz
- Maximum frequency 16000 Hz
- Frame length is 1024
- Number of samples between successive frames (hop-length) set to 512.

Once the preprocessing stage is completed, the preprocessed data is saved into TFRecord files which can then be used for training the model, as shown in Fig. 9. Preprocessing the data this way can improve both the loading speed and processing efficiency.

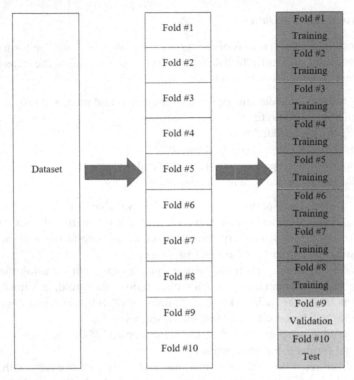

Fig. 7. Splitting a dataset into training, validation, and test sets.

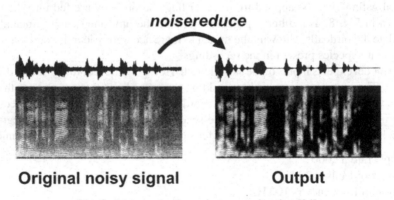

Fig. 8. Noise reduction using spectral gating [24].

4.3 Model Development, Training, and Evaluation

After analyzing and preprocessing the data, the last steps are training and testing the model. In this work, several configurations are explored; these configurations are as follows:

1. Randomly Initialized ResNet-50 Architecture

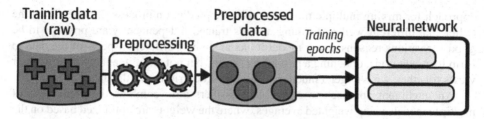

Fig. 9. Saving the preprocessed data into TFRecord files

2. Reusing Pretrained ResNet-50 Architecture
3. Reusing Pretrained ResNet-50 Architecture with Background Noise Filter
4. Reusing Pretrained VGG-19 Architecture with Background Noise Filter
5. Reusing Pretrained Xception Architecture with Background Noise Filter

All networks were trained on 23,255 spectrograms extracted from 400 audio recordings that comprises the training set. For validation, 2,071 spectrograms extracted from 50 audio recordings were used to monitor the training process and to apply early stopping if the validation error did not progress. In addition, 2192 spectrograms extracted from 50 audio recordings were used as a test set to test the model one last time when it is ready for prime time.

5 Results and Discussion

In this section, the results of each architecture are explained. These results are summarized in Table 1.

Table 1. Results for several model variants on the validation set

Architecture	Weights	Background Noise Filter	Training Time (minutes)	Macro F1-score
ResNet-50	Random	Without	29	76.88%
ResNet-50	Pre-trained	Without	53	81.15%
ResNet-50	Pre-trained	With	60	84.70%
VGG-19	Pre-trained	With	44	83.08%
Xception	Pre-trained	With	131	83.71%

It can be seen that, there is about a 5.55% F1-score improvement in ResNet-50 architecture just by using pre-trained weights instead of random initialization. Moreover, the use of a background noise filter raises the F1-score by 4.73%.

5.1 Model Ensembling

The main contribution of this work is to improve the performance even further. For this purpose model ensembling is implemented. Modeling ensembling is a machine-learning approach for mixing multiple models within the prediction process. It depends on the belief that different well-performing models trained independently are possible to be good for various reasons: every model looks at slightly different aspects of the data to form its predictions, obtaining a part of the "truth" but not all of it, and by pooling their views together, we will get a much more accurate description of the data.

An intelligent approach to ensemble classifiers is to combine the predictions of multiple models using weighted averages, where the weights are optimized based on the validation data. The following formulation describes the optimization problem.

$$W^* = arg\left(\max_W F\left(Y, W^T \widehat{Y}\right)\right) \tag{2}$$

Subject to

$$\sum_i W = 1 \tag{3}$$

where

$F \stackrel{\text{def}}{=}$ the macro F1 score.
$W \stackrel{\text{def}}{=}$ ensemble weights
$W^* \stackrel{\text{def}}{=}$ the best ensemble weights
$\widehat{Y} \stackrel{\text{def}}{=}$ prediction of classifier
$Y \stackrel{\text{def}}{=}$ actual labels

In order to avoid any possible local minima, a grid search method has been used to solve the optimization problem. This method involves testing various combinations of weights and selecting the combination that yields the best performance on the validation set. Once the best set of weights is found, the models are combined to create a final ensemble model, as shown in Fig. 10.

The usage of ensembling leads to improved performance and more robust models. However, the inference time of ensembling is slower than a single model due to the increased complexity of the ensemble model.

5.2 Testing Process

After training, the best-performing models are saved and combined into an ensemble to improve performance. The ensemble model is evaluated using a separate test set to ensure that the model is not overfitting to the validation data and can generalize well to new, unseen data. The ensemble model achieves an 89.66% macro F1 score on the test set, making it suitable for prediction and inference tasks.

6   Conclusion and Future Work

This work is oriented towards identifying birds from their calls using convolutional neural networks. Toward this end, a subset of the BirdCLEF 2022 dataset was used for model training and validation. The dataset was thoroughly examined, and several

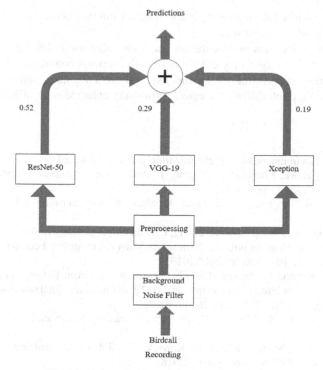

Fig. 10. Improving predictions with ensembling

challenges were discovered that make this task extremely difficult to tackle. These challenges concern the dataset's size, the varying waveforms' length, and the environmental noise that overlaps with bird calls. These difficulties, however, are addressed during the preprocessing stage by applying a background noise filter that relies on "spectral gating" to remove the unwanted noises, followed by zero-padding and splitting of the waveforms to have the same length, and then extracting the Log-Mel-Spectrograms. Once the preprocessing stage is completed, the preprocessed data is saved into TFRecord files to speed up loading the data into the model.

The results of the experiments show that adding a background noise filter significantly improved the performance of the resulting model. Furthermore, the experiments show that the ImageNet pre-trained model outperforms training from scratch, indicating that, despite the differences between the audio spectrogram and standard ImageNet image samples, transfer learning from the ImageNet dataset is an effective approach for birdcall identification tasks. Another important aspect that should be referred to is that, despite using different network architectures, they performed equally well; nonetheless, combining them into an ensemble led to even better performance; the optimized ensemble weights were calculated based on the validation set.

Moreover, in this study, only the magnitude of the spectrograms was utilized for classification, and the phase information was discarded. Further research is needed to explore the potential of incorporating phase information in spectrogram analysis and its impact on the model's performance.

In addition, three data augmentation methods were used: MixUp, CutMix, and SpecAugment. Surprisingly, they did not help in the variants conducted; it only resulted in a slight decrease in performance. Further exploration of augmentation techniques such as time stretching, pitch shifting, or equalization may enhance generalization.

References

1. Piczak, K.: Environmental sound classification with convolutional neural networks (2015)
2. Elias, S., Jaggi, M., Kilcher, Y., Hofmann, T.: Audio based bird species identification using deep learning techniques (2016)
3. Kahl, S., et al.: Large-scale bird sound classification using convolutional neural networks (2017)
4. Xie, J., Zhong, Y., Zhang, J., Liu, S., Ding, C., Triantafyllopoulos, A.: A review of automatic recognition technology for bird vocalizations in the deep learning era. Ecol. Inform. **73** (2023). https://doi.org/10.1016/j.ecoinf.2022.101927
5. Cakir, E., Adavanne, S., Parascandolo, G., Drossos, K., Virtanen, T.: Convolutional recurrent neural networks for bird audio detection. In: 2017 25th European signal processing conference (EUSIPCO), Kos, pp. 1744–1748. IEEE (2017)
6. Fritzler, A., Koitka, S., Friedrich, C.: Recognizing bird species in audio files using transfer learning (2017)
7. Kahl, S., Wilhelm-Stein, T., Klinck, H., Kowerko, D., Eibl, M.: Recognizing birds from sound - the 2018 BirdCLEF baseline system (2018)
8. ImageNet. https://www.image-net.org/. Accessed 8 Mar 2022
9. Konovalov, D., Sankupellay, M.: Bird call recognition using deep convolutional neural network, ResNet-50 (2018)
10. Szegedy, C., Ioffe, S., Vanhoucke, V., Alemi, A.A.: Inception-v4, inception-ResNet and the impact of residual connections on learning. In: Proceedings of the AAAI Conference on Artificial Intelligence, 2017 February 12 (2016)
11. Sevilla, A., Glotin, H.: Audio bird classification with inception-v4 extended with time and time-frequency attention mechanisms (2017)
12. Gao, H., Zhuang, L., Van Der Maaten, L., Weinberger, K.Q.: Densely connected convolutional networks. In: Proceedings - 30th IEEE Conference on Computer Vision and Pattern Recognition, CVPR 2017 (2017)
13. Conde, M.V., Shubham, K., Agnihotri, P., Movva, N.D., Bessenyei, S.: Weakly-supervised classification and detection of bird sounds in the wild. A BirdCLEF 2021 solution (2021)
14. Adavanne, S., Politis, A., Nikunen, J., Virtanen, T.: Sound event localization and detection of overlapping sources using convolutional recurrent neural networks. IEEE J. Sel. Top. Signal Process. **13**(1), 34–48 (2019)
15. Chollet, F.: Deep Learning with Python, United States of America: Manning Publications, p. 96 (2021)
16. Simonyan, K., Zisserman, A.: Very deep convolutional networks for large scale image recognition. In: 3rd International Conference on Learning Representations, ICLR 2015 - Conference Track Proceedings (2015)
17. Géron, A.: Hands-On Machine Learning with Scikit-Learn and TensorFlow: Concepts, Tools, and Techniques to Build Intelligent Systems. O'reilly Media, Sebastopol (2019)
18. He, K., Zhang, X., Ren, S., Sun, J.: Delving deep into rectifiers: surpassing human-level performance on ImageNet classification. In: 2015 IEEE International Conference on Computer Vision (ICCV) (2015)

19. Chollet, F.: Xception: deep learning with depthwise separable convolutions. In: Proceedings - 30th IEEE Conference on Computer Vision and Pattern Recognition, CVPR 2017 (2017)
20. Basha, S.M., Ahmed, S.T.: Mathematical Principles in Machine Learning (2023)
21. Thakur, A.: Approaching (Almost) any Machine Learning Problem, vol. 45 (2017)
22. BirdCLEF 2022, 15 February 2022. https://www.kaggle.com/competitions/birdclef-2022
23. canto. https://xeno-canto.org/. Accessed 22 Dec 2022
24. Timsainb/noisereduce: Noise reduction in python using spectral gating (speech, bioacoustics, audio, time-domain signals). https://github.com/timsainb/noisereduce. Accessed 9 July 2022

Automated ECG Classification for Myocardial Infarction Diagnosis Using CNN and Wavelet Transform

Hajer Albraki[✉] and Issmail Ellabib

Computer Engineering Department, Tripoli, Libya
{h.albraki,I.Ellabib}@uot.edu.ly

Abstract. In this study, we propose a methodologyfor classifying electrocardiogram (ECG) signals into normal and myocardial infarction (MI) classes. The methodology consists of three main steps: pre-processing, segmentation, and classification. ECG signals obtained from the PTB database are initially subjected to pre-processing using the Daubechies wavelet transform to filter out noise and enhance signal quality. Subsequently, the signals are segmented into 651-sample segments and further reduced to 500 samples per segment for dimensionality reduction. These segmented signals serve as input data for a convolutional neural network (CNN) model, which extracts relevant features and performs the classification task. The proposed methodology achieves an impressive classification accuracy of 97.8% for ECG signals. These findings highlight the effectiveness of our approach in accurately distinguishing between normal and MI ECG patterns.

Keyword: electrocardiogram (ECG) · myocardial infarction (MI) · convolutional neural network (CNN) · Daubechies wavelet transform

1 Introduction

Artificial Intelligence (AI) has revolutionized various domains of healthcare, and one area that greatly benefits from AI advancements is the classification and diagnosis of heart diseases. Electrocardiogram (ECG) signals, which represent the electrical activity of the heart, play a crucial role in understanding cardiac health and detecting abnormalities. ECG signals are recorded by placing electrodes on the patient's body, and they provide valuable information about the heart's rhythm, rate, and overall functioning.

The interpretation of ECG signals has traditionally relied on manual analysis by healthcare professionals, which can be time-consuming and subjective. However, with the advancements in AI and deep learning techniques, it is now possible to automate the analysis of ECG signals and improve the accuracy and efficiency of heart disease diagnosis.

In this paper, we aim to leverage AI algorithms, such as deep neural networks, to develop a system that can automatically process and interpret ECG signals. By extracting relevant features and patterns from the signals, the AI model can classify different types of heart diseases with a high level of accuracy. This AI-based approach eliminates the

T. A. T. Benmusa et al. (Eds.): ILCICT 2023, CCIS 2097, pp. 298–308, 2024.
https://doi.org/10.1007/978-3-031-62624-1_24

subjectivity and variability associated with manual analysis, providing consistent and reliable results.

By harnessing the power of AI, we can not only enhance the accuracy of heart disease diagnosis but also enable faster and more efficient analysis, allowing healthcare professionals to make informed decisions promptly. The automated classification and diagnosis of heart diseases using ECG signals have the potential to improve patient outcomes, facilitate timely interventions, and optimize the utilization of healthcare resources.

Through the utilization of comprehensive datasets, advanced deep learning models, and rigorous evaluation, this project aims to contribute to the ongoing efforts in leveraging AI for improving cardiovascular care. By developing a robust and accurate AI system for ECG signal analysis, we can augment the capabilities of healthcare professionals, enhance patient care, and ultimately save lives.

2 Related Work

In recent times, substantial advancements have been made in the development of deep neural networks (DNNs), leading to significant improvements in the accuracy of classifying various clinical tasks [1]. Among the methods used for analyzing biomedical signals, the convolutional neural network (CNN) has become increasingly popular in this field [7]. Numerous techniques have been proposed to overcome the limitations of manual electrocardiogram (ECG) analysis, with a particular focus on extracting meaningful information directly from the raw data. Effective feature extraction is achieved through techniques like wavelet transform (WT) [10]. Moreover, reduction methods such as principal component analysis (PCA) and meta-heuristic algorithms like particle swarm optimization (PSO) [11] are employed. The classification step involves various techniques such as neural networks (NN) [9], support vector machine (SVM) [10], and k-nearest neighbor (KNN) [9].

While these methods have shown promising performances, they do come with certain drawbacks. First, the inclusion of additional feature extraction and selection algorithms leads to increased computational complexity. Second, external factors such as age, sex, and pathological changes in myocardial infarctions (MIs) can influence ECG patterns, resulting in dynamic changes in explicit or implicit features. Predefined handcrafted features struggle to maintain generalization abilities in such cases. To effectively leverage information from different layers, Rajpurkar et al. [8] developed a 34-layer CNN to diagnose irregular heart rhythms based on single-lead ECG, achieving a maximum accuracy of 90.80% and surpassing cardiologists' performance. Similarly, Acharya et al. [7] proposed an 11-layer 1-D CNN for detecting MIs using lead II ECG signals, attaining a maximum accuracy of 95.22%.

In our proposed method, based on the aforementioned papers, we have incorporated a preprocessing step to denoise the signal and utilized the same CNN model. As a result, our method outperforms other existing methods and achieves an impressive accuracy of 97.8%.

3   Methodology

3.1   Method Overview

Our approach to effectively categorizing ECG signals into two classes, normal and MI, consists of three main steps: pre-processing, segmentation, and classification. To evaluate our method, we suggest utilizing the PTB database, which comprises 448 recordings. In order to mitigate signal noise, we apply the Daubechies wavelet transform with 6 to 10 levels for signal filtering. Each recording is then divided into multiple segments, with each segment containing 651 samples. To reduce dimensionality, we further truncate the segments to 500 samples before initiating model training. These processed samples are directly fed into a CNN model for feature extraction and ECG signal classification. For a visual representation of our proposed approach, please refer to Fig. 1.

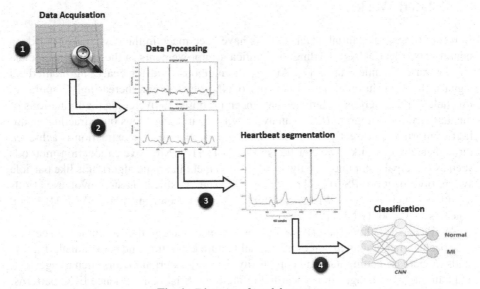

Fig. 1. Diagram of model structure

3.2   Data Acquisition

The PTB Diagnostic ECG Database holds a prestigious reputation as a carefully curated collection of electrocardiogram (ECG) recordings, recognized internationally. It serves as a vital standard resource for research and diagnosis, enabling the development of advanced algorithms and methods to analyze and classify ECG signals. This comprehensive database encompasses various ECG recordings, featuring both normal cases and data related to specific cardiac conditions, such as myocardial infarction (MI). Its impact on cardiovascular research and the improvement of heart-related disorder diagnosis and treatment is significant.

In the realm of MI diagnosis algorithms [1], the PTB Diagnostic ECG Database holds a distinguished position as the most extensively utilized resource. It comprises 549 12-lead records sampled at 1000 Hz, gathered from 290 patients. Among these records are 368 cases of MI from 148 patients and 80 records from 52 healthy control (HC) patients. Our research specifically focuses on the investigation of lead II records. The detailed characteristics of the PTB database, presented in Table 1, underscore its crucial role as a valuable asset in our work and the broader scientific community.

Table 1. The attributes of the electrocardiogram (ECG) data acquired from the PTB database.

	Normal	Mi
Minimum age	17	36
Maximum age	81	86
Average age	43.43	60.37
Number of males	39	110
Number of females	13	38

Our data was split into two sets: the training set, which comprised 80% of the data with 40,581 instances, and the test set, which comprised 20% of the data with 10,146 instances.

3.3 Data Processing

Precise identification and categorization of heart diseases based on electrocardiogram (ECG) readings are crucial. However, the ECG signal is susceptible to weaknesses and interference noises during acquisition, resulting from factors like equipment limitations, patient movements, or breathing. These noises present a significant challenge in analyzing the ECG signal, making a preprocessing step necessary for dependable classification. In this research, we adopt the Daubechies 6 wavelet transform with 10 levels of decomposition [7] to effectively remove noise from the ECG signal. The wavelet transform enables the identification of high-frequency coefficients, which indicate the presence of noise in the signal.

Subsequently, we employ a threshold processing technique to eliminate unwanted noise components, such as electromyography (EMG) noise and power line interference. Figure 2 illustrates the ECG beat signals before and after the denoising process, highlighting the effectiveness of our denoising approach.

3.4 Heartbeat Segmentation

According to [8], the wavelet transformation method proves to be highly effective in detecting R peaks in electrocardiogram (ECG) signals when compared with the Tompkins algorithm. This approach offers superior performance in accurately identifying the

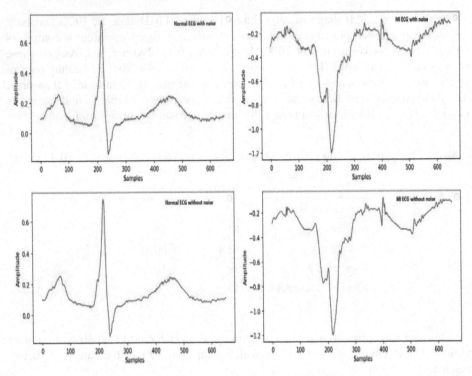

Fig. 2. The diagram of the denoising effect

significant points in the ECG waveform known as R peaks, which indicate the contraction of the ventricles.

To visually demonstrate this, Fig. 3 depicts the segmentation process using the 2-level Daubechies 3 wavelet transform. Each segment of an ECG beat consists of 651 samples, with 250 samples captured before the R peak and 400 samples taken after the R peak.

The wavelet transform successfully captures the distinct features of the ECG waveform, enabling precise detection of the R peak locations. By segmenting the ECG signal in this manner, the analysis can focus on specific regions of interest around the R peaks, thereby facilitating further examination and diagnosis of cardiac abnormalities.

3.5 CNN Architecture

In Fig. 4, it can be observed that a Convolutional Neural Network (CNN) typically comprises three main layers: the convolution layer, pooling layer, and fully connected layer. The CNN uses a fixed-sized filter matrix to convolve an input series of feature maps, thereby extracting high-level features. The pooling operation reduces the size of the feature maps while retaining important information. Additionally, it effectively captures dominant features that remain consistent regardless of rotation or position.

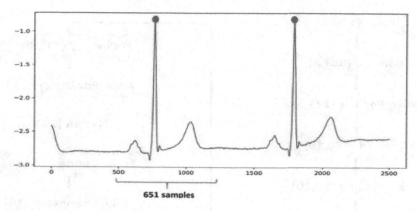

Fig. 3. Heartbeat Segmentation

The fully connected layer employs a multi-layer perceptron (MLP) and operates on the flattened input after multiple convolution and pooling operations, connecting each input to all neurons.

The model in this figure is composed of four convolution layers, four max-pooling layers, and three fully connected layers. The convolution layer uses a stride of 1, and the pooling layer uses a stride of 2. Max-pooling is performed after each convolution operation. Finally, the fully connected layer connects the neurons from the preceding layers to create a probability distribution over two classes: normal and MI (Myocardial Infarction). The initial layer (layer 0) undergoes convolution with a 102-sized filter, leading to the formation of the first layer (layer 1). Then, a max-pooling operation with a size of 2 is performed on each feature map, resulting in layer 2. This max-pooling reduces the number of neurons from 399×3 to 199×3.

Next, the feature maps of layer 2 are convolved with a 24-sized filter, generating layer 3. Another max-pooling operation is then applied to each feature map, producing layer 4. Subsequently, layer 4's feature map is convolved with an 11-sized filter, creating layer 5. Afterward, a max-pooling operation is performed on each feature map, reducing the number of neurons to 39×10 in layer 6.

Layer 6's feature map is convolved with a 9-sized filter, creating layer 7. Following this, a subsequent max-pooling operation is applied, resulting in layer 8. Notably, layer 8 is fully connected to layer 9, which consists of 30 neurons. Layer 9 is further connected to layer 10, containing 10 neurons, and finally, to the output layer, which has 2 neurons representing the "normal" and "MI" (Myocardial Infarction) categories.

In the Convolutional Neural Network (CNN), the activation function plays a crucial role in determining whether a neuron should be activated or not in response to a signal. It acts as a mathematical function that governs signal processing. One widely used activation function is the Rectified Linear Unit (ReLU), which sets negative results to zero. Mathematically, the ReLU function can be expressed as: $f(x) = max(0, x)$. In this study, the ReLU activation function is applied to layers 1, 3, 5, 7, 9, and 10. Additionally, the softmax function is used in layer 11 (the final layer) to provide a probability distribution for classification.

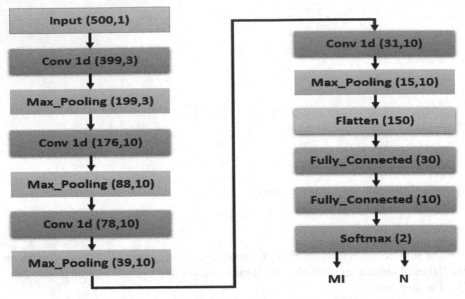

Fig. 4. Architecture of the proposed CNN model

4 Experimental Results

Our model was trained on a workstation equipped with an Intel(R) Core(TM) i5 6200U CPU running at 2.30 GHz and 8 GB of RAM. The experimental data used for training and testing was sourced from the widely recognized and precise MIT-BIH ECG database. This database is a standard resource in ECG research, providing comprehensive expert annotations.

To split the data for training and testing, we divided it into two sets, allocating 80% for training and 20% for testing. During the training process, we utilized 300 epochs, with each epoch consisting of a batch size of 32. This batch size was applied to the entire input data.

For optimization, a learning rate of 0.001 was employed to control the update step size during the training process. Additionally, before training, we performed signal rescaling to normalize the data and ensure it falls within the range of $[-1, 1]$. This normalization step proved beneficial as it improved the accuracy of the model compared to training without normalization.

Figure 6 illustrates the accuracy and loss curves for both the training and validation stages of our model. These curves provide insights into the performance and progress of the model during the training process.

To evaluate the effectiveness of our model, we employed several metrics: accuracy, specificity, and sensitivity. These metrics play a crucial role in assessing the model's performance in classifying ECG signals. The Eqs. (1), (2), and (3) represent the calculations for accuracy, specificity, and sensitivity, respectively.

In the experimental verification, our proposed CNN model achieved outstanding results. The accuracy obtained was 97.8%, indicating the percentage of correctly classified instances. The sensitivity, which represents the true positive rate, reached 97.0%, highlighting the model's ability to accurately detect positive cases. Furthermore, the specificity, which measures the true negative rate, was recorded at 97.32%, demonstrating the model's capability to correctly identify negative cases.

These high accuracy, sensitivity, and specificity values indicate the effectiveness and reliability of our proposed CNN model for ECG signal classification. The experimental verification results validate the model's ability to accurately distinguish between different cardiac conditions and contribute to improved diagnosis and treatment of heart-related disorders (Fig. 5).

$$accuracy = \frac{TP + TN}{TN + FP + TP + FN} \times 100 \tag{1}$$

$$specificity = \frac{TN}{TN + FP} \times 100 \tag{2}$$

$$sensitivity = \frac{TP}{TP + FN} \times 100 \tag{3}$$

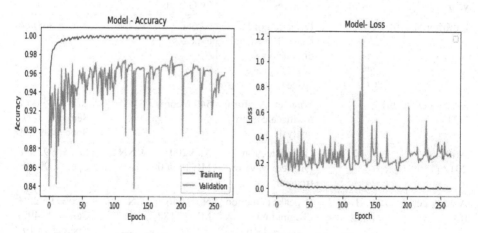

Fig. 5. Accuracy and Loss of the trained model

We have obtained the confusion matrix for our model, which serves as a solid confirmation of its performance. The confusion matrix allows us to assess how well the model is classifying instances by providing a breakdown of predicted and actual class labels (Table 2).

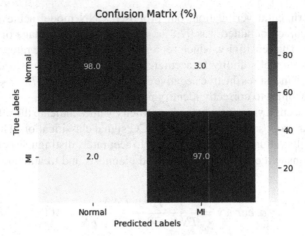

Fig. 6. Confusion Matrix

Table 2. Compilation of Chosen Research on MI Detection and Diagnosis Utilizing ECG Signals from PTBDB

Author, year	Number of leads	Notable Features	Number ECG beats	Classifier	Performance
Lahiri et al. [10]	12	Detection of R peaks The fractal dimension of ECG phase space	64 680 R-peaks	RNN	Acc = 96.00%
Sharma et al., 2015 [11]	12	Wavelet transform Multiscale energy analysis	549 records	SVM	Acc = 96.00% Sen = 93.00% Spec = 99.00%
Arif et al., 2012 [13]	12	QRS detection Discrete wavelet transform	N: 3 200 MI: 16 960	KNN	Sen = 99.97% Spec = 99.00%
Acharya et al. 2017 [8]	II	R-peaks detection (Tompkins) 11-layer deep neural network	N: 10546 MI: 40 182	CNN	Acc = 95.22% Sen = 95.49% Spec = 94.19%
Proposed Method	II	R-peaks detection: Wavelet transform Preprocessing: Wavelet transform No feature selection	N: 10 546 MI: 40 182	CNN	Acc = 97.8% Sen = 97% Spec = 97.32%

5 Conclusion

In conclusion, our methodology has demonstrated remarkable performance in the classification of electrocardiogram (ECG) signals into two categories: normal and myocardial infarction (MI). Through the integration of convolutional neural networks (CNN) and the Daubechies wavelet transform, we successfully extracted crucial features and achieved accurate differentiation between normal and MI ECG patterns.

The obtained accuracy of 97.8% signifies the model's ability to make highly precise classifications. This high accuracy rate has significant implications for improving the efficiency and accuracy of cardiovascular diagnostics, ultimately leading to enhanced patient care and treatment outcomes.

For future work, we have identified potential avenues for further improvement. Firstly, by incorporating a residual architecture such as ResNet or DenseNet, we can explore the benefits of deeper networks and residual connections to potentially enhance the model's performance. Additionally, increasing the size of the training data can contribute to even better accuracy by providing a more diverse and comprehensive representation of ECG patterns.

By continuing to refine our methodology through these future directions, we anticipate further advancements in ECG signal classification, ultimately leading to more accurate and efficient cardiovascular diagnostics in clinical practice.

References

1. Liu, W., Ji, J., Chang, S., Wang, H., He, J., Huang, Q.: EvoMBN: evolving multi-branch networks on myocardial infarction diagnosis using 12-lead electrocardiograms. Biosensors **12** (2022). https://www.mdpi.com/2079-6374/12/1/15
2. Dwivedi, R.K., Kumar, R., Buyya, R.: Gaussian distribution-based machine learning scheme for anomaly detection in healthcare sensor cloud. Int. J. Cloud Appl. Comput. (IJ-CAC) **11**(1), 52–72 (2021)
3. Ortega-Delcampo, D., Conde, C., Palacios-Alonso, D., Cabello, E.: Border control morphing attack detection with a convolutional neural network de-morphing approach. IEEE Access **8**, 92301–92313 (2020)
4. Kumar, A.: Design of secure image fusion technique using cloud for privacy-preserving and copyright protection. Int. J. Cloud Appl. Comput. **9**(3), 22–36 (2019)
5. Sedik, A., Iliyasu, A.M., El-Rahiem, A., Abdel Samea, M.E., Abdel-Raheem, A., Hammad, M., et al.: Deploying machine and deep learning models for efficient data-augmented detection of COVID-19 infections. Viruses **12**(7), 769 (2020)
6. Ramchoun, H., Idrissi, M.A.J., Ghanou, Y., Ettaouil, M.: New modeling of multilayer perceptron architecture optimization with regularization: an application to pattern classification. IAENG Int. J. Comput. Sci. **44**(3), 261–269 (2017)
7. Singh, B.N., Tiwari, A.K.: Optimal selection of wavelet basis function applied to ECG signal denoising. Digit. Signal Process. **16**(3), 275–287 (2006)
8. Acharya, U.R., Fujita, H., Oh, S.L., Hagiwara, Y., Tan, J.H., Adam, M.: Application of deep convolutional neural network for automated detection of myocardial infarction using ecg signals. Inf. Sci. **415**, 190–198 (2017)
9. Rajpurkar, P., Hannun, A.Y., Haghpanahi, M., Bourn, C., Ng, A.Y.: Cardiologist-level arrhythmia detection with convolutional neural networks. arXiv preprint arXiv:1707.01836 (2017)

10. Lahiri, T., Kumar, U., Mishra, H., Sarkar, S., Roy, A.D.: Analysis of ECG signal by chaos principle to help automatic diagnosis of myocardial infarction (2009)
11. Sharma, L., Tripathy, R., Dandapat, S.: Multiscale energy and eigenspace approach to detection and localization of myocardial infarction. IEEE Trans. Biomed. Eng. **62**(7), 1827–1837 (2015)
12. Kora, P.: Ecg based myocardial infarction detection using hybrid firefly algorithm. Comput. Methods Programs Biomed. **152**, 141–148 (2017)
13. Arif, M., Malagore, I.A., Afsar, F.A.: Detection and localization of myocardial infarction using k-nearest neighbor classifier. J. Med. Syst. **36**(1), 279–289 (2012)

Detecting Chest Diseases with Chest X-Ray Using Convolutional Neural Network

Malik Miloud Alfilali[1] , Yusra Maatug[2(✉)] , and Ismail Ellabib[2]

[1] Heriot-Watt University, Edinburgh, UK
ma2212@hw.ac.uk
[2] University of Tripoli, Tripoli, Libya
{y.maatug,i.ellabib}@uot.edu.ly

Abstract. Lung diseases, such as viral pneumonia, lung cancer, and the coronavirus, have caused significant deaths worldwide in the past year. The detection of such diseases by radiologists is a challenging task. However, by applying image processing and artificial intelligence techniques, the computer can help radiologists identify chest diseases more accurately. Our research work aims to propose a methodology to detect chest diseases using convolutional Neural Network (CNN) and image processing techniques more effectively. In this paper, two predefined CNN model architectures (VGG-16, and VGG-19) are applied with Contrast Limited Adaptive Histogram Equalization (CLAHE) as a pre-processing technique in order to enhance the chest X-ray images. Moreover, Gradient Weighted Class Activation Maps (Grad-CAM) were applied to localize the affected areas in chest X-ray images. The two models are trained on the COVID-19 Radiography Dataset provided by Kaggle. For the performance evaluation, the two CNN models are investigated and evaluated with the image-enhanced technique. The experimental work demonstrates a significant improvement in performance using the CLAHE technique for both models. The results show that the enhanced VGG-16 model achieved a 97% accuracy rate and a 97% precision rate. With the consideration of X-ray image enhancement, the VGG16 model performs well and is a very promising way to diagnose chest disorders and lessen the radiologists' workload.

Keywords: CNN · X-Ray · Chest diseases · GRAD-CAM · Image Processing · Image Classification

1 Introduction

Lung diseases killed more than 8,000,000 people in the last two years. As a result of the pneumonia epidemic, there were 800,000 deaths of children under the age of five every year, with nearly 2200 deaths per day that occurred from the disease. And coronavirus have caused the deaths of 6,800,000 people since the beginning of the pandemic [1]; The Global Burden of Disease Study reported that lower respiratory tract infections, including pneumonia, were the second leading cause of death in 2013 [2], and the coronavirus was the first in 2020 and 2021 [1]. The high number of deaths from lung diseases is prompting scientists around the world to propose more effective and acute

T. A. T. Benmusa et al. (Eds.): ILCICT 2023, CCIS 2097, pp. 309–321, 2024.
https://doi.org/10.1007/978-3-031-62624-1_25

methods of detecting these diseases. X-rays and computed tomography (CT) are two of the most common methods of imaging chest organs for diagnosing lung diseases, in addition to magnetic resonance imaging (MRI). A chest X-ray is the most cost-effective and practical method of diagnosing lung diseases because it is more readily available in hospitals, easier to use, and exposes the patient to less radioactive radiation than any other. X-Rays for different diseases, such as coronavirus, contain similar information about the region; thus, diagnosing lung diseases from radiographs is still a considerable task, even for very professional and experienced doctors. By using traditional methods, diagnosing pneumonia takes a lot of time and work, and it is challenging to distinguish between pneumonia and coronavirus by a standardized method. An automatic diagnosis of viral pneumonia and coronavirus using X-ray images is proposed in this paper using a Convolutional Neural Network (CNN) model.

2   Related Work

In recent years, several methods have been introduced to detect abnormalities from chest X-ray images, especially deep learning methods. One of these methods is Convolutional Neural Networks (CNNs), which, particularly in the area of medical imaging, have been effectively employed to enhance the efficiency of computer-aided diagnosis (CAD) technology. In 2017, the Authors [2] proposed a classical deep learning network named DenseNet-121 [3], a CNN model with 121 layers, to accelerate the diagnosis of pneumonia. It was observed that the framework scored higher on the F1 scale than experienced physicians. A weighted binary cross-entropy loss has also been introduced by the team as a means of mitigating the effects of unbalanced classes, whose difference from the binary cross-entropy loss comes from the way the unbalanced classes are weighted differently according to the number of each class in the model. According to their model, they achieved a recall rate of 96.7% as well as an F1 score of 92.7%. In [4], Verma et al. adopted transfer learning and fine-tuning to train two classical CNN models, Xception-Net and VGG16-Net, to classify images with chest diseases. In [5], four efficient CNN models are proposed, namely two pre-trained models, ResNet152V2 and MobileNetV2, a CNN architecture, and a Long Short-Term Memory (LSTM) network. A number of different parameters were also compared for each of the models that have been trained. They have been able to achieve an accuracy rate of more than 91% for each of their four models in terms of recall, F1, precision, and AUC. The authors [6] attempted to detect COVID-19, non-COVID, and Healthy cases from chest x-ray images. It was based on the RSNA Pneumonia detection dataset and the COVIDx dataset provided by the RSNA. A combination of Autoencoder and Deep CNN was used to extract information from the images in order to classify them. As a result of their proposed system, they found that it was accurate to 93.5%. The authors of [7] attempted to solve the problem of data imbalance in X-ray image classification. The proposed architecture was tested using two different benchmark datasets in order to see how well it performed. In CNN, features from different layers are dynamically combined in layers in order to improve the performance of the classification algorithm, and this has been designed to solve gradient descent problems. They were successful in achieving 99.6% accuracy with the architecture they proposed. In [8], Aparna et al. used a dataset from the COVID-19 Radiography

Database. In this work, they used different CNN models that were developed with the following features: Gaussian blur and weighted grayscale conversion. The dynamic dictionary was set to 512 entries. The optimization method used was stochastic gradient descent, with a batch size of 2. With this dataset, an accuracy of 93.3% and 91.6% for VGG-16 and MobileNet, respectively, was achieved. The author of [9] proposed a model called "CoroNet", a CNN model for COVID-19 diagnosis based on chest radiographs. Xception Architecture is a pre-trained model that utilizes the ImageNet dataset as a basis for training. This pre-trained model was then used to train on a series of publicly available datasets for research purposes, which were collected from various publicly available sources. It was found that the average result rate for the model was 89.6%, while the recall and precision rates for cases of COVID-19 were: 93% and 98.2% for the three classes of pneumonia (normal, COVID, pneumonia bacterial, and pneumonia viral), respectively. There is a 95% accuracy in classification performance for the classification of three classes (COVID, pneumonia, and normal). In [10], the authors proposed a transfer learning-based pneumonia and COVID-19 detection process from the chest X-ray image of the open-source dataset and achieved 98.2% accuracy in COVID-19 classification. In [11], the authors experimented with various convolutional neural networks to examine the images of chest X-Ray conditions related to COVID-19. The experiments showed that there was 68% accuracy of the results when images were processed with the help of a support vector machine network. The second experiment used VGG19, which pertained to the earlier results and therefore wasn't accepted. The third method, CLAHE, showed 84% accuracy. However, the neural network that the researchers designed was able to provide 91% accuracy. The proposed model was effective to use in hospitals, medicine clinics and radiology clinics.

3 Proposed Methodology

The COVID-19 Radiography Database [12] is used to train and evaluate the two models. We have collected a total of 21165 chest radiographs, which can be categorized into four different types of chest radiographs (COVID-19, Lung Opacity, Normal and Viral Pneumonia). Due to processing limitations of the GPU, 9945 images from the data set were used, and the set for Lung Opacity was excluded. Firstly, we applied image processing techniques to enhance image contrast without downgrading the image or adding any noise. After that, data augmentation techniques such as rotating, zooming, and flipping the image are then fed to the CNN model. Figure 1 describes the flow diagram of the proposed methodology. The two CNN architectures, VGG-16 introduced in [13] and VGG-19 introduced in [14] are trained and validated on the dataset to fine-tune the models' parameters. As a next step, we evaluated and compared the performance of the two different architectures using the test set obtained with the two different architectures. Finally, Gradient Weighted Class Activation Maps (Grad-CAM) introduced in [15] are used to localize the affected areas in chest X-ray images.

3.1 Dataset

This study used the publicly available dataset of chest X-rays, consisting of a total of 9945 X-ray images from the COVID-19 Radiography Database [12]. The dataset was randomly split into two folders, Train and Test, where 80% of the dataset was split into the Train folder and 20% into the Test folder. We resized all the images to a fixed size of 224 × 224 pixels. A total of 7956 images were used to train the system, which was divided into three sub-sets: normal images, pneumonia images, and covid images; the normal images consisted of 4000 images, the pneumonia images consisted of 1076 images, and the covid images consisted of 2880 images. There were a total of 1989 images in the test set; the normal set contained 1000 images, the pneumonia set contained 720 images, and the COVID set contained 269 images, respectively.

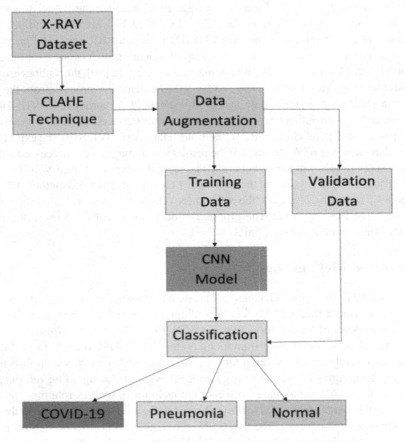

Fig. 1. System Flow Diagram of the Proposed Model

3.2 Image Enhancement

In the field of radiographic image processing, enhancing the image contrast is a vital pre-processing step to improve the accuracy of subsequent analyses. One of the renowned techniques employed to serve this purpose is the Contrast Limited Adaptive Histogram Equalization (CLAHE) [16]. This paper discusses the application of CLAHE to chest radiographs prior to applying data augmentation techniques [17]. CLAHE is a specialized method that operates by dividing the image into multiple non-overlapping, small regions referred to as 'tiles'. Each of these tiles is then processed individually for histogram equalization, thereby providing a customized, adaptive enhancement. The technique improves the local contrast of an image and brings out the details embedded in the varying regions of the image.

The CLAHE process can be dissected into four primary steps:

1. Division of the image into non-overlapping tiles.
2. Computation of the histogram for each tile.
3. Contrast limiting, where histogram bins that exceed a specified limit are clipped, and the surplus pixels are uniformly redistributed among other bins. This prevents over-amplification of contrast, mitigating issues such as the checkerboard effect and over-enhancement of noise.
4. Merging of the independently processed tiles using bilinear interpolation to prevent the generation of artificial boundaries.

Through this process, CLAHE is proficient in preventing the potential washout of image information due to the compression of low histogram components.

In the context of radiography, CLAHE proves to be effective in enhancing the contrast of chest radiographs. Figure 2 and Fig. 3 demonstrate the significant enhancement in image contrast. The grey and blurred regions in the images of Fig. 2 have been transformed into nearly black and white areas in Fig. 3, indicating the effectiveness of the enhancement technique. Moreover, crucial information hidden in the original images, such as bones, lung areas, and other tissues, is unveiled, which can greatly aid in the subsequent image processing tasks. The application of CLAHE as a pre-processing step

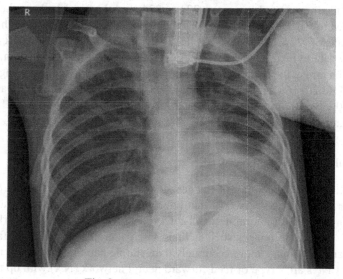

Fig. 2. Example of original image.

before data augmentation serves to improve the performance of the later stages of the image processing pipeline.

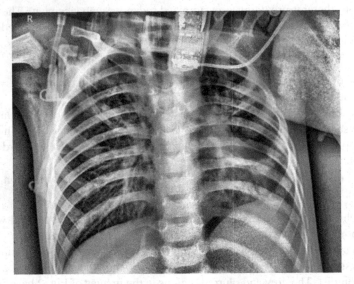

Fig. 3. Example of enhanced image.

3.3 Data Augmentation

The size of the image has been set to 224 × 224, and the pixel scale of the image has been changed to [0, 255] by dividing the maximum number of pixels in the image. A channel setting of [224, 224, 3] was applied to the images, as well as other techniques to augment the data to increase the robustness of the proposed models to be implemented. In the rotation range, the random rotation of the image will take place during training in the range of [0, 20]. As a result of using the zoom range, the image size was randomly scaled by 20% based on the zoom range. An image was randomly flipped horizontally using a technique called horizontal flip.

3.4 Convolutional Neural Network

In the detection and processing of images, convolutional neural networks (CNNs) are a class of artificial neural networks that have been developed for the enhancement of pixel data in the form of neural networks. The convolutional neural network is capable of detecting patterns in images such as lines, circles, gradients, and even face and eye features in an input image more accurately than simple neural networks. It is important to note that CNNs are a type of feed-forward neural network (NN) with up to twenty or thirty layers. The performance of CNN results from a particular type of layer called a convolutional layer. CNNs are made up of several superimposed convolutional layers, each capable of recognizing more complex structures. In this research, the first model architecture is based on VGG16 [12], with the last layers modified for training purposes. The VGG-16 model consists of thirteen convolutional layers as shown in Fig. 4, five maxpooling layers, and three fully connected layers. As a result, sixteen layers will be included in the model, including two fully connected hidden layers and one output layer. This will lead to a model with sixteen layers and tunable parameters. In both of the fully connected layers, the number of neurons is 4096, the same number as in the fully connected layer. Using the COVID-19 Radiography dataset as an example, the output layer consists of a set of three neurons representing the number of categories in the dataset.

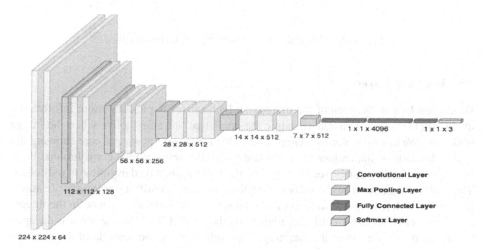

Fig. 4. VGG16-based model with last layers modified.

The second model architecture is based on VGG19 [13], with the last layers modified as well. This model is shown in Fig. 5. There will be sixteen layers of CNNs, three fully connected layers, and a final layer for the SoftMax function in a network constructed from sixteen layers of CNNs, as well as the same three fully connected layers for each of the architectures. Adam is employed as the optimizer to train the network from the beginning to the end. It is a stochastic optimization algorithm in which the weights of the CNN are multiplied by a small factor between 0 and 1 after each epoch for training the CNN; the weights of the CNN are decremented after each epoch; It is a technique used in order to regularize Neural Network training, along with batch size and dropouts. Choosing a weight decay method will allow you to use a larger initial value for the learning rate, which in turn will reduce the training time since a larger learning rate can be used. Taking into account the high imbalance between the Pneumonia case and the other cases, you should choose the categorical cross-entropy loss with weights defined for each class in the One vs. All case.

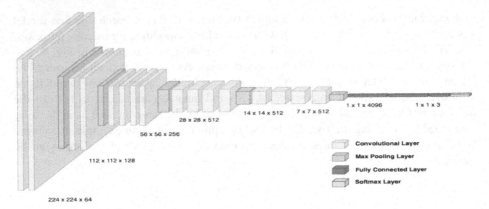

Fig. 5. VGG19-based model with the last layers modified.

3.5 Heatmap Layer

When you look at the area of the image in which the CNN picks up more information in a particular class, you can visualize the areas that are more active when the image is shown. We have developed a Grad-CAM [15] for this purpose. A figure showing the spatial location of the features that activate more intensely the final convolutional layer before classification can be seen in Fig. 6 by the regions displayed in yellow to red colors. The CNN can be seen in the COVID-19 X-ray image, identifying important features, including the left lung and the top of the diaphragm, which can be found in the image. However, the CNN can identify hot regions on the normal X-ray image, such as the apex of the heart and the top of the diaphragm, as well as a hot spot outside of the chest on the upper side. As a result of these images, we can gain valuable insight into what the

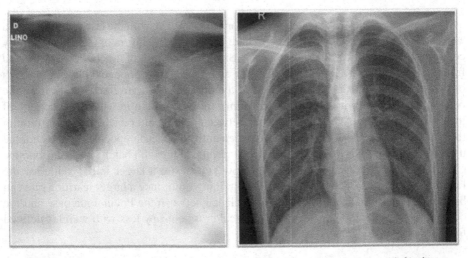

Fig. 6. Grad-CAM for a COVID-19 X-ray (right) and normal X-ray Image (left) class.

most essential features of the CNN are and how we should tune the model parameters to improve the training process for a great CNN.

4   Results

The terminology used for evaluating their performance: Accuracy, Precision, and F1-Score. Accuracy, commonly used in machine learning, is a measure of how frequently the model predictions are correct, which is determined by the ratio of instances correctly predicted to the total number of instances. Precision provides an assessment of the model's exactness or quality. Specifically, it is calculated as the ratio of true positives (items correctly identified as positive) to the sum of true positives and false positives (items incorrectly identified as positive). This metric offers insight into the number of correctly predicted cases that were positive. F1-Score, the harmonic mean of Precision and Recall, is a useful measure for situations with imbalanced data distribution. Recall is another significant metric that quantifies the number of true positive cases the model correctly identified. The F1-Score, ranging from 0 (worst) to 1 (best), provides a balanced view of Precision and Recall [18]. Given the terminology presented, below in Table 1 is a summary chart for an analysis of two models, VGG16 and VGG19. These models are evaluated with respect to an input shape of 224 and the Cross-Entropy Loss function (CCE), respectively. It is notable that the performance of these models, when pre-processed with contrast enhancement techniques, surpasses that of the original models without enhancement. Moreover, the table shows that the best results of accuracy of 0.97 and precision of 0.97 are obtained by the proposed model. It is also evident from Table 1 that the best results, in terms of accuracy, precision, and F1, are all obtained from models that have been preprocessed by methods that have been enhanced. The VGG16 is the most accurate and precise model when it comes to accuracy and precision.

Table 1. Summary of the performance of the two models

Model	Set	Accuracy	Precession	F1-Score
VGG-16	Original	0.95	0.95	0.95
	Enhanced	0.97	0.97	0.97
VGG-19	Original	0.94	0.94	0.95
	Enhanced	0.95	0.96	0.96

The accuracy of the trained and validated models can be seen in Fig. 7. In this figure, the x-axis generally represents the number of training epochs, where an epoch is a complete pass through the entire training dataset, and the y-axis typically represents the accuracy metric, which ranges from 0 to 1, with a higher value signifying better performance of the model. There is also Fig. 8 that displays the training and validation losses of the best-performer model, which is an enhanced version of VGG16, identified during the training procedure for 100 epochs.

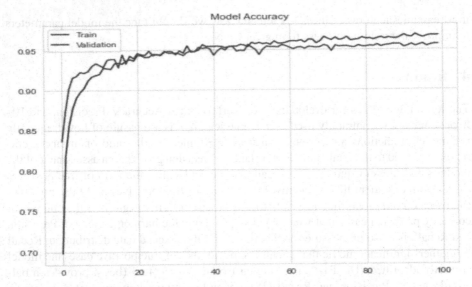

Fig. 7. Training and Validation Accuracy of VGG16

In Fig. 8, the x-axis again represents the number of training epochs, while the y-axis represents the loss value. The loss is a measure of how well the model's predictions match the actual values during training, with lower loss values signifying better model performance. A training accuracy of over 96%, a validation accuracy of over 95%, and a training loss of under 0.05 also suggest that the model has the potential to achieve excellent performance if properly trained and validated. A decreasing trend can also

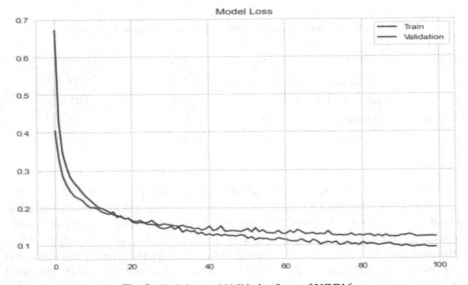

Fig. 8. Training and Validation Loss of VGG16

be seen in training accuracy as well as training loss during training. The result of this process was that the most accurate model after the last epoch of training was saved. In the experiment, the loss tendency showed an unstable oscillating tendency. This is probably related to the limited mini-batch size of the GPU computation source.

5   Confusion Matrix

By combining stacked convolution layers and pooling layers with SoftMax activation, we can predict the probability of CNN models being generated. Figure 9 shows the best-performing model prediction among the total of 269 pneumonia images, a total of 1000 normal images, and a total of 720 COVID images. Only 64 of the 1989 samples were misclassified; eight samples were misclassified from Viral Pneumonia images; 30 samples were misclassified from COVID, and 26 samples were misclassified from normal images. Figure 10 shows the confusion matrix of the enhanced VGG19 model. 111 were misclassified; seven samples were misclassified from Viral Pneumonia images; 55 samples were misclassified from COVID, and 49 samples were misclassified from normal images. These results shows that the enhanced VGG16 model outperforms the enhanced VGG19 model in detecting the normal and COVID images.

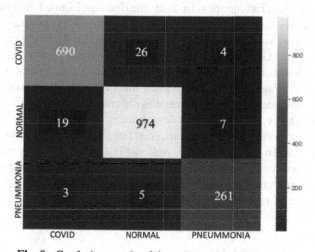

Fig. 9. Confusion matrix of the enhanced VGG16 model.

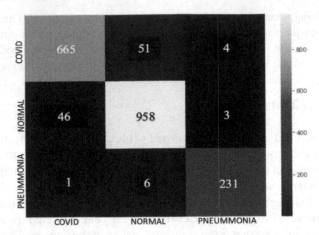

Fig. 10. Confusion matrix of the enhanced VGG19 model.

6 Conclusion

This paper describes CNN-based models for diagnosing pneumonia and coronavirus diseases based on chest radiographs. Initially, the Contrast Limited Adaptive Histogram Equalization (CLAHE) technique was applied to improve image contrast, and data augmentation techniques such as zooming, rotating, and image flipping were also applied. Then, VGG-16 and VGG-19 CNN models were trained and tested to extract the features needed to detect the diseases. These models contain sixteen and nineteen layers, respectively; combining a SoftMax activation function, a drop operation, and pooling layers. The performance of the two models was illustrated with and without the enhancement technique. The experimental work demonstrates that the enhanced VGG-16 model obtained an accuracy rate of 97% and a precision rate of 97%. This improvement demonstrated that the VGG16 model performs well and is a very promising method to detect chest diseases when considering the enhancement of X-ray images. Finally, more investigation of different image processing enhancement techniques is needed in future work in order to enhance X-ray images more effectively.

References

1. World Health Organization: WHO Health Emergency Dashboard (2022). https://covid19.who.int/. Accessed 2022
2. Zhang, D., Ren, F., Li, Y., Na, L., Ma, Y.: Pneumonia detection from chest X-ray images based on convolutional neural network. Electronics **10**(13), 1512 (2021). https://doi.org/10.3390/electronics10131512
3. Zhao, J., Yuan, Q., Wang, H., Liu, W., Liao, X., Su, Y., et al.: Antibody responses to SARS-CoV-2 in patients with novel coronavirus disease 2019. Clin. Infect. Dis. **71**(16), 2027–2034 (2020). https://doi.org/10.1093/cid/ciaa344
4. Verma, D., Bose, C., Tufchi, N., Pant, K., Tripathi, V., Thapliyal, A.: An efficient framework for identification of tuberculosis and pneumonia in chest X-ray images using neural network. Procedia Comput. Sci. **171**, 217–224 (2020). https://doi.org/10.1016/j.procs.2020.04.023

5. Yang, W., et al.: The role of imaging in 2019 novel coronavirus pneumonia (COVID-19). Eur. Radiol. **30**(9), 4874–4882 (2020). https://doi.org/10.1007/s00330-020-06827-4
6. Agarwal, C., Khobahi, S., Schonfeld, D., Soltanalian, M.: CoroNet: a deep network architecture for enhanced identification of COVID-19 from chest X-ray images. In: 71st Proceedings on Proceedings, pp. 1–10 (2021). https://doi.org/10.1117/12.2580738
7. Jia, G., Lam, H.-K., Xu, Y.: Classification of COVID-19 chest X-ray and CT images using a type of dynamic CNN modification method. Comput. Biol. Med. **134**, 104425 (2021). https://doi.org/10.1016/j.compbiomed.2021.104425
8. Aparna, G., Gowri, S., Bharathi, R., Vimali, J.S., Jabez, J., Ajitha, P.: COVID-19 prediction using X-ray images. In: 2021 5th International Conference on Trends in Electronics and Informatics (ICOEI), Tirunelveli, India, pp. 903–908 (2021). https://doi.org/10.1109/ICO EI51242.2021.9452740
9. Khan, A., Latief Shah, J., Bhat, M.: CoroNet: a deep neural network for detection and diagnosis of COVID-19 from chest X-ray images. Comput. Methods Programs Biomed. **196** (2020). https://doi.org/10.1016/j.cmpb.2020.105581
10. Mishra, M., Parashar, V., Shimpi, R.: Development and evaluation of an AI system for early detection of Covid-19 pneumonia using X-ray (student consortium). In: 2020 IEEE Sixth International Conference on Multimedia Big Data (BigMM) (2020)
11. Hussein, F., et al.: Hybrid CLAHE-CNN deep neural networks for classifying lung diseases from X-ray acquisitions. Electronics **11**(19), 3075 (2022). https://doi.org/10.3390/electroni cs11193075
12. Rahman, T., Chowdhury, M., Khandakar, A.: COVID-19 Radiography Database. Kaggle. https://www.kaggle.com/datasets/tawsifurrahman/covid19-radiography-database. Accessed 2022
13. TensorFlow. Keras Applications VGG19. https://www.tensorflow.org/api_docs/python/tf/keras/applications/vgg19/VGG19. Accessed 2022
14. Keras. VGG. https://keras.io/api/applications/vgg/. Accessed 2022
15. Selvaraju, R.R., Cogswell, M., Das, A., Vedantam, R., Parikh, D., Batra, D.: Grad-CAM: visual explanations from deep networks via gradient-based localization. Int. J. Comput. Vis. (2019). https://doi.org/10.1007/s11263-019-01228-7
16. Pizer, S.M., et al.: Adaptive histogram equalization and its variations. Comput. Vis. Graph. Image Process. **39**(3), 355–368 (1987). https://doi.org/10.1016/s0734-189x(87)80186-x
17. Reza, A.: Realization of the contrast limited adaptive histogram equalization (CLAHE) for real-time image enhancement. VLSI Signal Process. **38**, 35–44 (2004). https://doi.org/10.1023/B:VLSI.0000028532.53893.82
18. Japkowicz, N., Shah, M.: Evaluating Learning Algorithms: A Classification Perspective. Cambridge University Press, Cambridge (2011). https://www.cambridge.org/core/books/evalua ting-learning-algorithms/3CB22D16AB609D1770C24CA2CB5A11BF. Accessed 2023

Real Time Arabic Sign Language Recognition Using Machine Learning: A Vision - Based Approach

Shahd Elgergeni[✉] and Nabil Drawil

Computer Engineering Department, University of Tripoli, Tripoli, Libya
{s.elgergeni,n.drawil}@uot.edu.ly

Abstract. Dumb and hearing-impaired people are unable to communicate as well as normal people; thus, they must rely on sign language. Which is a visual or gestural form of communication. Unfortunately, sign language is neither common nor easy to learn. Consequently, deaf-mute people encounter many challenges in their daily communication. Hence, we proposed an intelligent system that employs a vision-based approach dedicated to Arabic sign language recognition (ArSLR). The system is aimed to recognize Arabic words expressed in dynamic sign language expressions and translate them into textural form. While maintaining natural and flexible translation, the system doesn't impose any hardware requirements, colored gloves, or limitations on the background. A custom dataset is utilized in the development process of the system. A significant amount of experimental work has been conducted to come up with effective and generalized algorithms for image processing, feature extraction, feature selection, and practical classification. Satisfactory results are achieved with the use of linear discriminant analysis (LDA) as a feature selection and dimensionality reduction method; where 100% accuracy is achieved with support vector machine (SVM) and logistic regression classification algorithms. An accuracy of 99.9% is obtained with a multi-layer perceptron (MLP) feed-forward artificial neural network and 99.6% with a decision tree classification. The impact of using principal component analysis (PCA) and LDA as a feature selection approach instead of raw data features is also presented. Finally, the system is validated in real-time with unseen data. It is evident from the validation and testing results that word-level ArSLR can be achieved robustly and accurately.

Keywords: Sign Language Classification · Machine Learning · Feature Selection and Reduction

1 Introduction

Sign language is a non-verbal language that represents an essential communication tool for deaf and mute people. It is based on visual cues through the hands, face, mouth, and body. Similarly to spoken languages, sign languages are composed of the following indivisible features: Manual features, i.e., hand shape, position, movement, and orientation of the palm or fingers; and non-manual features, namely eye gaze, head nods or shakes, shoulder orientations, and various kinds of facial expressions such as mouthing and mouth gestures [1]. Furthermore, since speaking in continuous sentences is quicker than spelling out every single word, people with hearing or speech impairments frequently communicate with others using words and continuous sentences. However, signers use fingerspelling if the desired word does not have a standard sign to represent. Fingerspelling involves only using manual features to represent the letters and numbers of a writing system, while a combination of manual and non-manual features is used to express words and sentences as well. Like spoken languages, there is no universal sign language; e.g., Arabic sign language (ArSL) is different from the sign languages approved by other countries. Furthermore, Arab countries have different sign languages; however, a unified dictionary for ArSL is produced by the Council of Arab Ministers of Social Affairs (CAMSA). ArSL is a manual language (i.e., it mostly depends upon manual features rather than non-manual features), but non-manual features may also be used to support the meaning.

Unfortunately, due to the complexity of sign languages in general and the lack of learning resources for ArSL in particular, most of the hearing majority tend to ignore this language; thus, deaf-mute people face many challenges in their daily life communication with the society and a human interpreter is needed. However, dependency on an interpreter has the problems of lack of availability and a privacy breakthrough. Therefore, there is a great need for an automatic translation of sign language.

This research focuses on word-level ArSLR that is built based on the unified dictionary for ArSL. The contributions of this research work are summarized herein. To prove the concept, a set of 25 signed words, which are commonly used in critical places, constitutes dataset classes. Furthermore, with the aim of flexible and natural translation, a vision-based approach is followed instead of impose wearable sensors or gloves, cf. [2,3]. With only a single 2D web camera, the proposed system is capable of real-time recognition. In order to isolate words, end point detection algorithm is developed with the help of background subtraction technique. A 3D pose estimation model is employed to extract 3D features from various parts of the body, which represent the elements of the sign, that is carried out over a number of captured frames. At the end of the sign, the extracted features are passed to the feature selection and dimensionality reduction techniques, where we have explored the use of both PCA and LDA. Finally, the selected features passed to the stage of the classification, where various classification algorithms have been experimented to end up with the best classification performance.

The remainder part of the paper is organized as follows. Section 2 explores some of the related research studies, Sect. 3 introduces the methodology behind the proposed Arabic sign language recognition system with the use of various feature selection and classification algorithms, Sect. 4 presents the implementation details, Sect. 5 provides experimental results and validation of the proposed approach along with the discussion of the results. Finally, Sect. 6 highlights the concluding remarks and recommends future research directions.

2   Related Work

In the domain of Human-Computer Interaction (HCI), automatic sign language recognition is a key research subject. Recent studies focus on all levels of intelligent machines, from preprocessing images through feature extraction and up to classification of patterns pertained to sign language, in an effort to replace sign language interpreters.

In [4], the authors present a real-time system for ArSL recognition. The system recognizes 30 isolated words from the standard ArSL signs using the dynamic time warping (DTW) algorithm based on the Kinect sensor for gesture acquisition. However, the system obtains a signer-independent recognition rate of 95.25% and a signer-dependent recognition rate of 97.58%. The system imposes the use of the hardware device (i.e., Kinect sensor), which is considered an extra cost. The number of the selected joints per frame is 12 out of 20, which are considered the more descriptive features for the selected signs – a deficiency that may limit the ability to extend the system to recognize more words with different key features. In addition, DTW has limitations represented in Lack of *Global Alignment* and *Alignment Path Ambiguity*: the former may limit the ability to deal with sequences with large variation in length and shape, and the latter may limit the system to be extended to patterns with a high degree of similarity. Furthermore, due to the absence of the depth feature of the joints, the researchers force a fixed position for the signer within the room to avoid the large variation of the x and y coordinates between the joints, which adds another constraint to the system.

For Egyptian Sign Language movements, in [5], the authors introduce a vision-based system that alternatively translates them into their isolated words. For categorization, they employed the Inception v3 Convolutional Neural Networks (CNNs) and Inception v3 CNN-Long-short-term memory (CNN-LSTM) architectures. The first architecture had a 90% accuracy rate. A 72% accuracy rate was achieved using the Inception v3 CNN-LSTM architecture. They concluded that CNNs are excellent at recognizing isolated signs, but CNN-LSTMs are excellent at recognizing continuous words. However, the researchers rely on the unprocessed video dataset that was gathered at various lighting conditions, viewing angles, and camera placements. Dealing with raw video signals is computationally expensive during the training phase because of the feature extraction process that is carried by CNN, in addition to the time and effort required for dataset collection to account for a wide range of environmental variations.

In [6], authors presented dynamic hand gesture recognition of ArSL by using deep CNNs. In this approach, a Microsoft Kinect V2 camera is used to build a dataset of RGB and depth videos, also, they proposed the use of four deep neural networks models using 2D and 3D CNN to cover different feature extraction methods and then passing these features to a recurrent neural network (RNN) for sequence classification. The reported research work presents the optimal multi-model ResNet50-BiLSTM-Normalization with 100% test efficiency without incorrect training, validation, and testing. Despite achieving high accuracy score, they depend on raw videos for the dataset creation, which causes some issues in form of large storage capacity and computational power needed during the training phase, a large dataset size of 14700 samples to cover all possible environmental variations, furthermore, to equalize the length of the collected videos during the preprocessing stage. In addition to the huge amount of time and effort spent on manually cleansing the irrelevant frames that are not part of the expressed sign instead of devicing an intelligent algorithm or tool to perform this task. Logical research practices, such as, analyzing the patterns pertained to the twenty-one classes in the feature space and evaluating the degree of similarity among the selected signs, can greatly reduce the cost of time and computation. In other words, such practices may lead to opt-out the choice of deep learning techniques and utilize a less expensive classifiers yet more effective.

In [7], the 3D-CNN is used for sign language recognition. The authors investigate the use of both single and parallel 3D-CNN architectures. Three different feature fusion techniques with parallel architecture are conducted and performances are compared for three different datasets. Authors conclude that parallel architecture as a feature extraction with Multilayer perceptron (MLP) for feature fusion and softmax layer for classification produces the highest accuracy scores at the level of the three datasets. The obtained recognition rates are 98.12%, 100%, and 76.67% on the three datasets, respectively, for the signer-dependent mode. For the signer-independent mode, the obtained recognition rates are 84.38%, 34.9%, and 70% on the three datasets, respectively. The authors reported that the aforementioned approach lacks the ability of real time recognition; therefore, researchers aim for further improve it to cover the real time recognition scenarios.

An automatic ArSLR system is proposed in [8], where a dataset of 30 isolated words covering the occlusion state scenarios was developed. Geometric features are used to construct the feature vector, and an Euclidean distance classifier is applied to the classification stage. The system achieved a recognition rate of 97% with a low misclassification rate for similar gestures. However, the mentioned approach follows the use of raw videos, and the extracted geometric features are dedicated to the hands without consideration of facial expressions or finger shapes, which may limit the capabilities of extending the system to the recognition of other signs.

3   Proposed Methodology

In this paper, we propose an intelligent real-time vision-based ArSLR system that guarantees a natural, flexible, and economical translation tool that does not impose hardware requirements, colored gloves, or limitations on the background.

The main components of the proposed system are represented by a data acquisition system, which is simply a 2D web camera that captures the sequence of the fingers and hand gestures, body movements, and facial expressions that express the Arabic word. Secondly, every captured frame passed through an end point detection and feature extraction algorithm; thirdly, by the end of signing, the sequence of captured features passed to a feature selection and dimensionality reduction algorithm; then, the selected features passed through the classification algorithm that represents the intelligence of our system. Finally, the predicted word is displayed on the screen of the smart device in its textural form. In the following sections, we present each of these components in details.

3.1   End Point Detection

In order to enhance the speed of the real time detection and recognition of the sign language expressions, a robust, generalized motion detection algorithm that is able to adapt to the variations of the scene's illuminations is required. Thus, to accomplish this task, the "Background sub-tractor Mixture of Gaussian Two (MOG2)" algorithm [9] is utilized. It is a pixel level background subtraction algorithm, where the scene model has a probability density function (PDF) for each pixel separately. The algorithm uses recursive equations to constantly update the parameters of a Gaussian mixture model (GMM) and to simultaneously select the appropriate number of Gaussian components for each pixel. Therefore, for every new pixel value, the pixel would be classified as a background pixel if it matches at least one of the background models; otherwise, it would be classified as a foreground pixel. In the proposed system, the end-point detection of the sign language expressions is done with the help of this algorithm. Practically, a motion is detected whenever a number of foreground pixels, above empirically-set threshold, are detected. This way, one can locate the sequence of frames contains the sign language gestures. Once the motion is detected, the features will be extracted from the received live feed frames.

3.2   Image Processing and Feature Extraction

Real time sign language recognition is a fairly complex task that requires live perception and tracking of face, pose and hands movements. Furthermore, dealing with raw video signals is a computationally expensive task that can lead to over-fitting and person dependence. On the other hand, the current state of the art pose estimation systems provide explainable, person independence, privacy preserving and the generalizations over the person's appearance and background – allowing us to focus on the recognition of the motion [10]. Therefore, Media pipe holistic model [11] is utilized as a main tool for feature extraction. It is a 3D pose estimation model that was designed as a multistage pipeline. It integrates separate models for pose, face, and hands, thus providing fast and accurate feature estimation.

In this research work, a media-pipe holistic model is used in video mode so that it continuously extracts the features from face, both hands and pose within the frame, with total number of 1662 features per frame (i.e., 132 features for pose that represent X, Y, Z and V values of each pose landmarks, 126 features for both hands that represent X, Y and Z values of each hand landmark, 1404 features for the face that represent X, Y and Z values of each face landmark). Figure 1 shows the models that are used to extract 3D features from various parts of the body, their end result, and the final output of the MediaPipe pose estimation model.

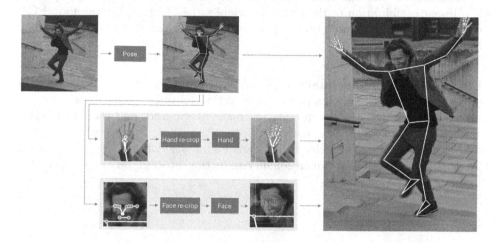

Fig. 1. 3D Pose Estimation Model: MediaPipe Holistic Model

3.3 Feature Selection

Dimensionality of the dataset refers to the number of input variables or features in the dataset. High Dimensionality of the data set may increase the complexity of the classification model thus increases the chance of over-fitting which dramatically decreases the overall performance of the classifier. Hence, to avoid these problems a feature selection and dimensionality reduction techniques are used. Feature selection refers to the techniques that reduce the number of non-informative and redundant features. While dimensionality reduction refers to the projection of the input data onto the new selected lower dimensional subspace. Therefore, due to the extensively large number of features extracted from each sequence or video of the sign language expressions (i.e., 49,860 features), feature selection and dimensionality reduction techniques are applied. By doing so, two main advantages are obtained:

- Ability to perform data visualization.
- Enhancement of the classification performance

Principal Component Analysis (PCA) and Linear Discriminant Analysis (LDA) techniques are frequently used in feature selection and dimensionality reduction. In the following, PCA and LDA techniques are briefly discussed.

Principal Component Analysis (PCA). PCA is an unsupervised machine learning technique and the most common approach to the dimensionality reduction. PCA can be defined as the orthogonal projection of the data onto a lower dimensional linear space, known as the principal subspace, such that the variance of the projected data is maximized [12]. Furthermore, PCA generates a new set of uncorrelated variables called principal components. Each principal component is a linear combination of the original variables (i.e., features). Therefore, PCA considered to be a suitable tool to perform feature selection and dimensionality reduction.

Linear Discriminant Analysis (LDA). LDA projects the data points onto a lower dimensional sub-space, the basis of this subspace called linear discriminants, such that the between class scatter is maximized, and the within class scatter is minimized. Scatter matrix expresses the same measure as the variance but on different scale. Therefore, LDA can also be considered as a good candidate for feature selection and dimensionality reduction process, but in a supervised manner.

3.4   Classification

ArSLR process is a supervised multiclass classification problem. A pattern is represented by a feature vector $x^{(i)}$ signifies the sequence of gestures of thirty frames. The classifier should predicts the sequence class as one of the selected twenty five classes (i.e., words) listed in Table 1. Some of The corresponding signs are presented in Fig. 2.

According to the pattern analysis and data visualization, presented in Sect. 4, the twenty-five class of interest do not exhibit considerable overlapping in the reduced feature space. This presentation encourages the utilization of inexpensive classifiers yet capable of handling linearly inseparable classes. For the purpose of performance comparison, four common machine leaning algorithms, fulfill the aforementioned conditions, are implemented, Namely, Logistic regression, decision tree, Support Vector Machine (SVM) and Feed Forward Artificial Neural Network (FFANN). In the following sections we discuss those algorithms in some of detail.

Logistic Regression. Logistic regression classifier is one of the binary classifiers by nature. Thus, we implemented logistic regression using one versus rest strategy, During the test phase, K different classifiers run in order to predict the label of the new example, each classifier provides the predicted probability that new example belongs to one of the K classes, the final predicted class by the algorithm will be the class of the highest probability.

Table 1. The Selected Arabic Words

Class Label	Arabic Meaning	English Meaning
0	حادث	Accident
1	طائرة	Airplane
2	سيارة إسعاف	Ambulance
3	وصول	Arrival
4	عمود فقري	Back bone
5	بنك	Bank
6	تحليل دم	Blood Analysis
7	طبيب	Doctor
8	ابتزاز	Extortion
9	استخراج	Extraction
10	إحساس	Feeling
11	أزمة قلبية	Heart Attack
12	جار	Neighbour
13	ممرض	Nurse
14	زيت	Oil
15	عملية	Operation
16	ألم	Pain
17	جواز سفر	Passport
18	موعد دقيق	Punctuality
19	تجديد	Renewal
20	تهديد	Threat
21	اختفاء	Vanishement
22	أراد	Wanted
23	ماء	Water
24	أين	Where

Decision Tree. The decision tree is one of the preferred algorithms due to its high performance. While a small dataset is available, it is fast to train, and it has an efficient memory storage requirement. During the test phase, starting from the top of the tree and at every node, the relevant features of every new sequence of frames would be tested until they landed into one of the leaf nodes, the assigned class label will be the label associated with that leaf node.

Support Vector Machine Classifier (SVM with a Linear Kernel). SVM has the advantage of effectiveness in high dimensional space, even when a small dataset is available. As the size of the dataset that we have is small compared to the total number of features, we implemented SVM with a linear kernel. However, SVM is a binary classifier by nature. Thus, for multiclass cases, it is implemented by using the one-versus rest technique. During the testing phase, for every new sequence, K different linear transformations are performed on the input feature vector using the K different learned parameters: the weight vector w, and the bias b. Finally, the sequence will be assigned to the positive class whose decision

Fig. 2. Sample of the Selected Arabic Sign Language Expressions

boundary results in the highest value of the linear transformation of the feature vector since it amounts to a high level of decision confidence.

Feed Forward Artificial Neural Network (FFANN). Multilayer perceptron (MLP) was implemented as a Feed Forward Artificial Neural Network (FFANN) with multiple layers of neurons, in training phase, the network uses Backpropagation algorithm with Adaptive Moment estimate (Adam) optimization algorithm [13]. Every input feature vector is fed to the input layer of MLP, where it propagates through the hidden layers. Set of linear transformations and nonlinear or nearly linear activation functions are to be applied at every hidden unit, In our implementation, ReLU is used at the hidden layers due to its desirable, close to linear and the avoidance of vanishing gradient properties that make linear models generalize well and are easy to optimize with the gradient-based methods; also, we used logistic activation function that has the property of a smooth gradient. For the output layer, it was implemented as a fully connected layer, with the Softmax activation function to provide the network predictions.

4 Experimental Work

This section introduces the implementation details related to the system components. As shown in Fig. 3 The system has two phases, with slight differences in the components and implementation of each phase. Where the first is the data collection phase and the second is the real time recognition phase.

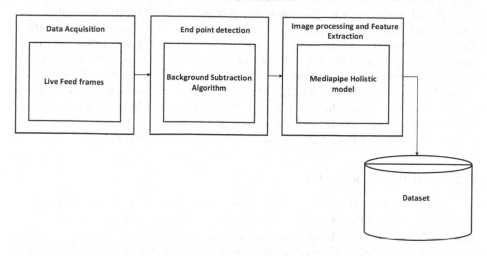

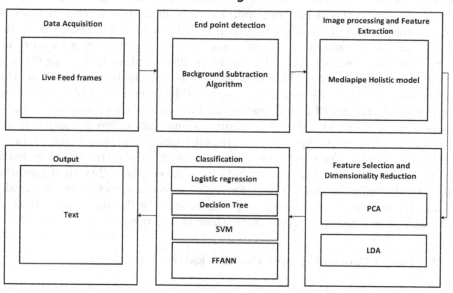

Fig. 3. Real Time ArSLR System's phases Implementation

4.1   Dataset Description

Due to lack of open source Word-level ArSL dataset, in this work, we create a custom dataset that is collected by a non-expert person, based on "The Arabic Dictionary of Gestures for the deaf" that is borrowed from "Al Amal center for the deaf and hearing impaired" in Tripoli, the dictionary contains a unified

Arabic sign language. Our dataset includes the sign language movements of the selected 25 Arabic words, the data set is collected in different lightening conditions and different backgrounds using a single 2D web camera by a vertical distance of 187 to 188 cm to the camera level. Basically, we utilize two main tools to collect the dataset: 1) Mediapipe holistic model as a feature extraction tool, thus, our dataset is the extracted coordinates values instead of raw videos, of total size of 864 MB, and 2) MOG2 algorithm in order to be used for endpoint detection of the signs. Dataset contains 90 samples per class, each sample represents a sequence of captured signs over 30 frames. Each frame contains 1662 coordinate values. Thus, each sequence has a total of 49,860 values.

4.2   End Point Detection

In order to enhance the speed of real time recognition and avoid introducing the classification algorithm with irrelevant frames which results in reduced performance of the system; end point detection technique with the help of the adaptive motion detection algorithm is implemented. The robustness of the algorithm is represented by its ability to adapt to the different illuminations and changes, thus, it helps to maintain the generalization gained from the use of Mediapipe model. Basically, this algorithm requires some training set (i.e., each of which is a pixel value) collected over an adaption period, thus, in this project, we specified 50 samples as the size of the training examples that is updated with every new pixel value is added, however, This size is specified empirically. Mainly, this algorithm is utilized to detect the foreground pixels (i.e. pixels represents a motion) based on some threshold value, that is specified by recording set of measurements representing number of foreground pixels in both cases i.e., movement and no movement in different lightening conditions and with different motion speeds. We assume that each type of measurements has a Gaussian posterior probability distribution, for every new measurement it will be considered to belong to one of the distributions that results in a higher probability than the other. By calculating mean and variance for each Gaussian, we set a threshold value. Thus, if the count of the movement pixels exceeds the threshold value, it will be considered as a movement, otherwise, there is no movement.

4.3   Image Processing and Feature Extraction

Due to the advantages of the current state-of-the art pose estimation systems, instead of dealing with raw video signals, we utilized the media pipe holistic model due to its fast and accurate estimations of the face, hands, and pose features. Furthermore, this model is designed in such a way that it is suitable for real time applications, which matches our needs. Media pipe holistic model is used in video mode, such that it will continuously extract the total of 1662 features from each single frame, which already containing the movement detected by the end point detection technique. However, as they have different signing speeds and lengths, this may result in each sequence having a different number of motion frames from the other sequences, even though they belong to the same class; thus, to avoid the bias of classification towards the majority class, we equalize the number of frames for all sequences for all classes to 30 frames, which is the maximum number of frames required by the selected signs; this is achieved by zero padding. Therefore, if motion is not detected, frames of 1662 zeros are appended to the sequence until the length of 30 frames is reached.

4.4 Feature Selection and Dimensionality Reduction

In this section, we introduce the implementation details of the dimensionality reduction techniques that are utilized in this experiment, namely, PCA and LDA.

Principal Component Analysis (PCA). PCA is utilized to reduce the dimensionality of the data. Prior to apply PCA, there is a preprocess step that is the standardization. Each sequence of the sign language expressions is represented as a single vector of N dimension (i.e., 49,860 features). The features of each pattern (i.e., sequence) are standardized with the following formula:

$$x^i = [\frac{x_1^i - m_1}{s_1}, \frac{x_2^i - m_2}{s_2}, ..., \frac{x_N^i - m_N}{s_N}] \tag{1}$$

where x^i, is a feature vector of sequence i, x_j^i is the jth feature of the sequence i, m_j is the mean of feature j, s_j is the standard deviation of the feature j and N is the number of features.

After the standardization, we end up with the data belongs to the standard normal distribution of zero mean and standard deviation of one. PCA results in a total number of PCs that is equal to the number of the original features, however, the goal of PCA is to reduce the dimensionality of original data, thus, a subset of PCs is selected. One of the popular criteria for principal components selection is the proportion of explained variance.

In this experiment, the first 60 components are selected which guarantees about 95% of the variance of the data is retained. The entire sequences which represent points in the N-dimensional space are projected on the new lower dimensional subspace of 60 dimensions. Figure 4a shows the retained variance ratio for each component individually and cumulatively. Furthermore, PCA is utilized in data visualization to get some insights into the data that we have, thus, it helps us to decide which classification algorithms need to be used. Figure 4b shows the results of data visualization using PCA. Where PC1, PC2, and PC3 represent the first three Principal components out of 60, which captures the direction of the first, second, and third maximum variance of the data respectively.

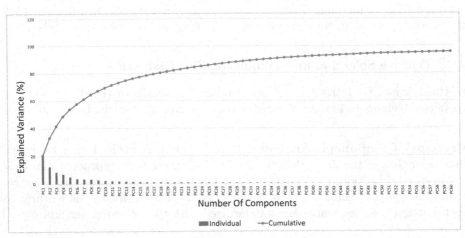

(a) Cumulative and Individual Explained Variance Ratios of PCA Components

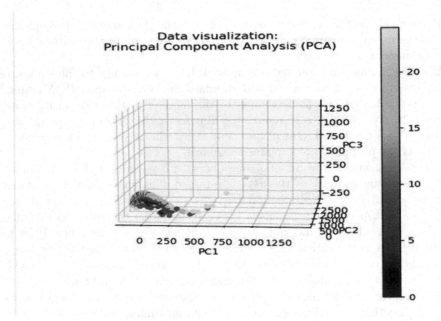

(b) Data Visualization Results of PCA

Fig. 4. Explained Variance Ratios and Data Visualization of PCA

Linear Discriminant Analysis (LDA). LDA is another dimensionality reduction technique that projects the data points onto dimensions of the new subspace that captures the direction of the maximum separation of the classes, it is a preferred technique for enhancing the classification performance. As we have 25 classes, the number of the selected dimensions that guarantees the maximum separation is equal to the number of classes minus one, that is 24 dimensions, and the total variance retained by those components is equal to 100%, Fig. 5a shows the explained variance ratio for each component individually and cumulatively. As shown in Fig. 5b, the overlap between data points belonging to different classes is highly reduced by the use of LDA, thus, we propose the use of the most popular machine learning algorithms that are mentioned in the previous section for the classification instead of following the deep learning approach.

4.5   Classification Performance with the Aid of PCA and LDA

The enhancement of classification performance is achieved by the projection of the original dataset onto a lower dimensional subspace using PCA and LDA dimensionality reduction techniques. For hyperparameter optimization and model performance evaluation, nested or double cross-validation with grid search technique is used.

In this experiment, for the outer loop of nested cross-validation, stratified 10-Fold cross-validation is used. While the inner loop is implemented as a stratified 5-fold cross validation using grid search for hyperparameter optimization, The final algorithm performance is the average performance of 10 best models.

Logistic Regression. The experiment is done with $L2$ penalty. For the strength of the regularization that is denoted as C, we explored the following values for the grid search: 100, 10, 1.0, 0.1, 0.01.

Decision Tree. The following settings are experimented: For minimum number of samples at leaf node, according to [14], the ideal possible values for leaf samples tend to be between 1 and 20 for the CART algorithm; however, one leaf sample can increase the risk of overfitting; thus, it is excluded. The sample counts of 2, 5, 10, 15, and 20 are explored. For The max depth of the tree is set to such a value that the nodes are expanded until all leaves are pure or contain a smaller number of samples than the minimum number of samples required to split the node, 5, 10, 15, 20 and 25. Finally, according to [14], the ideal minimum number of samples required to split the internal node tend to be between 1 to 40, thus, we predefine the following values: 5, 10, 15, 20, 25, 30, 35, 40.

SVM. Linear kernel is used. The optimized hyperparameter is the regularization parameter that is denoted as C, which is inversely proportional to the strength of regularization. Penalty, $L2$, as in logistic regression is applied by default, we selected the values 0.01, 0.1, 1, 10, 100, to form the grid points.

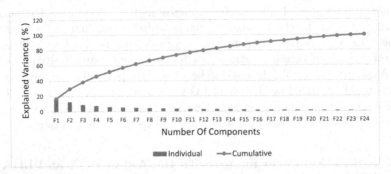

(a) Individual and Cumulative Explained Variance Ratios of LDA components

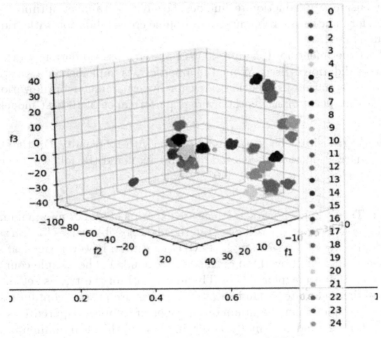

(b) Data Visualization Results of LDA

Fig. 5. Explained Variance Ratio and Data Visualization of LDA

FFANN. One of the common guidelines for choosing the optimal number of hidden units is stated in [15], who claims that this number typically falls between the input layer size and the output layer size. Therefore, one hidden layer is used for PCA. Furthermore, to change the complexity of the model, we experimented the following number of hidden units: 26, 32, 38, 44, 50, 56, 60. While, for LDA the number of the inputs features is 24 and number of classes is 25, thus, 24 hidden units is chosen for the single hidden layer. By these settings, the higher complexity models can be avoided. For both PCA and LDA data, we investigate both Logistic and ReLU activation functions for hidden units. Neural network is trained using Adam optimizer with the default settings ($\alpha = 0.001, \beta_1 = 0.9, \beta_2 = 0.999$ and $\epsilon = 10^{-8}$) as recommended in [13]. The maximum number of epochs is specified to be 500 epochs; however, in the interests of saving time and computational power, an early stopping criterion is used, such that it automatically sets aside 10% of the training dataset as a validation set. Thus, if the validation score does not improve by at least a tolerance of 10^{-4} for 10 consecutive epochs, the neural network training is terminated.

However, it is important to acknowledge a limitation of the current approach. The computational system utilized for this experiment encounters a constraint in its ability to implement cross-validation directly on the raw data, primarily due to the intricate nature of computational complexities involved with the use of FFANN.

5 Results and Discussion

The classification performance for the aforementioned classification algorithms is evaluated by the use of the accuracy measure that is defined with the following formula:

$$Accuracy\% = \frac{TP + TN}{TP + TN + FP + FN} \times 100 \tag{2}$$

Table 2, 3 and 4 list the accuracy scores that is achieved with the use of raw data, PCA and LDA features.

Table 2. Classification Performance Using Raw Data features

Classification Algorithm	Accuracy (%)
Logistic Regression	88.80
Decision Tree	79.02
SVM	83.20
FFANN	Can't be Evaluated

According to the recorded accuracy scores, as a feature selection and dimensionality reduction technique, raw data features result in a worse classification performance than PCA and LDA features. However, classification performance

Table 3. Classification Performance Using PCA features

Classification Algorithm	Accuracy (%)
Logistic Regression	89.4
Decision Tree	52.9
SVM	92.2
FFANN	87.5

Table 4. Classification Performance Using LDA features

Classification Algorithm	Accuracy (%)
Logistic Regression	100
Decision Tree	99.9
SVM	100
FFANN	99.9

presents the best accuracy scores with the use of LDA features. This can be justified by the fact that PCA projects the data points onto the direction of the maximum variation of the data and doesn't take account of the class labels. On the other hand, LDA projects data points onto the direction of the maximum separation of data, which makes it more suitable for the task of sign language classification than PCA. Furthermore, we conclude that SVM and logistic regression perform slightly better than FFANN and decision trees with the use of LDA features.

Based on those results, we validate the four classifiers with LDA features by performing real time test for fifty trials. Furthermore, we make the use of the following classification measures besides the use of accuracy measure to satisfy the robustness of the system,

$$Specificity\% = \frac{TN}{TN + FP} \times 100 \tag{3}$$

$$Precision\% = \frac{TP}{TP + FP} \times 100 \tag{4}$$

$$Recall\% = \frac{TP}{TP + FN} \times 100 \tag{5}$$

$$F1\_score\% = 2 \times \frac{Precision \times Recall}{Precision + Recall} \times 100 \tag{6}$$

In the following, Table 5 presents the overall Accuracy, Specificity, Precision, Recall, and F1_score classification measures for the system.

Table 5. Real Time Classification Performance Using LDA features

Classification Algorithm	Logistic Regression	Decision Tree	SVM	FFANN
Accuracy (%)	97.0	94.7	99.0	95.4
specificity (%)	98.4	97.3	99.5	97.6
Precision (%)	77.5	68.9	91.3	69.9
Recall (%)	82.0	34.0	88.0	42.0
F1_score (%)	88.5	38.5	84.7	43.2

6 Conclusions

This paper presents the implementation of an automatic real-time Arabic sign language translator, a crucial system for the deaf-mute community. First, we present the methodology of our implementation, where we address the algorithms and the methodology to be followed. Second, we deep dive into the details of the implementation of the system's phases, where we elaborate on the dataset gathering, classification performance tuning, and evaluation procedures. Finally, it is proven by both measurements and real-time experiments that satisfactory classification performance can be achieved with the use of LDA as a feature selection technique with an SVM classifier. It is evident from the results that real-time word-level ArSL recognition can be achieved regardless of the environment and/or user conditions.

Nevertheless, there are still issues that continue to hinder ArSL recognition, such as identifying a non-skilled signer and adding new classes (sign words) to the dataset to account for more generalization and real-world scenarios. Active learning algorithms are a tentative approach that may be used in conjunction with the proposed technique to categorize novel scenarios of known classes from unknown classes. Further research work is needed to address these issues.

References

1. Yang, Z., Tai, Y.-M., Shen, X., Shi, Z.: SF-Net: structured feature network for continuous sign language recognition (2019)
2. Elmahgiubi, M., Ennaja, M., Drawil, N., Elbuni, M.: Sign language translator and gesture recognition (2015)
3. Ambar, R., Fai, C.K., Abd Wahab, M.H., Abdul Jamil, M.M., Ma'radzi, A.A.: Development of a wearable device for sign language recognition. J. Phys. Conf. Ser. **1019**, 012017 (2018)
4. Abdel-Rabouh, A.S.A., Elmisery, F.A., Brisha, A.M., Khalil, A.H.: Arabic sign language recognition using Kinect sensor. Res. J. Appl. Sci. Eng. Technol. **15**(2), 57–67 (2018)
5. Elhagry, A., Gla, R.: Egyptian sign language recognition using CNN and LSTM (2017)
6. Ismail, M.H., Dawwd, S.A., Ali, F.H.: Dynamic hand gesture recognition of Arabic sign language by using deep convolutional neural networks, February 2022

7. Al-Hammadi, M., Muhammad, G., Abdul, W., Alsulaiman, M., Bencherif, M.A., Mekhtiche, M.A.: Hand gesture recognition for sign language using 3DCNN, 27 April 2020
8. Ibrahim, N.B., Selim, M.M., Zayed, H.H.: An automatic Arabic sign language recognition system (ArSLRS), October 2018
9. Zivkovic, Z., Heijden, F.: Efficient adaptive density estimation per image pixel for the task of background subtraction, 17 August 2005
10. Moryossef, A.: Evaluating the immediate applicability of pose estimation for sign language recognition (2021)
11. https://google.github.io/mediapipe/solutions/holistic.html. Accessed 29 June 2022
12. Bishop, C.M. (ed.): Pattern Recognition and Machine Learning. ISS, Springer, New York (2006). https://doi.org/10.1007/978-0-387-45528-0
13. Kingma, D.P., Adam, J.B.: A method for stochastic optimization. In: 3rd International Conference on Learning Representations, ICLR 2015 - Conference Track Proceedings, pp. 1–15 (2015)
14. Mantovani, R., Horváth, T., Cerri, R., Junior, S.B., Vanschoren, J., Carvalho, A.C.P.: An empirical study on hyperparameter tuning of decision trees, 12 February 2019
15. Silhouettes, P.R.: A graphical aid to the interpretation and validation of cluster analysis (1986)

Author Index

A

Abdalla, Mohamed A. E.   239
Abdelnabi, Esra A.   109
Abdo, Amina A.   239, 257
Aburas, Ali   145
Abuzaraida, Mustafa Ali   197
Alarabi, Ebtihal   173
Albar-Athe, Salma   248
Albaser, Marwa   42
Albraki, Hajer   298
Alfilali, Malik Miloud   309
Alfsai, Entesar H.   248
Algaderi, Omar Bouagila   3
Alharari, Alharari Alsouri   68
Ali, Salwa   42, 96
Alkawan, Sharafedeen   210
Alshwihde, Rayhan S.   269
Altaher, Ahmed   210
Al-Werfalli, Sarah   159

B

Bacanin, Nebojsa   81
Banini, Fatma   257
Bisevac, Petar   81
Bizzan, Sami Saddek   68
Bohalfaya, Huda M.   109
Bouchemha, Amel   20
Boumehrez, Farouk   20
Budalal, Asma Ali   55
Budalal, Rogaya A H   55

C

Chantar, Hamouda   42, 96

D

Djellab, Hanane   20
Drawil, Nabil   322

E

Elakeili, Salwa   159
Elbadri, Mohamed   210

Elberkawi, Ebitisam K.   248
Elbuni, Mohamed Samir   130, 221
El-Deeb, Fatma   248
Eldukali, Azer M.   284
Elgergeni, Shahd   322
Elhabrush, Hala   221
Elhawil, Amna   284
Ellabib, Ismail   309
Ellabib, Issmail   173, 298
Elmajpri, Howayda   159
Eltarhouni, Wafa I.   269
Emshiheet, Moad   27
Ezzedin, Abdullah   221

G

Gargoum, Bothaina F.   239
Gdura, Yousef Omran   130

H

Habberrih, Abdullah   197
Hewadia, Suleiman G H   55

I

Imbarak, Tariq   159

J

Jovanovic, Luka   81

K

Karghli, Qusay   257

L

Lahmer, Ibrahim E.   184
Lawgali, Ahmed   239

M

Maamri, Fouzia   20
Maatug, Yusra   309
Maatuk, Abdelsalam M.   109
Majouk, Ahmed   27
Mohamed, Abdelhafid Ali   257

N
Nagem, Tarek A. M.   248

O
Omar, Abdulmoied   68
Ounifi, Salma Salah   130

P
Petrovic, Aleksandar   81

S
Sahour, Abdelhakim   20
Salb, Mohamed   81

Saleh, Eiman M.   159
Salem, Yousef   96
Sati, Mohamed   27
Sati, Salem Omar   27
Sharif, Khaled Idris   55
Studiawan, Hudan   119

T
Toskovic, Ana   81

Z
Zatout, Abdulkhalek M.   3
Zivkovic, Miodrag   81